INVENTING TH

This book approaches Ulster Protestantism through its theatrical and cultural intersection with politics, re-establishing a forgotten history and engaging with contemporary debates. Anchored by the perspectives of ten writers—some of whom have been notably active in political life—it uniquely examines tensions going on within. Through its exploration of class division and drama from the early twentieth century to the present, the book restores the progressive and Labour credentials of the community's recent past along with its literary repercussions, both of which appear in recent decades to have diminished. Drawing on over sixty interviews, unpublished scripts, as well as archival material, we can see—contrary to a good deal of clichéd polemic and safe scholarly assessment—that Ulster Protestants have historically and continually demonstrated a vigorous creative pulse as well as a tendency towards class politics.

Connal Parr is Lecturer in History at Northumbria University. He studied Modern History at the University of Oxford and obtained his PhD in Ulster Protestant politics and culture at Queen's University Belfast in 2013. He was Irish Government Senior Scholar for 2014–15 at Hertford College, Oxford, and went on to teach at Fordham University's London Centre before joining Northumbria University as a Vice-Chancellor's Research Fellow in September 2016. Two years later he became Lecturer in History. A board member of Etcetera Theatre Company, he has published articles in *Irish Studies Review, Irish Political Studies*, and the *Irish Review*.

Inventing the Myth

*Political Passions and the Ulster
Protestant Imagination*

CONNAL PARR

OXFORD
UNIVERSITY PRESS

Praise for *Inventing the Myth*

'It is rooted in a wide range of primary sources, a large number of interviews and a grounding in scholarly literature on the modern social, cultural and political history of Northern Ireland. It is a courageous book in many ways . . . Parr has made a major contribution to a historically and culturally sensitive understanding of that community and in particular of its combative and progressive dimensions.'

Henry Patterson, *History Ireland*

'In exploring the social and political contexts of northern Irish Protestantism, its inheritance of dissent (what Dawn Purvis, former leader of the Progressive Unionist Party, refers to as "independent thought") and linking this history to the "literary imagination" and its "connection to the theatre", Parr has opened the door on the history of creative self-questioning and critical debate that is all so often passed by.'

Gerald Dawe, *The Irish Times*

'This is not only an excellent book to read but it is also very readable, being both well-written and informative . . . This is a book that deserves to be well read by anyone with an interest in Ireland, also by those with an interest in literature and its role in conveying a message to the outside world whilst also reflecting back to ordinary people the realities of their own space.'

James Dingley, *National Identities*

'unquestionably the product of many years of painstaking reading and reflection, a rarity amongst the vast splurge of books on Northern Ireland. Crammed full of original insight for scholars and students keen to rediscover the lost world of the Ulster Protestant imagination, Connal Parr has given us an indispensable addition to the very best scholarship on the intersection of culture and politics in this troubled part of the world.'

Aaron Edwards, *Irish Studies Review*

'comprehensive and meticulously—researched . . . *Inventing the Myth* raises many important questions . . . Parr deftly utilizes the texts of these authors' writing, exploring how their work fit within and critiqued the political contexts of their time . . . Parr's writing style is clear enough to be appreciated by a popular audience.'

Gladys Ganiel, *Slugger O'Toole*

OXFORD

UNIVERSITY PRESS

Great Clarendon Street, Oxford, OX2 6DP,
United Kingdom

Oxford University Press is a department of the University of Oxford.
It furthers the University's objective of excellence in research, scholarship,
and education by publishing worldwide. Oxford is a registered trade mark of
Oxford University Press in the UK and in certain other countries

© Connal Parr 2017

The moral rights of the author have been asserted

First published 2017
First published in paperback 2019

Published in the United States of America by Oxford University Press
198 Madison Avenue, New York, NY 10016, United States of America

British Library Cataloguing in Publication Data
Data available

Library of Congress Cataloging in Publication Data
Data available

ISBN 978–0–19–879159–1 (Hbk.)
ISBN 978–0–19–884775–5 (Pbk.)

For Kyra and Theresa

Acknowledgements

I owe a special debt of gratitude to my original PhD supervisor Professor Graham Walker, whose guidance, suggestions, and close reading of my doctorate and subsequent chapters has been invaluable. Similarly, this book would not be what it is without the help of Professor Roy Foster, my original thesis external examiner and postdoctoral mentor at Hertford College, Oxford. Like a generation of scholars, I am grateful for his encouragement and indelible imprint on Irish historical writing. I also want to specially thank Professor Richard English, Dr Marc Mulholland, Professor Paul Bew, Dr Margaret O'Callaghan, and Professor Henry Patterson, all of whom have made the study of Northern Ireland a serious pursuit and have directly inspired and aided my own progress. Professor Senia Paseta, Professor Fearghal McGarry, Dr Ben Levitas, and Dr Stephen Hopkins commented helpfully on draft chapters and have been supportive and friendly at all turns. Oxford University Press's anonymous readers made similarly constructive suggestions on receiving the original manuscript, and I also want to thank Jacqueline Norton and Aimee Wright for their help in bringing this book to fruition. Special thanks are also due to Jo Egan, Dr Aaron Edwards, Roy Garland, Dr Uwe Hild, the Reverend Chris Hudson, Professor W. J. McCormack, Dr Gareth Mulvenna, Bobby Niblock, Olivia Primanis and Christopher Hynes (for a wonderful stay in Austin), and the late Tony Rowe.

I hugely appreciate the award of a three-year PhD studentship from the Northern Ireland Department of Employment and Learning in 2010 to pursue the initial project, and the Andrew W. Mellon Foundation for a fellowship award to travel and carry out research at the Harry Ransom Center in Austin, Texas. This book would not have been possible without the participation of those who gave up their time to be interviewed. I consider myself very lucky, and am enormously grateful to: Glen Barr, Boyd Black, the late Pam Brighton, Robert Cooper, Julie-Anne Corr Johnston, Harry Donaghy, Sammy Douglas, Lord Reg Empey, Brian Ervine, Neil Faris, Jimmy Fay, Brian Garrett, Dan Gordon, Lord Grey Gowrie, Stuart Graham, David Grant, Maurice Hayes, Jackie Hewitt, Richard Howard, Billy Hutchinson, John Kennedy, Tony Kennedy, John Kyle, Mark Langhammer, the late Joe Law, Maurice Leitch, Martin Lynch, Seamus Lynch, Owen McCafferty, Colin McCusker, Stella McCusker, Chris McGimpsey, Douglas McIldoon, Billy McQuiston, James Magee,

Laine Megaw, William Mitchell, Carol Moore, Danny Morrison, George
Morrow, Patrick O'Kane, Richard O'Rawe, David Overend, Lynne
Parker, Tom Paulin, the late Lord James Prior, the late Bob Purdie,
Dawn Purvis, Robert Ramsay, Stephen Rea, Jackie Redpath, Robert
Rodgers, Patrick Sandford, the late William 'Plum' Smith, the late Hugh
Smyth, Andy Tyrie, Mark Williamson, Sammy Wilson, and Brenda Winter-
Palmer. Five people I especially want to thank are playwrights Ron Hutch-
inson, Marie Jones, Gary Mitchell, the late Christina Reid, and Graham
Reid. Each allowed me to draw on unpublished material and gave up time to
speak about their life and work. I am further indebted to their partners Alisa,
Ian, Alison, Richard, and Gwen, for their generosity and patience.

I am grateful to others in Belfast, Oxford, London, and beyond who
have helped in different ways including: Mark Adair, Nick Androulidakis,
Deidre Ashe, Professor Arthur Aughey, Kathryn Baird, Dr Sean Brennan,
Dr Edward Burke, Dr Seán Byers, the late Liam Clarke, Francis Devine,
Professor Paul Dixon, Jeff Dudgeon, Dr Sarah Ferris, Lisa Geary, Dr Isaac
Gewirtz, Dr James Greer, Paul Grubb, Professor John Harrington, Brian
Henry Martin, Erskine Holmes, Dr Matt Hunt, Dr Neil Jarman, Dr Wei
H. Kao, Diarmuid Kennedy, Professor Edna Longley, Ben Lowry, Ian
McElhinney, Dr Cillian McGrattan, Laurence McKeown, Alan Meban,
Dr Austen Morgan, Frank Ormsby, Dr Katy Radford, Aideen Reilly,
Professor Marilynn J. Richtarik, Tom Saunders, Dr Graham Spencer,
David Stevens, Brian Strong, Anne Tannahill, Iain Turner, the late Sabine
Wichert, Kathy and Professor Rick Wilford, and the staff of the Linen Hall
Library, Queen's University Belfast's Special Collections, the Berg Collec-
tion of the New York Public Library, and the Harry Ransom Center in
Austin, Texas.

My family including Moya, Patricia, Peter, Joe, Andy, Ceara, and Josh
have provided the surest emotional support anyone could hope for, as have
my parents Anne and Chris. Their unwavering belief has kept me on track
through a challenging but ultimately excellent few years. My late grandfather Paddy is much missed, the respect and affection he inspires on all
sides in Northern Ireland reflective of his compassion and giant heart.
Finally, this book ends with a chapter on two remarkable women and
I dedicate it to two others: my grandmother Theresa Devlin, still the
strongest person I know, who has helped in ways that can never fully be
repaid. Above all this is for Kyra, who has taught me so much and is my
companion.

                                                    Connal Parr

8 March 2017

The author expresses his thanks to the following:

The Estate of John Boyd for permission to quote from the John Boyd Collection held at the Linen Hall Library, Belfast.

The Special Collection of the McClay Library, Queen's University Belfast, for permission to quote from the collection of Forrest Reid and the Thomas Carnduff Archive. Additional thanks are due to Carnduff's Literary Executor Dr Sarah Ferris.

The Harry Ransom Center, Austin, Texas, for permissions to quote from the collection of St John Ervine.

The National Library of Ireland and the Sean O'Casey Estate for permission to quote from St John Ervine's letters to Sean O'Casey held in the Eileen O'Casey Papers.

The Estate of St John Ervine for permission to quote from the letters held at the Berg Library, New York, and other assorted correspondence.

The Estate of John Hewitt for permission to quote from the published works of John Hewitt and other materials held at the John Hewitt Collection at the University of Ulster, Coleraine.

The Estate of Sam Thompson for permission to quote from the unpublished plays and autobiographical script held at the Central Library, Belfast.

Contents

List of Figures

List of Abbreviations

BC	Berg Collection, New York Public Library
DUP	Democratic Unionist Party
FRP	Forrest Reid Papers, McClay Library, Queen's University Belfast
HRC	Harry Ransom Center, Austin, Texas
INLA	Irish National Liberation Army
IRA	Irish Republican Army
JBC	John Boyd Collection, Linen Hall Library, Belfast
MLA	Member of the Legislative Assembly
NILP	Northern Ireland Labour Party
NLI	National Library of Ireland, Eileen O'Casey Papers
PDP	Paddy Devlin Papers, Linen Hall Library, Belfast
PRONI	Public Records Office of Northern Ireland
PUP	Progressive Unionist Party
RUC	Royal Ulster Constabulary
SDLP	Social Democratic and Labour Party
TCA	Thomas Carnduff Archive, McClay Library, Queen's University Belfast
UDA	Ulster Defence Association
UDR	Ulster Defence Regiment
UVF	Ulster Volunteer Force
UWC	Ulster Workers' Council

Kilpatrick was murdered in a theatre, yet the entire city played the role of theatre, too, and the actors were legion.

Jorge Luis Borges, *Theme of the Traitor and the Hero* (1944)

Introduction

This book is a synthesis of the political and the creative, telescoping modern history and politics with theatre and television drama. It centres on ten writers: St John Ervine (1883–1971), Thomas Carnduff (1886–1956), John Hewitt (1907–87), Sam Thompson (1916–65), Stewart Parker (1941–88), Graham Reid (1945–), Ron Hutchinson (1947–), Gary Mitchell (1965–), Christina Reid (1942–2015), and Marie Jones (1951–). While never intending to ghettoize Protestant writers, or indeed suggest that only those from this background can write illuminatingly about it, one of the reasons the book does not focus on the work of a playwright like Donegal-born Frank McGuinness—especially *Observe the Sons of Ulster Marching Towards the Somme* (1985)—is that it is important to emphasize that writing *has* come from within the Ulster Protestant community itself. By failing to address this, academics and commentators continue to inadvertently maintain the fallacy that the Protestant working class in Northern Ireland has no culture but the Orange Order and Rangers F. C.,[1] a deficiency which has filtered through to historical writing and contemporary journalism, leading to an inaccurate, skewed vision of its history and potential.

Illuminating a diverse and inherently conflicted culture stretching beyond Orange parades, the weaving together of the lives and works of each of the writers considered in this book highlights mutual insights on this identity, as if part of some grander tapestry of alternative Protestant culture. It particularly seeks to re-establish the vibrant Protestant working-class theatrical heritage which has been deliberately downplayed by both Ulster Unionists and Irish Republicans in recent years. It is not just of course an assessment of this theatre but an illustration of how writers interact with, and influence, the politics of their time. There is no 'ivory tower' syndrome with the lofty scribe looking down from on high. Edna Longley once wrote that we need to look at Ulster Protestant writers

---

[1] See, for instance, Ronan Bennett, 'An Irish Answer', *The Guardian Weekend*, 16 July 1994, 6–10, 95.

because 'their political consciousness illuminates the darkest area',[2] and
the dramatists covered in this book work in shipyards and trades, run
guns, witness the 1916 Easter Rising, discourse with politicians, stand for
election, challenge Prime Ministers, pace the streets of the later Troubles,
engage with paramilitaries, and converse at all times with their audiences
and communities. To forget this tradition is to forget this wealth of
interaction and history, making the insistence of elected representatives
that working-class Protestants have no tradition of 'buying into' the arts or
participating in the theatre in Northern Ireland both inaccurate and
absurd.[3] Attempting to find some way beyond the violence, John Hewitt
called at a 1976 conference for the population of Northern Ireland to
create anew and 'invent the myth, invent the metaphor'.[4] This book is a
political and cultural exercise in how Ulster Protestants from a working-
class background have inclined towards this reflex for a whole century.

I have been fortunate in charting a set of men and women who also
brought voices onto the record which would otherwise not have been
heard. This naturally raises the issue of social class, and so apart from
Hewitt this book focuses on working-class playwrights. One academic has
argued that literature concerning sectarianism and strife within the Labour
movement means that 'working-class life and values have come to dominate our cultural life in Belfast'.[5] Leaving aside the fact that the middle
and upper classes actually dominate the arts throughout the United
Kingdom,[6] what this view fails to acknowledge is that working-class voices
were, and continue to be, rarely heard or represented in national news and
parliamentary chambers, thereby marginalizing the themes and issues
pertinent to their lives. The plays often capture those people not found
in official reports, Hansards, or even newspapers. 'The ordinary decent
little things that men and women do in their everyday lives are not
recorded as news', Thomas Carnduff observed many decades ago: 'You

---

[2] Edna Longley, 'Progressive Bookmen: Politics and Northern Protestant Writers in the
1930s', *The Irish Review*, No. 1 (1986), 50.

[3] The comments of William Humphrey, Democratic Unionist Party MLA (Member of
the Legislative Assembly) for North Belfast, quoted in *Belfast Telegraph*, 9 October 2013, 12.

[4] John Hewitt, 'A Question of Identity', in *A Critical Look at Independence: Papers from a
Weekend Workshop at Corrymeela* (Belfast: The Workshop, 1976), 4. Linen Hall Library
Political Collection.

[5] John Wilson Foster, 'Our Engineering Was Good Enough to Be Called Art', *Belfast
Telegraph*, 24 March 2012, 38.

[6] According to a 2015 survey conducted by Goldsmiths, University of London, the
University of Sheffield, LSE, and the arts organization *Create*, more than three-quarters (76
per cent) of 2,539 arts sector workers came from a middle-class background where one or
both of their parents held managerial or professional jobs. See the results available at: http://
www.createlondon.org/panic/survey/.

have to take note of them yourself.'[7] Social media may have partially altered the equation, but listeners to *Drumcree* (1996), a radio drama by Gary Mitchell about the Orange parading dispute running at the time, were reportedly relieved 'to hear the feelings of ordinary people about what was going on, not just officials and politicians'.[8]

On account of his class and poetry, John Hewitt appears the odd man out in this work. He was, however, something of a lost playwright, serving on the board of Belfast's Lyric Players' Theatre and writing plays under his own charge.[9] Hewitt's poem 'The colony' (1950) was called a 'dramatic monologue',[10] and in the 1930s he worked with unemployed youngsters on productions of *Doctor Faustus* and a left-wing play called *Where's the Bomb?*, which came to the attention of the authorities who forced him by law (Section 18b) to close it. In the context of this book, Hewitt's primary significance is as a symbol. He was, in James Simmons's phrase, the 'Protestant Prospero', representing, even to those who may not have realized it, 'a map, an example'.[11] Gerald Dawe credits Hewitt for inventing a 'new idiom, an imaginative space',[12] enabling new myths and Protestant identities. Ron Hutchinson encountered him as a fellow exile in Coventry, asking for advice as a young writer starting out. Unaware of his precise vocation at this stage, Hutchinson was penning short stories for magazines such as *Woman's Own* which were being rejected. Hewitt:

> gave me some of the most invaluable advice that any writer could ever be given. He said: 'Listen, the people writing those stories are writing at the top of their game. There's nothing else they can write and they are writing really at full stretch, so don't for a minute imagine that you could write those stories. Don't be dismissive of people who write those stories. Don't assume there's an ease writing those stories, because if you're not that kind of writer you'll never be able to write them, and you're wasting everybody's time trying.' It was practical advice from somebody who knew his way around even though he was a poet, who was able to talk very generously and wisely about the business of being a writer.[13]

[7] Thomas Carnduff, *Life and Writings*, ed. John Gray (Belfast: Lagan Press, 1994), 116. See also Harris Beider, *White Working-Class Voices: Multiculturalism, Community-Building and Change* (Bristol: Policy Press, 2015).
[8] Roland Jaquarello, *Memories of Development* (Dublin: Liffey Press, 2016), 233.
[9] Mary O'Malley, *Never Shake Hands With the Devil* (Dublin: Elo, 1990), 87, 95–6, 105, 121–2. See also John Hewitt, *Two Plays: The McCrackens and The Angry Dove* (Belfast: Lagan Press, 1999). Another Hewitt play, *The Bloody Brae*, was performed at the Lyric Theatre.
[10] Seamus Heaney, 'The Poetry of John Hewitt', in *Preoccupations: Selected Prose 1968–1978* (London: Faber and Faber, 1980), 207. Hewitt's biographer has unearthed and attributed a further play called *Africa Calling* (1926) to Hewitt, though there are other possible authors. See W. J. McCormack, *Northman: John Hewitt (1907–1987): An Irish Writer, His World, and His Times* (Oxford: Oxford University Press, 2015), 263–7.
[11] 'For John Hewitt', *The Linen Hall Review*, Vol. 4, No. 3 (Autumn 1987), 13.
[12] Gerald Dawe, *Against Piety: Essays in Irish Poetry* (Belfast: Lagan Press, 1995), 89, 101–2.
[13] Interview with Ron Hutchinson, Belfast, 2 August 2012.

Another intention of this book is to outline how Ulster Protestantism, contrary to cliché and stereotype, is prone to political division and dissent, shattering the conventional reading of a conservative monolith. The latter notion is frequently projected by Ulster Protestants themselves as part of a political culture where disagreement and disunion can be seen as a sign of weakness, and even treachery: 'There's this romantic notion within Unionism that we should all be united; that we should all hark back to those glory days when there's one Unionist Party and if there's more than one Unionist Party then they're traitors.'[14] The increasing use of the term 'PUL'—'Protestant/Unionist/Loyalist', as if all these identities are the same—is in many respects a desperate manifestation of this spirit,[15] even though it has been fairly stated that Ulster Protestantism's ideological dissension, encompassing Unionism, socialism, republicanism, anarchism, and liberalism 'might be seen as an underlying *strength* of Protestant culture'.[16]

While the thread of the Labour movement runs through, from St John Ervine's Fabian associations to independent Labour councillors on the Rathcoole estate, we should not forget murkier complexities. Aside from the violence of Loyalist paramilitaries, the phenomenon of 'Paisleyism'— where 'race memories snout blindly around'[17]—shadows many of the writers and political representatives under consideration. It is worth remembering, too, that Sabbatarianism was significantly stronger in working-class parts of Belfast than in their middle-class equivalent during the 1960s.[18] Coalescing with a deep-rooted British tradition of Christian socialism, this can also be seen as part of a typical grappling within Ulster Protestantism. The Northern Ireland Labour Party embodied some of these

[14] Interview with Dawn Purvis, Belfast, 20 January 2012.

[15] The term appears to have first come into use in 2001 when a Cookstown-based organization calling itself the 'PUL Group' organized a conference at the Waterside Theatre in Derry to discuss Protestant community relations (*Belfast News Letter*, 21 November 2001, 9). The group disappeared but the 'PUL community' is now regularly referred to by community groups, in media outlets, and even in academic circles, where it is taken to mean all Protestants, Unionists, and Loyalists as one.

[16] Edna Longley, 'Stereotypes of Northern Protestants Block Progress', *Irish Times*, 6 April 1995, 14. Longley's italics.

[17] Stewart Parker, 'The Tribe and Thompson', *Irish Times*, 18 June 1970, 12.

[18] In 1968 Belfast City Council conducted a mini-referendum to gauge opinion as to whether play centres should be allowed to open on Sunday. While solidly middle-class areas were supportive of opening, the only three areas out of twenty-one to oppose were the working-class principalities of Eastland Street, Hemsworth Street (both off the Shankill Road), and the Donegall Road and Castleton (off North Queen Street). Similarly, when it came to debates on social issues over Sunday drinking, working-class constituents were against the laws being brought into line with the rest of the United Kingdom. Marc Mulholland, *Northern Ireland at the Crossroads: Ulster Unionism in the O'Neill Years, 1960–9* (Basingstoke: Macmillan, 2000), 257.

tensions, especially around the time of the emergence of the civil rights movement. David Bleakley would retrospectively assert that his party presented the Unionist government with proposals closely resembling a civil rights charter several years before the advent of the Northern Ireland Civil Rights Association (NICRA).[19] This is correct, but Bleakley was certainly on the wing of the party, along with fellow lay preachers Vivian Simpson and Billy Boyd, who cautioned against becoming involved in the agitation of the late 1960s. While some of this was personally fuelled, the divide between the nonconformist Sabbatarian profile and the pro-civil rights contingent of Charles Brett, Tom Boyd, and Sam Napier revealed a party playing out a very characteristic schism of Protestant politics.[20]

All is intrinsically related to the community's fissiparous political nature which has hitherto been underestimated. It has, again, been left to dramatists like Gary Mitchell to identify that 'the diversity in the Protestant community is unbelievable and extraordinary. You don't have to go very far to get a fight in a Protestant community, you just have to make a statement and you've got ten different points of view within one house or within one street.'[21] It is that spirit located by John Morrow, flowing 'directly from the dissenting spirit that had sent Godgiven Kings to the block and, in 1798, had caused even Ireland to feel, however briefly, the breath of the Enlightenment'.[22] The 'importance of the individual conscience' and 'suspicion of concentrations of power' is held to define Protestant social teaching,[23] and this extends politically and creatively. Scholars have also located a general polarity between the 'creative' approach of the liberal Protestant churches (such as the Non-Subscribing Presbyterian Church) against the fixed literalism of the fundamentalist variants,[24] which may explain the politics and culture of a group capable of being both Left and Right. Mitchell confirms that theatre prospers from people not having 'the answers to anything', thriving on doubt and division rather than certainty: 'Great drama's all about conflict, and there's no more conflicted people than the Protestant

[19] Sam McAughtry, 'Northern Ireland Labour lives on', *Irish Times*, 20 May 1981, 12.
[20] C. E. B. Brett, *Long Shadows Cast Before: Nine Lives in Ulster, 1625–1977* (Edinburgh: John Bartholomew, 1978), 133. See also *Irish Times*, 26 May 1969, 14. The party's non-Protestant socialists such as Paddy Devlin, Eamonn McCann, and Michael Farrell were prominent in the civil rights campaign.
[21] Gary Mitchell, speaking on *Arts Extra*, BBC Radio Ulster, 2 March 2009.
[22] John Morrow, 'John Hewitt', *Honest Ulsterman*, No. 85 (Summer 1988), 28.
[23] David Stevens, 'The Social Thinking of the Protestant Churches', *Studies*, Vol. 80, No. 319 (Autumn 1991), 266.
[24] Graham Spencer, *Protestant Identity and Peace in Northern Ireland* (Basingstoke: Palgrave Macmillan, 2012), 72–5, 235.

community. Every person has a row every day, so there's great drama springing up all around you.'[25]

While such protestors certainly did not represent the Protestant working class in its entirety, an apparent measure of the receding radicalism of the constituency was on display in June 2013 when an anti-G8 march was jeered by a rump of protestors still demonstrating against Belfast City Council's restricted flying of the Union Jack from City Hall six months previously.[26] But countering the view of an inflexible and reactionary bloc, the current secretary of the Labour Party in Northern Ireland reminds us that while not everything is progressive in the Protestant working class, 'there's a lot progressive in it because it had the Presbyterian radical tradition in terms of land reform back in the late-nineteenth century'.[27] On 1 February 2014, over 120 people gathered in the Shankill Road Library to pay tribute to seven men from the area who fought for the left-leaning Second Spanish Republic during Spain's Civil War (1936–9).[28] Memorialized with a plaque courtesy of the International Brigade Commemoration Committee, the commemoration represented part of a wider recovery of working-class Protestant radicalism. Loyalists involved in trade unionism remembered that 'the Protestant community was always very socialist-minded',[29] and this book restores the lineage and returns throughout to the Labour element which, with one recent exception, has been thoroughly displaced from the annals of recent historical writing. The wilful, occasionally polemical dismissal of this vein—a process seemingly endorsed within the Protestant working class itself—negates a rich Labour (and literary) past representing a once formidable, now largely forgotten culture.

It is unsurprising for those politically hostile to the Protestant working class to have declared, at the height of the Troubles, that 'there is no point in appealing to them as fellow-workers because they have no working class consciousness. They see themselves as Protestants not as workers and they have no real hostility to the ruling class beyond a certain jealousy.'[30] More problematic has been the way the community itself has internalized the

[25] Interview with Gary Mitchell, Antrim, 6 June 2013.
[26] *Belfast Telegraph*, 17 June 2013, 12. By this stage the protestors comprised approximately 150 people. See Chapter 6.
[27] Interview with Boyd Black, Belfast, 10 October 2012.
[28] *Belfast Telegraph*, 1 February 2014, 12. Two of the seven were members of the Northern Ireland Labour Party, two were Communists, and the other three (including the most well known, Harry McGrath) were unaffiliated.
[29] Interview with William 'Plum' Smith, Belfast, 14 March 2012.
[30] Michael Farrell, *The Battle for Algeria* (Belfast: People's Democracy, 1973), 11. This polemic combines with deficient contemporary scholarship to recycle stereotypes of a whole working-class community defined by 'conservatism and sectarianism'. For an example see Michael Pierse, 'Labour and Literature One Hundred Years After the Lockout: Towards an Archive of Irish Working-class Experience', *The Irish Review*, No. 47 (Winter 2013), 54.

falsehood. James Hawthorne, controller of BBC Northern Ireland from 1978 to 1987, pondered 'the Protestant ethos': 'I suppose I have to concede that I was born into that tribe. Having been born into that tribe, I would be the first to admit that we lack a certain lyricism. The Catholic case is sometimes more lyrical, because it's about change. Whereas the conservatism of the Protestant ethos, not well-articulated, is of less interest to the ardent journalist and the dramatist.'[31] Along with the somewhat inaccurate reading of the Catholic Church in human history, it is striking how convinced many Ulster Protestants are of their inveterate conservatism and innate lack of lyricism. St John Ervine once perceived a 'general Puritan objection to the theatre', which is 'founded, and is still maintained, on the conviction that the mummer violates the commandment that we shall not make unto ourselves graven images',[32] and this appears to linger in the contemporary belief of many Protestants that they do not 'do' the arts just as they do not 'do' left-wing politics, both contentions proudly cultivated and reinforced by many of their own politicians. It is a thesis contravened by all the Ulster Protestant dramatists and writers considered in this book.

In contrast to the claim that Ulster Protestants lack a lyricism and have no tradition of writing plays or left-wing politics, these writers became part of the movement 'to formulate questions and construct counter-statements to the reigning pieties. Literature is dialogue; responsiveness . . . writers are makers, not just transmitters, of myths.'[33] There is something of this in John Hewitt's reminiscence from exile. Placed in charge of Coventry's Herbert Art Gallery and Museum in 1956, he strolled around his new home city:

> I found greatly to my delight that the name Hewitt figured in the history of Coventry, and I saw in the churches and graveyards headstones to John Hewitt. For instance, in the 15th and 16th centuries Coventry had a cycle of miracle plays, done on wagons and driven around streets, and the man who made the scenery and the properties was John Hewitt, and the man who composed the music and the songs they sang was James Hewitt, his brother. So I decided they were my ancestors. I've no evidence that they were, but as most people live by myths, that's my myth.[34]

[31] Speaking on *The Late Show: Telling the Troubles*, broadcast on BBC2, 21 September 1993.
[32] St John Ervine, *The Theatre in My Time* (London: Rich & Cowan, 1933), 18.
[33] Susan Sontag, 'Literature as Freedom', *Irish Pages*, Vol. 2, No. 1 Empire (Spring/Summer 2003), 183.
[34] Quoted in Ketzel Levine, 'A Tree of Identities, a Tradition of Dissent: John Hewitt at 78', *Fortnight*, No. 213 (4–17 February 1985), 17.

This was also understood by Stewart Parker, who enthused how 'Alternative versions of the historical myths sacred to each of the communities have been staged: not in a spirit of mockery but in a spirit of realism, and out of a desire to substitute vibrant and authentic myths for the false and destructive ones on which we have been weaned.'[35] Rather than simply redelivering the reigning mythologies, the dramatists considered in this book constitute a ferociously creative group of mythmakers and myth-breakers. They represent but one of Ulster Protestantism's alternative cultures.

DEFINITIONS AND SCHOLARLY LITERATURE

Sarah Nelson once excoriated how, with a few exceptions, 'studies of the Ulster Protestant community have been conspicuous by their scarcity, or by their cliché-ridden predictability'. With some exceptions since—including Nelson's own *Ulster's Uncertain Defenders* (1984)—this remains an accurate assessment, with such works continuing to suffer from 're-stating and reinforcing many of the familiar assumptions which most need critical examination'.[36] Whilst it is therefore understandable for studies to use the phrases interchangeably,[37] it is vital to clarify how 'Loyalist' and 'Protestant working class' are not the same and that a valuable etymological distinction should be made. A story involving Shankill community worker May Blood frames the issue. Approached for an interview by a senior American academic who assumed that being a Protestant automatically made her a 'Loyalist', she challenged him, asserting that because of Loyalism's paramilitarist associations she refused 'to be labelled in that way'. The academic was confounded by her antipathy for the word and questioned whether she would have at any time supported the 'defenderist' paramilitaries. 'No, never', she replied. The man then inferred that this might make her the exception to the rule. 'Oh no', Blood corrected: 'Many ordinary, decent working-class Protestants would want nothing to do with Loyalist paramilitarism. He was clearly quite confused by this.'[38]

[35] Stewart Parker, '*Dramatis Personae*: John Malone Memorial Lecture', in *Dramatis Personae and Other Writings*, ed. Gerald Dawe, Maria Johnston, and Clare Wallace (Prague: Litteraria Pragensia, 2008), 26. The lecture was given on 5 June 1986 at Queen's University Belfast.
[36] Sarah Nelson, 'Review: *The Protestants of Ulster* by Geoffrey Bell', *Fortnight*, No. 126 (7 May 1976), 14.
[37] Gareth Mulvenna, 'The Protestant Working Class in Northern Ireland: Political Allegiance and Social and Cultural Challenges Since the 1960s', PhD thesis, Queen's University Belfast, 2009, 8. Steve Bruce also uses the terms correspondingly throughout *The Red Hand: Protestant Paramilitaries in Northern Ireland* (Oxford: Oxford University Press, 1992).
[38] Baroness May Blood, *Watch My Lips, I'm Speaking!* (Dublin: Gill & Macmillan, 2007), 199–200.

Protagonists in the conflict also began to realize that the appellation 'Loyalist' became pejorative as well as a categorization along class (and behavioural) lines. In the wake of the violence of the 1970s, some ex-paramilitaries grasped how designations began to change:

> When I was arrested in 1973, I was called a 'Protestant gunman', a 'Unionist gunman'. When was Loyalism ever used? When the violence started, when people started getting arrested and the anger increased, all of a sudden the term 'Loyalist' began to be used. What the Unionist Party did was they distanced themselves from the violence. In order to distance themselves they started terming people 'Loyalists'. 'Loyalist gunman', 'Loyalist this, Loyalist that'. So the Unionists weren't culpable: it was 'Loyalist'. So what you get now is that anything that doesn't taste right, doesn't look right—they're called 'Loyalist'.[39]

Another ex-UVF (Ulster Volunteer Force) prisoner referred to how politicians who involved themselves in the Ulster Workers' Council strike of 1974 'are now thought of as Unionists rather than Loyalists. You won't hear now people calling Ian Paisley a Loyalist politician, but at that time, him and others were certainly labelled as Loyalist politicians.'[40] A Craigavon councillor for the Ulster Unionist Party concedes, 'Technically I'm a Loyalist. I'm in the Orange Order, I should be called a Loyalist—it just seems to be the way it's termed. Loyalism was like a working class Unionism.'[41] There is therefore a stigma attached to the word itself which, as the current leader of the Progressive Unionist Party admits, 'tends to be a derogatory term in this society'.[42] With this tainted and disputed phraseology in mind, this book focuses on the altogether broader and more capacious Protestant working class. 'Loyalist' will be used in the case of those associated with paramilitary groups.

In much the same way as many books written about Irish Catholics have been written about militant Republicanism rather than the political organizations which received the support of the clear majority of Catholics throughout the Troubles,[43] those books which have been written about Ulster Protestants have been written about the extremes and the minority involved in violence. One such work's description of UVF violence as

[39] Interview with William 'Plum' Smith, Belfast, 14 March 2012.

[40] Interview with William Mitchell, Belfast, 26 July 2012. See also the feature on Paisley, 'The Loyalist Who Came in from the Cold', in *Fortnight*, No. 60 (13 April 1973), 5–6.

[41] Interview with Colin McCusker, Portadown, 29 November 2011.

[42] Interview with Billy Hutchinson, Belfast, 12 November 2012.

[43] Richard English, *Irish Freedom: The History of Nationalism in Ireland* (London: Macmillan, 2006), 387–97.

'protestant terrorism' was as subjective, and objectionable, as calling the violence of the Provisional IRA 'catholic terrorism'.[44] The work of Patrick Buckland and A. T. Q. Stewart made strides, but by the mid-1990s Alvin Jackson identified that there was in fact 'a bias within much of the recent literature towards the consideration of radical loyalism', which 'tends to neglect centrist themes, and to favour the radical periphery of politics'.[45] The variable—and in some cases, poorly written—literature usually focuses on Loyalist paramilitarism,[46] accompanied by a glib journalism (or tabloidism) which charts the egregious violence and criminality of the same groups in detail.[47]

Branching out, Henry Patterson's early work *Class Conflict and Sectarianism* (1980) remains important, resonating to the present day in its cold examination of northern Protestantism's complex alignments which showed a class consciousness co-existing alongside sectarianism.[48] The Protestant working class displayed resentment at both Protestant elites (dominated by the Unionist Party) and Catholics. Critically, Patterson describes how Labour politics developed in a British framework, establishing that the commitment to the Union was 'not something imposed by the manipulation of a crafty bourgeoisie'.[49] The very theme he explored back in 1980, of dual class consciousness and sectarianism, is a theme northern society is still dealing with on the streets outside its political chambers. It was not until 2009, finally, that a comprehensive overview of the Northern Ireland Labour Party—an organization with a distinctly

[44] David Boulton, *The UVF 1966–73: An Anatomy of Loyalist Rebellion* (Dublin: Torc, 1973), 6.

[45] Alvin Jackson, 'Irish Unionism', in D. George Boyce and Alan O'Day (eds), *The Making of Modern Irish History: Revisionism and the Revisionist Controversy* (Abingdon: Routledge, 1996), 131.

[46] See for instance: Sarah Nelson, *Ulster's Uncertain Defenders: Protestant Political, Paramilitary and Community Groups and the Northern Ireland Conflict* (Belfast: Appletree Press, 1984); Steve Bruce, *The Edge of the Union: The Ulster Loyalist Political Vision* (Oxford: Oxford University Press, 1994); James W. McAuley, *The Politics of Identity: A Loyalist Community in Belfast* (Aldershot: Avebury, 1994); Graham Spencer, *The State of Loyalism in Northern Ireland* (Basingstoke: Palgrave, 2008); Lee A. Smithey, *Unionists, Loyalists, and Conflict Transformation in Northern Ireland* (Oxford: Oxford University Press, 2011); Peter Shirlow, *The End of Ulster Loyalism?* (Manchester: Manchester University Press, 2012).

[47] For the more sensationalist fare see Jim McDowell, *The Mummy's Boys: Threats and Menaces from Ulster's ParaMafia* (Dublin: Gill & Macmillan, 2008), and for necessary redress to this see Tony Novosel, *Northern Ireland's Lost Opportunity: The Frustrated Promise of Political Loyalism* (London: Pluto Press, 2013).

[48] Henry Patterson, *Class Conflict and Sectarianism: The Protestant Working Class and the Belfast Labour Movement 1868–1920* (Belfast: Blackstaff Press, 1980).

[49] John Whyte, *Interpreting Northern Ireland* (Oxford: Oxford University Press, 1990), 186.

Protestant ethos—was delivered.[50] Though it did not address the creative lights which were so intrinsic to the NILP (see Chapter 3), this was a significant offering to which there has been little follow-up, and there is little doubt that the shortcomings of much journalism and academic literature is connected to the way Protestant working-class communities feel alienated and apart from modern socio-political life. The widely held view is of a group which is reactionary, prone to violence, possessing little or no Left and Labour history, and nothing approaching a literary heritage. After surveying the contemporary cultural battlefield in its opening chapter, the rest of the book seeks to correct the misperception.

[50] Aaron Edwards, *A History of the Northern Ireland Labour Party: Democratic Socialism and Sectarianism* (Manchester: Manchester University Press, 2009). The four MPs the party had elected to Stormont in 1958 were all 'Protestants of notable piety, though of various kinds' (Brett, *Long Shadows*, 85–6), and in the following 1962 election the NILP gained over 25 per cent of the popular vote. By 1969 this had dwindled to 8.1 per cent.

1

Words as Weapons

Northern Ireland's Ongoing Cultural Wars

> Our people [Ulster Protestants] have accepted almost tamely the
> current cant that Eireans [Irish Catholics] can write better than they
> can; and because they have neither outlet for their work nor
> adequate criticism of it when it appears, it has become slight or
> paltry. But the stuff's there ... as our history plainly shows.

St John Ervine, Letter to John Boyd, 28 July 1950

> It goes back to something somebody said to me one time: 'You had
> all the jobs—we had the culture.'

Democratic Unionist Party MLA Sammy Douglas
(Interview with the author, February 2012)

When the Provisional IRA fire-bombed the Linen Hall Library at the start
of 1994, one commentator expressed surprise that it would attempt to
destroy an institution which 'includes in its collection the only comprehensive records of the IRA's own recent past', along with other precious
documentation relating to the United Irishmen Rebellion of 1798.[1] In
many ways, however, the action was completely rational. The fact the
Linen Hall contains such literature is precisely why a group engaged in an
ongoing campaign would attempt to obliterate it. In August of the same
year, the Provisionals called a major ceasefire as they reached the critical
juncture whereby their armed operations were being gradually wound
down in favour of a purely political, non-violent approach,[2] one which
would prioritize the role of culture. With the arts destined to become 'part
of that political struggle',[3] there is a 'culture war' going on in Northern

---

[1] Fintan O'Toole, 'Linenhall Attack Shows Final Incompatibility of IRA Aims', *Irish Times*, 5 January 1994, 12.

[2] See the comments of the late Brendan Hughes in Ed Moloney (ed.), *Voices from the Grave: Two Men's War In Ireland* (London: Faber and Faber, 2010), 291–3.

[3] Micheál Mac Giolla Ghunna, quoted in Bill McDonnell, *Theatres of the Troubles: Theatre, Resistance and Liberation in Ireland* (Exeter: University of Exeter Press, 2008), 116.

Ireland but, rather typically, many have misinterpreted what the exact nature of that conflict is.

Scholars and journalists have accepted without question the idea, propagated by Irish Republicans and Ulster Unionists alike, that Protestant culture is essentially embodied by the Orange Order. When the former First Minister of Northern Ireland claimed at the beginning of July 2014 that 'people will recognise the importance of having respect and tolerance for the cultural expression of our tradition',[4] he meant Orangeism. The Order has long staked claim to blanket representation of Ulster Protestants, but its recent emphasis as a cultural organization, courtesy of rebranding and a slicker public relations operation, is thought to have originated under the direction of its late grand secretary Drew Nelson.[5] This was initially designed to modernize the institution and move it away from being understood in solely religious and political terms, but ironically has instead fused the religious and political elements with culture. This has come to dominate perceptions of what constitutes Ulster Protestant culture generally (an outcome not dissatisfying to the Orange Order), pitched as 'a particular way of life' representative of a whole group.[6] Instead of challenging the crux of this claim by highlighting the presence of any other culture(s), academics and journalists dismiss the idea of a 'culture war' because there are more Orange parades and marches taking place now than at any other point in modern times.[7] This chapter argues that the main culture war is instead being fought through literature, and that it is underpinned by the very same political insistence that Protestants have 'no culture' other than Orange marching and parades.

CULTURAL DISPARAGEMENT

The new militarization of culture was exemplified by former paramilitary-turned-writer Ronan Bennett in an infamous article published in 1994. An opening salvo in the ongoing culture wars, Bennett outlined how Ulster Protestants existed in 'an intolerable mental world', with a culture

---

[4] Peter Robinson, quoted in *Belfast Telegraph*, 4 July 2014, 4.

[5] Sam McBride, 'Loss of Orange Order's Strategic Modernising Thinker Leaves a Chasm', *Belfast News Letter*, 11 October 2016, 6.

[6] Raymond Williams, *Keywords* (London: Fontana, 1988; 1st edition 1976), 90.

[7] See Paul Nolan, *Northern Ireland Peace Monitoring Report: Number Three* (Belfast: Community Relations Council, 2014), 157; Stephen McCaffery, 'Imaging NI—Part 2: Northern Ireland's "Culture War"? Don't Believe the Hype', *the detail*, 28 April 2015. http://www.thedetail.tv/articles/northern-ireland-s-culture-war-don-t-believe-the-hype. The main nationalist newspaper the *Irish News* agreed, pointing out that there were 2,120 marches in 2005 compared to 4,637 in 2013 (*Irish News*, 1 July 2014, 6).

limited to 'little more than flute bands, Orange marches and the chanting of sectarian songs at football marches'. West Belfast's Catholic community, on the other hand, was 'increasingly secular' and 'outward-looking (foreign—including English—visitors are encouraged)', blending 'traditional Gaelic and contemporary Irish influences in music, the visual arts, writing and dance with those of modern youth culture'.[8] This scene, Bennett contended, contrasted sharply with the 'exclusive and inward looking' Protestant working class. Any artists to emerge from this background had by necessity to leave, with fulfilment only achievable by looking 'beyond the confines of the Protestant world'. Aside from the naked sectarianism of such sentiments, this had followed more considerable voices within Irish academia such as Joseph Lee, who had enunciated in his major history of modern Ireland the general dearth of the Ulster Protestant 'imagination'.[9] The negation of this written culture—the poets, playwrights, and novelists to have emerged from an Ulster Protestant background—and the willingness to either ignore or disparage the cultural status of a whole group, naturally represents its own form of authentic political attack.

As has been noted, 'Bennett's tone indicates how much status rides on culture. It has certainly not been decommissioned by republicans. Nor is his patronage of Protestants new. Their inferiority was a tenet of Jacobitism; their heresy a theme of religious education.'[10] Such attitudes persevered throughout the twentieth century, St John Ervine picking up on a prevalent belief after the Second World War that:

> If you are a Socialist, you are a fine writer. If you are a Conservative, you're a deplorable writer. And, of course, the other way round. I have never yielded to this iniquity. Even when I was a member of the Fabian Executive, or perhaps because I was a member of it, I maintained that [Rudyard] Kipling was one of the world's greatest short story writers—maintained it against infuriated I.L.Pers [Independent Labour Party members] who would admit no virtue in Kipling whatever. In Ireland to-day, you're a finer writer if you're a Shinner and believe in the back-street republic; but you can't write at all if you're a Unionist and believe in the Commonwealth![11]

---

[8] Ronan Bennett, 'An Irish Answer', *The Guardian Weekend*, 16 July 1994, 8–10, 95. In 1974, at the age of eighteen, Bennett was wrongly convicted of killing a Royal Ulster Constabulary (RUC) police officer and spent eighteen months in Long Kesh Prison (*The Guardian Review*, 27 October 2007, 11).

[9] J. J. Lee, *Ireland 1912–1985: Politics and Society* (Cambridge: Cambridge University Press, 1989), 1–19.

[10] Edna Longley, 'What do Protestants Want?', *The Irish Review*, No. 20 (Winter–Spring 1997), 117.

[11] Letter to John Boyd, 22 July 1950. JBC.

Ronan Bennett's particular entitlement stems from being embraced by liberal, middle-class outlets such as *The Guardian* and *London Review of Books*, essentially telling their metropolitan readerships what they want to hear about Ireland and Ulster Protestants.[12] Specifically in response, Arthur Aughey published the pamphlet *Irish Kulturkampf* (1995), a reference to the decrees of Otto von Bismarck which attempted to diminish the power of the Roman Catholic Church and Polish nationality in Prussia. In Aughey's reformulation the term meant the same (literally 'cultural struggle') adapted to a Northern Irish context, critically identifying that 'It never occurs to Bennett that there might just be something wrong with a view of Protestantism which can only see flute bands, Orange marches and sectarian songs.'[13]

Aughey pinpointed Bennett's own view of culture as '*cultural nationalism*', with the conflation of community, religion, politics, and culture ensuring that 'What is distinctive of political Protestantism—its Orange marches, its flute bands, its lodge banners, its sectarian songs—is taken to be the sum of *all* cultural life in that community.'[14] BBC producers like Robert Cooper who worked with, and admired, Bennett had also worked with Stewart Parker, Graham Reid, and Gary Mitchell, meaning that he knew the depiction of Ulster Protestant 'culture' as defined by the Orange Order and sectarian songs was deceitful: 'There is lurking within the Protestant culture a fear that they don't have a culture, so I think that's what he was probably picking up on. I'm not sure that Northern Irish Protestants know what their culture is, and that's different from saying there is no culture.'[15] Novelist Maurice Leitch also weighed in pugnaciously several years later, ridiculing Bennett's sentimentalization of West Belfast (an IRA man's poem quoted as evidence of vibrant Catholic culture was 'the worst piece of crap I've ever read'), but also identifying that 'Ronan Bennett has his Ace of Spades: that if you denigrate the

---

[12] See Ronan Bennett, 'The Party and the Army', *London Review of Books*, Vol. 18, No. 6 (March 1996), 3–7. A similar problem hampers David Ireland's play *Cyprus Avenue*. The original production featured an extraordinary performance from Stephen Rea as Eric Miller, an Ulster Loyalist who convinces himself that his five-week-old granddaughter is Gerry Adams. He ends up butchering his entire family. However, because the play ran in Dublin and then London in the spring of 2016, it played on its audiences' inherent derision for a white working class whose sense of allegiance to Britain makes them 'insane' and murderous. David Ireland, *Cyprus Avenue* (London: Bloomsbury, 2016).

[13] Arthur Aughey, *Irish Kulturkampf* (Belfast: Young Unionist Council, 1995), 10.

[14] Aughey, *Irish Kulturkampf*, 13.

[15] Telephone interview with Robert Cooper, 15 August 2014. Cooper produced Bennett's *Love Lies Bleeding* as part of the BBC's *Screenplay* series, transmitted in September 1993.

opposition long enough they'll actually believe that they don't have any culture, that they can't produce any art.'[16]

Another consequence of the development of non-violent political competition has been the general marginalization of Ulster Loyalists, recognizable to other white working-class groups throughout the Western world. Tapping into a widely felt 'defeatism',[17] Bernadette McAliskey states:

> As the American system disgracefully refers to some of its poorest people as 'white trash,' loyalists are perceived within British nationalism as an underclass. Many from loyalist communities have internalized that themselves. When I work with people from that background I'm often surprised that they will set on the table first, 'Okay, so, we know we are no good.' I have talked to young loyalists who say, 'We know we are scum.' I don't understand any human being starting a conversation saying that they are not human. There is a clear lack of self-esteem and also a loss of confidence.[18]

This lack of self-esteem naturally filters through to a more general working-class Protestant belief, often passionately insisted on by individuals from within the group itself, that they have produced nothing of literary or artistic value. At a conference held at Queen's University Belfast to mark the fortieth anniversary of the Ulster Workers' Council strike, the following exchange took place between teacher and writer Henry Sinnerton, who was born and brought up in East Belfast, and drama lecturer Dr Mark Phelan (of Queen's University):

SINNERTON: The Protestant working class don't have a history of going to the theatre, or writing plays, or being involved in the theatre. Prior to Dawn Purvis's recent play in the Opera House,[19] in the street where she lives the people wouldn't go to the Opera House because it wasn't for them. It was just around the corner of the Donegall Pass.

PHELAN: That's actually a great myth.

SINNERTON: (*Taken aback*) It's not a myth.

PHELAN: Tom Carnduff, a working-class Protestant shipyard worker. Sam Thompson . . .

---

[16] Quoted in 'Closed Places of the Spirit: Maurice Leitch Interviewed by Richard Mills', *Irish Studies Review*, Vol. 6, No. 1 (1998), 67.

[17] Andrew Finlay, 'Defeatism and Northern Protestant "Identity"', *Global Review of Ethnopolitics*, Vol. 1, No. 2 (2001), 3–20.

[18] Quoted in 'Left Behind by Good Friday', *Jacobin*, Between the Risings, Issue 21 (Spring 2016), 87.

[19] This was a short play Purvis had written called *Picking Up Worms*, performed as part of a trilogy of short plays entitled *Flesh and Blood Women*. It ran at the Opera House from May to June 2014. See Chapter 7.

SINNERTON: Yes, but Sam Thompson stands out!

PHELAN: William Humphrey [of the Democratic Unionist Party] quite recently criticized the MAC [Metropolitan Arts Centre] and the Lyric for not doing enough for working-class Protestant audiences in this city. By his own admission he had never been to the Lyric or the MAC.

SINNERTON: That proves the point.

PHELAN: But from January until June [2013] there was an unbroken succession of working-class plays with working-class Protestants [at the Lyric]. We had Marie Jones, St John Ervine, Gary Mitchell, David Ireland, and a new Graham Reid play. In fact one constituency that wasn't represented on the Lyric stage in six months was a Republican working-class audience. There were more working-class Protestant playwrights than there are middle-class Protestant playwrights. We just don't know the history.[20]

Sinnerton sincerely believed that former politician Dawn Purvis was the first Protestant working-class person to write for the theatre, even though, as the following chapters show, a large number of dramatists and theatrical practitioners have emerged from a Protestant working-class background.

A 1993 report on Northern Irish community drama mentioned that attitudes towards the theatre in Protestant working-class areas were negatively defined by the middle-class associations of the Grammar School system,[21] attitudes which were more generally fostered by a local and external media. One journalist wrote how since Sam Thompson's debut, *Over the Bridge* (1960), 'Depictions of the Protestant Unionist family in the arts have fared badly.' Graham Reid's *Billy* plays, which aired on television from 1982 to 1984, 'were the exception rather than the norm. The Northern Irish Catholics had a better story to tell, or so it seemed from the outside.'[22] Following the death of Stewart Parker—another working-class Protestant dramatist— Mary Holland declared ('Certainly') that Ulster Protestants 'have had few dramatic voices to interpret the virtues of their tradition and, in so doing, to

---

[20] Speaking at the conference '40 Years On: The Strike Which Brought Down Sunningdale', held at Queen's University Belfast on 19 May 2014. Author's transcription. The sessions of this event were recorded and are available at: https://audioboom.com/playlists/1255041-uwc40-ulster-workers-council-strike-40th-anniversary-conference-at-qub. This panel—which Phelan chaired—concerned Stewart Parker, whose play *Pentecost* (1987) was set during the UWC strike. See Chapter 4.

[21] David Grant, *Playing the Wild Card: A Survey of Community Drama and Smaller-scale Theatre from a Community Relations Perspective* (Belfast: Community Relations Council, 1993), 41.

[22] David Sharrock, 'Nobody Knows the Troubles We've Seen', *The Guardian*, 23 April 1997, 10.

give them some new sense of their own identity and the possibilities that are now open to them. Those who have tried have been drawn, on the whole, from the nationalist tradition—Frank McGuinness . . . Brian Friel.'[23]

Aughey's original points concerning the 'experience of cultural humiliation and communal disparagement'[24] have become even more pertinent as time has passed, but what he and other Unionists miss is how culture functioned as an integral path for Irish Republicans to move away from physical-force methods. Republicans needed to discover other forms of resistance, quickly realizing that the arts represent a vital outlet and displacement. Consequently, some Unionists have reacted by abandoning (or ignoring) their literary heritage altogether, essentially arguing that concepts of the Enlightenment and science are Protestant while literature is a 'romantic art' for Catholics,[25] cementing the sectarian dichotomy and ignoring a plethora of Ulster Protestant playwrights, poets, and novelists. Indeed a major success of the Irish Republican strategy lies in the willingness of Ulster Unionists to accept that the Protestant community's main culture is indistinguishable from the Orange Order, and that its sizeable and diverse working class has no tradition of being involved in or going to the theatre. The year after Ronan Bennett's original attack, Edna Longley perceived that:

> Unionist politicians are equally to blame for misrepresenting the people they purport to lead. Their incapacity to argue the local cultural case makes it easier for Irish nationalism to claim, and grotesquely simplify, the island's culture. Thus, when a few unionists attempt counter-propaganda, they end up talking about 'Ulster-British' culture, as if this consisted of political manifestations like Orangeism.[26]

Little could Longley have known how comprehensively this was to dominate present conceptions of Protestant culture. Many Ulster Unionists are accordingly content to take their place in the culture wars on the back foot and along lines set out by Republicans, with their representatives complicit in the process 'because they are the mouthpiece for a lot of the Protestant population which just perpetuates the myth that they have no interest in the arts'.[27] It was telling that the same Unionist politician

[23] Mary Holland, 'Such Goodness Demands that We Respond', *Irish Times*, 9 November 1988, 14.

[24] Aughey, *Irish Kulturkampf*, 14.

[25] See James Dingley, *The IRA: The Irish Republican Army* (Santa Barbara, CA: Praeger, 2012), 67; Nelson McCausland, 'Patrick Murphy—the Irish News' Resident Cultural Bigot (2)', *Nelson's View* blog, 25 April 2014. http://nelsonmccausland.blogspot.co.uk/2014/04/patrick-murphy-irish-news-resident.html.

[26] Edna Longley, 'Stereotypes of Northern Protestants Block Progress', *Irish Times*, 6 April 1995, 14.

[27] Interview with Carol Moore, Belfast, 13 August 2014.

(Democratic Unionist Party representative William Humphrey) who in October 2013 publicly stated that Belfast theatres offered no 'tangible benefit' to the Protestant working class, when questioned on what kind of play he would like to see more of named only one: *Observe the Sons of Ulster Marching Towards the Somme* (1985) by Frank McGuinness.[28] No Protestant dramatists were mentioned, leading Gary Mitchell to point out in the local media that he had written around forty plays which had been staged in Europe, the United States, and Ireland, and that when Humphrey's DUP held the Culture, Arts and Leisure portfolio in Northern Ireland's power-sharing Executive, 'nothing happened'.[29] With the Assembly's Departments Bill of 2016 dissolving the entire Arts and Culture department and designating its duties to the Department for Communities, Unionists have proved themselves adept cultural warriors in their own right.

MODERN IRISH REPUBLICANISM AND WAR LITERATURE

At the 1978 Sinn Féin Ard Fheis in Dublin, Danny Morrison (1953–) was one of the northern personnel who spoke against Dáithí Ó Conaill's motion calling for 'open discussions with the Loyalist people'. 'The Protestant tradition of Republicanism has been killed by Loyalist violence,' Morrison proclaimed. 'How far will you get with Loyalists if you sit down at a table with them and start by saying you are against their idea of a six-county independent Northern Ireland?'[30] As a phase in the Gerry Adams–Martin McGuinness takeover, this also signalled an alteration in the party's philosophy: 'Ironically this new radicalized element inside the Provos was less inclined than their more traditionalist predecessors to contemplate doing deals with loyalism, believing instead in the incipient fascism of important strands in Northern Protestant politics.'[31] This conviction of the eventual leadership—Adams and McGuinness had gained complete control by 1983—represented a facile way of looking on the varied political aspirations of northern Protestants, and though this cadre eventually negotiated the Ceasefire and the 1998 Good Friday Agreement, the

---

[28] Quoted in *Belfast Telegraph*, 9 October 2013, 12.

[29] Quoted in *Irish News*, 10 October 2013, 9.

[30] Quoted in *Irish Times*, 23 October 1978, 8. The motion passed overall, but the Belfast delegates including Morrison, Gerry Adams, and Tom Hartley were 'vehemently opposed'.

[31] Andrew Pollak, 'The Left That Never Was', *Fortnight*, No. 196 (July–August 1983), 3.

shift reflected a refusal to contemplate the thinking of Loyalists and more broadly take into account Ulster Protestant perspectives.

Republicans have historically insisted that Ulster Unionism is essentially a 'false consciousness' imposed by the British state to divide and rule Ireland, and modern dissenters note how the 'fascist' label later allocated to Loyalists is in many ways ironic, as the designation could easily be applied to elements of Sinn Féin. Richard O'Rawe (1953–) recalls that in the early 1980s the constitutionally nationalist Social Democratic and Labour Party opened new offices in Mullholland Terrace, West Belfast, which 'kept getting burned, refurbished, burned, refurbished, burned, refurbished. In actual fact it was a fascism there, absolute fascism in that Republican people were not prepared to tolerate any other political persuasion or party in West Belfast.'[32] O'Rawe has himself challenged the narrative surrounding the 1981 Hunger Strike by revealing that Margaret Thatcher's government offered a deal which would have met three or possibly four of the prisoners' five demands on 5 July 1981, shortly before the death of the fifth hunger striker Joe McDonnell.[33] This offer was accepted, O'Rawe maintains, by the prisoners inside Long Kesh but countermanded by the 'outside' IRA leadership in the form of the 'H-Block Committee' (comprising Adams, McGuinness, Morrison, Tom Hartley, and Jim Gibney). His challenge to the received Republican version of events, O'Rawe believes, brings the 'fascism' of his old cohort to the fore:

> I still get ostracized by people who I knew very well. See if they thought that it wouldn't be political suicide, they'd be killing me. They'd be shooting me stone dead. The only reason I'm not being shot or disappeared—believe me, because I know these guys—is because of the profile that I have, and it would make the thing thirty times worse for them. See at the back of it all there's a real fascism and intolerance of other people and other opinions, and it's still there.[34]

While Danny Morrison has called specific IRA actions such as Bloody Friday—when the Provisional IRA exploded twenty-two bombs in July 1972—'unconscionable',[35] O'Rawe's contrition is more overwhelming and forthright. He speaks in a way the vast majority of Republican ex-combatants do not about the past: 'I think the whole campaign was a disaster and I'm sorry I was ever involved in it. I've said that a thousand

---

[32] Interview with Richard O'Rawe, Belfast, 18 January 2012.
[33] Richard O'Rawe, *Afterlives: The Hunger Strike and the Secret Offer that Changed Irish History* (Dublin: Lilliput Press, 2010), 2–4. See also *Blanketmen: An Untold Story of the H-Block Hunger Strike* (Dublin: New Island, 2005).
[34] Interview with Richard O'Rawe, Belfast, 18 January 2012.
[35] Interview with Danny Morrison, Belfast, 29 August 2013. See also his comments in *Belfast Telegraph*, 20 July 2012, 4–5.

times, I don't care who or what Republican likes it or doesn't like it. I'm so sorry for all those people that died.'[36] These are the comments of a man now stationed completely outside the historical narrative of the Provisional IRA, reflecting too a dissent linked to O'Rawe's writing:

> It enables me to write about anything and whatever I want. I am not encumbered or inhibited by party-political considerations. I fucking hate this hunger strike shit because it's like an anchor round my neck having to deal with it.[37] I'm in it and I have no choice, but I prefer creative writing. I couldn't write if I thought for one second that I had to take a party line; that I couldn't see or view the other guy's opinion. That's the only way you can approach writing. To approach it any other way is like cutting off one of your hands. You have to be liberated. You have to be free to write what you want, no matter how obnoxious the party may feel it to be. It has to be your line, how you see things.[38]

Morrison might well reply that he has, unlike O'Rawe, actually published novels and had a play staged, but O'Rawe's film work demonstrates a natural storytelling ability, inner conflict, and strong characterization. In *Greed*, a film O'Rawe has written based on the fallout of the 2004 Northern Bank robbery, a heist tale fuses with a negotiation of the internal politics of the Republican movement. Protagonist Ructions Rooney, fresh out of prison, comes to meet Eamonn O'Neill, leader of the Republican movement in Belfast:

15. INT. SIDE-ROOM. CONTINUOUS.

Eamonn O'Neill is looking up when Ructions enters. O'Neill comes around the table, and takes Ructions's hand in his two hands.

O'NEILL: Failte abhaile, A Sheamais. Good to see you back, James.
RUCTIONS: Go raibh mile maith agat, Eamonn. I'd like to say it's good to be home, Eamonn, but (*A beat*)... I'd be telling a lie.
O'NEILL: Sit down; take the weight off your feet.

Ructions sits.
O'Neill goes back to his chair.

O'NEILL: You liked America?
RUCTIONS: I loved it; loved everything about it.
O'NEILL: I was fund-raising in New York and Boston in the early seventies, and I enjoyed it myself. Americans are... full of life; there's not enough hours in the day for them. Would that be accurate?

---

[36] Interview with Richard O'Rawe, Belfast, 18 January 2012.
[37] See the exchange between Morrison and O'Rawe in the *Irish News*, 16 January 2012, 10 and 17 January 2012, 13.
[38] Interview with Richard O'Rawe, Belfast, 18 January 2012.

RUCTIONS: Absolutely. (*A beat*) Eamonn, you know me; I never was much good at ballsology...

O'NEILL: True.

O'Neill smiles.

RUCTIONS: ... so I'm going to be straight with you: I've given up on the struggle; I'd a good life in America, and I'd never have come back to Ireland by choice; it just wouldn't have happened. If I can swing it, I'll be heading stateside again.

O'NEILL: Look, I should be able to fix you up with a false passport and identification whenever you are ready.... If you need me, give me a ring.

RUCTIONS: Thanks, but I hope to sort out the documentation myself.

O'Neill wriggles his fingers for Ructions to draw closer.

O'NEILL: Don't get cocky, James, it's disrespectful.

RUCTIONS: Eamonn, I'd never disrespect you; you picked me up wrong.

O'NEILL: No, I didn't, but it doesn't matter. Son, you've been away a long time. Much has changed.

RUCTIONS: That's what everybody's keeps telling me.

O'NEILL: Well, it's true. (*A beat*) You think the people you left behind are the same?

O'Neill shakes his head slowly.[39]

Part of the quality of the scene stems from the knowledge that we know O'Rawe has been around conversations like this. The ambiguous portrayal of a Sinn Féin leader and a volunteer's slight flippancy towards him is startling and would be unlikely to emanate from the pen of one of the party's writers. In O'Rawe's case, to write is to dissent.

The difficulty for writers hoisted from the main political party of the Republican movement—whose status as writers has been validated by journalism and academia[40]—is that few 'alternative stories' or mentalities to Irish Republican beliefs and goals can seriously be highlighted or explored. The theatre and other creative platforms are in fact conceived as a mechanism and platform through which to advance and continue the

---

[39] Richard O'Rawe, *Greed* (Unpublished, n.d.), 31–4; original ellipses. O'Rawe has developed screen work with the provincial film and television agency Northern Ireland Screen. I am grateful to him for access to this script.

[40] John Wilson Foster, *Between Shadows: Modern Irish Writing and Culture* (Dublin: Irish Academic Press, 2009), 92; Fintan O'Toole, 'Escaping Reality into the Realm of Fiction', *Irish Times*, 12 October 1989, 10.

struggle. In such a vision, political opponents of the cause—be they the British security forces, the Royal Ulster Constabulary (RUC), Unionists, or any other group or individual perceived to be acting as a barrier to Republican aspirations—will seldom receive an empathetic portrayal because they block the end goal. Yet the most successful dramas usually 'take their shape from a conflict within the writer himself', a contest between 'mind and intuition. The most shapely plays emerge when the antagonists wrestle each other to a draw.'[41] This is especially so in the theatre which represents a 'safe thinking space' where the mind intuits 'no danger from the alternative actions, thoughts and feelings being presented'. While this is often cited as a weakness, because what the audience sees does not impact directly upon their lives, 'It is precisely because theatre does not directly affect our normal lives that our minds allow us the thinking space to experience and consider the alternative stories and behaviours in front of us.'[42]

Richard O'Rawe's willingness to break from the political movement is therefore reflected in his ability to write creatively: 'I don't think Danny [Morrison] can write, and that's not me being prejudicial to Danny because of all this Hunger Strike stuff. I just don't think there's a creative bone in his body.'[43] While this view is very likely informed by the dispute, it appears to be borne out by Morrison's fiction. His jail journal *Then the Walls Came Down* (1999) is an insightful and valuable memoir,[44] but problems arise when Morrison turns his hand to fiction. His novel *The Wrong Man* (1997) leads with its IRA protagonist Raymond Massey going out to attack 'the Brits', who to a man 'are evil bastards, every last one, without any redeeming features. Just like the RUC who squeeze poor Raymond's balls when they stop his car.' All those who live in West Belfast, on the other hand, possess 'a heart of corn. They are all decent, take-the-shirt-off-their-backs types; doting grandfathers, wise-cracking buddies, friendly winos.' A reviewer observed, 'It's as if in Morrison's blighted landscape, Protestants hardly exist. Apart from the sadistic RUC men, there's only one mention of a Protestant, a poor devil called Joe Powderly who has ventured into West Belfast and has the misfortune to be in the UDR [Ulster Defence Regiment].' Inevitably, 'Raymond and his

---

[41] Stewart Parker, '*Dramatis Personae*: John Malone Memorial Lecture', in *Dramatis Personae and Other Writings*, ed. Gerald Dawe, Maria Johnston, and Clare Wallace (Prague: Litteraria Pragensia, 2008), 25.

[42] Mick Gordon, *Theatre and the Mind* (London: Oberon Books, 2010), 13–14.

[43] Interview with Richard O'Rawe, Belfast, 18 January 2012.

[44] Danny Morrison, *Then the Walls Came Down* (Cork: Mercier Press, 1999); Eugene McEldowney, 'Jail Journal: From Elation to Despair', *Irish Times*, 13 November 1999, 51.

pals blow his head off.'[45] In an older novel, *West Belfast* (1990),[46] an uneven style charts 'the "exciting" exploits of goodies and baddies in which, as you might expect given the author's politics, the IRA are always the former, Loyalists and British Army the latter'. While the security forces are brutish and deplorable, 'only a handful of innocent civilians are murdered by Mr Morrison's heroes'.[47]

In fairness to Morrison, he has stipulated that this book was, in contrast to his later fiction, 'written with an agenda in mind. That should not have been a conscious contrivance on my part. I was following my political, ideological instincts and allowing them to override all creative possibilities.'[48] In *On the Back of the Swallow* (1994) Morrison attempted to broaden his scope by writing the novel from the perspective of a homosexual Protestant, both profiles 'other' to him. Yet gay rights campaigner Jeff Dudgeon found the book 'difficult to take as it was so Republican in tone. It was actually a prison story not a gay one.' Morrison was in prison when he wrote it so this was understandable, and the fact that Dudgeon is now an Ulster Unionist Party representative on Belfast City Council lends him his own partiality. Nevertheless, even his more impish points are valuable: 'Can rage write? The Provos were more armed Hibernians than Republicans which probably explains the lack of war literature.'[49] Other reviews corroborate Dudgeon's interpretation of *Swallow*, seemingly because Morrison could only reach the other while staring out through the familiar bars of a prison cell: 'The novel's irony is that the opposite persona turns ignominiously into just another victimised social martyr, the feminised unknown maladjusted becomes a surrogate for the minor republican other . . . We end up once more annihilated by the violence of the Crum.'[50] The unflinching continuance of Morrison's political commitment in his writing reflects just how deeply the values of the party have imprinted the entire vision of many involved, raising parallels with leaders of Western European Communist Parties for whom all writing is principally a form of official 'party history'.[51]

---

[45] Eugene McEldowney, 'Hearts of Gold, Bullets of Lead', *Irish Times*, 25 March 1997, 14. See Danny Morrison, *The Wrong Man* (Cork: Mercier Press, 1997).

[46] *West Belfast* (Cork: Mercier Press, 1990).

[47] John Dunne, 'No Depth Charge', *Books Ireland*, No. 141 (May 1990), 96.

[48] Interview with Danny Morrison, Belfast, 29 August 2013.

[49] Email correspondence with Jeff Dudgeon, 31 August 2011. See Danny Morrison, *On the Back of the Swallow* (Cork: Mercier Press, 1994).

[50] Medbh McGuckian, 'On the Back of the Swallow', *Fortnight*, No. 334 (December 1994), 47.

[51] Stephen Hopkins, *The Politics of Memoir and the Northern Ireland Conflict* (Liverpool: Liverpool University Press, 2013), 9, 22.

When Morrison adapted *The Wrong Man* into a play he found local and UK theatre companies unreceptive to it for years, claiming this was down to 'prejudice' against his past and the 'assumption that anything I write would be an apologia for the IRA'.[52] Morrison accompanied this with resentful reflections on how Republican informers have been lionized, naturally reflecting his political view that they are beneath contempt. Yet a playwright, or any other creative writer, must enter the shoes of the informer to understand why he or she betrays a cause, as Liam O'Flaherty did with one of his best-known novels.[53] Comments St John Ervine made when manager of the Abbey in 1916 speak to this too: 'Your dramatist must be a man with a cool mind, judging these things without prejudice. If you were angry with men, you could not possibly understand them.'[54] Morrison denies the stage version of *The Wrong Man* is hostile towards its eponymous figure, claiming that a lot of Republicans did not like the play 'because they thought it was anti-IRA. Some of my old jail-mates turned round and said to me "You shouldn't be writing a play like that there, the IRA doesn't come out well in it."'[55] It was turned down first by the Paines Plough company in London and then by Pam Brighton, of the West Belfast-based DubbleJoint group. Brighton was strongly pro-Republican in outlook, denying that her rejection of the play was because of its content: 'I turned it down with great regret. We could have used the PR.' Brighton originally claimed Morrison 'hounded me to do his play', but I don't think it's very good', retrospectively paying tribute to his 'great energy' and reiterating that the play 'just wasn't very good. I love his book that he wrote in prison, I thought it was fabulous. I remember how upset he was about the play. He's not a novelist, not a creative writer—but I think he is a brilliant diarist.'[56]

Some of Morrison's best writing is to be found in *All the Dead Voices* (2002), an evocative and carefully written memoir which reflects his thinking about life, death, politics, and art. He explains how his initial picture of writers was of 'angst-ridden, bohemian, eccentric, iconoclastic

---

[52] Quoted in Karen Fricker, 'Too Hot to Handle', *The Guardian—G2*, 16 March 2005, 12. See 'From Novel to Stage', in *The Wrong Man*: Theatre Programme (Belfast: New Strung Theatre Company, 2005), 6. Linen Hall Library Political Collection.

[53] Liam O'Flaherty, *The Informer* (London: Penguin, 1936). Morrison is kinder to political opponents in one of his memoirs, inferring that his most impressive writing voice is not creative. See *All the Dead Voices* (Cork: Mercier Press, 2002), 126–7.

[54] *Irish Times*, 12 February 1916, 4.

[55] Interview with Danny Morrison, Belfast, 29 August 2013. See also Morrison, *All the Dead*, 164, 166.

[56] Quoted in *The Guardian—G2*, 16 March 2005, 12; interview with Pam Brighton, Belfast, 25 March 2014. The play was eventually staged at London's Pleasance Theatre in March 2005.

individuals', jarring with his own 'fundamentalist disposition' and involvement in 'a struggle and a propaganda war in which words were weapons and language was finely calibrated'.[57] One contemporary reviewer correctly observed how it displays 'the interests and views of Republicanism throughout the book, but in the range of people and the travels he undertakes there is a growing sense that the writer is becoming aware of others'.[58] Like Morrison's similarly broad-minded reviews, it displays an open-mindedness and capaciousness his creative work lacks.[59] The quality which drives his best writing is when the critical voice merges with the political, as perhaps it did during the height of his political involvement. Though he maintains that he can be bound to the community and write, there is certainly an inner struggle going on which can hardly be concealed: 'I'm still a supporter of Sinn Féin, I do things whenever I'm asked to. But I always think about it before I do anything now instead of automatically doing things.' He remembers on his 1995 release from jail feeling torn between resuming his role for Sinn Féin and becoming a writer, knowing he could not do both. The leadership supported his decision, though Morrison remembers 'agonizing over it. I felt that I was betraying people who were still in jail.'[60]

CONFLICT DISPLACED

Most importantly of all, Morrison believes that 'art and culture can displace and replace conflict', contingent with 'political activity and opportunity', and it is hard not to agree that the energies and antagonisms which were once expressed through bombs and bullets have now been diverted into plays and books. Morrison is a founder and former chairman of the *Féile an Phobail* festival, which adopted from its very first event 'a political edge but not a party political edge'.[61] Leaving aside the doublespeak, this is not to be dismissed lightly. Morrison points out that the *Féile* was founded to counter the 'demonization' of West Belfast following the Corporals killings of March 1988 and to overshadow the annual disturbances which accompanied the August anniversary of internment (from 1971), all of which 'left a bad taste in people's mouths'. The specific date of the festival coincided with attempting 'to bring people away from street

[57] Morrison, *All the Dead*, 162–3.
[58] Paul Donnelly, 'With a Pen in One Hand...', *Fortnight*, No. 410 (January 2003), 29.
[59] See Morrison's eloquent review of Sam McAughtry's novel *Touch & Go*, 'Missing the Pierrepoint', *Fortnight*, No. 320 (September 1993), 48.
[60] Interview with Danny Morrison, Belfast, 29 August 2013.
[61] Jim Gibney, 'Potent Programme as Féile Turns 25', *Irish News*, 8 August 2013, 19.

conflict',[62] a significant factor in reducing violence and disorder in West Belfast and symbolizing the broader significance of culture and the arts in pacification and rechannelled political competition. 'You can't just stop the violence and put nothing in its place,' said the director of the Ardoyne Fleadh, which ran alongside the *Féile* in 1996.[63] Parallels between the original internment anniversary events and the annual July bonfires in Protestant areas were recently highlighted, with the caveat that 'Sinn Féin stamped out the nationalist bonfire tradition, marking the August anniversary of internment through a plan of community action. Unionists do not work like this. We sense that something is wrong and drift away quietly one by one.'[64]

Another playwright once involved with Republican paramilitaries who has since gone in another direction is Martin Lynch (1950–). In his view the *Féile* is:

> at its heart a manifestation of the Catholic train that's going. If the train's a load of carriages of different aspects of nationalism, there's at least one carriage there that's the *Féile an Phobail*. The same as the *Andersonstown News*, the same as the *North Belfast News*. They're all following a nationalist agenda really. I don't want us to sit here all afternoon talking about the Provies [the Provisional IRA]—the Provies have made great progress from where they were thirty years ago. But when you have two leaders like Adams and McGuinness who are essentially nationalists with a wee smattering of social consciousness, you know what you're going to get, and you get what you get—and that's the fucking drivers of that train. That's what's going to permeate all the way though.[65]

Back in the 1980s Lynch was himself a politically driven writer, aware of his own didacticism, and his current reading derives from his background in the Official IRA/Workers' Party, one-time political adversaries of the Provisional IRA from the time of the December 1969 split. His comments must be understood in this light, as he continues to claim that the modern leaders of Sinn Féin have not made 'anything like that journey' of his own Marxist comrades in the Workers' Party. But he also admires the modern politico-cultural project of nationalist West Belfast for how it has

[62] Interview with Danny Morrison, Belfast, 29 August 2013. The festival was unsurprisingly pro-Sinn Féin 'because it was set up by Republicans'.

[63] Quoted in *Irish Times*, 6 August 1996, 6.

[64] Newton Emerson, 'Bonfires Reflect Underclass Defiance More than Loyalism', *Irish Times*, 14 July 2016, 14.

[65] Interview with Martin Lynch, Belfast, 20 March 2014. Brian Hanley and Scott Millar, *The Lost Revolution: The Story of the Official IRA and the Workers' Party* (Dublin: Penguin Ireland, 2009), 353, 513, 597.

mobilized young people to become involved in the arts, and the way it functions as an outlet for former Provisional IRA volunteers:

> I think people like [Danny] Morrison, who's a very bright guy, if he lived in England would progress a lot faster than what he is now. His problem is he's the same as the Sinn Féin movement. He has the constituency and if he goes too far in front of that constituency he will find his life will be intolerable, and he's not prepared to do that. I mean the Officials [Official IRA] were the first to do it in the 1970s by saying 'We're not Catholics. We're not fucking doing that. We're not defending Oldpark because the Protestants are attacking it. We don't do that.' That was like ructions in the Catholic communities. We were ostracized, spat at, shouted at in the street. And even these dissidents nowadays have made radical steps, like Tommy Gorman and Anthony McIntyre and all them ones, and have had to leave their homes because they stood outside the Provie community quite forcefully.[66]

On the other hand as *Féile an Phobail* has evolved and raised confidence within the Catholic nationalist community of West Belfast, it has increasingly hosted voices from outside its comfort zone. In August 2006 the festival helped to stage Gary Mitchell's *Remnants of Fear* at the Rock Theatre in Whiterock after he and his family were attacked and forced out of the overwhelmingly Protestant Rathcoole estate.[67] While the play contained the line 'The only thing Protestant people need to be protected from is the UDA [Ulster Defence Association],' and so there was an element of 'the version of Protestantism that Republicans want to hear' (as well as what many would regard as a reasonable comment),[68] it is also a sign of increasing tolerance and a measure of how far the festival has moved since its early days as a simple Sinn Féin mouthpiece.

In August 2016 the *Féile* organized the staging of scenes from *The Man that Swallowed a Dictionary*, a play written by Loyalist ex-prisoner Bobby Niblock about the deceased Progressive Unionist Party leader David Ervine, who he knew in the compounds of Long Kesh.[69] Danny Morrison puts this down to the way 'nationalists are more confident—so therefore can take more slagging in a way, can take Loyalists coming into the area. There's a confidence there about taking criticism or letting it bounce off you.'[70]

---

[66] Interview with Martin Lynch, Belfast, 20 March 2014. Gorman and McIntyre are both former Provisional IRA members who have criticized the political trajectory of Sinn Féin. The latter's home in West Belfast was picketed during the 2000s.

[67] *Irish News*, 1 August 2006, 10.

[68] Gary Mitchell, *Remnants of Fear* (Unpublished: 4th Draft July 2004), 118; interview with David Grant, Belfast, 20 October 2015.

[69] The *Féile* also helped to stage Niblock's first play *A Reason to Believe* in the autumn of 2009.

[70] Interview with Danny Morrison, Belfast, 29 August 2013.

Unionist politicians and high-ranking Police Service of Northern Ireland officers have additionally been invited to speak on the *Féile*'s discussion panels, leading to the festival's organizers receiving a thinly veiled threat from a Republican prisoners' group in the summer of 2016.[71] None of this has prevented continuous attacks on the festival from Unionist politicians,[72] who persistently overlook how such cultural initiatives have helped to prevent street disorder and violence.

Pam Brighton, who was born and raised in Bradford, made the valuable point that plays written by Republican ex-prisoners which she directed through the JustUs and DubbelJoint Theatre groups in West Belfast were not bound by the need for balance because at the time 'There was no Republican voice.' Community plays like *Binlids* (1997), written by Christine Poland, Brenda Murphy, Jake Mac Siacais, and Danny Morrison, were 'about giving that Republican community a voice. It wasn't meant to be even-handed; it was about their experience. I just felt that the imbalance was so total here. People weren't writing Republican plays because where could they get them on?'[73] The BBC and Lyric Theatre in the 1980s did not promote drama with their line of politics,[74] so it was up to Republicans themselves to create their own work. Where Brighton and other nationalist supporters ran into difficulties—and outright falsehoods—was in their claims that there were 'no even-handed plays' or political dramas on television or stage per se. As the writers discussed in the rest of this book illustrate, many engaged politically with the Troubles and politics; just not in the way Sinn Féin Republicans might approve of.

TROUBLED PORTRAYALS

While it is part of a 'liberal fallacy that *all* drama must at *all* times express multiple viewpoints', as a simple extension of the politics, polemical plays and novels never succeed in allowing any 'thinking space' or 'moment to reconsider ourselves, to ask how we can be otherwise'.[75] Though some of

---

[71] *Andersonstown News*, 30 July 2016, 1. This was the Irish Republican Prisoners' Welfare Association (IRPWA). The *Féile*'s directors responded that the threat was 'anti-community'.

[72] Nelson McCausland, 'Feile an Phobail a Success Today Thanks to NIO Money', *Belfast Telegraph*, 6 August 2015, 23.

[73] Interview with Pam Brighton, Belfast, 25 March 2014.

[74] A notable exception was the forgotten *Horseman, Pass By* (1985) by Daniel Magee, a former Sinn Féin activist, depicting the dynamics of a Belfast Republican family. It was staged at the Lyric and directed by the theatre's artistic director at the start of 1985, predating the theatrical efforts of Morrison and Laurence McKeown by over a decade (interview with Patrick Sandford, London, 13 October 2015).

[75] Michael Billington, *The Life and Work of Harold Pinter* (London: Faber and Faber, 1996), 289; Billington's italics. Gordon, *Theatre*, 70.

the plays written by Republicans have been defended by sympathetic scholars as pieces of 'ideological ballast on behalf of the drowning',[76] the problem is when those on the end of the ballast become one-dimensional or dehumanized—a stereotyped portrayal many Republicans claim they themselves endured during the Troubles. This didactic theatre does not encourage empathy with opposing groups and, on the contrary, denigrates and vilifies them. In *Forced Upon Us* (1999), written by Christine Poland and Brenda Murphy, the fascinating fusion of real-life historical figures (Edward Carson, James Craig, Fred Crawford, MPs Joe Devlin and John W. Nixon), verbatim quotes, and contemporary modern political attitudes eventually leads to a frank demonization of the Protestant working class. In one scene a reporter sketches 28 September 1912:

> REPORTER: This morning in Belfast, Ulster Day dawned. I watched as a sea of people gathered in the fine clear sunshine. Two hundred and fifty thousand strong, they moved silently and solemnly behind the yellow flag last carried at the Boyne. Watching from the dome of the City Hall, I saw that everywhere in the square facing the building, was black with people, a human sea, wave after wave of people of all ages. With Drums and fifes and sashes they marched all day to queue to sign the covenant.[77]

These are Ulster Protestants, and though a 'progressive element within the Protestant working class, of socialist trade unionists who were as screwed by the one one-party state as anybody else' is sketched through the character of Wilfred,[78] when working-class Protestants appear they are rapists (of a Catholic woman in the opening scene), thuggish bigots, and gun-crazed sectarians.[79] In another scene two workers catch sight of a Catholic, Paddy, and accuse him of stealing the rope and bottle of paint-thinner he is carrying. They beat him to the ground. 'String the bastard up to that lamppost over there. Let's have a bit of fun,' says Billy. The two Protestants then pour the paint-thinner over Paddy and set fire to him: 'he is screaming as the lights go down'.[80]

The play closes with the elderly Mary, the voice of communal West Belfast, in contemporary 1999:

---

[76] McDonnell, *Theatres*, 174.

[77] Brenda Murphy and Christine Poland, *Forced Upon Us* (Unpublished, n.d.), 4. I am extremely grateful to Danny Morrison for tracking down this script and sharing it.

[78] Brenda Murphy, quoted in *Irish Times*, 29 July 1999, 14; Murphy and Poland, *Forced*, 24–6, 34–6.

[79] Murphy and Poland, *Forced*, 2, 15–16, 24–6, 31–2.

[80] Murphy and Poland, *Forced*, 7–8.

MARY: I learned to be a good Catholic, keep my head down, say nothing when they draped their union jack over my machine at the twelfth, smiled at the taig jokes. But as soon as I could I voted for republicans, and I will do it till I die. So when them Shankill butchers started up in the 70s I wasn't surprised. I wasn't even frightened. I had seen it all before—and worse—from their grandfathers. It was part of their tradition.[81]

The play ends on one final dig at then-Ulster Unionist leader David Trimble, his 1998 Nobel Peace Prize 'not too noble [*sic*] now after him getting one'. A controversy over *Forced Upon Us* sprung up when the Arts Council of Northern Ireland (ACNI) initially withdrew £18,000 of the money allocated to DubbelJoint productions after external readers of the script objected to its quality and 'cardboard' characters.[82] Though the play is powerful and an accurate reflection of how Republicans think about the foundation of Northern Ireland, its depiction of invidious Protestants is facile and repellent.

Initially some of the plays Brighton directed, especially work by former Provisional IRA hunger striker Laurence McKeown (1956–), might have suffered from a similar debilitation. *The Official Version* (2006) is one of several plays about the legacy of the 1980–1 Hunger Strikes, featuring a Protestant former prison officer Robert, who now acts as a guide at the Maze prison. Though it has been claimed that writers McKeown and Brian Campbell 'faced sharp criticism from the Republican community for their determination to recognize the complexity of Loyalist experience', Brighton explained how 'it doesn't lambast the prison officer for who he was; it lambasts him for what he thinks. It's saying what this guy thinks is crazy. In the end what Laurence intended was that you felt sorry for the guy for being such a fucking idiot.'[83] Whereas this would again appear to refuse to understand a non-Republican perspective, McKeown's recent short play, *Those You Pass On the Street*—first produced by Kabosh Theatre Company in 2014—is a sophisticated piece about how Northern Ireland deals with the past. Beginning with Elizabeth Farrell entering a Sinn Féin office to enquire if anything can be done about anti-social behaviour of kids in her area, we learn that her husband Michael was a Catholic RUC Superintendent shot dead by the Provisional IRA. Elizabeth's predicament is that people have no idea how it feels

[81] Murphy and Poland, *Forced*, 59–60.
[82] *Irish Times*, 6 August 1999, 7; McDonnell, *Theatres*, 176. See also Ian Hill, 'Double Trouble', *Fortnight*, No. 380 (September 1999), 21–2. Funding was eventually restored.
[83] McDonnell, *Theatres*, 199; interview with Pam Brighton, Belfast, 25 March 2014.

'To live amongst people and wonder if one of those you pass on the street, maybe who speaks or smiles or waves to you was the person who set your husband up, gave the information, pulled the trigger'.[84]

In many ways the play confirms that the political project is still paramount and its writers remain 'on message'.[85] We are constantly reminded that Sinn Féin get things done and put in the 'work on the ground'. Comic value appears in the form of Elizabeth's vacuous friend Ann, an archetypal Social Democratic and Labour Party supporter (in the Sinn Féin vision),[86] and the play functions in large part as an intra-communal challenge towards a middle-class Catholic constituency. The key character of *Those You Pass On the Street* is Frank, who initially receives Elizabeth in the office and helps to solve her 'anti-social' problem. In a conversation between the conventional Sinn Féin figure Pat and the more discerning Frank, the former reminds the audience that the IRA were not sectarian and killed people because they were in the security forces:

> PAT: All very nice to say they were just poor Protestants going about their work. It suits them to say he was killed because of his religion rather than admit he was part of an army keeping an eye on his neighbours, part of loyalist killer gangs, part of a group that harassed people day and night.[87]

A hallmark of these plays is to explain and, where necessary, justify why the IRA had to bomb and shoot to achieve their aims politically. Instead of any suggestion of remorse for the killing of Elizabeth's 'Real Castle Catholic' husband,[88] it is Elizabeth who must move and realize that Sinn Féin have changed and are good at what they do.

Pat is angry when he hears 'this "poor us" and the "big, bad IRA" and what they did or didn't do and them taking no responsibility for what they did or didn't do'. At the same time, he has accepted the rule of law and the Police Service of Northern Ireland's jurisdiction, serving on the local policing partnership, and so part of this theatre is also about holding the

---

[84] Laurence McKeown, *Those You Pass On the Street* (Unpublished, Performed Script 2014), 14. My thanks to Laurence McKeown for access to this play-script.

[85] The actor Stuart Graham judges that Republican drama 'fails to see the individual. It's all about the message passed down to them, and they are "on message" all the time.' Best known for his role as the prison officer in *Hunger* (2008), Graham says that 'All good drama centres around the human condition, individually. Drama isn't about telling people what to think: it's about making them think for themselves' (interview with Stuart Graham, Belfast, 8 October 2011).

[86] McKeown, *Those You Pass*, 1–4, 10–11.

[87] McKeown, *Those You Pass*, 16–18.   [88] McKeown, *Those You Pass*, 4.

base: 'A lot of our own people are still very shaky about where we're at. Decommissioning, Stormont, in bed with the DUP, policing. Sometimes I have to give my own head a shake about how far we've come.'[89] Furthermore, Frank is very gently asking questions and we learn later that his brother Gerard was executed by the IRA as an informer, appearing close to a sincere acknowledgement that the IRA's killings were disturbing and even immoral.[90] While the audience still needs to understand why violence was—to borrow the phrase of one study—'objectively necessary',[91] this is recognition of sorts. Towards the end we learn from Pat that Frank has suddenly died of a heart attack and how he and his parents never got over the killing of his brother. His mother 'was a life-long republican' who 'walked away from us', as had Frank, who 'reacted against the movement... Got into trouble, mostly with the Movement. Would get drunk, start fights'. Having lived abroad in the United States and England, he came back calmer: 'There were those who wondered why he would want to join Sinn Fein when it was the IRA shot his brother. I thought he was someone who had returned to his community and we needed to find a place for him.'[92] Emphasizing the group cohesion of West Belfast, this is also a tacit admission of responsibility, even if it relates to the killing of an informer rather than a 'Castle Catholic' or a Protestant.

GROUP WRITING

Even when Danny Morrison reaches a place where he feels more 'objective' following the 1994 Ceasefire, he is drawn back: 'There is a dependent relationship between a writer and his or her society. No artist functions in a psychological vacuum and there are pressures to represent the interests of one's community. Some writers simply "flee", believing they can transcend history, loyalty and communal solidarity, often to enjoy only illusory objectivity.'[93] This should not be underestimated, chiming as it does with what Gerry Adams once referred to as 'group Catholic thinking'.[94] The playwright Gary Mitchell, who was born and grew up on the mainly Protestant Rathcoole estate, understands this ethos and the protection it offers. In the case of his own community:

---

[89] McKeown, *Those You Pass*, 20, 24.   [90] McKeown, *Those You Pass*, 27–8.
[91] McDonnell, *Theatres*, 188. This prescriptive phrase is problematic, as most Ulster Protestants (and many Catholics) see the violence of the Provisional IRA as neither objective nor necessary.
[92] McKeown, *Those You Pass*, 28.   [93] Morrison, *All the Dead*, 166.
[94] Quoted in Fionnuala O'Connor, *In Search of a State: Catholics in Northern Ireland* (Belfast: Blackstaff Press, 1993), 87.

There's no structure to it and it's very individual—and this has always been the problem with the Protestant community. It's about one person deciding to do something or looking at a problem or a difficulty. You have a guy getting involved in the arts who wants to write everything, direct everything, produce everything, and decide everything. And next door to him could be another Protestant who wants to write, produce, direct, and star in his own thing—this is the problem. If you were to introduce the two of them and say, 'Oh do you realize you're both Protestants and you're both talking about the same thing?', they'd go 'Ah no, he's crap. Oh I hate him, don't listen to him.' And then you say to the other guy, 'But you do realize you're next-door neighbours?': 'Ah he's a loudmouth, he's a piece of shit. Don't listen to him. I'm the one.'

On the other hand:

If you were to look at the opposite, the West Belfast festival for instance, from a housing estate like Rathcoole or Carrickfergus, you look at that and go 'That's all Catholic.' But what it is, more importantly, is organized. It's together; it's coherent, and you can see very definite Catholic structures. Now if that goes on then to be blurred with nationalism or Republicanism, it's allowed and supported and it sort of flourishes. They prop each other up. They help each other, and you can see that some elements—even the tiniest elements—are being carried by the bigger, more powerful elements. If you look at Protestants doing the same things, or thinking about the same things, the reason that they're pathetic is it's one person trying to do it all by themselves.[95]

Mitchell is looking at this as an individual who was cast out from the group—he was driven out of his home by Loyalist paramilitaries at the end of 2005—and so is highly attuned to its power. At the same time, polemical writing from the modern Irish Republican movement is subsequently tied to a fluctuating political atmosphere of which it is itself an integral part. Thus Mitchell senses problems ahead for Republicans, with past certainties changing or dissolving:

In a way they're a bit trapped now, because now they've gone into government there really are big problems for writers like Danny Morrison. How can you talk about the army, the police, how can you write plays when you say in every play that the police and army are the bad guys? When someone comes to you and says, 'Now excuse me—we need our own police and our own army. Now when we build these, are they going to be the bad guys?' Or is there possibly a notion that, somehow, a person who wants to be a policeman could be a good person? Because if you look back, every policeman who has ever existed and every person who wanted to be a policeman in those plays is naturally a bad person. You suddenly need new work to explain all this. You suddenly need new work to encourage people to join the police, and where are we going to get that from?[96]

This also leads to the syndrome, upholding a group 'consensus', where activists are keen to convey how impressive the literature of their comrades is, promoting art which is 'all about community esteem'.[97] In the different but connected practice of memoir-writing, which Adams has himself industrially cultivated, writing is crucial in aligning the story and fortunes of individual Republican leaders with the entire Catholic nationalist community.[98] Writing in the newspaper most entwined with the Catholic communal mind of Northern Ireland, a Gerry Adams acolyte points out that the diary of Bobby Sands has never been out of print, lauding the 'content, fluency and style' of Sands's writings.[99] While debatable, such statements reflect a demonstrable belief in the value of writing itself, a recognition which has not always been granted the respect it deserves, especially against a broader philistinism which occasionally characterizes Northern Ireland.

Militant Irish Republican drama is nothing new. It began in a modern context with Seán O'Casey, who was a member of James Connolly's Irish Citizen Army and illustrated his political disillusionment through his plays, jarring later postcolonialists who could not quite reconcile the dramatic ability with the politics, the left-wing humanism with Irish nationalism.[100] O'Casey—along with other Republican writers of a previous age—were motivated by the wish to challenge, rather than affirm, communal consensus. Standing up to the crowd of Irish nationalists who attempted to prevent *The Plough and the Stars* from being staged in 1926, O'Casey explained—via his autobiographies' inimitable third person— how 'Sean knew well that . . . what concerned them was the implication of fear showing itself in the manner and speech of the fighting characters of the play; and in the critical way their patriotism was ignored, or opposed by Dublin's poor.'[101] But polemical literature of the kind Republicans in

---

[96] Interview with Gary Mitchell, Antrim, 6 June 2013. For a discussion of Mitchell see Chapter 6.
[97] Aughey, *Irish Kulturkampf*, 9.
[98] Hopkins, *Politics of Memoir*, 17–19, 27–9. See Gerry Adams, *Before the Dawn: An Autobiography* (Kerry: Brandon, 1996).
[99] Jim Gibney, 'Indomitable Spirit of Hunger Striker Lives On', *Irish News*, 13 March 2014, 19.
[100] See Seamus Deane, *Celtic Revivals: Essays in Modern Irish Literature 1880–1980* (London: Faber and Faber, 1985), 108–22.
[101] Sean O'Casey, *Inishfallen, Fare Thee Well: Autobiography: Book 4, 1917–1926* (London: Pan Books, 1949), 178.

Northern Ireland are writing also echoes the early pagan ideal of the hero in Ireland, exemplified by Cú Chulainn. It was the job of druids and *filid* (poets) 'to confer honour on the king or chieftain and to foster and perpetuate his fame: to ordain him hero'. Brendan Ó Magagáin argues that this 'surviving heroic tradition holds the key to an understanding of a very great deal in Irish culture right down to our own time', and so the modern Republican ideologue who doubles as writer can therefore be seen to represent a modern form of the bardic poet, upholding black-and-white heroism and/or villainy. The individual, meanwhile, is 'of no importance: merely a link in the all-important community-chain',[102] leading up to the King—or president.

LOYALIST LITERATURE

Writing in the year of the Good Friday Agreement, a journalist stated that one of the intriguing details of the Troubles was 'how little literature—well, writing anyway—has come from the Loyalists and how much from their adversaries: poetry from Martin McGuinness, plays and movies from Ronan Bennett, short stories and memoirs from Gerry Adams. Patrick Pearse would have approved.'[103] Temporarily leaving aside the Protestant working-class writers to be explored in this book, Loyalists did write (and think) creatively during the Troubles, and were more proximate to writers than is often credited. In a somewhat bizarre intersection, the former Supreme Commander of the UDA, Andy Tyrie, encountered the Irish novelist Francis Stuart in the mid-1970s:

> He was strange. He came up to talk to me, we had a bit of a yarn and he told me all about going to volunteer to do the propaganda for the Germans. They put him in jail so they did. They thought he was mad, absolutely mad. And he looked like the Gestapo—you know all the things you see? Tall, sort of aristocratic-looking person. He was a lovely man too. But he just had ideas about he could go and help the Germans to capture the world. He was just someone who had a fascination for this sort of thing, he maybe thought that he would have looked well in the SS uniform or something. In my journey I've met some fascinating people.[104]

[102] Brendan Ó Madagáin, 'Cultural Continuity and Regeneration', in M. A. G. Ó Tuathaigh (ed.), *Community, Culture, and Conflict: Aspects of the Irish Experience* (Galway: Galway University Press, 1986), 19, 21, 23–4.
[103] John Boland, 'Armalite into Word-processor', *Irish Times*, 3 January 1998, 31.
[104] Interview with Andy Tyrie, Dundonald, 9 August 2012. Stuart, who knew Yeats and married Maud Gonne's daughter Iseult, praised Tyrie as 'A very intelligent person and a

It is often forgotten that Tyrie, along with Sammy Duddy and Michael Hall, wrote a play concerning Ian Paisley's declared 'Day of Action' in 1981.[105] The idea came from a real incident when a young man from Dundonald went to parade in Newtownards with notions of blocking off the border to put a stop to violence. Tyrie relays the story that when the event ended, after rousing speeches, the young man asked one of the striped seniors,

> 'What bus have I to get on?' They said to him: 'Where do you live?' He says Dundonald, and the man said: 'Well you just get on the Dundonald bus and go on home, because it's over.' And he couldn't take that. He was sick of the whole situation and was simply told, 'This is a bit of play-acting, away home.' He was really hurt because he thought this was it.

This Is It!, complete with songs and archetypally black Belfast humour, was a response to those senior members of Protestant public life, Unionist politicians and Orange leaders, who whipped up others but ended 'queuing up to do nothing'. Writing a play represented 'the best way to get at them'.[106] At one stage a discerning UDA sergeant questions how many of the men in the main prisons of the Crumlin Road and Long Kesh are politicians:

> DAVE: Those ones out there on the platforms do all the mouthin'—
> (*THEN IN A PAISLEY VOICE*) 'Ulster will fight and Ulster will be Right' 'The Protestant People will not tolerate this any longer.' But who does the fightin! Us! The ordinary Prods! That lot keep their noses clean. What gets up my nose is after having goaded us into action, they turn round and fuckin' disown us. We're just dirt then![107]

Though some deduced that Tyrie was 'finding in fictions what they cannot find in reality',[108] the play became a vent for Tyrie's (and Loyalism's) ire towards provocative but well-heeled Unionist politicians—an immensely common Loyalist predicament. Dave also laments Britain's treatment of Ulster Loyalists, their reward for war service and loyalty the 'Worst bloody living conditions in Europe':

> DAVE: To be honest, I'm a Labour man. It's the Republican threat that always made me support the Unionists. But I'd no love for the

[105] Andy Tyrie, Sam Duddy, and Michael Hall, *This Is It!*, *Theatre Ireland*, No. 7 (Autumn 1984), 19–34. Sammy Duddy also published a poetry collection, *Concrete Whirlpools of the Mind* (1983).
[106] Interview with Andy Tyrie, Dundonald, 9 August 2012. Initially the UDA approached Martin Lynch to write the play, but this collaboration never materialized.
[107] Tyrie, Duddy, and Hall, *This Is It!*, 27.
[108] O'Toole, 'Escaping Reality', 10.

bastards. Most of their leaders were landed gentry—and I could tell
you what I think of the fur coat brigade![109]

This theme is echoed in unpublished poems written by Tyrie's one-time
UDA associate Glen Barr, also a trade unionist and first chair of the New
Ulster Political Research Group (NUPRG). Understandably better known
as a community worker and leader of the Ulster Workers' Council strike of
May 1974 (see Chapter 4), his poetry is passionate but crude. Though
Barr was a left-leaning Loyalist,[110] the verse highlights some traditional
problems. Ireland is, of course, a woman and a 'harlot' at that, with one
poem bordering on a strange sexualized view of the conflict:

> Oh England take care
> For this harlot has no affection for you.
> She uses her bed to sap your strength
> And when you awake in the morning
> To find yourself in her chains
> You will remember the words of warning that I spoke.
> She takes no pleasure from the orgy with you
> For it is me that she desires.
> She only fills your head with wine
> So that in your drunken stupor
> You lose your sword and drop your shield
> And my naked body is exposed to her.[111]

Despite this, the piece reflects the UDA's flirtation with the symbolism of
Cú Chulainn and confirms that Loyalists, like Irish Republicans, often
write out of a kind of grievance. Another poem echoes Tyrie's preoccupation with Protestant elites and the way Loyalists were cajoled by those
on 'higher ground' who,

> waved the biggest 'Union Jacks' and urged us to advance,
> But they did not move forward and left us to take the chance.
> Oh I surely recognised them, I'd seen them all before,
> If not on the television then Orange platforms in Dromore.[112]

There is the familiar contempt for 'Gaelic heroes' using 'all the worn out
clichés to move their forces on', but Barr also slates those who 'cringe

---

[109] Tyrie, Duddy, and Hall, *This Is It!*, 30. The 'fur coat brigade' was a derogatory term
for affluent members of the Official Unionist Party.

[110] *Irish Times*, 23 September 1977, 6.

[111] Glen Barr, 'The Lamentations of Mother Ulster' (n.d.). Barr was drafting the 1979
UPRG document *Beyond the Religious Divide* at the same time as he wrote this (interview
with Glen Barr, Derry, 28 November 2012).

[112] Glen Barr, 'The Ulidian' (1986), 1. I am very grateful to Glen Barr for sharing his
poems.

behind their castles and make us the sacrifice', before a final call to 'cast off all these ancient chains' and 'Be not a second class "Brit" or Gael but a first class "Ulidian"'.[113]

Brian Ervine, the brother of the former Loyalist political leader David (and a distant relative of St John Ervine), wrote his own play *Somme Day Morning*, which was staged through Tom Magill's Shankill Community Theatre Company in November 1994.[114] Ervine would lead the Progressive Unionist Party in the May 2011 Assembly election, when the party lost its only seat in East Belfast following a split Loyalist vote, but has always been fascinated by the theatre. In his office on the Albertbridge Road he described travelling down to Dublin to see Seán O'Casey's *The Silver Tassie* at the Abbey, which he found enjoyable and moving. He had looked up its intermittent production history and saw in the story resonances with present-day Northern Ireland:

> There was a message in it. Because the guys who were maimed, the victims—the guy was a great footballer, he was in a wheelchair, and another guy was blind—wanted the world to stop for them. They wanted to come and pick things up as it was before. And it could never be the same again. So his best friend is going to marry his ex-girlfriend, he's raging about that. They're feeling guilty and the nurse says: 'No. They have to find their own way, they have to find their own medal. And you have to get on with your living.' And I thought it was a great message for Northern Ireland. Because we can't be hamstrung by the victims of our troubles. The victims can't set the agenda or we'll never get anywhere. Now we facilitate the victims and sympathize with them as much as possible, but we have to draw the line and move on.[115]

The Historical Enquiries Team (HET) has been involved in individual prosecutions of Loyalists who committed killings during the Troubles, and Ervine confirmed how a grievance was arising—and remains ongoing[116]—because Republican paramilitaries are seen to be given a free ride by the authorities in return for their participation in political institutions.

At the same time the families of victims, including many Ulster Protestants, are less convinced of the need to 'move on'. Indeed part of the difficulty with 'ex-combatants' who have embraced storytelling through the arts is the risk of 'valorising terrorist narratives over the very real effect of

---

[113] Barr, 'Ulidian', 2. The Kingdom of Ulidia signified the 'lesser Ulster', with Ulidian translating here as 'Ulsterman'.

[114] McDonnell, *Theatres*, 154–7.

[115] Interview with Brian Ervine, Belfast, 28 January 2011.

[116] See, for instance, the case of ex-UVF prisoner Robert Rodgers, convicted in 2013 for the September 1974 killing of Eileen Doherty (*Belfast Telegraph*, 21 February 2013, 18).

violence on victims'.[117] This could not however be levelled at Brian Ervine, who also spoke of how O'Casey was a favourite of his father Walter, an intriguing character who passed on his books and socialism to his sons, sowing the seeds for their eventual dissent from mainstream Unionism and traditional assumptions. Inheriting his father's enthusiasm—and lack of interest in ever becoming a member of the Orange Order—Brian Ervine admired O'Casey for being:

> about the only one at that time from the Nationalist side to give the Unionist viewpoint. Of course he was a Dublin Protestant—John Casey, as you know—but his mother was a Loyalist! So he had that point of view and he gave it in *The Plough and the Stars* as well, when Bessie Burgess is united with them and says 'What about that, stabbing in the back the men that are dying for you in the trenches?' And that was the Unionist view of the 1916 Rebellion. In 1916, the 1st July, you had the Somme just after the Easter Rebellion. Ulster's blood sacrifice was given there.[118]

Ervine, finally, referenced Yeats's poem 'The Ghost of Roger Casement', adapting its refrain ('The Ghost of Roger Casement / Is beating on the door'): 'There are two houses in Ireland, and the ghost of Edward Carson is knocking on the other door; that's the problem. So you have all this glamour of the cause, and it's a lot of old twaddle when you think about it, "a terrible beauty is born". No terrible beauty at all—it's horrible, O'Casey says.' Though he rather glosses over the ambivalent 'terrible beauty' of Yeats's 'Easter 1916', the engagement with the original Protestant working-class dramatist O'Casey once again illuminates a unique collision of politics and literature, illustrating in Ervine's own words that 'our history and culture are not threadbare as some people believe', and that Loyalists, too, are not adrift from theatres and literature.

CONCLUSION

One renowned Belfast dramatist argues that Northern Ireland is:

> quite an anti-intellectual, anti-art place, and what has happened is that instead of an embrace of the openness of art there has been a push to control it. That's how stories are told. Like 'It's our story—we control the art, in the same way that we control our story.' As opposed to the art should just expand

[117] Aaron Edwards and Cillian McGrattan, 'Terroristic Narratives: On the (Re)Invention of Peace in Northern Ireland', *Terrorism and Political Violence*, Vol. 23, No. 3 (2011), 365.
[118] Interview with Brian Ervine, Belfast, 28 January 2011. On their father, see the comments of David Ervine in Moloney (ed.), *Voices*, 309–16.

everything and say: 'Maybe our story was wrong. Maybe what we thought all along was fucking wrong.' That control, that rigid type-thing—politicians here love that because that in itself is controllable. When the idea is like Picasso's fucking *Guernica*, you should be able to rip things asunder! That's what art's about.[119]

It would be unjust to measure Irish Republican writers by such a distinguished compass. Their project is different and ultimately linked to moving beyond the violence of the recent past. With the emergence of new initiatives there are signs that Loyalists are learning from this, and the late director Pam Brighton, who worked tirelessly for much of the latter part of her life in West Belfast, felt that the community needed to speak to itself first. She was 'fighting for a community's voice, and I knew from having worked in the BBC how impossible it was to ever hear it in that way. The people who needed to hear it was their own community.' Brighton elaborated how 'People say, "Oh John McGrath's plays are all about socialists," but socialists need to be reaffirmed. They *need* to know that other people think like them, in the way that I think Republicans desperately needed that at that point: "We're not crazy; there're loads of people who think like us."' When put to her that Seán O'Casey's plays, like many of the writers considered in the following chapters, offered a challenge to the political constituency he himself had emerged from, Brighton replied: 'I don't feel that that's my job. I would publicly support Sinn Féin like most people round here. They'd have a huge number of quibbles about what Sinn Féin's doing, but most people come out and vote for them because if you look around West Belfast, the amount of people that suffered is just incredible.' The experience of state brutality and those Republicans who served long prison sentences is what modern Sinn Féin 'came out of', and out of respect for this Brighton was prepared to give them the full benefit of the doubt.[120] Martin Lynch concurs that the communal aspect is crucial, with nationalists having come through 'this very painful struggle which has created a huge bond that I'm not a part of. But it's tangible. You can touch it, you can smell it, you see it all around you. And even people who aren't political will say "Well look, I'm with the lads."'[121]

---

[119] Interview with Owen McCafferty, Belfast, 28 March 2013. See his play *Scenes from the Big Picture* (London: Nick Hern Books, 2003).
[120] Interview with Pam Brighton, Belfast, 25 March 2014. This interview took place in West Belfast.
[121] Interview with Martin Lynch, Belfast, 20 March 2014.

As with the 1916 Easter Rising, the cultural and political movements are interlinked, though in Northern Ireland the cultural war followed the military conflict. The reverse had been the case earlier in the century, when plays such as Yeats's *Kathleen ni Houlihan* (1902) had 'made more rebels in Ireland than a thousand political speeches or a hundred reasoned books', helping to sow the seeds for violence.[122] The modern mainstream Republican movement, on the other hand, realized that culture and writing were ideal ways to disengage from physical-force methods. Danny Morrison, Laurence McKeown, and Ronan Bennett would all strongly deny that they are any less political than they were before they wrote. All are commendably honest about the indivisibility of their fiction from their politics. By his own admission Bennett believed 'that writing novels was not only something he felt driven to do, but an effective way for him to "play a part" politically'.[123] In Morrison's case: 'The stories that we pass on to the next generation we will carefully craft. They will contain self-justifications. Some aspects of the conflict—the heroism, the sacrifices—will be singled out, glorified; others, belonging to the darker side, will be suppressed or sanitized.'[124]

The debilitating and fallacious by-product, however, of the struggle continuing through art, literature, and culture has been the accompanying denigration of opposing groups to the extent that demoralization and a sense of defeatism is now prevalent in the Protestant working class. Though the idea that Protestants have 'no future' and 'no culture' is itself a fiction, 'it is one which some Protestants themselves have come to believe'.[125] It is no coincidence that Pam Brighton spoke of how the West Belfast Catholic community, compared to the Protestant working class,

> is just a much brighter community. It's a much sharper community that has a future and can see it. West Belfast has something to celebrate and East Belfast doesn't. I think the Protestant working class, as in East Belfast, is fucked on the whole: absolutely fucked. Unionism will not come to terms with the fact that the future ain't gonna be what it imagines.[126]

This bluntness may raise hackles but it accurately captures what many Irish nationalists think and are careful not to express in public. Neither are all Brighton's opinions completely without foundation. Her view that

[122] Lennox Robinson, *Curtain Up* (London: Michael Joseph, 1942), 17. See also F. S. L. Lyons, *Culture and Anarchy in Ireland, 1890–1939* (Oxford: Oxford University Press, 1979), 85–113.
[123] Paul Laity, 'The Controversialist', *The Guardian Review*, 27 October 2007, 11.
[124] Danny Morrison, 'Northern Futures', *The Irish Review*, No. 31 (2004), 81.
[125] Aughey, *Irish Kulturkampf*, 8. An anonymous musician from a Presbyterian background talked in the mid-1990s of 'dying' Protestant estates, and how 'a wee parade on the Twelfth, beating a drum and hating Catholics' was the sum of Protestant culture. Marilyn Hyndman (ed.), *Further Afield: Journeys from a Protestant Past* (Belfast: Beyond the Pale, 1996), 104.
[126] Interview with Pam Brighton, Belfast, 25 March 2014.

'Unionism/Loyalism, whatever you call it, has been so misled—I don't think any movement has ever had such rotten leaders', turns out to be surprisingly in tune with what Loyalist leaders of yesteryear think:

> Sinn Féin seem to have learned so much from their struggle, whereas our politicians learned very little. Because, to be honest, the Unionist politicians weren't in the struggle—the ordinary people were. We seem to carry this with us wherever we go. We find somebody who has a few bob and a stable and if they shout 'Right there's a war on, let's go', we all get behind them and go to war and once the war's over we take all our wounded back home again to the empty houses and bad conditions. And we start all over again.[127]

While the mythology that working-class Protestants are essentially an underclass with 'no culture' aside from the Orange Order and marching bands was always a possible runner in a post-conflict situation, what could not have been predicted was the extent to which Unionist politicians and leaders would embrace this mythology to become, in their own way, the greatest cultural warriors of all. No one is surer that Protestant culture is Orange alone. Factored in with the democratically secured removal of British symbols, provocative gestures such as the naming of children's play parks after Republican hunger strikers,[128] and long-standing feelings of alienation 'where declining working-class Protestant communities in areas such as Ardoyne and Tiger's Bay felt themselves losing out in a zero-sum conflict with Catholics',[129] and an angry defeatism is always liable to spike. One well-regarded writer perceives that the only way his former community believes they 'can fight back is by being really stupid and counter-productive, instead of actually sitting down saying "How can we combat this?"'[130]

Danny Morrison maintains that reading literature in prison enabled him 'to enter into the private minds of other souls—into the core—to understand motivation',[131] but this does not resound through his creative voice. He volunteers, tellingly, that he could not write a novel from a woman's perspective. Politically he now encourages Catholics to join the police force because Northern Ireland 'is not the place in which I grew up. There's nothing in this state which is not open to nationalists, which you could not have said thirty, twenty years ago.'

---

[127] Interview with Andy Tyrie, Dundonald, 9 August 2012.

[128] See, for instance, Newry and Mourne Council's vote to retain the naming of a children's play park after IRA hunger striker Raymond McCreesh (*Belfast Telegraph*, 4 December 2012, 7). McCreesh was arrested in possession of a rifle linked to the Kingsmills massacre of January 1976, when ten Protestant workers were shot dead.

[129] Henry Patterson, *Ireland Since 1939: The Persistence of Conflict* (Dublin: Penguin Ireland, 2006), 346–7.

[130] Interview with Maurice Leitch, London, 31 July 2015.

[131] Morrison, *All the Dead*, 160–1.

However, the likelihood of Morrison writing a novel or play which portrays the police even objectively remains dubious. In a strange sense the politics is more conciliatory than the culture, which is narrower. Inching political progress also appears forthcoming via initiatives like the 'Uncomfortable Conversations' series featuring the views of Unionists and non-Republican contributors, published in Sinn Féin's newspaper *An Phoblacht*.[132]

Overall Morrison appears to be aware of the quandary between culture and politics, noting that even in his current position within the movement 'the side of the [*Féile*] festival that I'm involved in is all the discussions and debates, plus also literary events—which shows you there's a division. I'm still caught between that dichotomy.' Morrison disagrees with Gary Mitchell's critiques that re-writing will be necessary and reminds us of the new dispensation, with Sinn Féin Republicans supporting the Police Service of Northern Ireland. What unsettles Ulster Unionists about the arts and literature, Morrison argues, is 'what is on the other side of the door. I think they're insecure. "Will I end up supporting a different point of view? Will I end up repudiating my past convictions?"' Put to him that the same thing could be applied to Irish Republicans if they took on the challenges of art, he replied:

> The difference is that politically that has already happened to nationalists and Republicans. The compromise has already happened. They've already crossed that bridge. The Unionists, in a sense, are still reluctant. They're still fighting the war. It's all about flags and 'How can we screw Sinn Féin continually?' This is where Republicans have the luxury of assuming that history's on their side.[133]

This negates that Republicans are also still fighting the war through books and politics, and are similarly fixated about flags (the original motion to remove the Union flag at Belfast City Council during mid-2012 was led by Sinn Féin).[134] And while the sense of community is formidable, and there can be consolation in upholding group allegiance because political choices have already been decided, one of the Protestant working-class dramatists in this book reminds us that the 'banishment from the tribe and the banishment from the self are interlinked. It gets dangerous when you can't live outside the tribe because you've not yet forged a complete identity for yourself.'[135]

---

[132] See Brian Kennaway, 'Reconciliation? We Need Genuine Words of "Abject and True Remorse" Demonstrated in Action', *An Phoblacht*, July 2015, 22.
[133] Interview with Danny Morrison, Belfast, 29 August 2013.
[134] *Belfast Telegraph*, 2 June 2012, 1.
[135] Interview with Ron Hutchinson, Belfast, 2 August 2012.

2

The Strange Radicalism of Thomas Carnduff and St John Ervine

I am studying life, not by culture,
But meeting it face to face.

Thomas Carnduff, 'A Worker's Philosophy' (1932)

MRS RAINEY: They'll have to mix in heaven, John.
RAINEY: This isn't heaven.

St John Ervine, *Mixed Marriage* (1911)

The London *Times* obituary of St John Ervine (Fig. 2.1), published as violence raged once more in his home place, referred to its subject's political individualism and withering criticism of the Irish government for its neutrality during the Second World War.[1] Little mention was made of Ervine's earlier associations, prompting Dame Margaret Cole—wife of Labour ideologue G. D. H. Cole—to publish a rejoinder obituary in the same newspaper one week later. Paying tribute to Ervine's 'early political radicalism, which was vigorous and of historical interest', Mrs Cole clarified that prior to the First World War Ervine had been 'an ardent Fabian' and a founder-member of the Fabian Nursery. As a one-time secretary of the Fabian Society, he had been guided through left-wing circles via the Fabian Executive Committee, chaired by George Bernard Shaw, who Ervine would form a long-lasting connection with as a friend and eventual biographer. Accepting that Ervine renounced socialism to become a forceful individualist, apparently on account of his personal dislike for Beatrice Webb, Margaret Cole also recalled letters from him as late as the 1950s which exhibited 'affectionate reminisces of some of his former Fabian comrades'.[2] One sensed an intrusion into the life Ervine had wished to leave behind.

---

[1] Anon., 'Mr St John Ervine: Playwright, Critic and Author', *London Times*, 25 January 1971, 12. See St John Ervine, 'Letter: Eire and the War', *London Times*, 6 March 1945, 5.
[2] Dame Margaret Cole, 'Mr St John Ervine: A Founder of the Fabian Nursery', *London Times*, 1 February 1971, 12. See St John Ervine, *George Bernard Shaw: His Life, Work, and Friends* (London: Constable, 1956).

Fig. 2.1. Photo of St John Ervine.
Note: Permission of the Estates of John Boyd

The turning point, as it was for so many, was Flanders. Immediately following his tenure managing the Abbey Theatre in 1916, Ervine enlisted as a trooper in the Household Battalion, going on to serve as a second lieutenant in the Royal Dublin Fusiliers. In an intriguing twist he joined an Irish as opposed to an English regiment after hearing a London crowd cheer the August 1916 execution of Roger Casement (Ervine would eventually refer to Casement as 'a piece of pestilential trash' and a 'traitor').[3] 'St. John wrote to me from the trenches. He does not seem to be anything like as miserable as some of my correspondents are', Shaw imparted to Ervine's wife: 'Happily he is not in a specially dangerous place.'[4] But his mentor had spoken too soon. Months later Ervine was shot in the knee, an injury eventually requiring the amputation of his leg and two operations before

[3] Patrick Maume, 'Ulstermen of Letter: The Unionism of Frank Frankfort Moore, Shan Bullock, and St John Ervine', in Richard English and Graham Walker (eds), *Unionism in Modern Ireland* (Dublin: Gill & Macmillan, 1996), 73; St John Ervine, *Craigavon: Ulsterman* (London: Allen & Unwin, 1949), 334.
[4] Letter to Leonora Ervine, 16 November 1917. HRC.

his release from Military Hospital.[5] He later regretted the 'great change in my life—I was a lover of long walks and swimming—and I had to give up much that I had previously enjoyed'. Ervine's problems with Beatrice Webb appear to have stemmed from her visiting him as he was recovering during this time, arriving on his ward 'determined to have me nominated there and then for a constituency [as a Labour MP] although I was not likely to be fit for any given work for a considerable period'.[6] As friends digested the bad news, Shaw consoled that Ervine was 'in bed . . . instead of under fire; and on the whole I think we must congratulate him', while Horace Plunkett invited him to recuperate in the sanatorium of his Foxrock home, a therapeutic escape from an Ireland 'enjoying an extraordinary mixture of political chaos, pseudo-militarism and economic prosperity. Heaven knows what is going to happen.'[7]

The extent of the physical trauma understandably hardened Ervine. When friends challenged his bad temper, displaying characteristics of 'phantom limb' syndrome, he replied: 'I never talk about it, but mebbe it's because never a day passes but I'm in pain from this leg . . . you know, I imagine it's still there.'[8] His novel *Sophia* (1941) opens on the moment its eponymous character dies of cancer, a great pain suddenly relieved. The wishful imagining of release is compounded by the ghost-narrator's later reference to an individual who had lost a leg in World War One, Tom Westlake assuring Sophia 'that it still felt as if it were on his body long after he had lost it. "And sometimes, Mrs. Alderson, I'd put my hand down to feel it, though I knew well enough it wasn't there!" That was the sensation she had now.'[9] Shaw also injected some typical gallows humour into the situation, asserting that Ervine losing a leg would actually put him 'in a stronger position'. For a writer, 'two legs are an extravagance: the Huns were nearer the mark when they attempted (as I gather from your wife) to knock off your head'.[10]

Ervine's later persona enables him to be seen, and caricatured, as part of a generation of Ulstermen shaped by the First World War, languishing in the ranks 'of returned veterans, the shell-shocked, the amputees, the blind and halt', with the conflict generally representing 'an immeasurable fracture into which were poured the consolations of religious solidarity

[5] *London Times*, 28 May 1918, 2.
[6] Letter to R. F. Rattray, 26 July 1955. HRC; Letter to R. F. Rattray, 20 July 1955. HRC.
[7] Letter to Leonora Ervine, 14 May 1918. HRC; Letter to St John Ervine, 22 May 1918. HRC.
[8] John Boyd, 'St John Ervine: A Biographical Note', *Threshold*, No. 25 (Summer 1974), 107. Original ellipsis.
[9] St John Ervine, *Sophia* (London: Macmillan, 1941), 1, 18–19.
[10] Letter to St John Ervine, 22 May 1918. HRC.

(for some) and the phoney wholeness of ethnic nationalism (for others)'.[11] However, because millions of this generation were annihilated on the Western Front, Ervine's view was no heroic naval-gazing or self-sustaining myth, *à la* Somme in the general Ulster Unionist mentality. He referred to the 'War which did no good to anyone' in his novels, seeing the bloodshed as culturally debilitating and archetypally inflicted on the young by older men.[12] By all accounts he appreciated the camaraderie of his fellow soldiers, and it was the experience of seeing crowds of men mown down by artillery which made him realize that 'organisation, efficiency and progress led to the crushing of countless individuals'.[13] Aftershocks persisted in recollec-tions of feeling 'perished in France in 1917–18, almost numb with the cold', chills which continued in Ervine's later years and which he claimed would prevent him from being able to write or return to 'the North'.[14] Though he rediscovered God in the trenches, Ervine retained a general pessimism for the 'Great European Disaster' which lingered throughout his life: 'Has not the war that was to end all war made war more probable?'[15]

BEGINNINGS

Ervine's political evolution could be tracked through his plays. Through tough realism and an acute ear for the Hiberno-English inflections of the Belfast working class, *Mixed Marriage* (1911) is a radical tragedy for the Irish Labour movement, brutally caught between the competing nation-alisms. G. K. Chesterton had been moved on seeing it in Dublin, but criticized a dramatist who 'seemed to resent a schism merely because it interfered with a strike'. Viewing the play alongside those which yielded their 'spirituality' for politics, Chesterton bemoaned that the resulting work 'is always a miracle play; and the name of its hero is Everyman'.[16] Flashing forward to 1947, Ervine's *Private Enterprise* opened at a time when Clement Attlee's post-war Labour government was in the process of restructuring British society and enacting a modern welfare state. Yet this play's hero, manager of the family-owned factory Edmund Delaware,

[11] W. J. McCormack, *Northman: John Hewitt (1907–1987): An Irish Writer, His World, and His Times* (Oxford: Oxford University Press, 2015), 252.

[12] Ervine, *Sophia*, 18; St John Ervine, *The Organised Theatre: A Plea in Civics* (London: George Allen & Unwin, 1924), 119.

[13] Maume, 'Ulstermen', 73.

[14] Letter to John Boyd, 25 January 1952. JBC. Original emphasis.

[15] St John Ervine, *Some Impressions of My Elders* (London: George Allen & Unwin, 1923), 47.

[16] G. K. Chesterton, *Irish Impressions* (Glasgow: W. Collins Sons & Co., 1920), 239–40.

clashes with striking trade unionists and is presented from the off with immaculate, almost regal deference, his looks '*not in the least like those of the business men imagined by cartoonists in Left Wing newspapers . . . He is a handsome, well-bred man.*' Edmund passionately extolls how 'individuals are more important than crowds. The freedom you and I enjoy wasn't won by crowds. It was won in spite of them. We fought the King: we fought the peers: we fought the manufacturers: we're fighting the state: and soon we'll fight our worst enemy—the working man.'[17]

Ervine's break with the Everyman accompanied an increasing 'journalistic knockabout and critical coat-trailing',[18] initially perfected as drama critic of the Sunday newspaper the London *Observer*. Holding a special venom for the Belfast-born author and politician Denis Ireland ('a third-class exhibitionist and a first-class shit'),[19] one of his favourite pastimes was comparing the merits of other Belfast writers with friends: 'Joe Tomelty has it, but that chap [Thomas] Carnduff hasn't. I say this to prove to you that I am not interested in creed in this matter.'[20] Carnduff (Fig. 2.2), for his part, had little time for Ervine either. During the Second World War he wrote to his wife mentioning the Belfast PEN society having 'their big dinner with St. John Ervine and all the big nobs there last Saturday'.[21] When the BBC was about to broadcast Ervine's popular play *Boyd's Shop* as part of its *Sunday Night Theatre* series in February 1954, Carnduff criticized the production in the press for failing to use actors from the Ulster Group Theatre. 'Carnduff drivelled about an insult to Ulster,' wrote Ervine.

> Why does that chap spout so much about things of which he is totally ignorant? Surely Carnduff has the common sense to realise that the engagement of fourteen or fifteen people from the Group would not only cost a devil of a lot of money in fares, maintenance and what not for about three weeks, but would also cause the Group to close its doors, probably for the whole of that period.[22]

Ervine, as we shall see, knew something about the management of theatres.

Born in Sandy Row in 1886, a year which saw extensive rioting in Belfast, to a mother from Newbridge, County Kildare, and a Presbyterian

[17] St John Ervine, *Private Enterprise* (London: George Allen & Unwin, 1948), 9, 80.

[18] Norman Vance, *Irish Literature: A Social History: Tradition, Identity and Difference* (Oxford: Basil Blackwell, 1990), 176.

[19] Letter to John Boyd, 13 October 1948. JBC. This was based on Ireland's own Ulster Presbyterian background evolving into support for Irish nationalism and Eamon de Valera.

[20] Letter to John Boyd, 28 July 1950. JBC.

[21] Letter to Mary Carnduff, 20 April 1942. TCA.

[22] Letter to John Boyd, 20 February 1954. JBC.

Fig. 2.2. Photo of Thomas Carnduff by Charley Haig.
Note: Permission of Queen's University Belfast McClay Library Special Collections

countryman father from Drumbo, County Down, Carnduff was educated
at Haslett's School in Eliza Street and then at the Royal Hibernian
Military School in Dublin (1896–1900).[23] Along with eight other
adolescents he formed the 'Pass Clan', a gang with a predilection for
confronting Catholics (though as much driven by 'protection as devil-
ment').[24] From the age of fourteen Carnduff entered work as, at various
times: a messenger boy, butcher's delivery boy, light porter, factory hand,
binman, shipyard catch-boy, and stereotyper. Like most males of his
background he signed the Ulster Covenant in September 1912, and the
following year started back at the shipyard as a helper, progressing to a
driller, before joining the Royal Engineers shortly after the outbreak of the
First World War. He had by this time begun writing, with memories of
his time in Ypres and Messines crystallizing into poems.[25] As significant

[23] James Quinn, 'Thomas Carnduff', in James McGuire and James Quinn (eds),
Dictionary of Irish Biography: Under the Auspices of the Royal Irish Academy: Volume 2
(Cambridge: Cambridge University Press, 2009), 354.
[24] Thomas Carnduff, *Life and Writings*, ed. John Gray (Belfast: Lagan Press, 1994), 70.
[25] See his 'Messines' and 'Ypres', dated to June and September 1917, in Thomas Carnduff,
Poverty Street and Other Belfast Poems (Belfast: Lapwing Productions, 1993), 42, 70.

was his membership of the Young Citizen Volunteers, an independent organization which later amalgamated with the Ulster Volunteer Force. He was involved in gun-running during the Home Rule crisis—his autobiographical account of the 'new spirit' of 1914 feels strangely formal, as if trying to protect himself (or others)—though Carnduff could certainly tell 'lurid stories of basements and attics packed with rifles in exclusive Belfast suburbs'.[26] In 1919 he demobilized and returned to troubles closer to home, helping Catholic workers escape across the River Lagan during the shipyard expulsions of 21 July 1920 when they were driven from the Harland & Wolff and Workman Clark's shipyards by armed men. Unionist leader Edward Carson had urged mobs to confront the Labour members who represented the 'Trojan Horse' of the IRA, leading to as many as 7,500 Catholics and 'rotten Prods' (Labour-supporting Protestants) losing their jobs.[27]

Many are familiar with St John Ervine's later incarnation as a pugnacious Unionist, but he had once furrowed a very different path. Born in 1883 to deaf-mute parents Sarah Greer and her husband William in East Belfast, Ervine's father died before he was three years old, constituting 'the deepest regret of my life' because he had 'no recollection of him'.[28] Like Carnduff, whose father had also died when he was young, Ervine retained 'a sense of grievance against God for not letting me know him. In my childhood, I used to shut my eyes and try to make myself remember him.'[29] His maternal grandmother stepped in, moving to the city from Donaghadee, County Down, to maintain a small hardware shop on the Albertbridge Road, thus rescuing Ervine from the orphanage (traces of this life were to be found in *Boyd's Shop*).[30] Though we must caution against some of the rosier recollections and memoir of later years, Ervine remembered 'relatives who were well-to-do and relatives who were very poor', relaying a 'happy life', brimming with character, women, and evangelical instruction.[31] One day his grandmother gave Ervine 'an object lesson in the dangers of drink', taking him out to the yard to experience what was known as 'the return room', pouring some liquor into a saucer: 'She then struck a match and set fire to the liquid. As the blue flames curled up from

---

[26] Carnduff, *Life*, 96–104; Anon., 'Portrait Gallery', *Irish Times*, 2 October 1954, 7.

[27] Austen Morgan, *Labour and Partition: The Belfast Working Class 1905–23* (London: Pluto Press, 1991), 265–84. This also included 1,800 women.

[28] Letter to John Boyd, 15 October 1960. JBC.

[29] Carnduff, *Life*, 63; Letter to R. F. Rattray, 1 August 1955. HRC. Rattray was a Unitarian minister and scholar.

[30] St John Ervine, *Boyd's Shop* (1936), in *Selected Plays of St John Ervine*, ed. John Cronin (Gerrards Cross: Colin Smythe, 1988), 197–284.

[31] Letter to Forrest Reid, 11 June 1940. FRP.

the saucer, she said to me "There, that's what a drunkard's inside is like!" and thereafter I never saw a drunk man without expecting, and even hoping, to see blue flames issuing from his mouth.'[32]

He had a tumultuous relationship with authority and was expelled from six different schools, only finding peace and vision at the Presbyterian-run Westbourne School on the Newtownards Road,[33] under the direction of an inspirational headmaster named Matthew McClelland. Ervine's grandmother passed away when he was ten, and he later rued how:

> we seemed to go to pieces thereafter. How often we find a whole group of people depending on the life of one person. I've seen group after group fall apart when the thole-pin, one person, was withdrawn. My mother's mother was such a pin. When she went, we all went. Quarrels and vanity and drink... these three destroyed us. I made up my mind to get out of it as quickly as possible. Belfast to me was only a long bitterness during that period of my life, though it had been a very happy place for me earlier on; and I would have moved the earth to get away from it.[34]

This time his mother cushioned the loss. She ran a boarding house for deaf mutes (both Protestant and Catholic) and despite never earning 'more than a pound a week in her life', Ervine sentimentally claimed that 'We had enough to eat and were never embarrassed by debt,'[35] even if the major casualty of this was his education and a place at Trinity College Dublin.

In the Theatre Royal, Carnduff and St John Ervine shared a favourite space. Located on Arthur Street in the centre of Belfast, it opened in 1871 and became the main dramatic venue in Belfast until 1909, when the Opera House increased its prices under the direction of J. F. Warden, who managed both venues.[36] The rise of the cinema meant that the Royal's last performance took place in March 1915 (and the whole building was ultimately demolished in 1961), but its imprint on Ervine and Carnduff's imagination is undeniable. Both recalled a predominantly working-class audience receptive to legendary actor-managers like Frank Benson and Henry Irving bringing Shakespeare and other classic plays to the city. Carnduff usually took his seat in the gallery,[37] in contrast to Ervine's spot

---

[32] Letter to R. F. Rattray, 26 July 1955. HRC.

[33] The Ulster History Circle Society unveiled a blue plaque to Ervine at this site in 2015, which was moved to the Presbyterian church itself following the school's demolition (*Belfast Telegraph*, 21 March 2015, 15).

[34] Letter to Forrest Reid, 11 June 1940. FRP. Original ellipsis.

[35] Ervine's *Autobiography*, quoted in Boyd, 'Ervine', 104.

[36] Ophelia Byrne, *The Stage in Ulster from the Eighteenth Century* (Belfast: Linen Hall Library, 1997), 25–8.

[37] Carnduff, *Life*, 135.

in the slightly more expensive stalls. The latter frequented the Royal with his aunt, though Ervine had trouble convincing her to see Irish plays like Dion Boucicault's *The Shaughraun* because of her fear that 'there might be a row in the gallery between the Papist and Orange corner-boys'. Some of these lads 'might have a rivet or two in their pockets, purloined from the shipyards on the Queen's Island, and how was she to know that I, who had a perfect genius for getting into the middle of any row or disturbance, might not find myself blocking the way of a rivet to the stage and have my eye knocked out?'[38] Carnduff confirmed his aunt's hunch that the shipyard men 'weren't too sweet' on Irish fare, striving 'to bring the play to an early conclusion. I was a catch-boy in the shipyard at the time, and we filled our pockets with suitable missiles, such as bolts, rivets, half-bricks and such things.'[39] One can imagine the two of them at the same performances, enraptured by Irving and Benson, or at the wilder Irish affairs when the rivets flew and the shipyard spilled onto the stage.

ORANGEISM

Carnduff spent almost four years serving in the Ulster Special Constabulary Northwest Brigade, before returning to the shipyard in the mid-1920s. This coincided with an economic downturn when he often went hungry and faced prolonged spells of unemployment (which stood at 18 per cent nationwide by 1923). The climate changed for him the following decade with the publication of his second poetry collection and the staging of his first play, *Workers*, at the Abbey in October 1932, the week after cross-community riots broke out against the parsimonious Outdoor Relief system in Belfast.[40] Speaking just before its opening, Carnduff remarked how 'Very few of the plays written about the working classes in a big city have been written by workers themselves. As a worker, I have made an attempt to dramatize the lives of that class; I have tried not to exaggerate anything, but to show it as it exists.'[41] *Workers* receives no mention in many histories of the Irish theatre and sections of the play have sadly been lost, though the authenticity of its portrait of 'a group of Belfast shipyard workers "hard-drinking, hard-swearing, hard-up", all of them struggling to

---

[38] St John Ervine, *The Theatre in My Time* (London: Rich & Cowan, 1933), 14–15, 29.
[39] Carnduff, *Life*, 125, 139.
[40] Paddy Devlin, *Yes We Have No Bananas: Outdoor Relief in Belfast 1920–39* (Belfast: Blackstaff Press, 1981), 116–36.
[41] Quoted in *Irish Times*, 12 October 1932, 5.

get out of the dole queue',[42] led to contemporary praise and designations of an 'O'Casey of the North'. Going up on stage to rapturous applause following the first performance, Carnduff exalted how 'Years of poverty, misery, disappointment, were forgotten in that solitary moment of Heaven. I, an unemployed shipyardman, became a playwright.' Carnduff never forgot that he had always 'had to start at the very bottom'.[43]

That same year Carnduff was elected Worshipful Master of Sandy Row True Blues, Independent Orange Lodge No. 5, which he had joined during the time of Lindsay Crawford in his teens (causing 'a bit of a family row' with his brothers, who were members of the main institution).[44] The Independent Orange Order (IOO) flourished from 1903 to 1908, under the aegis of Crawford and Thomas Sloan, and an active following persists in North Antrim where it once boasted the support of the late Ian Paisley.[45] Recent scholarship has effectively 'de-sectarianized' Crawford and his offshoot, showing how its philosophy clashed with the educational interests of both the Catholic and Protestant Churches. Certainly Crawford overestimated his powers in tackling these fixtures, but in offering 'secularist opposition to all forms of clerical power over civil matters', as opposed to mere anti-Catholic populism, the IOO appears even more radical than is often posited.[46] As a man with generations of family connections, the Order was in Thomas Carnduff's blood 'long before I was the age for joining', though he was fully aware that 'the landowning class and gentry realized the possibilities of exploiting 'the organisation as a first line of defence for their own particular interests'.[47] This was essentially why he had chosen Crawford's splinter, which recognized Irish identifications through an Orange prism. Crawford and Sloan's dissent along class lines in the early part of the twentieth century has been largely submerged in most histories, while the current manifestation of the main institution can also be set against the memories of those working-class men of a bygone era. Poet and memoirist Robert Greacen, also reared in East Belfast, recalled Orange familial traditions with ambivalence but

---

[42] Sam Hanna Bell, *The Theatre in Ulster* (Dublin: Gill & Macmillan, 1972), 54. His wife Mary pointed out that Carnduff simply 'wrote for the sake of writing and was not interested in what happened to his work after he finished it' (quoted in *Belfast Telegraph*, 30 October 1964, 15).

[43] Carnduff, *Life*, 111; letter to Mary Carnduff, 2 January 1941. TCA.

[44] Carnduff, *Life*, 78.

[45] Eric P. Kaufman, *The Orange Order: A Contemporary Northern Irish History* (Oxford: Oxford University Press, 2007), 14.

[46] Peter Murray, 'Radical Way Forward or Sectarian Cul-de-sac? Lindsay Crawford and Independent Orangeism Reassessed', *Saothar*, No. 27 (2002), 41.

[47] Carnduff, *Life*, 74, 76–7.

admitted to being 'a devotee of the bonfires, not so much for their political or religious significance as for their friendly pagan warmth'.[48]

Undoubtedly 'the Orange' has its fair share of responsibility in stoking violence, with contemporary echoes of the same violence springing up in the same Belfast areas where Catholic and Protestant neighbourhoods have interfaced since around 1813. The advent of the locomotive in the 1840s and 1850s was not welcomed by Protestant evangelicals (sinfulness on the Sabbath would result), and it also enabled the Order to transport thousands of Orangemen to annual celebrations across the province, an influx of outsiders which tended to disturb the 'territorial equilibrium' and rouse Catholic feelings of subordination.[49] The increasing unison of Anglicans and Presbyterians during the onset of the Home Rule movement entailed that the Orange Order 'did increasingly become the focus, not merely of negative anti-Catholic sentiment, but of positive identification with the Protestant myth', that is, the 'myth of siege'.[50] Never a member, St John Ervine had presented Orangeism in his first play *Mixed Marriage* as a divisive force within the working class, embodied by hardheaded patriarch John Rainey ('A'll have no Fenians here... she's a Cathlik, an' A'll nivir consent til a son o' mine marryin' her'), though his son Hugh also voices that Orangemen are 'brave, sensible men, a lot o' them, if they wur on'y let alone be them that's supposed t' be their betters'.[51] The child Ervine had been transfixed by the glittering parades, coming to admonish Protestant friends for their guarded view of the Twelfth of July: 'What right have you to have mixed feelings about it? Look first at the photographs of the men in the procession—decent workmen—and then remind yourself of what our fate would have been if William, a notable king whose early death was a disaster to this nation, had not kicked his bitter-minded father-in-law across the Boyne.' At least three of his uncles belonged to the Order, whose faults he claimed were the 'faults of humanity, not the faults of a particular group', and though appreciating the banners and regalia, 'it is the core of sound faith which impresses me and not the ritual'.[52]

This defensiveness taps into another critical and current detail: attacks on the Orange Order are always liable to strengthen its members' sense of

[48] Robert Greacen, *Even Without Irene* (Belfast: Lagan Press, 1995), 40.

[49] A. T. Q. Stewart, *The Narrow Ground: The Roots of Conflict in Ulster* (London: Faber and Faber, 1989; 1st edition 1977), 73.

[50] F. S. L. Lyons, *Culture and Anarchy in Ireland, 1890–1939* (Oxford: Oxford University Press, 1979), 136.

[51] Ervine, *Mixed*, in *Selected*, 46, 53. The original production was directed by Lennox Robinson.

[52] Letter to John Boyd, 16 July 1949. JBC; Letter to John Boyd, 27 July 1949. JBC.

loyalty. The frequent pounding by nationalist commentators,[53] in other words, serves only to perpetuate Orangeism: 'That's why people parade. They won't lie down, like croppies. They say "up yours".'[54] Carnduff agreed, outlining how the individual Orangeman may have Labour or liberal tendencies which clash with Orangeism's Tory elements: 'But let any outside criticise or abuse Orangeism because it is an Ulster product and he immediately becomes a defender of all it stands for.' Connectedly, 'The Catholic press in Eire, as well as in Northern Ireland, is too fond of applying the adjective "Orange" to every type of mob violence or political commotion which may crop up in any neighbourhood where Ulster Protestants predominate.'[55] Though the tensions between the two are profound, there are intriguing parallels between the banners used by trade unions and Orange organizations,[56] and Protestant workers often belonged to both. The distinctive Red Hand insignia associated with Ulster Loyalism also symbolized preferential treatment for union members at the dock gate, becoming commonplace through the 'New Unionism' of the 1890s, especially amongst previously unorganized carters and dockers. The most famous Irish Transport and Workers Union badge was the red hand with the letters I.T.W.U. and the year '1913', which became the emblem of resistance in the Dublin lock-out and the Irish Citizen Army badge.[57]

This symbolistic overlap chimed with Carnduff's claim that the iron discipline of the Lodge ensured that 'Orangemen make the best and most orderly trade unionists. No matter how they may dislike the Worshipful Master's ruling, they obey it.' Rejecting its image 'as a bulwark of landlordism and the Tory Party', Carnduff insisted that the Order's rank and file had repeatedly 'rebelled against their leaders. At the Act of Union, Orangemen in the main held aloof from interfering with the movement.'[58] The Grand Lodge tried to convince its Order to accept the Act in its entirety, but thirty-six Lodges in Armagh and thirteen in Fermanagh declared themselves against the Union. Such details were seemingly lost on the Order's critics, while Carnduff also pointed out that two of the most anti-Tory representatives of his time, Independent Unionists Tommy Henderson (1887–1970)

---

[53] See, for instance, Brian Feeney, 'Leaderless Loyalists March into Oblivion', *Irish News*, 30 April 2014, 20.

[54] Interview with Maurice Leitch, London, 31 July 2015.

[55] Carnduff, *Life*, 82.

[56] See Belinda Loftus, *Marching Workers: An Exhibition of Irish Trade Banners and Regalia* (Belfast: Arts Councils of Ireland, 1978), 25, 50–1.

[57] Francis Devine, 'The Red Hand of Union Solidarity', *Liberty*, 1913 Lockout Special, Vol. 12, No. 8 (October 2013), 29.

[58] Carnduff, *Life*, 75, 80.

and John Nixon (1880–1949), of Belfast's Shankill and Woodvale constituencies, were Orangemen.

THE ABBEY

Ervine landed a job in an insurance office after randomly joining a queue in the centre of Belfast, moving to London in 1901 for another clerkship. He swiftly jettisoned his religious affiliations, became a disciple of George Bernard Shaw, joined the Fabians (his real 'university'), and contributed to the modernist *New Age* journal and the *Fabian Nursling* typescript.[59] He also met W. B. Yeats and submitted what became his first play to the Abbey Theatre, where it was staged in March 1911. A work of assiduous realism, *Mixed Marriage* revisits James Larkin's 1907 dock strike, but also anticipated 'the coming hostilities',[60] namely further attacks on Catholics and trade unionists in the shipyards in 1912. The father of the household, John Rainey, objects to his son Hugh marrying a Catholic girl:

RAINEY: (*to* NORA) Ye're goin' til take him. A s'pose?

NORA: A am.

RAINEY: Ye're a Cathlik aren't ye?

NORA: Yes, A am.

RAINEY: Issen it agin yer religion t' marry a Prodesan?

NORA: It can be done, but A don't care.

RAINEY: Will ye turn Prodesan if ye marry him?

NORA: Naw, A wun't.[61]

Rainey's insistence that 'ye'd nivir by happy thegither. Ye ought t' marry a man o'er yer own faith' is grimly confirmed when Nora is shot amidst a sectarian street confrontation, symbolizing the fatality of non-sectarian radicalism approaching the third Home Rule crisis.

Regularly and wrongly described as a 'unionist playwright and an opponent of Home Rule',[62] Ervine in fact held pro-Home Rule views which envisaged that Ulster Protestants would unite with a new generation of Catholics to organize trade unions, deal with slums, secularize

[59] See Lauren Arrington, 'St John Ervine and the Fabian Society: Capital, Empire and Irish Home Rule', *History Workshop Journal*, Vol. 72, No. 1 (2011), 52–73; Vance, *Irish Literature*, 177.

[60] Ben Levitas, *The Theatre of a Nation: Irish Drama and Cultural Nationalism, 1890–1916* (Oxford: Clarendon Press, 2002), 186.

[61] Ervine, *Mixed*, in *Selected*, 44.

[62] Christopher Murray, *Twentieth Century Irish Drama: Mirror Up to Nation* (Manchester: Manchester University Press, 1997), 192.

education, and remove the clergy from Irish politics. Home Rule to Ervine was an anti-sectarian solution which would unite Protestant and Catholic workers 'in the struggle for economic equality'.[63] The resulting Ireland would be led, somewhat optimistically, by writer Æ (George Russell) and agricultural cooperative pioneer Horace Plunkett, while the physical force elements which accompanied the cultural volley were simply elided (along with the mainstream Irish Parliamentary Party's clericalism and conservatism). Because 'socialists of his generation often saw the Empire as a great developmental force',[64] Ervine continued to advocate a continuing link with Britain, retaining, even in his radical Fabian days, a conviction that Ulster people inherently knew in their bones how to handle machinery. This contrasted with the 'peasant' society of the rest of Catholic Ireland: 'We are mainly an industrial people: they are mainly an agricultural people. I have always maintained that N.I. is essentially different from the rest of Ireland for several reasons, the chief of which is not, as you might think, religious, but industrial. That is why I am a Unionist.'[65]

Mixed Marriage, *The Magnanimous Lover* (1912), *The Critics* (1913), *The Orangeman* (1914), and *John Ferguson* (1915) had already been staged by the time Yeats invited Ervine to run the Abbey Theatre at the end of 1915. It is famously repeated that during the Easter Rising, Ervine's one regret when the British gunboat *Helga* veered up the River Liffey to shell the General Post Office was that it 'had not paused and blasted the Abbey to pieces'.[66] This is normally couched as an example of Ervine's hatred of the institution, yet even this statement appears misinterpreted. Only the Abbey's windows were damaged in the rebellion and Ervine was expressing the wish that the theatre had been entitled to more recompense from the British government for the devastation wrought on central Dublin during the Rising. The compensation monies could then be used to upgrade its unimpressive premises,[67] rendering the implications of the reported *Helga* remark rather different. Some have stated that Ervine saw the Rising as 'the supreme betrayal not only of Britain but of civilianization', an overblown contention countered by what others have better put as his 'emotional admiration for the rebels while hating their worldview'.[68] His later denunciation of 'romantic idiots' seems light, and in a memoir-piece published the

---

[63] Jimmy Fay, 'St John Ervine: Director's Note', in *Mixed Marriage Theatre Programme* (Belfast: Lyric Theatre, January–February 2013), 13.

[64] Maume, 'Ulstermen', 73.

[65] Letter to John Boyd, 14 October 1953. JBC. See also Ervine, *Some Impressions*, 58.

[66] Hugh Hunt, *The Abbey: Ireland's National Theatre, 1904–1979* (London: Gill & Macmillan, 1979), 111.

[67] Gerard Fay, 'The Abbey Theatre', *Manchester Guardian*, 4 January 1952, 3.

[68] Boyd, 'Ervine', 114; Maume, 'Ulstermen', 73.

year after the Rising he reiterated his pro-Home Rule stance and insisted that 'there was nothing unclean or mean' about those involved. Though 'foolish', he admired their physical courage and how 'they were prepared to suffer the hardest test for it'.[69]

Scholars nevertheless persist in labelling Ervine a 'unionist manager' during 1916,[70] despite his yearning the previous year for a time 'when Protestants and Catholics, Orangemen and Ancient Hibernians put their hands together, and the four beautiful fields of Cathleen ni Houlihan become one pasture'.[71] He had argued in the same book that Edward Carson, whom he had met (and disliked), was the last 'stage Irishman'. Nevertheless, Ervine has been written out of most histories of the Abbey—one even refers to him as a 'rabid pro-Englishman'[72]—despite being its manager in the period leading up to and during the seminal event in the founding of the modern Irish state. We know that following A. Patrick Wilson's resignation in a letter on 19 July 1915, Yeats broached the subject of Ervine taking over the theatre in October because of his administrative capabilities, inexpensiveness, and familiarity. Shortly after, Fred Harris wrote offering him the job, outlining the economic constraints reflective of the Abbey's strained finances.[73] Ervine accepted without hesitation, and with the backing of the directors tried to forge closer links with British provincial theatres. It was his disastrous relationship with some of the Abbey's actors, however, which was key to the eventual fracture. Part of Ervine's problems unquestionably stemmed from the 'clash of temperaments' involved in running theatres: 'Anybody who spends any time with the Abbey knows it's fraught with politics, like any big building is once you involve a lot of people in decision-making. There's a temperament between actors and managers that even now is a hard balancing act.'[74] On the other hand Ervine stabilized the Abbey's finances, securing new advertisement contracts and producing popular satirical comedies, eradicating the financial morass he inherited.[75]

---

[69] St John Ervine, 'An Onlooker's Tale', in Keith Jeffery, *The GPO and the Easter Rising* (Dublin: Irish Academic Press, 2006), 184. The article was originally published in *Century Magazine* in November 1917.

[70] Nicholas Allen, 'Cultural Representations of 1916', in Richard S. Grayson and Fearghal McGarry (eds), *Remembering 1916: The Easter Rising, the Somme and the Politics of Memory in Ireland* (Cambridge: Cambridge University Press, 2016), 173.

[71] St John Ervine, *Sir Edward Carson and the Ulster Movement* (Dublin: Maunsel, 1915), 122.

[72] Peter Kavanagh, *The Story of the Abbey Theatre* (New York: Devin-Adair, 1950), 103. See also Sean McCann, *The Story of the Abbey Theatre* (London: Four Square Books, 1967), 78.

[73] *Abbey Theatre Minute Book* (1912–39), 21, 23–4. NUI Galway—Digital Collections.

[74] Interview with Jimmy Fay, Belfast, 25 November 2014.

[75] For this he was awarded a £50 bonus by the directors. Robert Welch, *The Abbey Theatre, 1899–1999: Form and Pressure* (Oxford: Oxford University Press, 1999), 69.

Lennox Robinson pointed out that although Ervine 'did his best', the Abbey 'at this time was suffering from a severe criticism from Sinn Fein, they were down on the Theatre and the houses were bad'.[76] A possibly apocryphal story of Sir John Maxwell, then in charge of the garrison in Ireland and later to hand out death sentences to the Easter rebels, being invited into the Green Room is occasionally attributed to Ervine, though Lady Gregory's friend and Abbey advisor W. F. Bailey was the man who most likely invited Maxwell in.[77] This had upset the actors and Ervine also took the blame for a reduction in their salaries, despite this being nego-tiated prior to him taking up the job (it had also helped balance the books). Though frequently called a Rising of poets, 'playwrights and actors were far more prominent', with several of its leaders involved in the theatre.[78] Seán Connolly, who had starred in his namesake James's play *Under Which Flag?*, was due to appear in the Abbey's revival of Yeats's *Cathleen ni Houlihan* on Easter Monday 1916 and instead became the first rebel casualty of Easter 1916 when he was shot down during the occupa-tion of City Hall. Ervine called Connolly a 'capable actor' and saw him march a company of men towards Liberty Hall on Easter Sunday, 'a most, quiet, kindly man of honest desires . . . I nodded to him and he waved his hand to me. The next day he was dead,'[79] a memory at odds with his later polemic against Irish nationalists.

In the following days volunteers were shot and died outside his door, and he was forced to cancel the *Cathleen* performance when a stagehand ran into his office informing him that 'there's a rebellion or something on, sir—anyway the Sinn Feiners are out!'[80] This found its way into his novel *Changing Winds* (1917), and as fire engulfed the city centre later in the week, Ervine saw O'Connell Street and the surrounding buildings 'roaring and rattling as roofs fell in a whirlpool of sparks that splashed high in the air. The finest street in Europe was consumed in a night.'[81] Writing to Lady Gregory soon after, Ervine conveyed that 'this business has brought the Abbey much nearer to disaster than even the European War, as, of course, it is impossible to open while Martial Law prevails. As the area

---

[76] Lennox Robinson, *Ireland's Abbey Theatre: A History, 1899–1951* (London: Sidgwick & Jackson, 1951), 68.

[77] Fearghal McGarry, *The Abbey Rebels of 1916: A Lost Revolution* (Dublin: Gill & Macmillan, 2015), 266; Robinson, *Ireland's Abbey*, 100.

[78] R. F. Foster, *Vivid Faces: The Revolutionary Generation in Ireland 1890–1923* (London: Allen Lane, 2014), 112. Another actor involved in the Rising was Arthur Shields, whom Ervine had brought into the Abbey just a few months before.

[79] Letter to Lady Gregory, 5 May 1916. BC; in Jeffery, *GPO*, 165.

[80] Max Caulfield, *The Easter Rebellion* (London: Frederick Muller, 1964), 132, 187.

[81] Ervine, in Jeffery, *GPO*, 182.

around the Abbey is either demolished or tottering, it is highly improbable that anybody would venture near us.'[82]

Trouble was also brewing within. On becoming manager Ervine laid down the law from the off: 'If players persistently come late to rehearsals, or are in any other way insubordinate, I shall suspend them for a week or two, and they will be the losers.'[83] Salaries were further trimmed and he clamped down on misuse of the Green Room, which 'has been treated as a kind of club', while other cutbacks on telephone calls and electricity soon targeted the actors, who needed to 'realise that their inconsiderate conduct has in every way, large and small, added to the burden of the Directors'. Ervine clearly excelled at rubbing people up the wrong way, insisting that players should rehearse two plays a day, and promoting—as he had been since 1914—his Birmingham-born actress wife Leonora to parts beyond her range.[84] A matter of days into his appointment Ervine confronted Arthur Sinclair for being 'very vain and very stupid, and still obsessed by the belief that the Theatre will fail without his support. I told him very frankly that his acting had deteriorated in the last two years, and by the time he left me he was a little more humble than he was when he came.'[85]

By May 1916 Ervine broke the news to Lady Gregory that he was having 'trouble with certain of the players', warning of the need for 'a very drastic change'. When the actors did not turn up to a special rehearsal of Synge's *Playboy of the Western World* he complained how they 'have been allowed to do exactly what they like, to attend rehearsals when they pleased . . . and although I hoped that the bad habits accumulated during the past ten years could be broken, and new ones put in their place, I am afraid this is not possible'. Consequently, Ervine urged the dismissal of several of the major offenders (including Sinclair) but his failure to get actor and Abbey founder Willie Fay back with the rest of the company to fulfil the Music Hall commitments spelt doom. 'I am sorry to say that I see no hope of anything with the present crowd,' Ervine lamented. 'I have done my best to keep this Theatre going during the recent crisis, but not one of the Players has done anything to help: indeed, some of them have done all they could to hinder . . . my feeling is that I am wasting my time here trying to keep together an unmanageable group of people.'[86]

---

[82] Letter to Lady Gregory, 5 May 1916. BC.
[83] Letter to W. B. Yeats, 1 November 1915. BC.
[84] R. F. Foster, *W. B. Yeats: A Life II: The Arch-Poet, 1915–1939* (Oxford: Oxford University Press, 2003), 23, 42.
[85] Letter to W. B. Yeats, 4 November 1915. BC. Sinclair had played John Rainey in the original *Mixed Marriage*.
[86] Letter to Lady Gregory, 22 May 1916. BC.

On Sunday 28 May 1916, visitors to the Abbey were met by members
of the company who handed out bills declaring that they would not appear
again under Ervine. Disparaging his public statements and 'dabbling in
politics', the players vowed to form their own company to tour the music
halls in the summer.[87] Ervine had delivered notice to the actors the
previous night and came down to the Abbey early on Sunday to get letters,
where he found several actors 'hanging about' the theatre and Green
Room. One, Sidney Morgan, was 'extremely abusive', assuring him that
'they would see that I was dismissed'. Ervine then told the dozen or so
members of the public who had arrived in the auditorium that the
performance had been cancelled and they would be refunded.[88] The
following month Lady Gregory began pushing for Ervine's removal, and
Yeats was despatched to initiate the severance 'as you engaged him'.[89] On
5 June 1916, the Abbey board met to discuss the company's 27 May
dismissal and, deliberating the best means of getting a new company
together, agreed that it would be closed for 'an indefinite period'. Ervine's
own resignation letter was read at a meeting (not attended by Yeats) the
following month, where it was accepted by the rest of the board.[90]

The more militant Abbey actors rejoiced—part of Ervine's mistake had
been to assume that the players would choose their careers over political
commitment[91]—but if Ervine bore any grudge it was short-lived. Though
he would later have the correspondence between Yeats and Sean O'Casey
over the Abbey's rejection of *The Silver Tassie* (1928) published in the
Observer (on account of it being 'of public interest'), Ervine spoke respect-
fully of Yeats all his life and commended the Abbey's founders for providing
a platform for Synge, O'Casey, Robinson, and T. C. Murray, who would
otherwise 'have found no place for their plays and little inducement to
write'.[92] His works continued to be staged at the national theatre until the
era 'that discredited politician' Ernest Blythe became a director.[93]

Ervine's trajectory from Labour-minded Home Ruler to obsequious biographer of Unionist Prime Minister James Craig was sealed, via France, when
he claimed to have heard Eamon de Valera publicly contemplate the 'whole-
sale deportation of Ulster Unionists and Protestants' from Ireland during a
function at the Commodore Hotel in New York a few years after the war.[94]

[87] *London Times*, 31 May 1916, 10.
[88] Letter to Lady Gregory, 29 May 1916. BC.
[89] Quoted in Foster, *Yeats: Arch-Poet*, 53.   [90] *Abbey Minute Book*, 26–8.
[91] McGarry, *Abbey Rebels*, 53, 181.
[92] Letter to Sean O'Casey, 6 June 1928. NLI; Ervine, *Theatre in My Time*, 156.
[93] Letter to John Boyd, 20 August 1955. JBC.
[94] Letter to Mr Sandford, 10 March 1941. JBC. Ervine reacted venomously to de Valera
throughout his life, lashing the 'dull Spaniard' and 'third-rate usher from a second-rate

His voyage was, however, defined by culture. Ervine was fundamentally out of step with the prevailing tune that Ireland needed heroic, mythical plays, something Yeats and Lady Gregory, despite their innate grandeur and haughtiness, understood very well. On 11 February 1916, he delivered a lecture to the Dublin Literary Society in which he reminded his audience that three months prior to his arrival the Abbey was in a perilous financial situation. Things had turned around, but Ervine feared that 'When a nation was healthy and vigorous, that nation could stand strong plays. But when a nation was weak and decadent, that nation could not stand strong plays... that was the state Ireland was in now.'[95] He envisaged his own realist work taking its place in a canon made up of writers attempting 'to do what no English dramatist does, write out of our own experience and knowledge', a new line hailing from Irish cities and small country towns, in tandem with Cork realists Robinson and Murray.[96]

Yeats also grasped the commercial potential of this new form, even though it was overtaken by the pressures of the age, one which also represents the limits of culture (plays have to be cancelled when buildings are on fire) and the extent of it (the writers and actors being intimately involved). Ervine could never be 'part of a literary revival that preferred romanticism to realism. Nor could the reality of the North of Ireland be accommodated by a cultural nationalism directed from Dublin.'[97] Having read a hundred plays since he had taken over (accepting three), Ervine had a very clear understanding that the 'literary ability' of the Irish people presently:

> expressed itself in terms of violence. A great many people in Ireland wrote historical plays. What was wanted was to get people to think about their own time, to forget Sir Edward Carson or Mr John Redmond, to forget that they were Protestants and Catholics, and to remember that they were Irishmen. (Applause.) But at this moment Ireland was a sick nation, very nearly a lunatic nation. The reason was that men could not talk for ten consecutive minutes about their own country without losing their tempers. Dramatists must remember that they had got to forget their bad temper. They had to cool their brains before they took their pens in their hands.[98]

Much as Ervine would later assert that Ulster people were as one with machinery in a way the 'Southern Irish' could never understand, so he too

---

academy in Blackrock', a stance Sean O'Casey challenged him on: 'I don't think Dev is quite so bad as you think him to be... an honest fellow, and he has intelligence' (letter to St John Ervine, 25 November 1933. HRC).

[95] *Irish Times*, 12 February 1916, 4.   [96] Welch, *Abbey*, 58, 65.

[97] John Wilson Foster, *Fictions of the Irish Literary Revival: A Changeling Art* (Dublin: Gill & Macmillan, 1987), 176.

[98] *Irish Times*, 12 February 1916, 4.

could not appreciate that much Irish literature was entwined with the oncoming militancy. In a strange way *Mixed Marriage*, which the Abbey revived until 1940, anticipated the above and provided his own revolutionary statement; the 'appeal for tolerance which is at the heart of it',[99] still meaningful and radical on the streets of Belfast.

TAKEOVERS

Thomas Carnduff was a committed member of the York Street Non-Subscribing Presbyterian Congregation, referring reverentially to 'the Boss' ('many's the time I've defended him without his knowledge. I act the fool a lot, but never when it is a question of loyalty').[100] Tapping in to the aforementioned myth of siege, Carnduff's unperformed *The Last Banshee* seems a variant on what has been termed 'Protestant gothic'.[101] Encapsulated in the fictions of Irish Ascendancy Protestants whose sense of fear could be attributed to the 'threat of a takeover by the Catholic middle class' (and peasantry), authors like Bram Stoker and Sheridan Le Fanu had been responsible for some of the best-known gothic fiction of the nineteenth century.[102] Unlike these writers Carnduff was a northerner, working class, and a dramatist, though his dabbling in such quintessentially Irish mythology resurrects Protestant gothic with an Ulster stamp. Set and probably written during the months following the end of the Second World War (November 1945), *The Last Banshee* also attempts to expand Carnduff's horizons outside Belfast, to the north Antrim coast of Ballycastle. His ear for the inflections is suitably sharp and there is even a political row between John, the son of the house, and Jim, their nephew from Belfast (both in their twenties):

JIM: Have ye no Trade Union up here at all?

JOHN: Trade Union! Ye mean one of them Socialist clubs in Belfast?

JIM: Socialist m'foot! A trade union exists to see every worker gets a fair deal. It protects ye from the employer. It keeps yer wages high enough to give ye a decent way of living.

JOHN: We live alright here.[103]

[99] Interview with Jimmy Fay, Belfast, 25 November 2014.

[100] Roger Courtney, *Second Congregation Belfast 1708–2008* (Belfast: All Souls' Non-Subscribing Presbyterian Congregation, 2008), 85; Letter to Mary Carnduff, 8 October 1940. TCA.

[101] R. F. Foster, 'Protestant Magic: W. B. Yeats and the Spell of Irish History', in *Paddy and Mr Punch: Connections in Irish and English History* (London: Allen Lane, 1993), 220.

[102] Foster, 'Protestant Magic', 214, 219.

[103] Thomas Carnduff, *The Last Banshee: A Tragedy of County Antrim Life in Three Acts* (Unpublished, n.d.), 1, 41. Linen Hall Library—Theatre Collection.

The play depicts the family's domestic life in the face of an oncoming haunting, with the local Presbyterian Reverend Norman McKenzie arriving to defend the McMullen family:

> *The wailing sound of a single cry is heard approaching, but as MCKENZIE'S earnest voice is raised louder in supplication the wailing voice gradually fades into the distance and ceases.*

We are but puny mortals, weak in flesh and lacking in courage to combat the servants of Satan.

This First Act ends with Jim staring towards a door in defiance of the spectre, glancing round at the others '*as they kneel or stand in attitudes of prayer*', with the play closing on another relative quoting scripture in further Protestant defiance of a ghostly menace.[104] Notions of takeover characterize another unperformed Carnduff piece, *The Stars Foretell*. Read in 1938 at the Young Ulster Society—which Carnduff chaired—it never received a full production but acquired a semi-legendary status which meant that it was still mentioned in newspapers some years after its author's passing. In 1968 the *Irish Times* referenced a 'dramatic fantasy about an Ireland in which the South has become royalist and Tory, while the North, radical and Tone-y, couldn't endure this and the upshot of the ideological conflict was a civil war in which the North tried to take over and re-form the South'.[105] Carnduff scores a number of points at the expense of both the Irish Free State, which had developed along decidedly apostolic lines, and the northern statelet that had bred its own self-reinforcing parochialism. One senses, however, that Carnduff is having particular fun at the expense of the Six Counties, as led by new Prime Minister James Graham, who addresses his Irish counterpart:

GRAHAM: Some time ago—three months to be exact—we overthrew [the] government and the people of Northern Ireland placed their confidence in myself as leader of the Young Ulster Party. We gained a sweeping majority throughout the six Counties. The members of the former government have now gone into retirement—for ever. Few of them were under seventy. The people had grown like them, old and tired. Ulster has taken a new lease of life. No member of my cabinet is over forty. We are ambitious to do something to rouse in the Irish people a new spirit of progress and adventure. Your Government, Sir, and, to some extent, your people, block out advance. Thirty-seven

---

[104] Carnduff, *Last Banshee*, 17–18, 60.
[105] 'An Irishman's Diary', *Irish Times*, 8 August 1968, 15.

years ago your people, and your party, were striving to establish an
Irish Republic. You are still striving. But you have lost all manifest
spirit in the ideal. You still commemorate Easter Week and bawl out
the old slogans of fighting days. But the fight's knocked out of you.
In plain words, it is high time you joined the official party in
retirement.[106]

The timing of the play, appearing the year after de Valera's 1937 Constitution, only sharpens the satirical bite.

Carnduff's earlier poems, especially those inspired by his war experience, displayed a symptomatic chauvinism. 'Graves of Gallipoli' was
addressed to 'Mr Turk':

> You can keep your smug-faced friendship,
> And your blood-besmeared hand;
> You can raise your crescent banners,
> You can give Mohammed praise;
> But we don't forget our comrades of Gallipoli days.[107]

Though these 'jingoistic poems' of his first collection are important 'because
they represent the baseline of Carnduff's consciousness',[108] a different,
perhaps more expansive individual emerged through further reading and
writing. Quotes from the Qur'an and Bengali poet Rabindranath Tagore
banner later poems, and Carnduff's increasing metropolitanism was evident
when he sent his wife translations of Indian, Persian, and Greek writers he
admired: 'They never boast about their own greatness but the greatness of
God, and the glory and beauty of life. You and I may never reach their
understanding.'[109] In December 1942, at a PEN function in Belfast's
Union Hotel, he met Czech Foreign Minister Jan Masaryk, though Carnduff later lamented an event 'crowded with third-rate writers and a host of
non-writers', as well as 'flousy-flocked and uninteresting old ladies who
seemed to be in the majority'. Carnduff sensed he was in the presence of a
magnetic figure but criticized an unreceptive local audience who failed to
shine 'even when the Czech leader rose to inspiring heights when portraying
the persecution of the Czechs and Jews. Masaryk appealed to the Belfast P.E.N.

---

[106] Thomas Carnduff, *The Stars Foretell: A Play in Three Acts* (Unpublished, n.d.), 6.
Linen Hall Library—Theatre Collection. Tinderbox Theatre Company also staged a
reading of the play in April 1993.
[107] Carnduff, *Poverty Street*, 32.
[108] Colin Graham, ' "port-lights / Of a ghost-ship": Thomas Carnduff and the Belfast
Shipyards', *UCDScholarcast*, Series 7 (Spring 2013), 5.
[109] Carnduff, 'Yesterday' and 'Shipyard Philosophy', in Thomas Carnduff, *Songs of an
Out-of-Work* (Belfast: Quota Press, 1932), 42–3; Letter to Mary Carnduff, 18 February
1942. TCA.

to help on the restoration of European culture after the war. It was like appealing to the ocean to cultivate apples.'[110]

Aside from his plays, the record of such encounters—and sharp asides—lends credence to justifiable claims of Carnduff's 'value as a social and cultural commentator',[111] especially during Belfast's blackouts, rationing, and politics during the Second World War. The prevalence of foodstuffs in the city led him to contemplate the 'good deal of illegal traffic going on across the border, and nobody seems to worry much whether the Black Market supplies the necessities, so long as they materialise. It has become quite a common habit to travel to Dublin for odds and ends which are only obtainable here by producing the required coupons.'[112] His correspondence became in fact increasingly political as the war progressed. He noted pro-communist sentiment in Belfast, while the resignation of Harry Midgley (1893–1957) from the Northern Ireland Labour Party led Carnduff to explain the 'dividing line' amongst its members: 'The Catholic members always leaned towards the Republican ideal, the Protestants cleaved naturally towards a closer union with the British Labour Party. Midgley challenged the issue and they expelled him. Now Midgley aspires to lead an imperialist Labour group in Ulster. I think Labour on the whole will suffer. They were never too strong in Belfast.'[113] Midgley previously won plaudits from the Left for his pro-Republican activism during the Spanish Civil War, clashing with the pro-Franco Catholic Church and associated *Irish News* in the process, and Carnduff might have appreciated that he won the seat of Belfast Willowfield on the back of 'Loyalist Labour' votes in a 1941 by-election. What he could not forgive was Midgley's 'wrecking the Labour Party' and joining Sir Basil Brooke's new government as a Unionist minister eighteen months later.[114]

JEMMY HOPE AND CASTLEREAGH

James 'Jemmy' Hope (1764–1847) takes on mythical status for several of the writers considered in this book. He appears in Stewart Parker's *Northern Star* (1984) as a common-sense 'Everyman' figure, while John Hewitt praised him as 'the archetypal Ulsterman, because he believed in

[110] Letter to Mary Carnduff, 19 December 1942. TCA. Original emphasis.
[111] John Gray, 'Thomas Carnduff', *Linen Hall Review*, Vol. 3, No. 3 (Autumn 1986), 18.
[112] Letter to Mary Carnduff, 10 April 1942. TCA.
[113] Letter to Mary Carnduff, 19 December 1942. TCA. See Graham Walker, 'The Commonwealth Labour Party in Northern Ireland, 1942–4', *Irish Historical Studies*, Vol. 24, No. 93 (May 1984), 69–91.
[114] Letter to Mary Carnduff, 1 May 1943. TCA.

the rights of the common people and he conceived of a social organisation'.[115] Though personally close to Henry Joy McCracken and Samuel Neilson, Hope, 'weaver of Templepatrick', was the United Irishman most interested in social and economic issues, possessing the 'class politics of a proto-socialist'.[116] Hewitt, Parker, and Carnduff all seconded Hope's view that 'there could be no solid foundation for liberty' until the people had achieved 'the right of deriving a subsistence from the soil on which their labour was expended'.[117] Hope thus remains symbolically potent, though also overwhelmed by the status quo. In April 2014 one of the Ulster History Circle's distinctive blue plaques bearing his name was vandalized in Mallusk Cemetery, reflective of how brightly his star burns in modern Northern Ireland.[118]

While most of the United Irishmen's leaders, including McCracken and Neilson, were well heeled, Hope was 'at the other end of the social ladder' as 'a northern weaver, whose views envisaged more sweeping changes in the social order'. He was friendly but not influential with the leadership; it was 'among his own northern fellow-weavers [that] he was well respected'.[119] This is explored by Carnduff in what he described as 'my supreme effort at playwriting', *Castlereagh*, which opened at the Empire Theatre in Belfast on 21 January 1935 and would visit the Abbey the following month. Through Viscount Castlereagh's relationship with his adviser Alexander Knox, we learn that the latter fears Hope more than the other United Irishmen because his name 'is a rallying cry for the work-people of Antrim and Down. His influence amongst his class is greater than any other member of the United Society.' The men are consequently aware, as Castlereagh puts it, that 'If we were to prosecute this man Hope and fail to get a verdict they would arraign us as persecutors of the working class.'[120]

Sam Hanna Bell picked up on the original production's loyalty to the 'Bloody Castlereagh' epithet: 'an appellation cordially accepted by a large part of the audience. I can recall [Richard] Hayward throwing open a

---

[115] Stewart Parker, *Northern Star*, in *Plays: 2* (London: Methuen, 2000), 9–20, 54–60; quoted in *Irish Times*, 5 July 1974, 14.

[116] Fergus Whelan, 'Jemmy Hope—the Most Radical United Irishman', *Look Left*, Vol. 2, Issue 7 (2009), 25.

[117] James Hope, *United Irishman: The Autobiography of James Hope* (London: Merlin Press, 2001), 59.

[118] *Belfast Telegraph*, 25 April 2014, 7.

[119] Gearóid Ó Tuathaigh, *Ireland Before the Famine 1798–1848* (Dublin: Gill & Macmillan, 1972), 12.

[120] Carnduff, *Life*, 113; Thomas Carnduff, *Castlereagh* (Unpublished, 1935), 8–9. Linen Hall Library—Theatre Collection. Richard Hayward and J. R. Mageean, of the Belfast Repertory Theatre, took the roles of Castlereagh and James Hope.

lattice and with a wave of his hand to the scenic backcloth crying: "They lie who say I do not love this country!!"—a declaration which we in the Gods received in silence broken by a storm of jeers, groans and orange peel.'[121] Though concurring that Castlereagh appeared too much of a villain in the first half, a Dublin critic praised Carnduff's 'courageous' step up from his previous plays, arguing that its author had almost succeeded 'in showing us a man who, in spite of his apparent cynicism and brutality, really was actuated by a wrong-headed idealism, and even by a love of Ireland'.[122] This quality is also hinted at by the play-text, even if it is clear where Carnduff's sympathies lie, as a play ostensibly about Castlereagh becomes a vehicle through which to introduce Belfast audiences to Jemmy Hope:

> CASTLE: (*A far-away look in his eyes*) We could build a great Kingdom out of these islands, an Empire that would rule the world. No nation in Europe, no race on the face of the earth would dare question its power!
> HOPE: The people's power?
> CASTLE: (*Looking up surprised*) What people?
> HOPE: The common people who till the soil, who labour the looms, who carry your arms in battle! Do they count for nothing in your Lordship's estimation?
> CASTLE: They are as God made them.
> HOPE: And God made them after his own image. (*With great feeling*) The day is not far distant when your Lordship and those who rule with you will be subject to those people you now persecute—take care, when that day comes, they do not deal as harshly with you as you have with them!
> CASTLE: We do not fear the rabble.
> HOPE: You feared them in the American war.[123]

In the context of 1930s Belfast, of recession and high unemployment, the play illuminates the class conflict of the time. Castlereagh—who underestimates Hope—claims to 'have no wish to deal severely with people of your class. We realise the majority of you people are peacefully inclined when not incited to violence by others,' sounding much like a patrician Unionist politician in the face of the industrial strife of the Depression era. This would also manifest during the Second World War when Carnduff, by then a sardonic Air Raid Precautions warden, observed a general 'dissatisfaction with the Northern Government. It is held in contempt

---

[121] Bell, *Theatre*, 55.   [122] *Irish Times*, 19 February 1935, 8.
[123] Carnduff, *Castlereagh*, 7, 20–1, 48, 58–9. Castlereagh and Hope probably never met in person.

by every person. We haven't a solitary person in the cabinet who holds the confidence of the people.'[124] However, the non-sectarian promise of the Outdoor Relief riots of October 1932, when Catholic and Protestant workers marched (and rioted) together against the penurious dispensations of the Poor Law guardians, was always liable to be overtaken by communal furies. Carnduff recalled his son Jim working in a Catholic district of Belfast at the time and being accosted at his workplace by two Republicans who ordered him to vacate at gun-point. Not dissimilar to the visitations faced by Catholic workers in July 1920, his son 'was given five minutes to leave the premises and did the job in five seconds. He had never been much of a politician up till then. In three weeks' time, he was an Orangeman'.[125]

THE LATER MAN

St John Ervine had been in touch with Northern Irish novelist Forrest Reid as early as 1926, praising his autobiography *Apostate*—published the same year—and attempting to arrange a meeting. This never transpired, though Ervine poured forth his thoughts in an extraordinary letter in the summer of 1940, written from his 'Honey Ditches' house in Seaton, Devon. Praising Reid's follow-up memoir *Private Road*, Ervine urged him to write a realist novel, before turning to writer and mystic Æ (George Russell). The latter was deferential around Yeats, whose aristocratic manner forced him to 'suddenly remember that he had been a shop assistant'. Ervine apportioned no blame to Yeats for this and thought Æ, whom he still admired, 'did it all himself. His last years were unhappy, I fear.' Through the recollection, Ervine proceeds to delineate himself:

His roots were being taken away from him. He had spent his life in demanding a national being, and when he got it, it killed him. What a pity he ever went to Dublin. He should have gone to Belfast. You say in your book, that you never really felt any difference between North and South in Ireland. That surprises me. I have never felt at home in Southern Ireland, not for a single second. Cork was as alien to me as a village in the Syrian desert. I felt myself more at home in Vienna and Copenhagen than I felt in Dublin. I don't like the Southern Irish, whether they are Protestants or R.C.'s. I do like the Northern Irish, no matter what their religion is. The best friend, the nearest to me in every way, that I had in Belfast was a Roman Catholic, called Tom Kane. He disappeared from my life when I was a boy—I don't know why—I think his people 'flitted' to some other place—and I never saw or

---

[124] Carnduff, *Castlereagh*, 11; Letter to Mary Carnduff, 3 April 1943. TCA. This unpopularity is confirmed by Graham Walker in *A History of the Ulster Unionist Party: Protest, Pragmatism and Pessimism* (Manchester; Manchester University Press, 2004), 93–6.
[125] Carnduff, *Life*, 114.

heard of him again, but he stays in my memory more than any other person I knew in those days—the one lad in Belfast of my acquaintance whose mind was akin to my own.[126]

Quite why Ervine opens up in this way to another writer who he was not close to (there is no evidence they ever met) is unclear. Over a decade later he confided to another friend that *Apostate* was the only Reid book he rated, that he had 'no great wish to meet him, and I find difficulty in reading his novels, several of which I possess'.[127] Writing to him personally, however, he enthused about Reid's memories of the Ulster Literary Theatre scene involving David Parkhill (Lewis Purcell) and the journalist W. B. Reynolds, who was most after Ervine's heart: 'At least one of his ideas has long been mine—that the Ulster Theatre should have built or bought a theatre. It's failure to do so, a failure with which I have long reviled its members, is the explanation in my mind, of its ineptitude. The means those people wasted... well, well, it's useless to talk of that now.'[128]

Politically, Ervine's dismissal of accusations of gerrymandering and discrimination in Northern Ireland looks like a normative oversight, the mention of 'overgrown schoolboys' who 'cannot think of anything better to do than organise raids on military barracks' a clear reference to attacks leading into the mid-1950s IRA 'Border Campaign'.[129] The context of these attitudes must, however, be understood. Ervine delighted in pointing out the interference of the Catholic Church in politics, referring to newspaper reports of Belfast trade unionist William McMullen being denounced by a priest 'because he is a Protestant', and his flinty public letters earned responsive sparks from Irish representatives like Senator Frank MacDermot, who denounced Ervine as emblematic of the 'highly artificial little State' of Northern Ireland and its 'Orange policy and Orange manners'.[130]

In June 1948 Ervine headed back to Belfast for a Reform Club lunch party in his honour, with Prime Minister Basil Brooke present. He also visited Stormont, where the sight of Independent Unionist MPs Tommy Henderson and John Nixon ('who looks like something out of Walt

[126] Letter to Forrest Reid, 11 June 1940. FRP.

[127] Letter to John Boyd, 1 April 1953. JBC.

[128] See Eugene McNulty, *The Ulster Literary Theatre and the Northern Revival* (Cork: Cork University Press, 2008), 60–7; Letter to Forrest Reid, 11 June 1940. FRP. Original ellipsis.

[129] St John Ervine, 'Letter: The Elections in Ulster', *London Times*, 16 February 1949, 5; Letter to John Boyd, 20 August 1955. JBC.

[130] Letter to John Boyd, 12 August 1953. JBC; Frank MacDermot, 'Letter: Ireland and Eire', *London Times*, 7 May 1938, 8. MacDermot had led the National Centre Party before it merged into Fine Gael, though he would join de Valera's Fianna Fáil in 1937.

Disney') and the Irish Labour Party's Jack Beattie left him distinctly unimpressed: 'Henderson suffers from labial diarreheea—I can never spell that word—and Nixon—well, Holy Jase!' Ervine wanted an Opposition to form naturally in the Northern Irish parliament, apparently sincere in his desire for 'R.C.'s to enter Stormont as serious Ulstermen and not like dry goats, such as Cahir Healy, and people who fancy they're thinking when they're only farting'. He thought the First Inter-Party Government of Ireland (1948–51) showed promise, initially regarding Taoiseach John A. Costello as intelligent, but eventually concluding that it was being 'led by that synthetic Frenchman, [Seán] MacBride, son of a mindless lout and an English exhibitionist'. More considerably, Ervine remembered telling Brooke,

> that he ought to encourage a society of Unionist Micks in Ulster. There are some, and they could easily be more. That's what I'd do. I'd elect them to membership of the Ulster Club and the Reform. I hate all this religious segregation, though no man despises the R.C. [Roman Catholic] religion, in most of its respects, than I do. I have many R.C. friends, all of whom are well aware of what I feel about their faith, but that fact does not prevent me from liking them or, I think, being liked by them. I cannot see why a Prod and a Mick who both believe that the Union between Great Britain and Ireland is good for Ireland should not vote together on that principle. I hate hereditary Nationalists and hereditary Unionists.[131]

Though this illuminates an inclusive kind of Unionism which does not square with a bigotry he was occasionally charged with, the problem arrived when those same 'Micks' (or 'Prods') might believe that political unity of the island was preferable. Unlikely as this prospect has ever seemed, the very mention of the aspiration drew occasionally demented fire from Ervine.

Elaborating that he 'used to argue with Craigavon about Donegal', Ervine once advised the Northern Ireland Prime Minister 'that he ought to have held on to it', tongue-in-cheek maintaining that British forces could have made use of Lough Swilly and Donegal Bay during the Second World War: 'But Craigavon feared the inclusion of a large number of semi-illiterate Micks in his community. My retort to that was that we should make life so good for the Micks in Donegal that they would not want to be put in that back-street republic, Eire.'[132] Here appears the

---

[131] Letter to John Boyd, 19 February 1949. JBC. Of Sean MacBride's father John, Ervine continued: 'Yeats used to be very funny in his accounts of Maud Gonne trying to civilianise the bogtrotter she'd married, by taking him round the European picture galleries. The poor lout, whose only virtue was animal courage, trailed round with his tongue hanging out in a terrible drouth for a pint!'

[132] Letter to John Boyd, 16 July 1949. JBC.

authentic Craigavon Ervine so doughtily championed in his biography, a choice of subject bemusing to George Bernard Shaw, who queried how Ervine could spend time researching 'that walking monument of obdurate mindlessness. Not even a reactionary, for reaction means movement and he was immoveable.'[133]

Like a relative who delights in telling the same story over and over again, almost every letter Ervine wrote to playwright John Boyd mentions his admiration for Joseph Tomelty ('the best actor we've produced'),[134] another indicator that he was no narrow-minded bigot. The correspondence between Ervine and Boyd is candid, bitter, and humorous. It is one self-proclaimed Ulsterman, who left the domain at seventeen never to return, justifying his cantankerousness to a liberal Northern Irish Protestant who stayed to disdain the Unionism of his own tribe. 'Although his character was something of an enigma to me, I admired his forthrightness, his gusto, his good humour, his kindness,' Boyd remembered, and Ervine in turn enjoyed taking him to task for being 'so god-damned contemptuous of your own people and so god-damned full of pity for the poor wailing, snivelling Gael! You make me feel wild when you practically apologise for being a Protestant and one of the people who converted tracts of slob into a great city and centre of industry.'[135] He was by now constantly disparaging former Independent Labour Party comrades, while his play *Private Enterprise*, which opened on 25 November 1947 at the St James's Theatre in London, suggested that the British would soon be as 'slaves' to Labour interests. Ending with the Delaware family's promise to defy Attlee's iniquitous government, which is due to take over their factory and end life as they know it, *Private Enterprise* also features digressions on 'those who aspire to something better than themselves', an oddly pertinent debate about 'getting on in life' the British Labour Party is still, interminably, having.[136]

As might be expected, the *Manchester Guardian* acknowledged the battle lines, labelling *Private Enterprise* 'a counterblast from the Right' with 'grave faults'.[137] Though praising its allusions to John Galsworthy and impressive performances (in a cast which included Charles Lloyd-Pack, Elizabeth Allan, and Nicholas Hannen), an anonymous critic in the London *Times*—not a paper known for its left-wing sentiment—observed that the championing of the bourgeois family's combative tradition

---

[133] Letter to St John Ervine, 26 July 1949. HRC. Even the Craig family were said to be uncomfortable at its strident tone (for examples see Ervine, *Craigavon*, 312, 531, 572–3). See also Gillian McIntosh, *The Force of Culture: Unionist Identities in Twentieth Century Ireland* (Cork: Cork University Press, 1999), 148–56.

[134] Letter to John Boyd, 13 February 1957. JBC.

[135] Boyd, 'Ervine', 102; Letter to John Boyd, 16 July 1949. JBC.

[136] Ervine, *Private*, 20, 62. See *The Observer*, 20 December 2015, 38, 44.

[137] P. H.-W., 'Free Enterprise', *Manchester Guardian*, 27 November 1947, 3.

('We fight, father') had 'the effect of blurring the dramatic values of the industrial issue', exacerbated by the 'disappointing' and 'rather cheap sneers at the Labour Party incidental to [the play]'.[138] There are unsubtle digs along the lines of Churchill's 'some kind of Gestapo' denunciation of Labour, at the austerity of Chancellor Stafford Cripps, and gibes like 'Father used to say that when a Conservative couldn't get a job from his own party he joined Labour.'[139] Two shallow and vindictive trade unionists called Selby and Snoddy also appear, leading Shaw, rather devastatingly, to inform Ervine that the play had 'no curtain: the combatants are left stranded with the contempt you have felt for them all through'.[140] Ervine's interpretation of Attlee's administration seems oddly similar to playwright John Osborne's description of his dreaded mother living out her final years on a private income: 'Fearing neither death nor illness, she lived in terror only of the Labour Government.'[141] In private, too, Ervine had become increasingly acerbic, castigating in letters the 'cliché-mongers and yappers of stale slogans on the Labour benches of the House of Commons'. Nationalized industries were merely 'subsidised workhouses', the trade unionists and workers on whom Ervine once staked the future now retrograde: 'I've no use for the Little Man. To hell with him.' Ervine even claimed to have met and challenged the future Labour Chancellor of the Exchequer Denis Healey, 'one of the young Labour intellectuals' (and then rather left-wing), for his criticisms of Ulster Unionist MPs who were propping up Tory governments: 'He changed his note . . . when I asked him if it was Labour's intention to disenfranchise every constituency which elects anybody who is not a Socialist.'[142]

Even the statement of Ervine's noteworthy debut atrophied into whimsical naysaying. 'I'm opposed to mixed marriages', he wrote in the autumn of 1948, 'because I find that one of the parties, or both, perhaps, has so little hold on faith that he or she will abandon it and embrace its opposite merely to get into bed and have a good bout of what Justin Martyr calls carnal concurrence.'[143] He pondered writing vituperative plays about Karl Marx ('God must have taken great joy in running him to hell') and Oscar Wilde, and was a signatory of the Individualist Group manifesto during the Second World War: a conflict which reminded him of the First and his time in the Irish Division when 'I thought that we'd bring off a union, but

[138] 'St James's Theatre: Private Enterprise by St John Ervine', *London Times*, 26 November 1947, 7.
[139] Ervine, *Private*, 13, 33, 43, 54, 61, 98.
[140] Letter to St John Ervine, 17 August 1948. HRC.
[141] John Osborne, *A Better Class of Person* (London: Faber and Faber, 1981), 210.
[142] Letter to John Boyd, 27 July 1949. JBC; Letter to John Boyd, 14 October 1953. JBC.
[143] Letter to John Boyd, 13 October 1948. JBC.

something went wrong...I don't know what...and disunion came instead.'[144] The tantalizing 'what' was of course Irish nationhood and partition. The influence of his wife Leonora, who patiently guided him and shared in vast and powerful social contacts, had subsided to a new affectedly English outlook, the mentality of another country:

> In the last war, I used to deride men who were the age I am now, when I heard them say they could neither work nor sleep for thinking of the sufferings of the soldiers in France. That was, I told myself, stuff and nonsense—old men trying to humbug young men. But it's true. I find myself lying awake at night, with my thoughts going round and round and round, as I think of our men at sea and in France. Dunkirk nearly killed me.[145]

The Second World War was similarly critical for Thomas Carnduff. Northern Ireland's contribution is remembered as backbone personified, though Carnduff's cynical dispatches, again, offer an alternative view:

> The people are bored stiff with the war. But merchants and business men wax fat on war, and munition workers rarely look on their labour as a patriotic gesture. The majority of people these days seem to think war a good investment and are not worrying very much whether it continues a few more years. Air raids upset them a little but they soon forget and just at present everyone seems quite contented to make money while the goings [*sic*] good.[146]

Carnduff also found himself headhunted by the Northern Ireland Labour Party, who 'were after me again to help them to visualise their aspirations'.[147] Despite the respective breakaways of Harry Midgley and Jack Beattie, the NILP grew steadily during this time, achieving some success in concentrating the electorate on social and economic matters.[148] Though a member and impressed by its flurry of 'whist drives, dances, rambles, debates, reading circles', Carnduff politely declined active involvement: 'I don't like politics. I told them so. They say it's not politics they want me for, but cultural activities!'[149]

---

[144] Letter to John Boyd, 19 February 1949. JBC; *Manchester Guardian*, 13 August 1942, 2; Letter to Mr Sandford, 10 March 1941. JBC. Original ellipses.

[145] Letter to Forrest Reid, 11 June 1940. FRP.

[146] Letter to Mary Carnduff, 21 March 1942. TCA. For a laudatory view of Ulster's wartime input see Ervine, *Craigavon*, 576–7.

[147] Letter to Mary Carnduff, 14 February 1943. TCA.

[148] Russell Rees, *Labour and the Northern Ireland Problem 1945–1951* (Dublin: Irish Academic Press, 2009), 36.

[149] Letter to Mary Carnduff, 14 February 1943. TCA.

He received a serious scare in 1941 when his serving son Joseph was captured and held at the German Dulag Nord camp.[150] By the time he was freed four years later, Carnduff had moved with his wife to a small flat above a photography studio on Royal Avenue in the centre of Belfast. The overall effect of the war on his family was 'similar to the records of many other families. The war had finished our home life.'[151] It also appeared to finish his theatrical life. Despite mentions of prospective projects in his letters (especially a piece called '*Derry*'), no play of Carnduff's was produced between the end of the war and his death in 1956. This last part of his life was testament to his battles against the stultifying social snobbery of middle-class Ulster, epitomized by numerous references to lacklustre Queen's lecturers and the 'usual woe-begone looking features staring back at me' as he presided over meetings of the Young Ulster Society.[152] Foreseeing future economic slumps after the war ended, Carnduff's pessimism was such that when the Beveridge Report was published in 1942, he claimed 'few of us have much faith in the sincerity of the proposals' because 'vested interests are ridiculing the effort. Most profits are made through ordinary peoples' [*sic*] fear of <u>what</u> might happen to them. If you take that fear away there would be no need to invest savings against bad times, there wouldn't be any bad times.'[153] As his own lights faded, Carnduff still had an eye on the bigger picture.

CONCLUSION

Because of his membership of the Independent Orange Order, Carnduff has occasionally been claimed by mainstream Unionist politicians,[154] and he was intriguingly rediscovered by one of the more discerning Loyalist leaders of a later era. Billy Mitchell (1939–2006) had been involved in UVF violence in the 1970s, but after incarceration in Long Kesh under the guidance of Gusty Spence (a choice text of the Loyalist prisoners was St John Ervine's *Craigavon* biography),[155] Mitchell re-emerged to work in

---

[150] G. Webb (Commodore, Royal Naval Barracks), Letter to Thomas Carnduff, 28 July 1941.

[151] Letter to Mary Carnduff, 26 July 1941. TCA; Carnduff, *Life*, 115.

[152] John Gray, 'Introduction' to Carnduff, *Life*, 56; Letter to Mary Carnduff, 3 April 1943. TCA.

[153] Letter to Mary Carnduff, 5 December 1942. TCA. Original emphasis.

[154] Nelson McCausland, 'Orange Order is Going Strong and Can Contribute to a Shared Future', *Belfast Telegraph*, 23 October 2014, 27. McCausland was a Democratic Unionist Party representative for North Belfast and a former Northern Ireland Executive Minister.

[155] Roy Garland, *Gusty Spence* (Belfast: Blackstaff Press, 2001), 113.

cross-community schemes. He told the story of Irish Republican-socialist icon Peadar O'Donnell on leave from the Curragh Prison Camp, taking the journey home to West Donegal and stopping in Belfast to meet Carnduff. 'This is the one time that an Orangeman's handshake is better than a papal blessing,'[156] joked O'Donnell. The former had been a regular visitor to O'Donnell's Dublin house, once presenting his host with an Orange Sash which was placed in a glass case and proudly exhibited. O'Donnell publicly voiced his admiration of 'the sturdy healthy mind of Mr Carnduff', regarding 'him as one of the great Irishmen',[157] and the tale had enabled Billy Mitchell to come to terms with his own 'Irishness'. The understanding that political opponents 'need not dehumanise one another' had been important for Loyalists as they entered into a new arrangement with their adversaries after the 1998 Good Friday Agreement, though Mitchell also expressed sadness

> that working class Protestants such as Thomas Carnduff have been relegated to the margins of politics, culture and literature. Misunderstood by those of us who for so long swallowed the bitter pill of anti-Catholic sectarianism, and rejected by others whose bitter anti-Protestant sectarianism refused to acknowledge that anything good could be said or be written by an Orangeman.[158]

An *Irish Times* feature on Carnduff a few years before he passed away was surely correct to challenge the 'O'Casey of the North' label. The latter was 'a world figure; Carnduff an Irish dramatist who has never succeeded in projecting the drama of Belfast's shipyards further than the stage of the Abbey Theatre, Dublin'.[159] But this was a high measure and one Carnduff deserved based on the plays which survive. The same piece hoped that despite his lifelong poverty he had received consolation on his final stage, the Linen Hall Library, where he saw out his days as caretaker. His eternal money worries meant he never came close to being able to afford a house, calculating in one of his more affluent spells that after rents and tax he had 'about 30 shillings to swim the channel with'. Changing digs with regularity, he once rented a home in a road opposite Skegoneill Avenue, North Belfast, writing to Mary how it was 'not a safe area. I want you to be in a

---

[156] Billy Mitchell, 'The Orangeman's Handshake', *The Blanket* (January 2002). Mitchell was behind the policy document *The Principles of Loyalism* (2002).

[157] Amy Costello, Letter to Mary Carnduff, 15 October 1956. TCA.

[158] Mitchell, 'Orangeman's Handshake'. Carnduff's poem 'Men of Belfast' is viewed thousands of times a week by visitors to the *Titanic Belfast* exhibition, inscribed along a compass on the atrium floor: 'From the night of moving shadows / To the sound of the shipyard horn; / We hail thee Queen of the Northland, / We who are Belfast born' (*Poverty Street*, 53).

[159] Anon., 'Portrait Gallery', *Irish Times*, 2 October 1954, 7.

safe area.'[160] The same widow—and muse—remembered that 'though he lived among working class people all his life, he never failed to see the drabness of it'.

> Nights are drear in Poverty Street—
> Drear and lone;
> Scarcely a shadow you chance to meet
> Except your own.[161]

What Carnduff built was cultural capital, fantasizing if he ever came into any money of 'building a little theatre for Belfast' to see if 'We might manage a centre like the Abbey Theatre where some sort of academy could be formed to give recognition to artists, writers, and similar workers.'[162]

Despite their extensive correspondence, John Boyd (1912–2002) described St John Ervine as 'not a writer of the first rank. Indeed most of his imaginative work will probably not last.'[163] Boyd appreciated the caricature presented to him in letters, confirming as it did his own political hostility to Ulster Unionism. Though Ervine was anti-Irish in his later rhetoric, he was also critical of the insularity of Stormont, which he considered 'a glorified county council'.[164] Ervine's plays received little respect from Mary O'Malley's Lyric Players Theatre in Belfast, another pie Boyd had his finger in, though *Boyd's Shop* became a staple of the Ulster Group Theatre and kept it financially viable when it appeared.[165] And for a man with such a high opinion of his own plays (see the opening of Chapter 5), Boyd's downplaying of Ervine's creative work was well wide of the mark. A production of *Mixed Marriage* opened at the Lyric in January 2013, directed by Dubliner Jimmy Fay, who took charge of the whole theatre the following year. Running at the height of the Flag Protests of 2012–13 ('that was real street theatre', Fay joked on his appointment), the play appeared to him synonymous with the 1913 Dublin Lock Out centenary.[166] Though out of time with the Revival, Ervine shared Sean O'Casey's realist focus, informing the latter that his work was 'often in my mind' and supporting him during

---

[160] Letters to Mary Carnduff, 15 September 1942 and 30 July 1941. TCA.

[161] Quoted in *Belfast Telegraph*, 30 October 1964, 15; Carnduff, 'Poverty Street', in *Songs*, 36.

[162] Carnduff, *Life*, 116–17; Letter to Mary Carnduff, 11 February 1941. TCA.

[163] Boyd, 'Ervine', 113.

[164] Letter to John Boyd, 14 October 1953. JBC. Ervine also disapproved of Stormont's low salaries, deterring those who could not rely on private incomes from entering politics.

[165] See John Keyes, *Going Dark: Two Ulster Theatres* (Belfast: Lagan Press, 2001), 63. Boyd was the Lyric's 'Literary Advisor' and an Honorary Director. Not until 1981 was Ervine's *Boyd's Shop* staged there, featuring the company's acting institutions and newer talent including one Sarah (Marie) Jones.

[166] Quoted in *Irish Times*, 5 July 2014, 45; interview with Jimmy Fay, Belfast, 25 November 2014.

The Silver Tassie controversy, when Yeats rejected the Dubliner's anti-war play. However, a spat over derogatory remarks the Dubliner made about Ulster culture in the press burnt that bridge too, and Ervine may have prospered from his own advice to O'Casey following the *Tassie* affair: 'I hope … when your justifiable anger has subsided, that you will remember that you are an Irish dramatist.'[167]

Ervine's place in the Irish theatrical canon was sealed when a biographical capsule and extract from *Mixed Marriage* were included by erstwhile political adversaries of a later era in the second volume of the *Field Day Anthology of Irish Writing* (1991)[168]—a belated recognition that Ervine had once been a different person. He encouraged the portrait of calcified Unionist, yet Margaret Cole had been correct to credit his Fabian roots. In the spring of 1954 he wrote of the Fabian Society having 'no nonsense in its head about the mob', and his later individualism appeared more emotional than ideological. 'I don't want everything to be in uniform,' he professed. 'I became a Fabian because I realised that there are certain things all human beings have in common such as ample and good food, and that a world in which masses of men and women were not obtaining their share of these common needs was not fit for a good Tory to inhabit.'[169]

Ultimately *Mixed Marriage* survives, and enjoyed good audiences in Belfast over a hundred years after its appearance, because its themes are still achingly resonant (a well-received production also ran at London's Finborough Theatre in October 2011).[170] Ervine's old doyen Horace Plunkett saw it in the West End a matter of months after the signing of the Anglo-Irish Treaty, and was struck by a piece both timely and prescient:

> I treated myself to your play at the Ambassadors the other night. How tragically pertinent to the awful situation of the moment. It seems to me that [British Prime Minister David] Lloyd George has made it almost hopeless by his consistent refusal to consider any but the violent in his Irish policy. Nothing but violence counts with him throughout or will with us, I fear for a long time to come.[171]

---

[167] Letter to Sean O'Casey, 13 July 1932. NLI; 'Mr Ervine Retorts', *The Spectator*, 30 November 1945, 14; Letter to Sean O'Casey, 6 June 1928. NLI.

[168] Seamus Deane (gen. ed.), *Field Day Anthology of Irish Writing, Volume 2: From Poetry and Song (1880–1980) Through Prose and Fiction (1880–1945)* (Derry: Field Day, 1991), 712–16, 719.

[169] Letter to John Boyd, 25 March 1954. JBC; Letter to R. F. Rattray, 1 August 1955. HRC.

[170] Michael Billington called the production, directed by Sam Yates, 'the most compelling play in London' (*The Guardian*, 11 October 2011, 46).

[171] Letter to St John Ervine, 10 March 1922. HRC.

As one prominent critic put it in 1939, the year before *Mixed Marriage* was last performed at the Abbey, 'Ervine's problems remain to be solved; and until they are solved the greater problem of Ireland will remain.'[172] Even in the peacetime of post-Troubles but still-divided Northern Ireland, only one in ten marriages are mixed. Distantly related Brian Ervine, who led the Progressive Unionist Party from 2010–11, saw the Lyric production and spoke of being impressed by its socialism and anti-sectarianism, with themes that 'sadly still echo our day'.[173]

Ervine's own sadness was compounded towards the end when Leonora passed away in 1965 ('What the devil would become of you without her?', Shaw had once queried), though he maintained 'no illusions about myself. I was lucky and people were good to me.' Several years before his mind sunk into dementia, Ervine wrote dejectedly of theatre in Northern Ireland. The Group Theatre had just been rocked by a controversy over a new play written by a strong-willed shipyard worker from Ballymacarrett, East Belfast, by the name of Sam Thompson, and Ervine admitted to now knowing 'nothing about the Group. It was hellbent for ruin when it began to be commercial. Sooner or later, altruistic enterprise become money-mad, and immediately afterwards they are as dead as the dodo.' He expressed his customary admiration of Joe Tomelty ('I always liked him'), scorned the 'Dublin gawks' who could not understand that Ulster people were fundamentally in tune with machinery, and discussed rewriting the autobiography which was never published, before concluding with the recommendation that 'If anyone wishes to be successful as an author, he must first learn to loathe his family, and especially his father and mother. I have failed lamentably to do this. I still love my elders who could not have been kinder.'[174]

---

[172] Andrew E. Malone, 'The Rise of the Realistic Movement', in Lennox Robinson (ed.), *The Irish Theatre* (New York: Haskell House, 1939), 113.
[173] Speaking on *BBC Newsline*, 5 February 2013.
[174] Letter to John Boyd, 15 October 1960. JBC.

3

John Hewitt, Sam Thompson, and a Lost Labour Culture

A writer is not accepted as part of the community. If you are a writer and you speak your mind, you're a danger here.

Sam Thompson (1961)

Thomas Carnduff admitted to finding the membership of the Young Ulster Society dominated by 'those dull expressionless features which seem to be the make-up of the intelligentsia. I find the most intelligent features amongst those who are still searching for knowledge, not those who fancy they have acquired all that is needed.'[1] This disillusionment with the more gentrified patrons of the arts scene was shared by another shipyard playwright, Sam Thompson (Fig. 3.1), manifesting in the dialogue of his drama: 'The quality of speech of the working class is rich and varied. Middle class speech is stereo-typed, dull and lacks vitality.'[2] Thompson admired Carnduff's work but where he differed was in taking up the Northern Ireland Labour Party offer and involving himself directly in politics. Rising unemployment through the decline of traditional industries contributed to the NILP's growth in the late 1950s, but it was the party's apparent fusion of trade unionism and the arts which revealed its emphatic vision, for these were 'the only two fields of Ulster life from which sectarianism was wholly absent; in each, Catholic and Protestant could mix quite naturally and unselfconsciously as they could do almost nowhere else'.[3] The 'arts leanings' of other members such as the solicitor Brian Garrett ensured that he 'spent a lot of time and nights not with other lawyers but with actors, and I preferred that work. So then I was in the Labour Party.'[4]

---

[1] Letter to Mary Carnduff, 10 April 1943. TCA.
[2] Eamonn McCann, 'Sam Thompson: An Appreciation', *The Northern Review*, Vol. 1, No. 2 (1965), 97.
[3] C. E. B. Brett, *Long Shadows Cast Before: Nine Lives in Ulster, 1625–1977* (Edinburgh: John Bartholomew, 1978), 65.
[4] Interview with Brian Garrett, Belfast, 28 March 2011.

Fig. 3.1. Photo of Sam Thompson.
Note: Permission of David Stevens

Thompson also attended the Workers' Educational Association (WEA) class of John Hewitt (Fig. 3.2), and would almost join his tutor as a casualty when Unionist censorship threatened to prevent his first full-length play *Over the Bridge* (1960) from being staged.[5] Both Thompson and Hewitt were Belfast-born and in different ways very much of the city, while their political lives countered the Unionist hegemony of Sir Basil Brooke's Northern Irish state. The *Over the Bridge* controversy can therefore be viewed contiguously with the decision to overlook Hewitt as Director of Ulster's Museum and Art Gallery in 1953, an experience which sealed Hewitt's flight from Belfast to Coventry in 1957, though he would return in 1972 to earn 'the honours which had eluded him in his earlier years'.[6] Conceding that the 'Socialists of my time' were 'never really significant in the Northern situation', Hewitt located how:

---

[5] James Ellis, *Troubles Over the Bridge* (Belfast: Lagan Press, 2015), 25–108.
[6] Patricia Craig, 'Visiting John Hewitt', Lecture delivered at the Crescent Arts Centre, 27 October 2011.

Fig. 3.2. Photo of John Hewitt by Dermot Dunbar.
Note: Permission of Keith Millar

Always overriding was the choice of the people to ignore economic and social matters and concentrate on the danger from the South, or the danger from Stormont. Even when the Labour Party were in favour in the mid-Sixties, and gained four seats at Stormont and held out to the Unionists the promise of constructive opposition Terence O'Neill set out to smash them. Inevitably the Socialists were driven out of Northern politics. In the old days Sam Kyle left to become a Dublin senator, Billy McMullen went south to work in the trade union field. Good men driven away, I think, by despair. We who tried so hard live with despair.[7]

Their public run-ins with the Unionist bloc ensured that both writers retained a visceral contempt for establishment politics which never wavered. 'It was typical of the Unionist Party that they were always marching somewhere—not forwards of course, but always backwards into history,' declared Thompson in 1962,[8] and Hewitt never shed his animosity either. In 'Lines for a Dead Alderman', republished in his penultimate collection *Loose Ends* (1983), Hewitt taunts the deceased Unionist councillor (and shirt

---

[7] Quoted in *Irish Times*, 25 July 1983, 10.
[8] Quoted in *Irish News*, 27 September 1962, 9.

manufacturer) Percy Tougher, who undermined his application to become Director of the Ulster Museum:

> Justice is done in the end,
> the rascal who had his day,
> to party and prejudice friend,
> lodged in non-partisan clay.[9]

Following St John Ervine's Fabian associations and Carnduff's sympathies, the essence of this chapter is the underestimated influence of Labour politics on John Hewitt and Sam Thompson, and how this embedded itself in their creative work. Paul Arthur correctly argues that 'too little attention has been paid (to Hewitt) as a political animal—"political" in the ancient Greek sense, which considered citizenship as the highest end of man',[10] and much the same can be said of Thompson. The key to addressing this lies in Eric Hobsbawm's statement of how 'in creating the world's memory of the Spanish civil war, the pen, the brush and the camera wielded on behalf of the defeated have proved mightier than the sword and the power of those who won'.[11] It is in this context that Thompson's and Hewitt's impact and Labour identifications can also be reassessed.

The literary component of the NILP's life was a major part of its ethos, as emphasized by a former secretary: 'That was the whole thing about us. Unionism was staid, formal. To be a Unionist was boring. We were fractious and effervescent, and it's a shame it didn't work out.'[12] It is striking how many of those who were to walk away from the NILP, exasperated by a political culture 'trying to find a solution with guns and bombs',[13] took refuge in writing and literature. David Bleakley authored multiple pamphlets and biographies of figures including Saidie Patterson, Brian Faulkner, and C. S. Lewis, while along with the memoirist Sam McAughtry—who penned manifestos and campaigned for the NILP in Castlereagh—both Sam Napier and Paddy Devlin wrote creatively following their retirements from active politics, Napier publishing short stories and Devlin with his 1984 play *Strike!* The latter also adapted *Over the Bridge* for the Belfast Civic Arts Theatre in September 1985, and was followed by his daughter Anne—one-time member of the Falls delegation—who continues to write short stories. Sam Hanna Bell was a part of this culture too, corresponding with the NILP's heavyweights and

[9] Unless otherwise indicated all poetry is dated to its first publication and taken from *The Collected Poems of John Hewitt*, ed. Frank Ormsby (Belfast: Blackstaff Press, 1991).
[10] Paul Arthur, 'Taking a Leaf out of Hewitt's Book', *Irish Times*, 8 August 1989, 10.
[11] Eric Hobsbawm, 'War of Ideas', *The Guardian Review*, 17 February 2007, 6.
[12] Interview with Douglas McIldoon, Belfast, 27 January 2012.
[13] Sam Napier, quoted in *Irish Times*, 27 April 1984, 7.

professing electoral support for it years after it had ceased in relevance.[14] The late Charlie Brett's numerous books on architecture—and an enigmatic memoir—mirrored the adult educationalist R. H. Tawney's view that culture was an 'engine of the soul', which was why he and Bleakley were so dedicated to aesthetically improving Northern Ireland's public spaces and buildings, lifting citizens with civic plans and urban greenery. Overall, therefore, the NILP has been acknowledged as 'a tremendously important asylum to the artistic', entwined with a socialist identity capable of breaking down sectarian barriers.[15]

OVER THE BRIDGE

Sam Thompson makes the crossover between politics and the arts particularly explicit because he both wrote plays and stood for election. His education began when he left school at fourteen to apprentice in the shipyards, taking a place with Bob Richardson as one of the 'Shithouse Orators'. Formative was their attendance at Hewitt's aforementioned WEA class, as recalled by Richardson:

> Our first class was an 'Appreciation of Art' under the learned and quiet guidance of the late John Hewitt. The class was about half 'white-collared' workers, the rest tradesmen. John Hewitt's search for sincere questions, and the desire to observe and learn was *untiring*. There must be many, many people in this country who owe a debt to this man. He gave us a new view. He showed us how to look at visual art, guiding the class to an understanding that our minds and eyes had not known.[16]

Thompson had worked with David Bleakley in the shipyard engine shop and was later recruited into the NILP by Paddy Devlin, who also persuaded him to run as the party's candidate for South Down in the October 1964 general election.[17] During the campaign, Thompson's Ulster Unionist opponent Captain Lawrence Orr and Prime Minister Terence O'Neill paid

---

[14] Sam McAughtry, 'A Good Mark', *Irish Times*, 22 May 1985, 11. Another member of the NILP literati was dramatist John D. Stewart, who was the party's final nomination as Senator to Stormont's Upper House. He never faced election because of the parliament's prorogation. Aaron Edwards, *A History of the Northern Ireland Labour Party: Democratic Socialism and Sectarianism* (Manchester: Manchester University Press, 2009), 188–9.

[15] John Wilson Foster, *Between Shadows: Modern Irish Writing and Culture* (Dublin: Irish Academic Press, 2009), 213.

[16] Robert Richardson, 'Sam & Me: Recollections of Belfast and Playwright Sam Thompson in the 1930s', *Krino*, No. 4 (Autumn 1987), 21–3, 26, 28. Both Thompson and Richardson were lifelong friends of the Communist Party's Betty Sinclair.

[17] *Belfast Telegraph*, 26 January 1985, 11.

special attention to Thompson, launching attacks on the writer who had lost himself in 'their' woods. Orr proclaimed that the people of South Down had nothing to learn from Belfast playwrights: 'Politics is not a play—it is concerned not with fiction but with fact.'[18] Earlier in the year O'Neill lamented the presence of 'a certain Mr. Sam Thompson, whose past experience was in producing works of fiction',[19] and when the playwright dismissed a trip to the United States in the spring—during which he met President Lyndon Johnson and Jackie Kennedy—as an 'Ulster blarney tour', O'Neill repeated how 'unlike the works of the playwright, the work of the politician is concerned with facts. On this visit to North America, I made a speech on Ulster which was broadcast throughout Canada from the Atlantic to the Pacific. I addressed one of the most distinguished business audiences in New York.'[20] O'Neill was ruffled by Thompson's assertion that the Premier did little during his trip other than talk about the 'ten American Presidents of Scots-Irish descent', who also 'probably had to emigrate for the same reasons as our young people who are emigrating to-day'.[21]

Fellow NILP alumni judged that as an 'archetypal Belfastman' the 'scattered villages and towns of South Down were not his milieu', and so Thompson lost his deposit.[22] Riots in Divis Street earlier in the month contributed, along with O'Neill's targeting of the party, to the marginalization of the Labour vote in the election.[23] Certainly there were elements inside the NILP repugnant to Thompson, and he was more a part of the 'Sunday Swings' story of November 1964—when the party's Woodvale representative 'voted to lock the swings and it became more associated with Sabbatarianism than Socialism'[24]—than is often remembered. Thompson had been approached by some in the party to run for West Belfast,

---

[18] Quoted in Maura Megahey, *'The Reality of His Fictions': The Dramatic Achievement of Sam Thompson* (Belfast: Lagan Press, 2009), 204.

[19] Quoted in *Belfast News Letter*, 9 April 1964, 5.

[20] Quoted in *Belfast News Letter*, 4 April 1964, 1.

[21] Quoted in *Irish News*, 10 April 1964, 5.

[22] McCann, 'Sam Thompson', 97. Thompson received 6,260 votes to Orr's 32,922.

[23] *Belfast News Letter*, 1 October 1964, 1; Brett, *Long Shadows*, 131. Graham Reid—who almost adapted Roy Bradford's novel *The Last Ditch* (1981) for television—recalls being told by Bradford that O'Neill urged him to stand for Belfast Victoria in the Stormont election the following year, saying: 'You won't win it, but just damage the Labour vote' (interview with Graham Reid, London, 17 May 2012). Bradford narrowly won the seat at the expense of David Bleakley, who later claimed that the 1965 election 'stopped the momentum of change and released most unfortunate forces in our community which have so far not been contained'. Quoted in *Socialist Commentary* (March 1973), 26.

[24] Anne Devlin, 'The Voice of Many Men', *Fortnight*, No. 473 (October/November 2010), 20.

a constituency tailor-made for him, a sprawling working-class area, often the cockpit of religious strife but with a strong Labour tradition. However, the reactionary wing did not relish the prospect of a fiery, emotional radicalism being let loose in an urban constituency, and Alderman William Boyd, who in a subsequent controversy revealed his conviction that the foundations of civilization would crumble if children were allowed to swing on Sunday, was selected by 9 votes to 7.[25]

Eamonn McCann was expressing in the above the kind of caustic disillusionment which would lead to his own expulsion from the NILP. His identification of an 'ultra-right lay-preacher element who courted orange support' is exaggerated but also not without basis, at least insofar as Boyd (and Bleakley) represented Protestant constituencies in East and West Belfast and were sensitive to the more socially conservative elements (they were later credited by the party's more secular wing with being 'much more in touch with where the Protestant working class was coming from', and would be again when the civil rights movement surfaced in the late 1960s).[26] McCann claimed that Thompson allied 'himself with the liberal against the reactionary wing', waging 'fierce war against those who introduced intolerance into the Northern Irish Labour Party itself',[27] the latter of which is certainly the case. One of the party's former candidates and executive members, Yorkshire-born David Overend, occasionally found that NILP activists 'didn't take kindly to the English accent. Sam did. Treated me like a brother.'[28]

At this stage it is necessary to outline the very real political impact of *Over the Bridge*. Ironically supporters of O'Neill used the scandal to discredit and eventually dislodge Sir Basil Brooke as Prime Minister, the controversy illuminating a warehouse of intra-Unionist Party discontent which began when Thompson accosted James Ellis on Bedford Street in the centre of Belfast, between the Ulster Hall and the premises of BBC Northern Ireland: 'I have a play here you won't touch with a bargepole.'[29] As director of production at the Group, Ellis had accepted, cast, and publicized *Over the Bridge* at a press conference, before the Group's directors elected by six votes to two to withdraw the play just a fortnight before its opening night in May 1959. John Ritchie McKee (a former estate agent and golfing companion of Brooke) underhandedly acquired a copy of the script, which Ellis had initially denied him—maintaining that

---

[25] McCann, 'Sam Thompson', 97.
[26] Douglas McIldoon, quoted in Edwards, *History*, 99.
[27] McCann, 'Sam Thompson', 95–6.
[28] Interview with David Overend, Belfast, 28 April 2015.
[29] Ellis, *Troubles*, 25. See also Paddy Devlin, 'The "Over the Bridge" Controversy', *Linen Hall Review*, Vol. 2, No. 3 (Autumn 1985), 4–6.

the dramatic subject 'wasn't any of his business'—and demanded cuts which Thompson rebuffed.[30] The opposition to Ellis and Thompson may have been Unionist, but the Group's original Board of Directors included Unionists. More debilitating was McKee's power serving simultaneously on the Group Theatre's Board, as President of the Council for the Encouragement of Music and Arts (CEMA), and as national governor of BBC Northern Ireland (his brother was also the Unionist Lord Mayor at the time).[31]

Thompson went round to McKee's home with Ellis to listen to the broadcast of his radio play *The Long Back Street* before they discussed how they were going to proceed with *Over the Bridge*: 'I let him have his say. He wanted the mob scene out and the language curtailed. In his opinion the religious references in the play were blasphemous. McKee told me in forceful terms that if the play went on in full, the guns would be out, the blood would flow and the theatre would be wrecked by mobs.'[32] Following the breakdown of talks, McKee and the directors (whose inferred position was 'There *was* no sectarianism in the shipyards') released a statement to the press: 'The Ulster public is fed up with religious and political controversies. This play is full of grossly vicious phrases, and situations, which would undoubtedly offend and assault every section of the public ... It is the policy of the directors of the Ulster Group Theatre to keep political and religious controversies off our stage.'[33] Thompson proceeded to sue the company for breach of contract, receiving an out of court settlement.[34]

Much as the Unionist establishment publicly campaigned against *Over the Bridge* being staged—McKee's brother threatening that 'Plays with sectarian themes make it difficult for Lord Mayors to give money to the arts'[35]—so prominent friends within the artistic community including John Boyd and Louis MacNeice mobilized to back Thompson. Sam Hanna Bell, who had first encouraged him to write following a meeting in the Elbow Room bar, joined MacNeice and Douglas Carson in supporting Thompson in the private corridors of the BBC and publicly, much to the corporation's irritation.[36] With Ellis and some of the Group's

---

[30] *Belfast Telegraph*, 8 May 1959, 1; *Belfast Telegraph*, 14 May 1959, 1; speaking at 'An Evening with Jimmy Ellis', 12th Belfast Film Festival, 9 June 2012.

[31] John Keyes, *Going Dark: Two Ulster Theatres* (Belfast: Lagan Press, 2001), 82–7; *Belfast Telegraph*, 27 February 1964, 2. CEMA was a forerunner of the Arts Council.

[32] Sam Thompson, 'Autobiographical Script' (1960). Sam Thompson Collection. Central Library, Belfast.

[33] Keyes, *Going Dark*, 83; quoted in *Irish Times*, 14 May 1959, 9.

[34] *Belfast Telegraph*, 16 May 1959, 1; *Irish Times*, 10 July 1959, 1.

[35] Quoted in Keyes, *Going Dark*, 85.

[36] John Boyd, *The Middle of My Journey* (Belfast: Blackstaff Press, 1990), 117.

actors, Thompson founded the new company 'Ulster Bridge Productions Ltd' and finally staged the play in January 1960 at the Empire Theatre (owned by a Dublin-based company), where it was seen by an estimated 42,000 people over the course of six weeks.[37] Scenes of blunt sectarianism jarred those who insisted such bigotry was not commonplace.

> RABBIE: (*agitatedly*) If a man is elected on to the district committee and does a good job, I don't give a damn if he's a Catholic or a Rumanian hemstitcher.
> ARCHIE: Well, don't say I didn't warn you. When the time comes for a showdown we'll not only number the Popeheads of the enemies of Ulster, but we'll have to take into account mealy-mouthed Prods like you who aid and abet them. We're not standing for a Fenian like O'Boyle sitting on the district committee who takes his instructions from an illegal organisation or some ould black crow of a Jesuit.[38]

Thompson defended, in response to accusations that the play itself was 'vicious sectarianism', that 'all sectarianism is vicious. I try to show what is good and bad on both sides.'[39] *Over the Bridge* toured profitably to Dublin, Edinburgh, Glasgow, and Brighton, but lost the money it had made when it arrived to uninterested audiences in London (its revolving set also broke down), and the affair was not without casualities. It led to the permanent exile of its director James Ellis, another fiery East Belfast native, who feared that 'having made a stand against the Establishment over the play, he wouldn't be welcomed back'.[40] Though he thought the battle worth fighting—and was surely mistaken in believing that Thompson's working-class following meant that he had things easier—Ellis always felt more isolated, and could only approach the episode some decades later in his own poetry:

> I crossed a bridge and thought to shake the dust
> From off my feet, but it was not to be;
> I fled across the Irish Sea,
> Nursing resentment and profound disgust
>
> That individuals had betrayed their trust
> And held the public stage in ignominy.[41]

[37] *Belfast Telegraph*, 7 March 1960, 4.
[38] Sam Thompson, *Over the Bridge and Other Plays* (Belfast: Lagan Press, 1997), 39–40.
[39] Quoted in *Belfast Telegraph*, 7 May 1959, 1.
[40] Ellis, *Troubles*, 13, 102–8; Robina Ellis, quoted in *Belfast Telegraph*, 4 April 2014, 32. Prompted by the desire to challenge 'the speculative and inaccurate accounts that have cropped up over the decades', one detects in Ellis's posthumously published memoir a desire to reinsert himself into a narrative which has been so naturally dominated by Sam Thompson.
[41] Ellis, *Troubles*, 15; James Ellis, 'Over the Bridge', in *Domestic Flight* (Belfast: Lagan Press, 1998), 55. Ellis landed the role of Bert Lynch in the BBC television series *Z Cars*

The NILP's Martin McBirney proclaimed that *Over the Bridge* 'knocked down the kitchen wall and brought the streets and the shipyard on to the stage', and Thompson could finally catch his breath and ponder his next move. A few months later a journalist asked him whether he thought the communal violence of the kind depicted in the play could ever recur. 'You never know. But we hope it won't,'[42] he fired back.

ACTIVISM, REGIONALISM, NATIONALITY

In the midst of the vast unemployment of the 1930s, imagery of empty slipways, and 'Men with great skills standing at corners everywhere',[43] John Hewitt helped to found the Belfast Peace League in 1934. It was during his work for the latter that he met his wife Roberta, who served as the organization's secretary. Hewitt wrote the League's recruiting article stressing the group's 'non-sectarian and expressly non-political nature', something he later recognized as 'a cruel paradox: working for international peace' while 'at the same time in my native city, Catholics were burnt out of the York Street area and fled to the new houses of the Glenard Estate'. Hewitt simultaneously became involved with the National Council of Civil Liberties, which was devoted to an investigation of the Special Powers Act. His rejection of this 'reactionary repressive weapon' led to his 'first acquaintance with the nature of state authority and its techniques of the opened letter and the tapped telephone'.[44] When the Spanish Civil War broke out in 1936, Roberta assisted with fundraising for the beleaguered Republic and the Hewitts took in two young Basque refugees to their Westland Drive home.[45]

That same year Hewitt wrote *The Bloody Brae*, though it was not broadcast on radio until 1954 (and not staged at the Lyric until 1957).[46] It depicts the fictional early seventeenth-century meeting of John Hill and Bridget Magee; the former is a Cromwell trooper who has killed Catholic peasant Bridget and her suckling child, condemning Hill's spirit to wander

---

from 1962 to 1978. He returned to Northern Irish terrain in Graham Reid's *Billy* plays (1982–4). See Chapter 5.

[42] Quoted in Hagal Mengal, *Sam Thompson and Modern Drama in Ulster* (New York: Peter Lang, 1986), 249; quoted in *Irish Times*, 12 March 1960, 10.

[43] Richardson, 'Sam & Me', 21.

[44] Sam Burnside, 'Preparing Lonely Defences', in Hewitt: A *Fortnight* Supplement (July/August 1989), III; John Hewitt, 'No Rootless Colonist' (1972), in *Ancestral Voices: The Selected Prose of John Hewitt*, ed. Tom Clyde (Belfast: Blackstaff Press, 1987), 150–1.

[45] W. J. McCormack, *Northman: John Hewitt (1907–1987): An Irish Writer, His World, and His Times* (Oxford: Oxford University Press, 2015), 53.

[46] For the text see Hewitt, *Collected Poems*, 400–16.

the same east Antrim territory as a revenant, unable to leave until he has earned forgiveness: 'I murdered pity when I murdered you, and reason and mercy and hope for this vexed land.' *The Bloody Brae* confronts Hewitt's own guilt, even if it 'dramatizes a spiritual condition in which Protestant guilt is objective'.[47] Allowing for 'the moral possibility of a change of heart',[48] Magee forgives him, though Hewitt realized that not everyone would embark on the reconciliation process. Another ghost trooper, Malcolm Scott, joins them, remaining loyal to the original antagonism between English soldier and 'renegade' peasant. When it was republished in *Freehold and Other Poems* (1986), Hewitt was struck by its continuing appositeness, adding the introductory sonnet 'Four decades on, the heartbreak's relevant'.

Hewitt spoke later of addressing Northern Ireland Labour Party meetings during the Great Depression, writing 'a great deal of political poems in those days, including one about an election in which Harry Midgley, the socialist who later turned Tory, was involved'.[49] Hewitt confirmed in a 1964 letter that he was always more attached to democratic socialism than communism: 'Although I have read a good deal of Marxism and still find the dialectic a handy if not all-purpose tool I have never been a Communist. Indeed I should best be described as a Utopian Socialist. The only Irish political group I subscribe to is Noel Browne's.'[50] Much as recent work acknowledges the generational influence of Louis MacNeice's father, so the significance of Hewitt's socialist father 'who was only illiberal, it seems, on the subject of strong drink' has often been highlighted.[51] The younger Hewitt was also a well-known frequenter of Davy McClean's Progressive Book Shop on Union Street in Belfast.[52] Despite his 'hierarchy of values' being regularly quoted, he was still happy to outline it as late as 1985:

> I belong to the north of Ireland and all the complexities of its occupation. I was born before partition when Ireland was a complete unit, so I'm an Irishman in that way. But I was born in the British Isles and I speak English

---

[47] McCormack, *Northman*, 54.

[48] Terence Brown, 'Review: *Freehold and other Poems*', *Poetry Ireland Review*, No. 16 (Summer 1986), 79.

[49] Quoted in *Irish Times*, 25 July 1983, 10. This appears to be 'A Labour Victory: *an election incident*' (1928).

[50] Letter to John Montague, spring 1964. The Hewitt Archive, Library of the University of Ulster, Coleraine.

[51] David Fitzpatrick, *'Solitary and Wild': Frederick MacNeice and the Salvation of Ireland* (Dublin: Lilliput Press, 2012). See also Patrick Walsh, '"Too Much Alone": John Hewitt, Regionalism, Socialism, and Partition', *Irish University Review*, Vol. 29, No. 2 (Autumn–Winter 1999), 341–57.

[52] John Kilfeather, 'Remembering John Hewitt', *Threshold*, No. 38, Hewitt Edition (Winter 1986/7), 33.

and I know no other tongue, so I'm British. And because we're an archipel-
ago to the west of Europe, I'm European. So that's my hierarchy: I'm an
Ulsterman, an Irishman, British and a European. And I believe anyone in
my condition who attempts to skip one stage of that is falsifying the family
tree, the ancestry of his thought. You get it with the Ulster Unionists who
say they're not Irish—they are of course, but they say they're not, so
they're falsifying it. The Gaels say they don't belong to the British Isles, so
they're falsifying it, they don't have a true appreciation of the family tree
for our area.[53]

It has rarely been noted that the high watermark of Regionalist thought
coincided with the radical measures of the UK's post-war Labour government, a condition which undoubtedly facilitated Hewitt's inclusion of
Britishness into his hierarchy, as Clement Attlee's socialist government
promised to seriously disorientate the Unionist establishment.[54] Prior to
this the Second World War had been paramount in the development of
Regionalism, with Hewitt one of many prevented from travelling in
Europe to holiday locally in Ulster. As well as delivering a boom period
for readings, concerts, and plays, the influence of the war 'encouraged
people all over Europe to think deeply about the problems associated with
nationalism'.[55] In response Hewitt was to request a federated British Isles
('or a federal Ireland') along with a culture 'individual and distinctive, a
fine contribution to the European inheritance and no mere echo of the
thought and imagination of another people'.[56] Some contended that
Regionalism represented an evasion of the north's hard political realities,
but looking back in 1972 Hewitt ideologically justified 'that in this
concept might be found a meeting place for the two separated communities' where 'the older and the less old peoples might discover a basis for
amity and co-operative progress'.[57]

However, little materialized in the way he hoped. Attlee's Labour administration passed the 1949 Ireland Act, cementing their positive relationship
with Unionists at Stormont (as even St John Ervine acknowledged), due in

[53] Quoted in Ketzel Levine, 'A Tree of Identities, a Tradition of Dissent: John Hewitt at
78', *Fortnight*, No. 213 (4–17 February 1985), 16.
[54] See Russell Rees, *Labour and the Northern Ireland Problem 1945–1951* (Dublin: Irish
Academic Press, 2009), 33–63; Graham Walker, *A History of the Ulster Unionist Party: Protest,
Pragmatism and Pessimism* (Manchester; Manchester University Press, 2004), 100–18.
[55] Tom Clyde, 'A Stirring in the Dry Bones: John Hewitt's Regionalism', in Gerald
Dawe and John Wilson Foster (eds), *The Poet's Place: Ulster Literature and Society: Essays in
Honour of John Hewitt, 1907–1987* (Belfast: Institute of Irish Studies, 1991), 250–1;
Hewitt, 'No Rootless Colonist', 152.
[56] John Hewitt, 'Regionalism: The Last Chance' (1947), in *Ancestral Voices*, 125.
[57] See Barra Ó Seaghdha, 'Ulster Regionalism: The Unpleasant Facts', *The Irish Review*,
No. 8 (Spring 1990), 54–61; Hewitt, 'No Rootless Colonist', 153.

large part to the post-war government's appreciation of Northern Ireland's industrial war effort.[58] Hewitt too would distance himself from the specifics of Regionalism, turning in a poem of 1949 'to the landscape because men disappoint me',[59] but the notion of an independent Ulster identity came to be construed by Roy McFadden, John Montague (who travelled round with Hewitt on the 'Planter and the Gael' tours), and nationalist-minded critics as an enlightened kind of Unionism.[60] Precisely not this categorization, it is at this point that his foundations in the Northern Ireland Labour Party must be acknowledged. Hewitt laid this out quite plainly:

> it seemed evident that the Unionists were a right-wing offshoot of the British Tory Party, who at home fought every election on the border, and that the Nationalists, the representatives of the Catholic minority, were merely obsolete clansmen with old slogans, moving in an irrelevant dream, utterly without the smallest fig leaf of a social policy. So my concern went to the Labour Party—I was branch delegate at one annual conference—the party of Sam Kyle and Billy McMullen, who had a policy about 'the ownership of the means of production, distribution and exchange'.[61]

Aside from a natural response to the attention Hewitt has received, the reaction against is based on his refusal to embrace a uniquely 'Irish' appellation. At an extreme, Hewitt's life and work could be spectacularly misunderstood by a southern poet like Thomas Kinsella as little more than an exhibition 'of the colonial mentality'.[62] Derek Mahon captured the original objection: 'Why did he never consider a United Ireland? I fail to see why his chosen "region" should have been Ulster instead of Ireland as a whole: a point on which we stuck more than once.'[63] When discussing a forthcoming John Hewitt Summer School, Mahon was heard to joke in private that 'the next gathering discuss Hewitt's Protestant inheritance with reference to South Africa or the Southern states', and he was irked by

---

[58] St John Ervine, *Craigavon: Ulsterman* (London: Allen & Unwin, 1949), 531; interview with John Kennedy, Holywood, 17 June 2014. See also Rees, *Labour*, 152.

[59] In an interview the year before his death Hewitt backtracked, commenting 'Ireland is not a region, it is many regions' (quoted in *Irish Times*, 18 March 1986, 13).

[60] John Montague, *The Pear Is Ripe: A Memoir* (Dublin: Liberties Press, 2007), 140, 147. David Trimble has made scattered references, but the only mainstream Unionist politician to have shown any sustained interest in John Hewitt is Mike Nesbitt, MLA for Strangford, who led the Ulster Unionist Party from 2012 until 2017. A former television anchor for the BBC and UTV, as well as the first leader of his party not to be a member of the Orange Order, Nesbitt claims to find 'a cultural home in the poetry of John Hewitt' (*Belfast Telegraph*, 3 April 2012, 31).

[61] Hewitt, 'No Rootless Colonist', 149.

[62] Thomas Kinsella, *The Dual Tradition: An Essay on Poetry and Politics in Ireland* (Manchester: Carcanet Press, 1995), 118–21.

[63] Derek Mahon, 'An Honest Ulsterman', *Irish Times*, 1 January 1988, 29.

the way Hewitt's 'regions never seemed to get past Scotland'.[64] Aside from
the way Hewitt's regions, in both his travels and his poetry, repeatedly
went beyond Scotland—he was memorably in Hungary when British
troops fanned through the streets of Derry and Belfast in August
1969—the criticisms completely ignore Hewitt's much-quoted hierarchy
as well as a designation embraced in one of his most famous poems. When
in London years later, Hewitt was adamant about watching 'the King's
horses / going about the King's business, never mine' (1974).

Undoubtedly the most powerful, and considered, of these voices was
Seamus Heaney's. In later years Heaney had credited Hewitt for viewing
Northern Ireland's 'colonial predicament', but continued to object to his
gaze ('more Belfast's shipyard than Derry's Bogside') as well as the way in
Hewitt's mind, 'the Catholics in the North, and the Irish south of the
border, remained definitively "other"... nothing in him could altogether
flow towards them. He was laureate of the reformed conscience, the
embattled Ulsterman in stand-off from both England and Ireland.'[65] This
is a revision of his previous, more interesting assessment. Back in 1972
Heaney suggested Hewitt was the 'two-way pull', whose work revealed 'a
quest for personal identity that must strike many of Hewitt's fellow-
countrymen as a remembrance, full of a stubborn determination to belong
to the Irishry and yet tenaciously aware of a different origin and cast of
mind'.[66] In Gerald Dawe's subtler formulation, which expands on the
original reading and locates a political reflex, Hewitt 'estranged himself
from the other perceptions made of the common Irish inheritance, acknowledged the conflicting versions of history in his country and embodied these
in his poetry'.[67]

It is here that his socialist convictions were most revealing. Robert
Greacen accurately grasped how, as a left-winger, Hewitt could hardly
admire a state 'that was not only overwhelmingly Catholic but dominated
by the Catholic Church'.[68] Hewitt himself clarified: 'I would not advise
the Protestants to become part of a state that writes the law of one church
into its constitution. I would not myself become the citizen of a state that
makes literary censorship legal.'[69] The later Heaney overlooks the socialist

[64] Hugh Maxton (W. J. McCormack), *Waking: An Irish Protestant Upbringing* (Belfast: Lagan Press, 1997), 211.
[65] Quoted in Dennis O'Driscoll, *Stepping Stones: Interviews with Seamus Heaney* (London: Faber and Faber, 2008), 331–2.
[66] Seamus Heaney, 'The Poetry of John Hewitt', in *Preoccupations: Selected Prose, 1968–1978* (London: Faber and Faber, 1980), 208–9.
[67] Gerald Dawe, *Against Piety: Essays in Irish Poetry* (Belfast: Lagan Press, 1995), 95, 99.
[68] Robert Greacen, 'John Hewitt: The Search for Identity', in *Rooted in Ulster: Nine Northern Writers* (Belfast: Lagan Press, 2000), 119.
[69] Quoted in *Irish Times*, 25 July 1983, 10.

vein running through (in his own phrase) 'Hewitt's peculiar mixture of lyric-tenderness and secular tough-mindedness', and could outright misread him as an exemplar of the 'feeling of possession and independence of the empowered Protestants with their own Parliament'. Further rebuking Hewitt in the same November 1993 lecture for a vision 'more capable of seeing over the water than over the border',[70] Heaney somehow passed over the view facing back over that border of a state characterized by the conservatism of the Catholic Church. Hewitt's aversion to Catholicism was political, not religious, stemming from 'the opposition between secularism and "received truth", that is, between the atheist and Catholic, rather than the Protestant and Catholic'.[71] This secularism accounted for his rejection of the time when Irish politics 'took on a sectarian bias, when nationalism became equated with a Jansenist Catholicism, and Protestantism became evangelical and royalist'.[72]

Excepting the way Unionists marked Hewitt 'as an intractable enemy' from the early 1930s (leading to his eventual departure),[73] questions of Irishness and Britishness veil Hewitt's authentic identity: Left. *Both* nationalities were reconciled but 'Growing up in Ireland of the thirty-two counties, until I first set foot outside I never consciously thought of myself as Irish or of any nationality at all. I accepted Sir Edward Carson and his twin, John Redmond, as men from the same country as myself, who had diverging ideas about the governance of it.'[74] Writing from his Postbridge Road address in Coventry, Hewitt described the American socialist Upton Sinclair's anthology *The Cry for Justice* (1915) as 'one of the books that shaped my thought', and while Dublin was a 'literary capital', Hewitt insisted 'our politics looked beyond to the world. Sacco and Vanzetti were, for us, far more significant that any of the celebrated "felons of our land".'[75] So quickly are tribal allegiances allotted in Irish cultural debates that many have obscured the internationalism of the Labour movement.

[70] Seamus Heaney, 'Frontiers of Writing', in *The Redress of Poetry: Oxford Lectures* (London: Faber and Faber, 1995), 195–6, 198.
[71] C.L. Dallat, 'A Single Flame', in Eve Patten (ed.), *Returning to Ourselves* (Belfast: Lagan Press, 1995), 124–7. Hewitt donated his body to Queen's University for research (*Irish Times*, 30 June 1987, 5).
[72] John Hewitt, 'A North Light' (1961), in *Ancestral Voices*, 34–5. This essay was later published as the more comprehensive memoir *A North Light: Twenty-Five Years in a Municipal Art Gallery*, ed. Frank Ferguson and Kathryn White (Dublin: Four Courts, 2013).
[73] Paddy Devlin, 'No Rootless Colonist', *Threshold*, No. 38, Hewitt edition (Winter 1986/7), 22.
[74] Hewitt, 'No Rootless Colonist', 148–9.
[75] Letter to John Boyd, 14 September 1970. JBC; Hewitt, 'No Rootless Colonist', 150.

The political consciousness of both John Hewitt and Sam Thompson was actually punctuated by the same foreign event, Italy's 1935 invasion of Abyssinia. Thompson personally witnessed the concurrent stream into the shipyards of Protestant gangs who persecuted Catholic workers, somehow aligning them 'with Mussolini's imperialist ambitions', at the same time as Hewitt campaigned for international sanctions against Italy because of its incursion into Abyssinia.[76] The internationalism of the NILP's more progressive practitioners led to the party gaining a reputation as 'a vector for civilization, the outside world', a quality expressed in Michael Longley's paean to his 'twin' Thompson, who opened 'a way over the bridge / For Jews and gypsies, all refugees / Persons displaced by our bigoted / Hometown'.[77]

Insightful is the kind of symbolic Irish figure Hewitt venerated. Cúchulainn was 'a very dirty fighter', but—as with Thomas Carnduff— the socialist-republican Peadar O'Donnell was a friend and inspiration. Hewitt did not distinguish between what he regarded as the insular conservatism of Ulster Unionism and the equivalent of Irish nationalism, referring to audiences at his talks in October 1971 as '100% RC [Roman Catholic]', from the south where 'I am afraid that the people...are as backward and tied to the ancient tradition'.[78] Sam Thompson also reflected this perspective, echoing the views of many in the north's Labour movement in a sequence from his television play and final work *Cemented with Love*. As a Unionist song '*merges*' into the nationalist 'Kevin Barry', the stage changes: '*The Union Jack on the table has gone and now there is a green cloth with a harp: the banners held by the crowds—almost as if they were the same banners reversed—now read* "Up the Republic", "Sinn Fein", "The Border Will Go".'[79] Both writers viewed nationalism and Unionism as a mirror image, thriving on each other's intransigence. NILP candidates were aware of specific instances of Unionist electoral fraud disenfranchising thousands of Labour voters during elections in the 1960s, while 'personation' was commonplace by Republican activists as late as 1992.[80]

---

[76] Paddy Devlin, 'Introduction' to *Over the Bridge* Programme (Belfast: Civic Arts Theatre, September 1985). PDP; Hewitt, 'No Rootless Colonist', 151.

[77] Interview with Bob Purdie, Belfast, 25 April 2012; Michael Longley, 'The Poker', in *A Hundred Doors* (London: Jonathan Cape, 2011), 31.

[78] Letter to John Boyd, 11 December 1971. JBC.

[79] Thompson, *Cemented with Love*, in *Over the Bridge*, 188.

[80] Interview with David Overend, Belfast, 28 April 2015. Overend stood in North Belfast in the March 1966 Westminster election, gaining 19,927 votes. See also *Irish News*, 13 December 2010, 2. For Republican 'personation' see the testimony of Brendan Hughes in Ed Moloney (ed.), *Voices from the Grave: Two Men's War in Ireland* (London: Faber and Faber, 2010), 274.

POKING THE FIRE

Louis MacNeice believed that *Over the Bridge* could be understood in India because it too had experienced communal strife in 1947, but there was no getting away from the fact that Thompson was 'born and bred a Protestant'; the play 'was his "J'accuse" and what he is accusing is religious bigotry, primarily Protestant'.[81] Thompson defended his straight-talking pugilism by saying, 'I am a Linfield supporter and a good Ulsterman, but I do not see any sense in trying to censor what has actually happened', and his objections to establishment Unionism were logically rooted in the hardship of his early life. In the radio play *The Long Back Street* a voice at the back of the crowd shouts, in response to a Unionist whipping up a mob with talk of 'Popish plots' and the siege of Derry: 'You can't ate Derry's walls when you're hungry.'[82] His literary executor confirms how much *Over the Bridge* was 'definitively against the regime', but also that 'Sam did feel Protestant; he felt betrayed by that type of Protestantism'—a sentiment exploited by future productions:

> The problem with *Over the Bridge* was that when the Troubles came we were getting these applications and I saw this production which was frankly just anti-Protestant. It took two or three lines out and they turned it round into the 'terrible Prods'. This would be about 1968, it was near Dundalk. I couldn't believe it. Quite well-acted, but [it] was certainly not the message, and from then on I thought, well ok we're going to license these people to play it.[83]

In a scene from the unfinished play *The Masquerade*, Thompson would go as far as to equate Orange tradition with totalitarianism. Set during the Second World War, the character of Grant, a Dublin Protestant, is holed up with Nazi fantasist Frank in a London flat. Grant refers to King William of Orange being 'resurrected every year' and explains to Frank what gerrymandering is:

FRANK: (*Excited*) We must inform the Fuhrer about this. I bet that's one angle he hasn't thought of. Now, how about traditional tunes?

---

[81] Louis MacNeice, 'Out of the Deadpan', *The Observer*, 31 January 1960, 23.
[82] Quoted in *Belfast Telegraph*, 7 May 1959, 1; Sam Thompson, *The Long Back Street* (n.d.), 33. Sam Thompson Collection, Central Library, Belfast. One of Thompson's biographers argues that the voice of the heckler represents 'the voice of Sam Thompson', compounded by the way Thompson often voiced or acted this part himself (Mengal, *Sam Thompson*, 213).
[83] Interview with Brian Garrett, Belfast, 28 March 2011.

GRANT: Oh, I see what you mean. The hit parade number one for the past forty years has been 'The Sash My Father Wore'.

FRANK: Is it a marching-tune of the Government? The same as the Horst-Wessel-Lied is for National Socialism?

GRANT: Aye, for marching to the Field on the Twelfth of July.[84]

After the whirlwind generated by his first play, Thompson's second major play, *The Evangelist*, opened at the Grand Opera House in June 1963. Driven by a bravura central performance from Ray McAnally, the play also ran successfully in Dublin. Though some have argued that Thompson took the sting out of the piece by switching the protagonist from an Ulsterman to a Bible-belt preacher of the Deep South (James Ellis dissuaded him from any possible allusions to the Reverend Ian Paisley),[85] he nonetheless continued—in Michael Longley's tribute—to 'poke the fire'. Instinctively provocative (poking the fire keeps it burning), Thompson renamed CEMA the 'Council for the Encouragement of the Migration of Artists' and informed the *Irish Times* two years before the play's opening that it concerned 'a high-pressure revivialist preacher and the trail of havoc he leaves behind him among the simple people who attend his missions. It's a universal theme... and if they think that *Over the Bridge* was hard-hittin', wait'll they see this one!'[86] Contemporaries observed that Thompson 'liked shocking people', and the play's director fanned the flames further at a subsequent press conference when he spoke of how certain Christian leaders in Ulster were 'misguided', using 'the type of salesmanship associated with the advertising of patent medicines. They have an amazing influence with many decent people.'[87] *The Evangelist*'s protagonist outlines the importance of competing 'for those Souls to win them for the Lord', faith intertwined with finance:

> EARLS: (*He points and shouts at crowd*) Satan is standing beside you right now. He is holding your hands in your pockets. He doesn't want the Lord to get your money. He wants it all for himself. (*Shrieks*) Cast him out of your midst... this rally calls out for money. Give it to the Lord, friends. Give until it hurts. (*People begin to panic and reach forward to buy records. EARLS has them worked up. EARLS points into the distance*) There he goes. Look at him running—you've chased Satan back to hell.[88]

---

84 Sam Thompson, *The Masquerade* (n.d.), 40. Sam Thompson Collection, Central Library, Belfast.

85 Megahey, *Reality*, 166; Ellis, *Troubles*, 129.

86 Quoted in *Irish Times*, 2 August 1961, 8.

87 Interview with Brian Garrett, Belfast, 28 March 2011; Hilton Edwards, quoted in *Irish Times*, 18 June 1963, 11.

88 Thompson, *Evangelist*, in *Over the Bridge*, 115, 158. Original ellipsis.

When the Evangelical Protestant Society demonstrated outside the theatre on the eve of *The Evangelist*'s opening, Thompson declared that while the turmoil of the 1920s was seemingly over, 'there are people in our midst, professing to be Christians, who, it would seem, are never content unless our community is divided into religious combat units'.[89] It is hard to understate how much Thompson's presence shook up the political climate of the day. His pronouncements slamming CEMA board members for knowing 'as much about culture and the arts as businessmen from the Malone Road'[90] constituted a genuine class shock. Thompson castigated the BBC and ITV for failing to address Northern Irish themes in their broadcasting as well as Stormont for being generally uninterested in the arts, also drawing abuse from more sinister quarters, including an anonymous threat following derogatory comments about the Twelfth of July festivities: 'The next few months will be critical for you,' ended a letter which was passed over to the police. Thompson, however, was defiant: 'I am not so easily intimidated. I am afraid my enemies will have to do better than this. I am a "Queen's-man", reared in the Tough School of the Queen's Island. Obviously the letter was written by somebody who crawled out of a sewer.'[91]

Thompson's *Cemented with Love*, which some see as his most accomplished work,[92] was televised in 1965. In the theatrical manuscript which became the broadcast piece, he continued to depict the facile, violent reductionism of Northern Irish politics. Questioned during an election if he is an atheist the character of O'Brien objects 'My religious associations are my own business,' to which he is assured 'Not around here. You're either a Republican or a Loyalist.' Later claims to be 'a progressive' earn him accusations of being 'worse than a Popehead...a United Irishman'.[93] Right until the end, political controversy tailed Thompson's creative output. The BBC postponed the showing of *Cemented with Love* before the 1964 Westminster election, apparently under the impression that its theme of 'personation' was too sensitive an issue for a provincial audience (despite the fact that such practices were a long-established pattern of Northern Irish elections, with many voters joking of their prerogative to 'Vote early, vote often').[94] Writing in the Unionist *Belfast News Letter* Ralph Bossence argued, 'If events in the campaign were accurately foreshadowed by

[89] Quoted in *Belfast Telegraph*, 7 June 1963, 2.
[90] Quoted in *Belfast Telegraph*, 24 April 1962, 7.
[91] *Irish News*, 8 December 1961, 2; quoted in *Belfast News Letter*, 25 October 1962, 7.
[92] Mengal, *Sam Thompson*, 447.
[93] Sam Thompson, *The Border Line: A Play* (n.d.), 51. Sam Thompson Collection, Central Library, Belfast. Original ellipsis.
[94] *Irish Times*, 25 November 1964, 12.

Mr Thompson that is a reason for putting his play on—not taking it off,' and Thompson himself was 'convinced there is always political pressure brought to bear on plays here. There is censorship within our own BBC by people who think they are carting around the conscience of the Ulster people as to what they should and should not see.'[95] Days later Thompson died of a heart attack following an Executive Committee meeting in the Waring Street offices of the Northern Ireland Labour Party in Belfast.[96] 'What does that say?', pondered a crestfallen Sam Hanna Bell in his diary. Stewart Parker thought that it represented the loss of 'a sane and compassionate leader for the Protestant working class. There is no knowing how Sam Thompson would have fared in this perhaps impossible position, but he remains the nearest thing to such a man that we have yet seen.'[97] After the play was finally televised, from Coventry Hewitt wrote to a friend: 'We enjoyed *Cemented With Love*. Was there a row? I didn't take it as a comedy but as social idealism. The only man so far to mention it here, remarked: "It was like what you have said. Funny that politics never entered it—just religion."'[98]

CLASS

Sam Thompson, so the story goes, would explain to new apprentices who entered the workplace that membership of his Painters' Union was compulsory, along with a fee of a shilling. In return he handed new members a copy of Robert Tressell's *The Ragged-Trousered Philanthropists* (1914), the famous novel about painters and decorators exploited under the capitalist system.[99] As an autodidact who joined the Left Book Club (like Hewitt) and built up his library 'to *learn*', Thompson was particularly troublesome because he dissented from the community that Unionism claimed to monopolize. His trade union background and membership of

[95] *Belfast News Letter*, 14 December 1964, 4; quoted in *Belfast Telegraph*, 10 February 1965, 4.
[96] Interview with David Overend, Belfast, 28 April 2015. Overend remembers Vivian Simpson, Paddy Devlin, and himself all present. See also *Belfast Telegraph*, 15 February 1965, 1. Thompson had already suffered two heart attacks and repeated health scares.
[97] Quoted in Fergus Hanna Bell (ed.), *A Salute from the Banderol: The Selected Writings of Sam Hanna Bell* (Belfast: Blackstaff Press, 2009), 180; Stewart Parker, 'Introduction to Sam Thompson's *Over the Bridge*', in *Dramatis Personae and Other Writings*, ed. Gerald Dawe, Maria Johnston, and Clare Wallace (Prague: Litteraria Pragensia, 2008), 62.
[98] Letter to John Boyd, 8 May 1965. JBC.
[99] Former managing director of Blackstaff Press Anne Tannahill recalls this story from her father, a painter and decorator at Harland and Wolff, stressing that she has no way of verifying the story and no reason to doubt it either (email correspondence with the author, 3 November 2016).

the National Council of Labour Colleges, which took him to both France and Russia before the Second World War, 'were anomalous for an East Belfast Protestant whose allegiance should have focused on the Unionist Party and the Orange Order'.[100] Dissenting from the tribe was a rare, potent prospect. The playwright (and founder member of the Alliance Party) Robin Glendinning recalled the ferocity of his Unionist aunt to Thompson during the 1964 election campaign: ' "That bloody man thinks he's Shakespeare", and then all the venom came out. There was a grave distrust for Thompson, not simply because he was standing for the Labour Party but because he dared to write about contemporary Belfast, about sectarianism, about the darker side of Ulster life.'[101] This was unquestionably linked to social class.

Thompson's unperformed teleplay *The Tea Breakers* sketches the class gradations of Ulster Protestantism on the cusp of the 1960s. The aspirational middle classes are represented by estimator Arthur Price and his wife Charlotte, who openly despise the house painters ('layabouts') sent to decorate their property. Charlotte later proclaims, 'It's not the customer who's always right now, it's the worker. Before we know where we are, they'll be hoisting the red flag on our house.' The painters are well aware of the Prices' attitudes:

STEVENSON: I'm sick of this estate, anyway. There's nothing in it for anybody. These people are living from hand to mouth.

CLEGGHORN: (*Very dramatic*) But it's the airs they put on that takes me to the fair, and them up to their eyes in Hire Purchase debt, with their Venetian Blinds, three seater settees, twenty one inch television sets, fitted carpets, chiming bells, and if you fainted outside their front door, they couldn't afford to make you a cup of tea to bring you round again.[102]

The estate is a microcosm for Ulster as a whole, and though the province experienced comparatively little industrial dispute in these years, the row is resolved only following concessions from the Prices. The implication is that the 'tittle tattle' and 'Idle gossip' of Ulster's middle classes—in the words of the boss of the firm Foster—signals future trouble on the estate, and when the crisis arrives it will occur within Protestantism.

'Relations were improving. The annual processions / began to look rather like folk festivals', lines from John Hewitt's 1969 poem 'The coasters',

---

[100] Richardson, 'Sam & Me', 25 (Richardson's italics); Philip Johnston, *The Lost Tribe in the Mirror: Four Playwrights of Northern Ireland* (Belfast: Lagan Press, 2009), 32.

[101] Quoted in Marilyn Hyndman (ed.), *Further Afield: Journeys from a Protestant Past* (Belfast: Beyond the Pale, 1996), 234.

[102] Sam Thompson, *The Tea Breakers: A Play for Television* (n.d.), 4–5, 8, 39, 46. Sam Thompson Collection, Central Library, Belfast.

echoed eerily the thoughts of Reverend Principal J. E. Davey in a BBC
broadcast review of Thompson's *Over the Bridge*. Davey praised the play
but qualified, 'it seems a pity to anticipate such failure where things are, in
fact, improving steadily on both sides'.[103] Despite the privilege of his own
background, Hewitt followed Thompson's focus on class rather than constitution, emerging most strikingly in the way he referred to the Ulster
Workers' Council strike of May 1974. The NILP opposed the UWC
stoppage which toppled the Sunningdale Executive, but speaking as part
of an extraordinary symposium organized by Eavan Boland featuring writers
Francis Stuart and Thomas Kinsella, and members of the Provisional IRA
and UDA, Hewitt remarked: 'I would say that the mood of Belfast changed
during the strike... by degrees, we began to understand the reasoning
behind it. And I want to say that the strike was magnificently run.'[104]

With this in mind, 'The coasters', an address to the Protestant middle
class, reflects a crucial class dimension:

> You coasted along
> to larger houses, gadgets, more machines,
> to golf and weekend bungalows,
> caravans when the children were small,
> the Mediterranean, later, with the wife.

The poem directly concerns the period of O'Neillism (1963–9) and is
quoted as such at the outset of studies of the civil rights movement.[105]
Nevertheless it takes on added resonance as an expression of Hewitt's class-
conscious take on the UWC strike, which can now be seen as a continuum.
The target remains the very same band who overlooked him to be Director
of Ulster's Museum and Art Gallery in 1953, appointing instead an English
candidate with no university degree or publishing experience. A letter from
the Irish director and Lyric Theatre founder Mary O'Malley supporting
Hewitt was brandished by Unionist councillors around Belfast City Hall
'as an indication of "the type of person that was backing Mr Hewitt"'.
O'Malley—a member of the Irish Labour Party—was accused of being a
'member of the "Tomelty gang"', a black mark referring to the playwright
Joe Tomelty ('a Catholic, like myself').[106] A Hewitt biographer has reasonably pointed out the tactlessness of O'Malley's original letter to the

---

[103] Quoted in *Belfast Telegraph*, 7 April 1960, 2.
[104] Quoted in *Irish Times*, 4 July 1974, 12.
[105] Bob Purdie, *Politics in the Streets: The Origins of the Civil Rights Movement in Northern Ireland* (Belfast: Blackstaff Press, 1990), 9.
[106] Mary O'Malley, *Never Shake Hands With the Devil* (Dublin: Elo, 1990), 64–5. Not to be confused with the NILP, the Irish Labour Party had organized in Belfast from 1949 and gained several municipal seats in wards with predominantly Catholic constituents.

Council indicating her support,[107] but the upshot failure brought him 'nearer to suicide than I shall ever be again', a prospect he seriously contemplated on the boat between England and Ireland, stopping to look down at the sea: 'In the weeks which followed my return my wife and I felt utterly alone.'[108] Four years later they moved to Coventry where he took up the post of art director at the Herbert Art Gallery.

While friends concurred that Hewitt 'was scuppered by the kind of insidious sectarianism against which he had always made a stand', John Montague thought that the experience 'was, in a way, a homecoming for the more English part of his psyche, and the rehabilitation of the city after the wartime bombings, with the new, very modern cathedral soaring from the ruins, appealed to his socialist side'.[109] The Hewitts attended ward Labour Party meetings on Ireland and protested against the Vietnam War and the Coventry Corporation when it brought police in from outside the city to move travellers from Balsall Common.[110] 'An Irishman in Coventry' (1958) finds Hewitt contemplating the city's 'famous steeples and its web of girders, / as image of the state hope argued for', concomitant with a new empathy for his old Catholic neighbours ('a people endlessly betrayed by our own weakness'). The change of scenery also inspired the highly political poetry constituting the *An Ulster Reckoning* (1971) collection, which Hewitt conceded he could only have written in exile. Pointing out that Hewitt's exaltation of the city 'must be one of the few poems that lauds the comprehensive school', a former NILP member links the poetry with Labour: 'To me the elements in "An Irishman in Coventry" reflect the optimism of the Left still in the fifties, "the clockwork horse, the comprehensive school", talking about how we're moving forward and can see a better society coming. That to me is more than either Unionist or Nationalist, and that's Labour politics.'[111]

Yet the Ulster Museum trauma remained with Hewitt. Mary O'Malley received his letters but sensed 'deep down he missed the North', while Heaney pointed out that he named a poem '1957–1972' as if the period in Coventry was 'a lost life'.[112] In 'The Search' (1967), Hewitt acknowledges that he ultimately 'will regret the voyage, / wakening in the dark night to

[107] McCormack, *Northman*, 135.
[108] John Hewitt, 'From Chairmen and Committee Men, Good Lord Deliver Us' (1968), in *Ancestral Voices*, 49, 51–2, 54–5.
[109] Craig, 'Visiting John Hewitt'; Montague, *Pear*, 141.
[110] Letter to John Boyd, 8 May 1965. JBC; Burnside, 'Preparing Lonely Defences', III.
[111] See Barre Fitzpatrick (ed.), 'Beyond the Planter and the Gael: An Interview with John Hewitt and John Montague', *The Crane Bag: The Northern Issue*, Vol. 4, No. 2 (1980–1), 87; interview with Tony Kennedy, Belfast, 14 June 2012.
[112] O'Malley, *Never Shake Hands*, 121; O'Driscoll, *Stepping Stones*, 332.

recall that other place'. Shortly after the election of Gerry Fitt to Westminster in the spring of 1966, Hewitt wrote to John Boyd on developments and the strong showing of the NILP's East Belfast candidate:
'Paisley is making the wee North notorious, only partially redeemed by
the West Belfast result. We were pleased to see that Martin McBirney
polled so well.'[113] Paisley had lit the touch-paper, meaning that by the
time of Hewitt's return to the north in 1972, the deadliest year of the
Troubles, 'the fever' was 'high and raging':

> who would have guessed it, coasting along? . . .
> The cloud of infection hangs over the city,
> a quick change of wind and it
> might spill over the leafy suburbs.
> You coasted too long.

Hewitt sympathized with the symbolic power of the 1974 UWC strike: an
assault on complacent middle-class Unionism as much as nationalists in
government, the cloud of infection finally spilled over the suburbs as a
generation of Unionist politicians quietly cowered. A former secretary of
the NILP recalled 'a total panic in the operations of Unionism that for the
first time ever the initiative had been wrested from them and had been
taken by people they were actually scared of. The genie had been let out of
the box, and they had to put it back in the box pretty quickly.'[114]

The director of the John Hewitt Society articulates how with pay
equivalent to the English civil service scale, combined with a lower cost
of living—and following the cessation of city-centre bombings in the mid-
1970s—the more affluent citizens of Northern Ireland could ignore the
Troubles and live 'quite happily'.[115] The same kind of class attitudes
prevailed as in England, except that in availing of grammar schools and
not paying public school fees for the likes of Charterhouse and Eton, the
coasters were even wealthier than their English counterparts. 'Minister'
(1969), Hewitt's poetic portrait of Brian Faulkner, who led the short-lived
Sunningdale Executive, is also worth considering in this light. The poem
cracks the class whip once again:

> Not one of your tall captains bred to rule,
> that right confirmed by school and army list,
> he went to school, but not the proper school . . .
> his father's money grew from making shirts.

---

[113] Letter to John Boyd, 21 April 1966. JBC. McBirney's 45.3 per cent of the vote in
East Belfast—to his Unionist opponent's 54.7 per cent—was the NILP's best ever Westminster result.
[114] Interview with Douglas McIldoon, Belfast, 27 January 2012. See Chapter 4.
[115] Interview with Tony Kennedy, Belfast, 14 June 2012.

Faulkner was mercantile class as opposed to landed gentry and he had missed war duty in a reserved occupation, grating with traditionalists in his own party.[116] Building his reputation as a dynamic Minister of Commerce generating investment in the 1960s, he lost the leadership contest of the Unionist Party in 1963 to O'Neill and again six years later to James Chichester-Clark: 'the door he planned to enter, twice / . . . slammed by the establishment'.

The award of the Freedom of the City of Belfast to Hewitt on 1 March 1983 took on political resonance when, in a manner uncharacteristic of the Council to the present day, members from across the parties combined to force the honour past a Unionist bloc that Hewitt had opposed his whole life. This took the form not just of the barriers he faced in Basil Brooke's Northern Ireland but in an inveterate kind of philistinism, the kind of which the dramatists of the previous chapter reckoned with too. 'I want us to remember our artists a little more and our industrialists a little less,' St John Ervine once wrote to a friend.[117] Hewitt always saw his work in museums as 'an integral part of democratic civilization', and he was exasperated by a story of Craigavon Council being offered a bust of the Lurgan-born writer and theosophist Æ (George Russell), only to be asked by a Democratic Unionist Party councillor: 'Was this man a British subject?' An incensed Hewitt raged: 'He was the greatest man who ever came out of Lurgan, it's absurd!'[118] Hewitt was aware his poetry was 'not speaking to my people . . . it is an inescapable thing. But linked with it is the important fact of the total lack of literacy interest among unionists of the north, the lack of any fixed literacy tradition', and he was fond of quoting Æ's rhetorical maxim: 'Name, if you can, a single Unionist writer of genius?'[119] When driving for Hewitt's Freedom of Belfast, trade unionist and councillor Paddy Devlin remembered how, following the Ulster Museum episode, with Labour colleagues 'we were bitterly disappointed that such an able man should be lost to Belfast by the Unionists in the City Hall', becoming 'resolved if the occasion arose, to bring John Hewitt back to haunt them'. By the early 1980s the Unionist members had indeed forgotten, and as Devlin's own political life as an independent socialist was drawing to an end, 'It was a great consolation to me that

---

[116] Interview with Maurice Hayes, Belfast, 26 November 2012; Paddy Devlin, *Straight Left: An Autobiography* (Belfast: Blackstaff Press, 1993), 151. It must be pointed out that because of his attacks on O'Neill, Faulkner was at this stage regarded as a hardliner.

[117] Letter to John Boyd, 30 October 1948. JBC.

[118] Burnside, 'Preparing Lonely Defences', III; quoted in *Irish Times*, 18 March 1986, 13.

[119] Quoted in Fitzpatrick (ed.), 'Planter and Gael', *Crane Bag*, 91; John Hewitt, 'The Bitter Gourd: Some Problems of the Ulster Writer' (1945), in *Ancestral Voices*, 114.

Belfast City Council in my time had recognized the achievements of our great poet.'[120]

Hewitt dismissed the 'Ulster Independence' ideas floating around Loyalist paramilitary groups—producing documents like the UDA's *Beyond the Religious Divide* (1979)—as it omitted a step in his 'hierarchy', the connection with Britain, thereby 'falsifying' the situation.[121] But while Hewitt's attachments should not be over-romanticized, he could be close to the pulse of the Protestant working class. In February 1949 Hewitt struck up an intriguing correspondence with a trade unionist from Belfast's Sandy Row, Robert McElborough, who spent his life working in the gas industry and on the tramways (McElborough entrusted him with his diaries which were deposited in the Public Records Office in 1956).[122] Hewitt aligned this with a Marxist view of the community: 'economically we have belonged to the British industrial complex. And then out of the economic involvement grew up the conception of loyalty. They were working for the British market so they were British. It wasn't the Irish market so they weren't Irish.'[123] The escalating violence of the Provisional IRA from 1970 further roused his empathy for its (frequently Protestant) victims. In a letter outlining his public appearances speaking to 'Catholic laymen' in Birmingham in October 1971 and before at an anti-Internment function, Hewitt 'found that the audience were of the old republican line, blank to my insistence that the Planters had their rights too, and wouldn't be swept into the tide. Where's "the terrible beauty" now? A seven month old child carried dead in a blanket in the Shankill Road.'[124] His hierarchy, meanwhile, is commemorated to the present day by a mural, courtesy of the community activist George Newell, at the bottom of East Belfast's Albertbridge Road.

FINAL YEARS: POSTSCRIPT 2010

Playwright John Boyd—who shared his socialist sympathies—noted Hewitt's view of the Soviet Union as a beacon of progress dimmed by the disclosure of Stalinism's atrocities, though they still discussed Gramsci,

---

[120] Paddy Devlin, 'John Hewitt—The Ulster Poet' (n.d.). PDP.

[121] Paul Arthur, 'John Hewitt's Hierarchy of Values', in Dawe and Foster (eds), *Poet's Place*, 283–4.

[122] Montague, *Pear*, 148; Robert McElborough, *Loyalism and Labour in Belfast: The Autobiography of Robert McElborough, 1884–1952* (Cork: Cork University Press, 2002), 2, 69.

[123] Quoted in Levine, 'Tree of Identities', 16.

[124] Letter to John Boyd, 11 December 1971. JBC. The victim, Colin Nicholl, was in fact seventeen months old.

and Boyd noticed how personally content Hewitt was in the last part of his life. The Hewitts rejoined the NILP, though Roberta was 'actually the more active, committed Labour person' at meetings of the South Belfast Windsor-Cromac branch,[125] passionately discoursing as Hewitt fiddled with his pipe. Despite the loss of his influential companion to cancer in 1975, grief gave way to 'his poetry, his trusteeship of the Lyric Theatre and his enjoyment of friendship'.[126] Neither was he finished politically. In 1979 Hewitt refused an OBE on account of it being offered by the Conservative government of Margaret Thatcher, and he cast his vote in the June 1984 European election—an acquaintance claimed—for the Workers' Party's Seamus Lynch because 'he could not bring himself to vote for either a Unionist or what he called the Nationalist SDLP'.[127] Right to the end Hewitt could be seen on demonstrations against Apartheid and the US invasion of Grenada in October 1983, as well as attending punk concerts in the Botanic area of Belfast.[128]

Other writers believe that, having left (or escaped), John Hewitt should never have gone back to Northern Ireland.[129] At the time, however, Hewitt's return at the height of the Troubles was viewed by fellow poets as 'an enormous endorsement' and 'a very important moment for the community',[130] signalling that artists could stay and survive the larger fire. This was possibly more important than his actual poetry and led to the genuine affection he continues to inspire; less 'The daddy of us all', and more 'blunt, stubborn and angular' archetype of a new Protestant identity, present and loyal as his city burned, wandering around writing poems about vicious sectarian killings in the newsagents where he bought his tobacco.[131]

A year prior to his death he was still responding creatively to political developments such as the 1985 Anglo-Irish Agreement, an atmosphere 'thick with bitter cries / As baffled thousands dream they are betrayed', the regionalist philosophy continuing to penetrate his verse:

---

[125] Interview with Neil Faris, Belfast, 29 July 2014. Faris later became General Secretary of the NILP.

[126] Boyd, *Middle*, 199.

[127] Geraldine Watts, 'Letter: John Hewitt's Politics', *Irish Times*, 31 July 1993, 11.

[128] Burnside, 'Preparing Lonely Defences', III; interview with Christina Reid, Belfast, 24 June 2013.

[129] Interview with Maurice Leitch, London, 31 July 2015.

[130] Michael Longley, quoted in *Honest Ulsterman*, No. 78 (Summer 1985), 22.

[131] James Simmons, 'Flight of the Earls Now Leaving', *Irish Times*, 4 June 1974, 10; interview with Tom Paulin, Oxford, 7 July 2015. See Hewitt's poem 'At the newsagents' (1981).

> Slave to and victim of this mirror hate,
> surely there must be somewhere we could reach
> a solid track across our quagmire state,
> and on a neutral sod renew the old debate
> which all may join without intemperate speech.

Hewitt frames an island 'split by belief, by blatant pageantry / ... alone among the nations and afraid', a vision of international isolation previously announced with some foresight by Thompson in 1962: 'we are in a danger of ending up as a tribal community of processions and primitive celebrations ceremonies—International freaks with half of the community on the road to starvation and the other half emigrating.'[132]

Many held that *Over the Bridge* would remain relevant as long as sectarianism scars Northern Irish society, and so it proved when the play was revived by Martin Lynch in March 2010 at the Waterfront Hall in Belfast. The production's historical adviser observed 'the impact it had on people who had not lived through that period of the early Troubles in Northern Ireland. I noticed a lot of young people coming out deeply affected by it, so its life was still there.'[133] Ostensibly about a Protestant mob intimidating a lone Catholic man in the shipyard, Lynch believes 'You can take all that away. It's about a mob against one man and that man's spirit to face up to the mob.' Admitting that his version was informed by seeing how such mobs behaved at the end of the 1960s, Lynch compared the gang menace of *Over the Bridge* with 'Turf Lodge in 1969—they behaved exactly the same when they went to attack the Protestants who arrived into the area, being aided and abetted and encouraged by each other to do even worse than what they would probably do individually'.[134] The Lord Carson Memorial Flute Band provided the crowd in the original production (the Irish Army took these roles in Dublin),[135] but the invidious Mob Leader inevitably takes on paramilitarist overtones in Lynch's adaptation:

LEADER: It's lucky for you I'm standing between you and that crowd out there. They wanted to tear you apart as soon as they laid eyes on you, but I stopped them and advised them to wait until ten-past-one to see what you intended to do.[136]

---

[132] Quoted in Purdie, *Politics in the Streets*, 67.
[133] Interview with Brian Garrett, Belfast, 28 March 2011.
[134] Interview with Martin Lynch, Belfast, 20 March 2014.
[135] Ellis, *Troubles*, 82.
[136] Thompson, *Over the Bridge*, 78; Lynch, *Over the Bridge* adaptation (Unpublished, 27 February 2010, Clean Act 2—Scenes 1–5), 14–15.

As with St John Ervine's *Mixed Marriage*, part of *Over the Bridge*'s power is its anticipation of conflict, and for natural reasons it will always be seen in light of the Troubles it preceded. Lynch thus had the mob singing 'The Billy Boys',[137] and while this is still the kind of sectarian chant echoing down the capital's streets, the long-standing difficulty remains the identification of sectarianism with one community. At the unveiling of a plaque to Thompson in Belfast's John Hewitt bar in April 2014, one local historian talked of the play as an attack on sectarianism 'in all its flag waving forms' (a contemporary reference to Loyalists involved in the Flag Protests of 2012 onwards),[138] ironically emblematic of the kind of partisan spite Sam Thompson and Jimmy Ellis—both proud East Belfast men—were taking a stand against. As old NILP colleagues made clear at the same event, *Over the Bridge* is 'against all intolerance', with Davy Mitchell's ultimate message: 'There's nothing civilised about a mob . . . be it Protestant or Catholic.'[139] Lynch studied the audience reaction to his adaptation closely and was delighted by how well it was received by working-class Protestant audiences, including a group of women from an East Belfast community group based on Templemore Avenue, off the Newtownards Road. Questioning them after the show about whom they empathized with, they replied, 'Oh, we were with Davy and the Catholic man. They [the mob] were bastards,' all of which conveyed to Lynch that 'People will always look on what they think is the side of justice.'[140] He also played up the IRA 'Border campaign' elements of the 1950s in his adaptation (the original script refers to the violence of the 1930s), and it was pointed out by veterans of the same ill-fated campaign (1956–62) during a discussion following one of the 2010 performances that *Over the Bridge* had 'caused more discomfiture' to the Unionists in 1960 'than anything they were doing blowing up lighthouses or telephone poles'.[141]

The Labour dignitaries who attended his funeral were long gone but Thompson's impact on Northern Irish politics and society was acknowledged by the presence of frontline Sinn Féin politicians—including Gerry Adams, Danny Morrison, and then-Lord Mayor of Belfast Tom Hartley—at the July 2010 recommemoration of his grave. The Sinn Féin-linked *Féile*

---

[137] 'The Billy Boys', featuring the lyrics 'We're up to our necks in Fenian blood / Surrender or you'll die', originated in Glasgow and is associated with fans of Rangers football club.

[138] *Irish News*, 3 April 2014, 11. John Gray's talk was printed in the Communist Party of Ireland's Belfast magazine. See 'Sam Thompson', *Unity*, Vol. 26, No. 15 (19 April 2014), 6–7.

[139] Thompson, *Over the Bridge*, 63–4.

[140] Interview with Martin Lynch, Belfast, 20 March 2014.

[141] Interview with Harry Donaghy, Belfast, 24 February 2014.

an Phobhail festival had generously paid for the event, but it must be remembered that Thompson's disdain for the Unionist establishment rivaled his rejection of sectarian nationalism on the Republican side.[142] Thompson liked to tell a story of his father, a part-time lamplighter in Belfast, working in both Catholic and Protestant parts of the city during the 1930s, being followed around by the armed vigilantes from both communities. Each set of gunmen put the lights he was illuminating out because 'they preferred it that way. They preferred the darkness.'[143] Hewitt, too, maintained a critical Protestant perspective on the conservative tenets of Irish nationhood. Sinn Féin continues to object to the extension of the 1967 Abortion Act to Northern Ireland, and it resonates to hear Hewitt commenting, through intermittent check-ins to the *Irish Times* column of Sam McAughtry, on the September 1983 referendum to prohibit abortion from ever being introduced into Ireland's constitution: 'As far as I am concerned the life of the mother is sacred. It is ridiculous to pretend to indignation on behalf of the unborn. This is the sort of thing that makes unity of the island recede further and further away.'[144]

CONCLUSION

Through their political and creative lives, John Hewitt and Sam Thompson promoted a progressive, socialist version of Protestantism quite distinct from Ulster Unionism. This is something missed by those keen to penetrate Hewitt's 'mythologies' and 'relevance as a superlative Protestant culture tsar',[145] for the point was that his alternative myth was one which enabled other visions to emerge. Gerry Dawe championed Hewitt for reasserting 'the possibility of actually having "roots" in a Belfast Protestant background that will not necessarily lead to the stranglehold of bigotry, or half-baked and ludicrously gentrified "Anglo" self-images'.[146] Hewitt was aware of his own potential for mythmaking at the same time

---

[142] Devlin, 'Voice of Many', 21–2. The NILP's leader Tom Boyd, Paddy Devlin, Sam Napier, and Martin McBirney were among those present at the original funeral (*Belfast News Letter*, 18 February 1965, 1).

[143] Speaking in *Sam Thompson: Voice of Many Men*, directed by Donald Taylor Black, aired 29 November 1985 (Channel 4).

[144] Quoted in *Irish Times*, 5 September 1983, 12.

[145] Sarah Ferris, *Poet John Hewitt, 1907–1987 and Criticism of Northern Irish Protestant Writing* (New York: Edwin Mellon Press, 2002), 184.

[146] Dawe, *Against Piety*, 89, 101–2. See also Glenn Patterson's remarks in Patrick Hicks, 'A Conversation with Glenn Patterson', *New Hibernia Review*, Vol. 12, No. 2 (Summer 2008), 108.

as being stringent in his assessment of the past,[147] claiming to be the first to apply the phrase 'crisis of identity' to Ulster Protestantism. His very use of 'Planter' instead of Protestant highlighted that the contemporary 'meaning of the latter is not reflected in the attitudes of those who assume the name'.[148]

Edna Longley was referring to Hewitt (and could also have been to Thompson) when she claimed that his intention was 'to widen the imaginative franchise of the Ulster Protestant society into which he was born', exemplifying 'the secular and socialist transformation of Protestantism, giving them a rarely heard Northern Irish accent'.[149] Thompson's voice was especially treasured because he represented 'the voice of all that is civilized and decent in Belfast working-class life, the embodiment of its impassioned common-sense and derisive good nature',[150] something reflected by the kind of audiences who went to the theatre to see *Over the Bridge* as middle-class audiences stayed away. When the play was first published, its launch took place in the building where Thompson died. At the same gathering, one of the NILP's last elected representatives, Vivian Simpson, spoke emotionally of Thompson's commitment to the party and of his wider contribution to Belfast.[151] He did not live long enough—as Parker mourned—to emerge as a leader for the Protestant working class, a void filled in part by the clamour of 'that noisy preacher' Paisley, glanced at with guarded admiration by Hewitt's coasters: 'Later you remarked on his vehemence . . . / But you said, admit it, you said in the club, / "You know, there's something in what he says."'

At the unveiling of a plaque for Thompson in (of all places) the John Hewitt bar in April 2014, Brian Garrett—a friend and literary executor of both Thompson and Stewart Parker—wisely warned the gathering not to 'beatify' Thompson, and neither should criticism of Hewitt be off limits. When Maurice Leitch (1933–) found out that Hewitt disliked his novels he felt 'very pleased because—I'm going to be brutal now—I found him a very boring old pipe-smoking fart. And bitter because he never got the job

---

[147] At an Irish Labour History Society conference in Belfast in 1981, Henry Patterson gave a talk about the Belfast Labour leader William Walker in which he referred to 'Walkerism'. 'Walker wasn't an "ism",' protested Hewitt: 'He was a man. He lived down our street. I used to see him going to work. He wore a high white collar.' *Fortnight*, No. 254 (September 1987), 31.

[148] Hewitt, 'No Rootless Colonist', 146; Robert Johnstone, 'John Hewitt: A Protestant Atheist', *Fortnight*, No. 157 (11–24 November 1977), 6.

[149] Edna Longley, 'The Planter's Rights', *The Times Literary Supplement*, No. 4203 (21 October 1983), 1162.

[150] Stewart Parker, 'The Tribe and Thompson', *Irish Times*, 18 June 1970, 12.

[151] *Irish Times*, 8 December 1970, 10.

in the museum that he wanted. A charmless man.'[152] Hewitt appeared to
relish unsettling people, heckling academics during talks, 'coming up and
saying "I have a bone to pick with you", that kind of thing'.[153] These
attitudes are flavoured by personal animus but are reflective of an occasionally self-defeating grouchiness and jealousy (Hewitt may also have
behaved this way because he found it amusing). In Thompson's case there
was undoubtedly something adolescent, as well as courageous, about his
anti-authority approach. 'There's no doubt the controversy went to Sam's
head. It didn't depress him; it exhilarated him, made him more excitable.
And in the end, possibly, it didn't do him an awful lot of good. Had he
been allowed to develop in a more rational and calmer way to write, he
might have been all the better for it,' observed the man who first encouraged him to write.[154]

Furthermore, Thompson was still discovering himself as a dramatist.
Louis MacNeice had pointed out in his original review that *Over the
Bridge* would benefit from trimming, and Martin Lynch duly obliged in
his 2010 adaptation. Lynch recalled a story the late James Ellis told him
about going to Thompson's home in Craigmore Street, East Belfast, with
pages of *Over the Bridge* strewn all over the floor: 'We could have just lifted
the fucking script, threw it up, let it come down, and performed what was
there—I think that's what we did in the end!' At the same time Thompson
was still apprenticing and 'means something to us because he had something to say and he had the balls to say it'.[155] The director of the Lyric
Theatre's 1990 production of the play agreed that 'what it has at its centre
is the visceral passion of truth', continuing to mesmerize audiences
through its 'unique sense of shared experience'.[156]

Going over the bridge, however, often symbolized crossing over to the
other side. Seán Lemass and Terence O'Neill famously met each other,
but only the Taoiseach, whom Thompson had met in Dublin, sent
condolences to the Thompson family on his death.[157] Connectedly, the
Over the Bridge controversy uncovered an inveterate cronyism but damaged only the sectarian part of the equation, not the condition itself. James
Ellis remembered that a few powerful individuals were emotionally and
financially supportive of Thompson during the affair, including the
Governor of Northern Ireland Lord Wakehurst, who attended *Over the
Bridge* with his wife and laid on a party for the production in the Empire's

---

[152] Interview with Maurice Leitch, London, 31 July 2015.
[153] Interview with Tom Paulin, Oxford, 7 July 2015.
[154] Sam Hanna Bell, speaking in *Voice of Many Men* (Channel 4).
[155] Interview with Martin Lynch, Belfast, 20 March 2014.
[156] Roland Jaquarello, *Memories of Development* (Dublin: Liffey Press, 2016), 168–9, 172.
[157] Megahey, *Reality*, 272; *Irish Times*, 9 April 1960, 11.

stalls bar afterwards.[158] The episode exposed a more local web of networks and established toadying, often connected in one way or another with Queen's University ('the place to make connections in addition to receiving an education').[159] *Over the Bridge* ruptured the Protestantism of this world; the mediocracy itself remains intact, as in some way testified by the entourage of Sinn Féin Republicans present at the recommemoration of Thompson's grave, by then governing at Stormont and constituting their own kind of elite.

In many ways the successful battle against Unionist censorship represents the apogee of the Northern Ireland Labour Party, which had been made the official opposition at Stormont two years before *Over the Bridge* was staged. It is in this context that Thompson's involvement in public life can be grounded. Slating O'Neill for 'still carrying on the tradition of revitalising other countries with the best of our youth and highly skilled craftsmen', he pronounced, 'Any industrial development for Northern Ireland under a British Tory Government is impossible. Our hope lies in the return of a Labour government under the leadership of Harold Wilson and his go-ahead Cabinet.'[160] Hewitt's immediate influence is cloudier and something of an unfinished project. He had more time, of course, and while his example may be celebrated at the annual John Hewitt International Summer School, 'Who needs to be there?' queried C. L. Dallat. 'Who needs to re-examine their assumptions about identity? Certainly not just the artists and speakers who generate and contribute to advancing the discussion.' Instrumental are 'those with secure identities who are incapable of seeing how their cultural trappings and assumptions impact on neighbouring contested areas'.[161] In 2012, however, Sinn Féin's Minister for Culture, Arts and Leisure Carál Ní Chuilín opened the same event. Ní Chuilín quoted the poetry of Bobby Sands and not John Hewitt, but the engagement complements what one of the School's coordinators conceives of as the task 'to reinforce people that are actually prepared to reach out, keep their confidence up and keep them believing that they want to do something'.[162]

The NILP's refusal to acknowledge the sectarianism of the political culture accounted in large part for its eventual extinction, even if, as we

---

[158] Ellis, *Troubles*, 87–8.

[159] Marilynn Richtarik, 'Stewart Parker at Queen's University, Belfast', *The Irish Review*, No. 29 (Autumn 2002), 58.

[160] Quoted in *Belfast News Letter*, 24 March 1964, 9.

[161] C. L. Dallat, 'What Identity Crisis?', *Fortnight*, No. 442 (March 2006), 17.

[162] *Belfast Telegraph*, 24 July 2012, 2; interview with Tony Kennedy, Belfast, 14 June 2012. The DUP's Arlene Foster, who became First Minister of Northern Ireland in 2015, followed Ní Chuilín to speak at the 2013 event.

shall see, its mythology lingered on. By the end the party is the narrowing group at the close of Thompson's most celebrated play getting 'smaller and smaller', until one morning it is just the individual who journeys over the bridge. Some authors located Hewitt's most transcendent work in the confines of 'historical isolation and private loneliness',[163] and far from 'I found myself alone' representing a reversal of his hierarchy—Europe to Ulster and 'its relentless conclusion . . . the lonely, isolated self'[164]—the aphorism stands as a solo cry of defiance. It was noted at a time in the early 1980s when no party would back the campaign that Hewitt was one of the few public personalities who supported the European court case which would lead to the decriminalization of homosexuality in Northern Ireland.[165]

One of the artists Eric Hobsbawm was referring to who found them-selves on the losing side politically but managed to frame the culture was Luis Buñuel, who once expressed doubts 'about the benefits of money and culture'. Thompson agreed:

> Let us have artists on our cultural committees, not business tycoons who would rather have an OBE hanging on their chest than an oil painting painted by a struggling artist hanging on their drawing room wall. They could not run an Arts Council like a limited company. We must not condemn business people who are genuinely interested in the arts. But don't let's confine it to privilege or the middle classes.[166]

Hewitt too was keen to highlight 'the lop-sidedness of the treatment of Artists against the "old fogy" Military Generals and Unionist Party flunkies' at the special meeting convened by Belfast City Council for his Freedom of the City award.[167] This appreciation of the arts and creativity went back to his WEA classes and tutoring of workers, ultimately signal-ling dissent not just from Unionism but also from Irish nationalism. Thompson, too, extolled the virtues of the Republic in the press but in private reflected a more critical view of the Irish cultural establishment, lashing the Abbey's managing director Ernest Blythe as a 'bamstick'

[163] Eavan Boland, 'John Hewitt—An Appreciation', *Irish Times*, 30 June 1987, 8; Heaney, 'Frontiers', 197–8.

[164] Walsh, 'Too Much Alone', 357. 'I found myself alone' is a line from Hewitt's poem 'Because I paced my thought' (1944) and was also the title of an Arts Council-funded 1978 short film on him.

[165] Jeff Dudgeon, 'Advances Made but the Fight for Rights Not Over', *Belfast Telegraph*, 29 July 2011, 37.

[166] Luis Buñuel, *My Last Sigh* (Minneapolis: University of Minnesota Press, 2003; 1st edition 1983), 158, 170, 182; quoted in *Belfast Telegraph*, 16 November 1963, 6.

[167] Devlin, 'John Hewitt—The Ulster Poet'. PDP.

(a Scottish word roughly translating as 'idiot') who had myopically advised him to set all his dramas in one room.[168]

Following a commanding 44 per cent share of a public vote, a new bridge stretching over the Connswater River connecting the old shipyards to Victoria Park was named after Sam Thompson. At its opening in April 2014 Unionist politicians were present along with a Sinn Féin Mayor, though former First Minister Peter Robinson was naturally more interested in the commercial and health benefits of the bridge than in any symbolism of the deceased playwright. The nationalist SDLP councillor Claire Hanna commented that Thompson was a 'good example of the fact our history hasn't always been about conflict and strife'.[169] His most significant plays, as well as the circumstances in which *Over the Bridge* was brought into being, can only contradict the assessment of this estimable representative who had played a major role in the campaign to call the bridge after the playwright, ensuring that his name lives on while the names of those who obstructed the play and trounced Thompson at the ballot box are long forgotten.

---

[168] Vincent Dowling, *Astride the Moon: A Theatrical Life* (Dublin: Wolfhound Press, 2000), 232.

[169] Quoted in *Irish News*, 5 April 2014, 3.

4

Stewart Parker, the UWC Strike
of May 1974, and Prisons

It isn't true to say they forget nothing. It's far worse than that.
They misremember everything.

Henry Joy McCracken, in Stewart Parker, *Northern Star* (1984)

As a general overview of the political shifts which had taken place in
Ulster politics, Marc Mulholland has captured how Unionism 'had traditionally been led by a social elite distant from the rank and file. The
leaders had made up for this, however, by paying a populist attention to
the opinions, attitudes and prejudices of their loyalist constituency. By the
1960s, however, the middle-class establishment had accepted a liberal
consensus, which believed that battles over the border had been left in
the past.' Terence O'Neill was consonant with this consensus and won
the leadership of the Ulster Unionist Party in 1963 as the candidate best
equipped to steal 'the NILP's technocratic, economically modernizing
clothes'.[1] This attracted 'liberal' middle-class Unionists who had kept
outside O'Neill's party due to its traditionalist Protestant associations,
but working-class liberals, who supported O'Neill's reforms and many of
the civil rights demands, remained largely steadfast in the NILP. From the
beginning of O'Neill's tenure, therefore, the '"liberalism" of his Unionism
was identified with the protestant middle class'.[2] The same consensus
continued into the 1970s, O'Neill identifying 'remnants of the middle
class moderation he had fostered' in the 1973 Sunningdale Agreement.[3]
This is important because while the man himself had left the stage, the
experiment was looked on as his apex by those who sought to demolish it.

---

[1] Marc Mulholland, *Northern Ireland at the Crossroads: Ulster Unionism in the O'Neill
Years, 1960–9* (Basingstoke: Macmillan, 2000), 199.
[2] Frank Wright, 'Protestant Ideology and Politics in Ulster', *European Journal of Sociology*,
Vol. 14, No. 2 (December 1973), 272.
[3] Marc Mulholland, *Terence O'Neill* (Dublin: University College Dublin Press, 2013), 94.

For his part, O'Neill was acutely aware of the contempt in which he was held by the emergent Loyalist groups. Referring to the 'so-called' Ulster Volunteer Force, he condemned that by drawing on 'a revered name in Ulster they were in a position to get support from unthinking, militant Protestants'. Outlawing it in 1966 under the Special Powers Act—which he knew would be traumatic for those who regarded the legislation as principally reserved for use against the IRA—O'Neill commemorated the fiftieth anniversary of the Battle of the Somme in Paris with a crowd of Ulster veterans shortly after, clarifying how 'these old boys knew the difference between the real UVF and its new namesake'.[4] When the Ulster Protestant Volunteers (UPV) bombed a large electricity substation in Castlereagh three years later, the first of six such attacks on water pipelines and electricity stations, O'Neill sensed immediately that it was not the work of the IRA. Informing a senior Royal Ulster Constabulary officer of his suspicions that an 'extreme Protestant organization' was responsible, the detective refused to believe it and replied to the effect 'that loyalists would never destroy their own country'.[5]

O'Neill was also on the radar of a young writer from Sydenham, East Belfast, by the name of Stewart Parker (Fig. 4.1), who had not forgotten the Premier's clashes with Sam Thompson. Parker assessed that while O'Neill had been 'Bridge building', Thompson had been 'Going Over the Bridge', the latter expedition requiring 'an integrity which public life in Ireland has failed to cultivate'. Thompson 'coaxed, commanded, persuaded and implored his mulish fellow countrymen to make the journey. He wasn't a captain or a king but a shipyard painter and they listened to him. They knew the reality of his fictions.'[6] Parker admired Thompson's 'integrity, his anti-sectarianism, humanity, sense of humour', and above of all how he had transformed hardship into craft.[7] Born within sight of the cranes of Harland and Wolff, Parker was perfectly placed to survey the ongoing fragmentation of his own community. The East Belfast Protestant background blurred notions of one identity, lending him a kinship with Belfast's small Jewish community. Furthermore, being working class added another dimension, 'because you are alienated from the Unionist establishment. You feel conversant with all of these things, but not obliged

[4] Terence O'Neill, *The Autobiography of Terence O'Neill* (London: Rupert Hart-Davis, 1972), 81–2.
[5] O'Neill, *Autobiography*, 122–3.
[6] Stewart Parker, 'Introduction to Sam Thompson's *Over the Bridge*', in *Dramatis Personae and Other Writings*, ed. Gerald Dawe, Maria Johnston, and Clare Wallace (Prague: Litteraria Pragensia, 2008), 55.
[7] Interview with Lynne Parker, Dublin, 24 March 2012.

Fig. 4.1. Photo of Stewart Parker by Jack Chambers.
Note: Permission of George Parker

to any of them.' At least, Parker joked, the ensuing 'No man's land' gave him 'a hell of a lot to explore'.[8] He was a sickly youngster who had, in a curious echo of St John Ervine, a leg amputated at the age of nineteen due to a rare form of bone cancer.

Parker's grandfather was a signatory of the 1912 Ulster Covenant, like John Hewitt's uncle (who had also been an 'original' UVF man), and latter-day Loyalists also make their presence felt in his work.[9] And whereas some writers in this book ultimately develop an emotive frustration with their background's more stifling elements, Parker's niece Lynne—artistic director of the Rough Magic Theatre Company—believes that her uncle's:

> feelings were an awful lot more mixed, and he absolutely believed in the integrity of the *Everyman* who is the worker, which is why he was so passionate about Sam Thompson. At the same time he despised the elements within the community who were selfish and grandiose and destructive but recognized that they were part of the same deal. His socialist politics were

---

[8] Stewart Parker, 'State of Play', *The Canadian Journal of Irish Studies*, Vol. 7, No. 1 (June 1981), 9; quoted in Marilynn Richtarik, *Stewart Parker: A Life* (Oxford: Oxford University Press, 2012), 86.
[9] Stewart Parker, 'An Ulster Volunteer', in *Dramatis Personae*, 38. See the Trick Cyclist doubling as the paramilitary in *Spokesong*. Stewart Parker, *Plays 1* (London: Methuen, 2000), 50–1.

that as long as the political and social system remains iniquitous then the common man is going to be abused. I think Stewart really admired someone who lifted themselves out of the ignorance that the rest of that class was subject to. To some extent that's what he did as well because, not that our family was ignorant or poor, but we were a working-class family and he was the first of us ever to go to university. Now his parents made every effort for him to do that and it was the generation, but he was unusual and I think that created a bit of a barrier between him and the rest of the family. The life that he was now leading—the intellectual exposure he had—was so very different from theirs. So he understands people like Sam Thompson and Jemmy Hope, not from the vantage point of the university graduate but from someone who'd made the same journey.[10]

A member of Philip Hobsbaum's 'Belfast Group' of writers at Queen's University Belfast—Seamus Heaney always suspected he was the tutor's favourite—Parker was also involved, prior to the lift-off of his writing career, in the campaign against the Belfast Urban Motorway and the debilitating impact of urban planning.[11] John Hewitt had previously identified 'the crippling and retarding effect' of redevelopment on Ulster's artists, and it was widely thought that the transport policies of successive Unionist governments were favouring the motor car with disastrous implications for Belfast's urban working class, old-aged pensioners, one-parent families, the unemployed, and the mentally or physically disabled who were unable to drive.[12]

Prior to this, Parker lived in the United States and taught English at Hamilton College, a liberal arts institution in picturesque New York, but he continued applying for jobs in Ireland and the United Kingdom, asking a correspondent for a reference for the post of Curator to Yeats's recently restored Thoor Ballylee (because 'it might give me time and silence in which to write'). As with Hewitt he could not conceal how much he missed his home city, noting from what he had read about the Arts Festival and Grove Theatre 'that Belfast is really awakening at last'.[13] A few years later Parker had moved on to Cornell University and, in between wry observations of his new colleagues ('brainy but deadly—like academics the world over'), he again admitted to 'really miss[ing] Belfast this time', earmarking a return in June 1969: 'Maybe people will begin to

[10] Interview with Lynne Parker, Dublin, 24 March 2012.
[11] Dennis O'Driscoll, *Stepping Stones: Interviews with Seamus Heaney* (London: Faber and Faber, 2008), 74, 76; Marilynn Richtarik, 'Beyond the National Question', in *The Parker Project: Spokesong and Pentecost* (Belfast: Lyric Theatre, 2008), n.pag.
[12] Sam Hanna Bell, 'Introduction' to Sam Hanna Bell, Nesca A. Robb, and John Hewitt (eds), *The Arts in Ulster: A Symposium* (London: George H. Harrap, 1951), 14.
[13] Letter to John Boyd, 21 November 1965. JBC. The Grove Theatre was badly damaged in fire-bomb attacks during the Troubles, and the site is now a Lidl supermarket.

realise that there is more to the place than ugliness and bigotry—that you can love it and hate it with the same degree of intensity.'[14] Parker suitably returned home in the summer of 1969, as the Troubles sparked to intensity.

ATMOSPHERE

It is very much the case that Parker conceived of the theatre and chose it over other mediums as the forum where he could put into practice his wish to break down 'the deepest, most enduring and least tractable evil in our inheritance': sectarianism. Rather than merely talking about ending it, the theatre offered Parker the chance of 'actually embodying that unity, practicing that inclusiveness', achieved through 'an act of the imagination'.[15] He pondered the concept of theatre-making itself with great seriousness, was highly attuned to its Irish lineage—which came to full fruition with *Northern Star* (1984)—and was aware of the accompanying pressures which had driven Sam Thompson into an early grave. Like most writers in this book, Parker was also exasperated by the local Northern Irish scene. He had written poetry first, admitting to being more influenced by novelists like Joyce and Flann O'Brien, and when he began writing plays he encountered a brick wall of nil enthusiasm from the province's main venue. 'There's just one theatre here', Parker told a journalist, months after his first play *Spokesong* had opened in London, 'and I think it's unhealthy for any theatre to have a monopoly. I sent my first play to the Lyric in 1967 and if they read this they might care to return the manuscript. That put me off the theatre. This city should have another outlet.'[16]

Parker was so scarred by the experience that he brought his own directorial and acting team with him when the Lyric premiered *Northern Star* in November 1984,[17] and his breaks came in London and Dublin, the latter beginning an important association in this book with the Peacock Theatre. Parker's *Catchpenny Twist* (1977) and *Nightshade* (1980) debuted at the Peacock, which as the experimental stage of the Abbey would also host the early work of Graham Reid and the key plays of Gary Mitchell, making it 'consistently the conscience of the north in

---

[14] Letter to John Boyd, 29 January 1968. JBC.
[15] Stewart Parker, 'Signposts', *Theatre Ireland*, No. 11 (Autumn 1985), 28.
[16] Quoted in *The Guardian*, 6 December 1976, 8. See Parker's poem 'Fitts' in Padraic Fiacc's anthology *The Wearing of the Black* (Belfast: Blackstaff Press, 1974), 125–6.
[17] Interview with Patrick Sandford, London, 13 October 2015.

theatre terms'.[18] Named after its distinctive colour scheme, it had been conceived as a space where 'new playwrights could be tried out and older and less fashionable plays could be replayed', a practice intensified from 1978 under the Abbey's artistic director Joe Dowling and script editor Sean McCarthy to the extent that it offered something of a counterculture to the main stage.[19] Parker's development was further facilitated by Michael Heffernan, a young BBC drama producer from Kilkenny (via Cambridge University), who arrived in Belfast in the early 1970s and began cultivating a new crop of playwrights.[20] Heffernan helmed the first production of *Spokesong* (1975), establishing Parker's enduring obsession: 'the link between the past and the present. How do you cope with the present when the past is still unfinished? This is what this whole situation is about.' The famous opening stage direction of *Northern Star* is, of course, '*Ireland, the continuous past*'.[21]

In Parker's final play, *Pentecost* (1987), the politics of the UWC strike of May 1974, when the story is set, 'were illuminated through the microcosm of the four characters and the ghost of the fifth—whose house they inhabit and whose bitter sectarian world they had inherited'.[22] *Pentecost* also contained the framework for its author's 'constant preoccupation: how ordinary Belfast people, especially women, live their lives in a hellish situation'.[23] The play was composed during the agonized Unionist response to the 1985 Anglo-Irish Agreement, which evoked to Parker the atmosphere of 1974. Its main characters are a mixed couple who have inherited a house following the death of its sitting tenant Lily Matthews, a Protestant working-class lady who had lived there since her marriage after the First World War, while the structure was handed to Parker by the coincidental timescale: the actual dates of the UWC strike coincided with the feast of Pentecost. Lily, an embattled revenant of the Protestant working class, was burnt out of her house by a Catholic mob in 1921, and is a voice resounding somewhere in Parker himself, emerging from the brickwork to deliver the line which seems to define her community's

[18] Interview with David Grant, Belfast, 20 October 2015.

[19] Sean McCann, *The Story of the Abbey Theatre* (London: Four Square Books, 1967), 61; Fintan O'Toole, 'Today: Contemporary Irish Theatre—The Illusion of Tradition', in Tim Pat Coogan (ed.), *Ireland and the Arts* (London: Namara Press, 1983), 135.

[20] Telephone interview with Robert Cooper, 15 August 2014. Heffernan died prematurely in September 1985, aged thirty-eight, following heart problems.

[21] Quoted in *The Guardian*, 6 December 1976, 8; Stewart Parker, *Northern Star*, in *Three Plays for Ireland* (Birmingham: Oberon Books, 1989), 9.

[22] Nicholas Kent, 'A Wonderfully Brave Ending', *Fortnight*, Stewart Parker Supplement 278 (September 1989), XI.

[23] Keith Dewhurst, 'Obituary: Uniting Irishman', *The Guardian*, 5 November 1988, 39.

intransigence: 'I don't want you in my house.'[24] The playwright's niece
Lynne, who has regularly directed productions of her uncle's work,
discerns that Parker is in fact present in most of the characters in *Pentecost*
but perhaps most in Marian, who is 'a huge part of the Stewart Parker
voice and psyche; really legitimately, intellectually engaging with the
whole dilemma'.[25]

> MARIAN: So why should Lily Matthew's home and hearth be less special
> than Lord Castlereagh's or the Earl of Enniskillen's? A whole way of
> life, a whole culture, the only difference being, that this home speaks
> for a far greater community of experience in this country than some
> transplanted feeble-minded aristocrat's ever could.[26]

Seemingly thrown together, the characters of *Pentecost* can instead be seen
to represent the full panorama of the Northern Irish Protestant spectrum
of experience.

As Field Day Theatre Company toured *Pentecost* around Ireland in
1987, the play sought a return 'to the individual, to the "Christ in
ourselves", as the source of regeneration and change'. Religion was not
shunned but, as the ending makes clear, part of the solution. Parker's own
proximity to death—he died of cancer the year after the play first
appeared—heightened this conviction, with *Pentecost*'s 'final cure' resting
'not in political action or even social agitation but in a fundamental
engagement which alone can give change'.[27] A number of years later
Seamus Deane argued that the play sidestepped politics by promoting
the notion that an individual is unable to find harmony in a group,[28]
leading Lynne Parker (who thinks Deane is partly 'talking through his
arse') to explain:

> The person at the centre of *Pentecost* is in a state of crisis in her own head and
> what she does is enter the whole life of someone else as an investigation to
> help her come through the trauma that she's experienced. What Marian does
> is step right across the community divide to investigate someone whose
> whole history is totally different to her own. How that becomes abnegating
> yourself from political responsibility I do not know. The play is about each of
> those characters coming to terms with each other, within this tiny place—
> which is a metaphor for the whole bloody thing! The point that Stewart's

---

[24] Richtarik, *Parker*, 308–9; Parker, *Pentecost*, in *Three Plays*, 155.
[25] Interview with Lynne Parker, Dublin, 24 March 2012.
[26] Parker, *Pentecost*, in *Three Plays*, 178.
[27] Elmer Andrews, 'Stewart Parker', *Pentecost* Theatre Programme (Derry: Field Day, 1987), n.pag.
[28] Seamus Deane, 'Irish Theatre: A Secular Space?', *Irish University Review*, Vol. 28, No. 1 (Spring/Summer 1998), 167–72.

making is not that you shouldn't engage with society; the opposite. What he's saying is: 'You need to sort yourself out first. You need to be going out into society having worked out your own problems, and not be carrying your own prejudices around, because otherwise you're just going to spread more mayhem.'[29]

There is a strong echo of the latter syndrome in *Northern Star*, where it is intimated that Henry Joy McCracken's personal idiosyncrasies may have sown the seeds for his public downfall, and Field Day founder Stephen Rea concurs that while *Pentecost* may have turned away from some kind of collective reconciliation, this was countered by the language of reconciliation it did present.[30]

THE STRIKE

The Ulster Workers' Council strike of May 1974 toppled the Sunningdale Executive and curtailed the prospect of devolved power-sharing in Northern Ireland for a generation. Its success and defiance of the UK, Irish, and Northern Irish legislatures, as well as the British Army and the RUC, led the stoppage to be labelled 'without doubt the most successful political action carried out by any European working-class since the World War'.[31] Other commentators who witnessed the turmoil at first hand argued that 'A people has brought down a Government by showing its will on the streets: the first such event in Europe since December 1970 in Poland.'[32] Yet scholars and journalists have subsequently delivered a mainly paramilitarist and thus quite unrepresentative analysis of 1974. In this reading the strike succeeded because of the muscle of the Ulster Defence Association (UDA) alone. However, as former Republican members of the Irish Transport and General Workers Union (ITGWU) note, the largely Protestant 'bone' of the trade union movement was instrumental to the strike's success.[33] The claim of an Irish Labour historian that 'The Ulster Workers' Council had nothing to do with trade unions. It simply deepened divisions,'[34] simply defies fact. Harold Wilson's press secretary

[29] Interview with Lynne Parker, Dublin, 24 March 2012.
[30] Terence Brown, 'History's Nightmare: Stewart Parker's Northern Star', *Theatre Ireland*, No. 13 (1987), 41; interview with Stephen Rea, Dublin, 14 August 2014.
[31] Tom Nairn, *The Break-Up of Britain* (London: Verso, 1981), 242.
[32] Neal Ascherson, 'The Republic of Hawthornden Road', *The Observer*, 2 June 1974, 11.
[33] Interview with Seamus Lynch, Belfast, 19 January 2012.
[34] Francis Devine, *Organizing History: A Centenary of SIPTU, 1909–2009* (Dublin: Gill & Macmillan, 2009), 601. Two-thirds of the UWC Committee was drawn from the trade unions, the Loyalist paramilitaries providing the other third.

offered the more refined assessment that the action 'had demonstrated that the Government's writ did not run in Ulster if the Protestant workers decided they were not going to man the power stations'.[35] A large number of community and voluntary organizations were similarly active during May 1974 alongside the trade union element.[36]

The strike has therefore proved especially problematic for writers from the British and Irish Left to comprehend, contravening as it does long-standing notions of a reactionary, uncomplicated Protestant bloc. The weakness of analysis so far has been to simplify and homogenize what was in actuality a complex phenomenon, either with facile labels such as 'fascist' or through nonsensical interpretations of a 'lock-out'.[37] Ironically mirroring the then-Secretary of State Merlyn Rees's insistence that the stoppage was 'not normal industrial action',[38] the failure to realize that the opposition to Sunningdale was motored by trade unionists from an Ulster Protestant background reflects many of the contemporary problems which have arisen through the ongoing politicization of history. At the height of the stoppage it was announced that the British Trades Union Congress's Len Murray was to lead a 'back-to-work' march,[39] an event which attracted little more than a few hundred people (swiftly pelted with rotten fruit and vegetables by Loyalist activists).[40] The bright but eccentric British and Irish Communist Organization (B&ICO) cheekily said, via its 'Strike Bulletin', that Murray should 'either keep quiet about N. Ireland, or else find out something about it',[41] and its bitterness had a ring of truth. Geoffrey Bell wrongly took the episode as evidence that 'The great body of Protestant trade unionists rejected the official leadership and showed by their absence that the trade union movement was of no relevance in the existing political crisis.'[42] Such claims were made in spite of the trade unionists in the leadership of the strike, with there being

[35] Joe Haines, *The Politics of Power* (London: Jonathan Cape, 1977), 133.

[36] Louis Boyle, 'The Ulster Workers' Council Strike: May 1974', in John Darby and Arthur Williamson (eds), *Violence and the Social Services in Northern Ireland* (London: Heinemann, 1978), 159–60.

[37] Geoffrey Bell, *The Protestants of Ulster* (London: Pluto Press, 1976), 82; Ronaldo Munck, 'A Divided Working Class: Protestant and Catholic Workers in Northern Ireland', *Labour, Capital and Society*, Vol. 13, No. 1 (April 1980), 131–2. A lock-out can only be orchestrated by management.

[38] 'Press Notice' (17 May 1974), Statement by the Secretary of State for Northern Ireland, PRONI OE/1/16.

[39] *London Times*, 22 May 1974, 1.

[40] T. E. Utley, *Lessons of Ulster* (London: J. M. Dent, 1975), 119.

[41] Workers' Association (B&ICO), *Strike Bulletin No. 1* (Belfast: 19 May 1974), 4. These bulletins were written by Brendan Clifford. See his '1974 Strike 40 Years On', *Irish Political Review*, Vol. 30, No. 8 (August 2015), 17–24.

[42] Bell, *Protestants*, 81.

'a lot of people involved in it who were trade unionists, and who would remain trade unionists after it'.[43] Others attribute the conditioning of trade unionism, 'where they got to learn about working class issues— wages, employment rates, conditions in work', to the strikers being able to draw on their 'unionized training' to drive the stoppage.[44]

On 14 May the *Belfast News Letter* carried what was regarded as a fairly innocuous warning calling for new elections and a stoppage of industry if a motion condemning Sunningdale was defeated in the Assembly, which it comfortably was.[45] The date was selected well in advance by the leaders, who agreed that it could not mirror the Vanguard strikes of 1972 which lasted a matter of days and resulted simply in lost wages. The Loyalist Association of Workers (LAW) under Billy Hull and other members of the original Committee lacked a 'reason' to call a strike, leading Derry trade unionist and UDA adviser Glen Barr to identify a moment: 'They were just going to pick out a date to hold the strike and tell the people "We're against this", and I said if we're going to go down this road, if we're going to commit our organization to it, there's one day coming up in which will be our excuse.'[46] The strike planners anticipated that the Sunningdale Agreement would be supported on 14 May owing to 'the head count', handing the UDA and its leader Andy Tyrie (1940–) their chance. Shipyard shop steward Harry Murray[47] announced on television that the stoppage would commence the following day.

The first day of the strike—which Barr confessed to being shambolic— seemed to go unheeded, with most workers showing up to work. Absenteeism was estimated at less than 5 per cent of the total labour force and confined to the Lagan Valley engineering firms (embarrassingly for the UWC, most of the Harland and Wolff shipyard workforce ignored the call).[48] At the same time a key asset of the organization, a union organizer from East Belfast called Billy Kelly, was about to start shutting down

---

[43] Interview with Joe Law, Belfast, 26 June 2013. Law, who died in September 2016, was a trade unionist from the largely demolished Agnes Street area of the Lower Shankill.

[44] Interview with William 'Plum' Smith, Belfast, 14 March 2012.

[45] John Laird's motion condemning the Sunningdale Agreement was defeated by forty-four votes to twenty-eight.

[46] Interview with Glen Barr, Derry, 28 November 2012.

[47] Harry Murray (1921–98) was a key spokesman during the 1974 stoppage. Always uneasy about Loyalist paramilitary involvement, he resigned from the UWC two months after the strike following a speech in Oxford in which he announced that he would negotiate with the Provisional IRA if they laid down their weapons. The following year he stood for the Alliance Party in a Bangor by-election and reconstituted the UWC with original colleagues in 1981 to promote worker unity and job-creation (*The Guardian*, 28 February 1981, 24).

[48] Paddy Devlin, *Straight Left: An Autobiography* (Belfast: Blackstaff Press, 1993), 235.

Northern Ireland's electricity generators. Kelly was a leading power worker who managed to convince colleagues at Ballylumford—where 70 per cent of the province's electricity was generated—to reduce the power supplies to a third of capacity, maintaining key services but not industry. From the start of the stoppage Sunningdale Chief Executive Brian Faulkner pressed Secretary of State Merlyn Rees to protect the power workers from intimidation, which the latter refused 'point-blank' to do.[49] By early afternoon of the first day power started flickering as Kelly's men began shutting down the electricity grid. Derry was particularly badly hit with the power workers dwindling the city's supply to a quarter and cutting the province as a whole to 40 per cent. Though this appeared a 'doomsday' scenario to many on the ground, Charlie Brett—whose office was affected by sewage flooding—discerned that 'the power workers were in fact nursing their plant at minimum power with very great skill, in such a way that no irreparable damage was done'.[50] On the second day the paramilitaries got into gear as several thousand workers at Harland and Wolff were called to a meeting to be told that any vehicles left in the car park after lunchtime would be burned. There were similar scenes at Mackie's engineering plant as all afternoon workers headed home, factories and businesses closed, and buses and lorries were hijacked and used to block roads.[51] Transport ground to a halt in Belfast, while the second largest port of Larne was entirely sealed off and shipping halted.

On 20 May, Stewart Parker delivered his radio play *The Iceberg* to the BBC, cycling through the streets to arrive at a disquieting scene of the Corporation 'in darkness. All these producers sitting in rooms, with candles. Petrol stations being taken over by hooded men with guns and a kind of vision of Armageddon being promulgated over the radio, the feeling that the whole structure of society had broken down.'[52] Though Parker naturally found the climate sinister, *The Iceberg*—which is set during the building, sailing, and sinking of the *Titanic*—appears to reference May 1974 in its conversation between the ghosts of two workers who died during the construction of the ship. As Hugh and Danny discuss the possibility of meeting other apparitions aboard the maiden voyage, the former mentions men who had 'the sense to strike, at least'.[53] Parker was

[49] Brian Faulkner, *Memoirs of a Statesman* (London: Weidenfeld and Nicolson, 1978), 264.

[50] *The Guardian*, 15 May 1974, 1; C. E. B. Brett, *Long Shadows Cast Before: Nine Lives in Ulster, 1625–1977* (Edinburgh: Bartholomew, 1978), 88, 90.

[51] *The Guardian*, 17 May 1974, 1; Faulkner, *Memoirs*, 261.

[52] Quoted in Richtarik, *Parker*, 130–1.

[53] Stewart Parker, *The Iceberg* (Unpublished, 1974), 56. Stewart Parker Theatrical Archive—Linen Hall Library. It was broadcast on Radio 3 on 7 January 1975.

particularly taken with the politico-religious overtones of the UWC strike, embodied by the aforementioned Kelly, who was a Pentecostalist. Other leaders regarded Kelly as 'a clown' for his role in the attempted repeat of the strike three years later,[54] but Kelly insisted to journalist Robert Fisk that he could apply biblical verse to the action, specifically the Books of Daniel, Ezekiel, Thessalonians, and Revelation, all of which contain themes of the transience of earthly regimes and the fear of God.[55] While this should not be overstated, Kelly's pronouncements at the time highlight a distinct class sway. Appearing on television, he declared that the UWC was not affiliated to any party and 'only an organisation for the working class people'.[56]

Another of the strike's organizers was Jimmy McIlwaine, a shop steward in the largely Protestant Sirocco engineering works in Belfast, who later came to the conclusion that all the Unionist politicians—Bill Craig, Harry West, and Ian Paisley—had betrayed the workers. Strongly evangelical, McIlwaine would eventually agitate for Catholic workers to be given union cards to work in Sirocco.[57] The profile of Sabbatarianism combined with socialism might seem outlandish but was in fact a core component of the Northern Ireland Labour Party, which just the previous decade had made serious inroads into the urban Unionist vote. In tandem with the Methodist roots of the Labour Party in the UK, the Moral Re-Armament movement which originated in Oxford had inspired people to 'get involved in society but with a mission as well'.[58] The potential of the party to enact change in society brought this group into Labour in the late 1930s, manifesting through the lay preacher profile within the NILP itself.

This economically Left and socially-conservative strain of Christian socialism was personified in Northern Ireland by David Bleakley. Admired by Stormont officials for his frugality and having been in a 'proper job',[59] he had won the Belfast Victoria seat at the third time of trying in 1958, lost it to Roy Bradford seven years later, and recovered to gain the NILP's only seat for Belfast East in both the 1973 Assembly and 1975 Constitutional Convention. Though a passenger on Len Murray's beleaguered

---

[54] Interview with Glen Barr, Derry, 28 November 2012. See *Irish Times*, 7 May 1977, 4.
[55] Robert Fisk, *The Point of No Return: The Strike Which Broke the British in Ulster* (London: André Deutsch, 1975), 174–5.
[56] Quoted in 'BBC Scene Around Six—13 May 1974', PRONI OE/1/16.
[57] Ciaran McKeown, *The Passion of Peace* (Belfast: Blackstaff Press, 1984), 273.
[58] Interview with Neil Faris, Belfast, 29 July 2014. See also Terence Brown, 'The Majority's Minorities: Protestant Denominations in the North', *The Crane Bag: Minorities in Ireland*, Vol. 5, No. 1 (1981), 23.
[59] Interview with John Kennedy, Holywood, 17 June 2014. Bleakley (1925–) had worked as a Harland and Wolff electrician and was educated at Ruskin College, Oxford, where he befriended C. S. Lewis. Made Minister of Community Relations by Brian Faulkner in 1971, he resigned in part over the introduction of Internment without trial.

'back-to-work' march, Bleakley was singled out for praise in the B&ICO-
assembled *Strike Bulletins* for proposals which 'would have averted the
crisis', after calling for power-sharing—which he maintained after the fall
of Sunningdale was still widely supported—to be separated from the
Council of Ireland.[60] In January 1974 he could be found spearheading a
motion in the new Assembly criticizing the low level of student grants,
calling on the British government 'to guarantee a regular cost of living
review which will enable students to maintain a satisfactory standard of
living during their years of study'. The 'impecunious conditions' many
students lived under, Bleakley believed, would jeopardize 'the national
need for a highly-trained labour force'.[61]

Attempts to mediate between the government and the UWC were
conducted by another NILP figure, solicitor Brian Garrett. During the
middle of the action Garrett was selected at a meeting in a Quaker hall by
a group of South Belfast's more affluent citizens to set up lines of dialogue
between the government and strikers. He went to see Minister of State
Stan Orme, who 'started on about how they were going to defeat these
"fascist" Loyalists, and I remember saying to him broadly: "If you go about
thinking like that, you will create an army of fascists." I used that language,
and we left in high tension, really very angry on both sides.' At the original
Quaker hall meeting Garrett pointed out that the strike's core members
at the start were not paramilitary: 'Therefore, one of the aims of our
government ought to be to separate the reasonably democratic from the
paramilitary.' Trade unionist Harry Murray fell into the former camp and
with Garrett sensing the possibility of a formula to divide the strikers along
these lines, he met with Murray—who he could tell was against the use of
force—and told him that while the government's communication had
been poor, it would be 'a terrible failure' to bring down Northern Ireland's
first power-sharing government. Garrett subsequently met with James
Allan, Assistant Permanent Secretary in the Northern Ireland Office
(NIO), and Merlyn Rees to inform them of a formula he had agreed
with the strike committee, accompanied by a prospective statement to be
issued referring to 'no hardship, no violence'. The NIO pondered the idea,
but Garrett was soon contacted by Allan who,

---

[60] Workers' Association, *Strike Bulletin, No. 5—Fascism* (Belfast: 24 May 1974), 4;
David Bleakley, 'Prospects for the Ulster Convention', *Socialist Commentary* (May 1975), 8.
The leader of the UDA at the time claims that had the Council of Ireland—which
essentially gave the Irish government a consultative role in northern affairs—been dropped,
'the whole business was over. We could've went back to work' (interview with Andy Tyrie,
Dundonald, 9 August 2012).
[61] Quoted in *Irish Times*, 30 January 1974, 9.

rang me up to say thank you very much for all my efforts and, as he knew I was going back to see this committee, to tell them to go back to work. No agreed formula; no meeting, and I remember actually expletives, 'How the fuck can you go back to Hawthornden Road and tell them to go back to work? You come down and tell them to go back to work!' Anyway I did go back, shyly saw Harry Murray and said, 'Look they won't agree the formula.' He just accepted it, and that was it.[62]

With petrol distribution in the hands of the strike committee, the para-militaries arranged for the delivery of essential food supplies and recreated what some regarded as a 'blitz spirit'. Hot weather, the avoidance of conflict with the security forces, and the decision of Paddy Devlin as Minister of Health and Social Services to dispense unemployment benefit all sustained the stoppage. The latter gesture guaranteed that the British taxpayer essentially subsidized the strike, which would eventually have run out of gas (to use an operative phrase) without financial support.[63]

In order to avoid the semblance of a sectarian action, Harry Murray ensured that foodstuffs were allowed into certain Catholic areas and directed the first fuel tanker very deliberately to West Belfast. As noted by John Hewitt at a symposium a few months later, the Falls Road was the one part of the city to receive an uninterrupted bus service throughout the strike.[64] Outside the Falls, however, Northern Ireland was a daunting place to be for many during those two weeks in May 1974. To the civil servant Patrick Shea the time represented 'the most bewildering and in some respects the most frightening experience of my life', his South Belfast suburban existence violated by 'raw Nazism'.[65] Two days into the action, a series of UVF car bombs ripped through the centre of Dublin at the height of rush hour, and in Monaghan one hour and a half later, leading to the eventual loss of thirty-three lives.[66]

Journalist Nell McCafferty sympathized with Loyalist resistance to an Executive 'foisted' on the Protestant population, but painted an alarming picture of Derry's 'erratic' electricity supply, petrol queues, and gas for cooking and heating run dry.[67] A UWC *Strike Bulletin* had proclaimed the arrival of the much-feared 'Protestant backlash', triumphantly querying:

---

[62] Interview with Brian Garrett, Belfast, 28 March 2011. See also Fisk, *Point of No Return*, 84–5.

[63] *The Guardian*, 9 July 1974, 15.   [64] *Irish Times*, 4 July 1974, 12.

[65] Patrick Shea, *Voices and the Sound of Drums: An Irish Autobiography* (Belfast: Black-staff Press, 1981), 199–200.

[66] Glen Barr remembered questioning: 'If the UVF had the technical know-how to build bombs such as that, why aren't they building them now?' He was 'convinced it was not a Loyalist paramilitary organization' and speculated on the involvement of outside agents (interview with Glen Barr, Derry, 28 November 2012).

[67] Nell McCafferty, *Nell* (Dublin: Penguin, 2005), 290.

'Where is the burning and looting: where are the pogroms and assassinations? The "Protestant backlash" has now been in full swing for eleven days. But you are safer in your houses and on the streets than you were before it began.'[68] However, the 1974 strike was not, as the Supreme Commander of the UDA contemporarily claimed, a 'bloodless revolution'.[69] Aside from intimidation and multiple road blocks in towns and villages, two middle-aged Catholic brothers were shot dead by UDA men just outside Ballymena when they refused to close their family pub, an incident which 'put a black mark on the whole thing, because it was meant to be without violence'.[70]

'SPONGERS'

In a statement on Saturday 25 May 1974, Brian Faulkner highlighted the potential loss of hundreds of thousands of jobs and warned that 'If the present deadlock continues much longer we will all be the losers in time to come.'[71] A matter of hours later British Prime Minister Harold Wilson took to the screens to deliver what became infamously known as the 'spongers' broadcast. Many Loyalists were expecting him to intern them; instead Wilson railed at how:

> British taxpayers, have seen their sons vilified and spat upon—and murdered. They have seen the taxes they have poured out almost without regard to cost—over £300 million a year...going into Northern Ireland. Yet people who benefit from this now viciously defy Westminster, purporting to act as though they were an elected government; people who spend their lives sponging on Westminster and British democracy...Who do these people think they are?[72]

Wilson later conceded that his words may have been 'provocative and bitter', but justified that 'the idea I was seeking to get across was that Ulster was always ready to come to Auntie for spending money, expressing

---

[68] Workers' Association, *Strike Bulletin, No. 7—Wilson Backs Down* (Belfast: 26 May 1974), 2.

[69] Quoted in *The Observer*, 2 June 1974, 11.

[70] Interview with Glen Barr, Derry, 28 November 2012. Tyrie also now regrets this 'bad incident' (interview with Andy Tyrie, Dundonald, 9 August 2012). See David McKittrick, Seamus Kelters, Brian Feeney, Chris Thornton, and David McVea (eds), *Lost Lives: The Stories of the Men, Women and Children Who Died as a Result of the Northern Ireland Troubles* (Edinburgh: Mainstream, 2008; 1st edition 1999), 447, 454–6.

[71] Broadcast by Brian Faulkner, Chief Minister, Saturday 25 May 1974, PRONI OE/1/16.

[72] Harold Wilson, Transcript of Televised Address, 25 May 1974, http://cain.ulst.ac.uk/events/uwc/docs/hw25574.htm (accessed 13 October 2012).

their thanks by kicking her in the teeth'.[73] Local civil servants remain bemused at the specific 'sponging' phrase, having perused a version of the speech the same morning which made no reference to it at all.[74] However, there was something especially potent in the spectacle of a Labour Prime Minister, a man who helped to establish the modern-day welfare state through his work on the 1942 Beveridge Report, addressing this section in such derogatory terms. Its economic tone, reminiscent of successive British governments up to the present day, was designed for an English audience but also calculated with maximum contempt for the Protestant population and all it entailed. A notable piece of high theatre, it invites *all* Northern Irish citizens to consider their status within the UK and its economy. Within Ulster, most agreed that the speech swung any waverers behind the strike, Glen Barr joking that they would make Wilson 'an honorary member of the UDA after this'.[75] Between this whirlwind and the Provisional IRA's continued bombing campaign, Sunningdale was unsustainable. Three days after the broadcast, Brian Faulkner and the five other Unionist ministers resigned, collapsing the Executive.

In Stewart Parker's *Pentecost*, after listening to the speech an enraged Ruth labels Wilson a 'smug wee English shite with a weaselly voice' who has failed to understand the sacrifices and work ethic of Ulster Protestants, 'British taxpayers just the same as they are . . . for five long years now we've watched it rent asunder, pulverised into rubble by the real spongers, cruel and murderous bastards.' When she is challenged by Peter, who fears raw sewage flooding the streets ('and it won't be the English who die of typhoid'), she defies that 'They can't take on an entire community. The strike is theirs.'[76] This defiance was not to pass unpunished. Wilson triumphantly withheld a £9 million subsidy from Harland and Wolff, clearly inferring that the Yard and other industries seen as too close to the strike were to take a hit in the coming years.[77] The following year the Labour government vowed that 'in future the company's losses in any year will have to be met from the Northern Ireland Exchequer Budget for that year', with others detecting how this instability coincided with the Wilson government's murmuring about withdrawal, 'and the signal that seemed most significant was the closure of Rolls-Royce in Dundonald in 1975,

---

[73] Harold Wilson, *Final Term: The Labour Government 1974–1976* (London: Weidenfeld and Nicolson, 1979), 77. To complicate matters, it was around this time that the paranoia later credited for his early exit from Downing Street was disturbing Wilson (David Pallister, 'Ulster "dirty tricks" File Sent to PM', *The Guardian*, 26 June 1985, 1).
[74] Interview with Maurice Hayes, Belfast, 26 November 2012.
[75] Quoted in Peter Taylor, *Loyalists* (London: Bloomsbury, 2000), 137.
[76] Parker, *Pentecost*, in *Three Plays*, 183–5.   [77] Wilson, *Final Term*, 75, 77.

which could be interpreted as getting the key installations out as part of a withdrawal plan'.[78] Against the pleas of the Executive's Minister of Commerce John Hume, Harland and Wolff was actually excluded from subsequent plans to nationalize British aircraft and shipbuilding industries.[79] Andy Tyrie remains proud that his community 'were the first group that ever took the British government on and won a strike',[80] but it was in some ways a pyrrhic victory, offering a wounded Labour government the chance to begin eroding its financial contributions to the bedrock of Protestant working-class employment. The broader energy crisis and quadrupling of oil prices further compounded the depressing impact on the local economy.

BANDITRY

One of the other more ominous consequences of the UWC strike period was the systematizing of criminal underworlds. The thin line between vigilantism—which has a long history in Belfast—and criminality was regularly blurred, in a dynamic further exacerbated by the political distress engendered by O'Neill's tenure. This resonates with Eric Hobsbawm's assessment that banditry fundamentally challenges 'those who hold or lay claim to power, law and control of resources', in a dynamic intrinsically related to 'class divisions'.[81] The criminality tar had initially been used by the SDLP to differentiate itself from the Provisional IRA, but the clash between law and lawlessness was always more pronounced in the Protestant population for the simple reason that it maintained a closer relationship with the state than its nationalist counterpart. Loyalists could also count, occasionally, on the RUC '"not noticing" their exploits'.[82]

An unchecked thesis fostered by contemporary Loyalist leaders proposes that the 'cancer' of criminality only entered Protestant areas with drug-dealing in the early 1990s,[83] despite these activities beginning decades before. As a former leader of the Ulster Unionist Party outlines:

---

[78] *Fortnight*, No. 103 (25 April 1975), 4–5; interview with Boyd Black, Belfast, 10 October 2012. Black was a former member of the B&ICO and is currently Secretary of the Labour Party in Northern Ireland.

[79] *Fortnight*, No. 98 (7 February 1975), 8; *The Guardian*, 3 June 1976, 5.

[80] Interview with Andy Tyrie, Dundonald, 9 August 2012.

[81] Eric Hobsbawm, *Bandits* (London: Abacus, 2000; 1st edition 1969), 7–9.

[82] Dervla Murphy, *A Place Apart* (Harmondsworth: Penguin, 1979), 146–7.

[83] See the comments of Jackie MacDonald in Peter Shirlow, *The End of Ulster Loyalism?* (Manchester: Manchester University Press, 2012), 115.

When they did start up, their activities in Loyalist areas weren't confined simply to fighting Republicans. They were involved in rackets, they were involved in criminality and those sort of things discredited them in front of the ordinary people because their activities in Loyalist areas had the effect in some instances of destroying the quality of life. They had Shebeens, they had protection rackets, they were throwing their weight around locally and just generally upsetting people. And the idea that they would actually fire on and attack police goes against the grain.[84]

The UDA was always heavily absorbed in criminal enterprises, and the difference between it and the UVF in this regard (as in others) has often been elided. From the beginning of its existence it attracted a gangsterist element who saw the organization as 'an easy way to good cars, thick gold jewellery and winter holidays in Spain', and a prevalent belief among UVF ex-combatants is that many who joined the UDA were driven by the basic desire for individual aggrandizement. This is seen to persevere in the form of present-day UDA spokesmen who only get involved in community projects and schemes when it is 'personally and financially beneficial' to them.[85]

Though the UVF's notorious east Antrim wing was also immersed in criminality from the early 1970s, there is much to be said for the view that the UDA's activities were comprehensively expanded during May 1974. These exertions had of course begun years prior to the UWC strike but, undisturbed by security forces, a generation of UDA leaders—including Jackie McDonald and John 'Grug' Gregg—cut their teeth in the stoppage.[86] During the manning of barricades, fuel smuggling, extortion, and black markets all flourished, generating some of the more unpropitious images associated with Loyalism to the present day. The situation may also be connected to the limitations of 'unimaginative politicians' who lack the vision or willingness 'to address the great structural inequities . . . upon which crime and instability thrive'.[87] In *Pentecost*, as the UWC tightens its grip on Northern Ireland, Peter delineates the atmosphere around the centre of its headquarters in East Belfast, not far from the gates of Stormont:

PETER: Is this what you want?—the apemen in charge, shops without food to sell, garages without petrol . . . there's a mile-long queue of doctors

[84] Interview with Lord Reg Empey, Belfast, 11 November 2011.

[85] Steve Bruce, 'It's Terrorism as Usual', *The Guardian*, 12 August 1992, 17; interview with William Mitchell, Belfast, 26 July 2012.

[86] Ian S. Wood, *Crimes of Loyalty: A History of the UDA* (Edinburgh: Edinburgh University Press, 2006), 40–1. Despite the input of the UVF's Ken Gibson, the strike was primarily associated with the UDA.

[87] Misha Glenny, *McMafia: Crime Without Frontiers* (London: The Bodley Head, 2008), 394.

and nurses and social workers, and lawyers, up at Hawthornden Road, queuing up to beg for a special pass to get them through the barricades to their patients and clients, and from who?—from the wee hard men who can barely sign their name to their special bloody passes, from shipyard bible-thumpers, unemployed binmen, petty crooks and extortionists, pigbrain mobsters and thugs, they've seized control over all of us.[88]

In fairness to the UDA, its spokesmen owned up to these activities to an almost comical degree. One public relations officer admitted that the outfit had originally 'incorporated among many of our companies and brigades gangsters, petty thieves and so on', and that after attempting 'to put forward some sort of political initiative this organisation has been very disappointed at the public response. We deduce from this that the only thing that pays in this country is violence.'[89] To the dismay of those strike leaders with trade union backgrounds, the UDA realized it was better at racketeering than socialism.

LONG KESH

Even those who have written intelligently about Ulster Protestantism are under the impression that during the 1970s, 'The IRA used the prison as their university, whereas all my lot did was body-building and look at porn. That tells you a lot.'[90] Representing the antithesis of this image, the 'Long Kesh University' presided over by Gusty Spence (1933–2011) bore the fruit of politically engaged and conciliatory Loyalists during the 1990s peace process. One of these men was David Ervine (1953–2007), who outlined Spence's Socratic opening salvo: 'The first question Gusty asked me was "why are you here?" and I said "possession of explosives", to which he said, "no, I'm asking you why are you here?"' This initially dejected Ervine, 'But it made me think about the police, army and judge who put me there because they were defending their country—which was exactly what I thought I'd been doing.'[91] Another ex-UVF inmate recalled:

> Because he controlled things there was a younger element that always wanted to usurp, undermine, disrespect him. And I wouldn't have been the most respectful of people towards him. But you realize you're wrong when you talk to him. Like most things, you realize you're not seeing the full picture.

[88] Parker, *Pentecost*, in *Three Plays*, 184.
[89] Sammy Duddy, quoted in *The Guardian*, 15 August 1979, 24.
[90] Interview with Maurice Leitch, London, 31 July 2015.
[91] Quoted in *The Guardian—G2*, 8 December 1994, 3.

From the time that I met him in Long Kesh, Spence would ask everybody how we got there, then say: 'Don't blame the cops. Don't blame Catholics, don't blame RUC, don't blame British Army. You put yourself here and when you get out you've to decide if you want to go through the same thing again or if you want to move on and make something of your life. Don't come back in with a bad attitude, hating people, hating everything—when you know you put yourself here.'[92]

While a one-sided contest between politics and criminality played out in Loyalist paramilitary groups from the early 1970s onwards, the former stood some chance of winning out in the prisons. The thinking emanated from inside: 'If Gusty had've been outside with the political thought, he might have been rejected. But whilst he was in there and had gathered round him similar-minded people, it was easier.'[93]

Contacts with the Official IRA were subsequently opened up in the compounds, both organizations united by their contempt for the Provisional IRA and an old vein of working-class socialism. Seamus Lynch remembered returning to Long Kesh after his own internment for a discussion convened by the Northern Ireland Office, which was where he first met a sharply suited Spence (whom he initially mistook for a prison governor). Because 'Gusty started engaging with the right people in political debate, reading and discussing, that led to the Ervines of this world—because he was an icon and had the capacity to take those boys under his wing and start to develop them politically,'[94] something reinforced by outside incentive. A triumvirate of the Reverend John Stewart,[95] Jim McDonald, and David Overend—all aligned to the Northern Ireland Labour Party—contacted the prisoners and helped nurture the acceptance of devolved power-sharing amongst discerning Loyalists at a time of vacuous Unionist integrationism (i.e. politics being solely decided at Westminster). Cautiously aware that 'prisoners came first', Overend made sure that the welfare of Loyalist prisoners was drafted into the

---

[92] Interview with George Morrow, Bangor, 18 June 2014.
[93] Interview with Robert Rodgers, Belfast, 15 August 2012.
[94] Interview with Seamus Lynch, Belfast, 19 January 2012.
[95] The Reverend John Stewart (1929–77) was a Methodist preacher in the mainly Protestant Woodvale area. He was one of the first people into the rubble of the Shankill Road's Mountain View Tavern to retrieve the dead and wounded after it was bombed by the IRA in May 1975, the kind of incident which led to his reliance on tranquillizers. Stewart worked as a missionary in the West Indies in 1953 and tutored the emergent leaders of the independence movement in socialist thought, meaning that when Antigua received its independence in 1981, his widow Beatrice was invited back 'as a personal guest of the Prime Minister in recognition of [his] contribution to the Antiguan struggle' (Roy Garland, 'Scattered Seeds Bearing Fruit in Strange Places', *Irish News*, 11 December 2006, 2; interview with Douglas McIldoon, Belfast, 23 January 2012).

constitution of the soon-to-be-founded Progressive Unionist Party,[96] with developments reflected in the 'Sharing Responsibility' document which gestated from 1977 onwards.

Consequently, when Martin Lynch's *Chronicles of Long Kesh*—depicting both Loyalist and Republican prisoners—premiered in 2009, many of the former were aggrieved by their presentation. Loyalists felt that the worth and complexity of their compound life (such as differences between the UVF and UDA) were negated,[97] objecting in particular to the play's depiction of a stand-off between Loyalists and the prison authorities on the morning of 12 July over the right to drink alcohol.[98] All seemed to confirm the Loyalist objection that when Lynch came to writing the play 'he couldn't but avoid that the story of the jails was ultimately an IRA story'.[99] Lynch, who has always been up front about his involvement with the Official IRA, justified that while his method was not strictly scientific he interviewed an equal number of Loyalists to Republicans when researching *Chronicles*. Yet:

> If you look at the statistics, it was hugely imbalanced in favour of the Provos [the Provisional IRA]. That kept staring me in the face and there was no way I could avoid that in terms of writing the play, so I zoned in and gave the majority of it to them. The other element which drove the play was that in the Republicans' stories which were coming back to me—Provos, Officials and INLA—there was a lot of humour. When it came to the Loyalists, there was a lot of reluctance. I put two guys together in the John Hewitt bar, two ex-UDA men, and I saw one of them tick-tacking [nudging] the other guy, saying he had gone too far in what he was saying. I can only say that the Loyalist experience wasn't better articulated to me. There was the issue of segregation as well but—maybe I met the wrong guys—when the Provies were going on about their escape, the most profound story I heard [from Loyalists] was the UDA barricading themselves into their cells for a day or so because they weren't allowed to celebrate the Twelfth and have some booze and sing their songs.[100]

Spence's disciplinarian regime, designed to keep the inmates physically and mentally agile, and in a broader sense start thinking, counters Lynch's portrayal of Loyalists in Long Kesh. The popular myth of thugs pumping

[96] Interview with David Overend, Belfast, 28 April 2015. Jim McDonald was the Chairman of both the PUP and the Loyalist Prisoners Welfare Association. See also Tony Novosel, *Northern Ireland's Lost Opportunity: The Frustrated Promise of Political Loyalism* (London: Pluto Press, 2013), 90–6.
[97] Interview with Bobby Niblock (ex-UVF volunteer), Belfast, 30 August 2012.
[98] Martin Lynch, *Chronicles of Long Kesh* (London: Oberon Books, 2010), 61–3.
[99] Interview with Danny Morrison, Belfast, 29 August 2013.
[100] Interview with Martin Lynch, Belfast, 9 November 2011.

iron and gaining little more than tattoos is rather belied by the evidence. Handicraft workshops, leatherworking classes, and mural paintings honouring Shankill artist William Connor stimulated creative spirit, while Loyalists received visiting lectures from academics (including Frank Wright and Miriam Daly) and poets like Michael Longley, who wrote warmly outlining his apologies for missing a few visits and suggesting some future sessions at the end of 1973.[101] UVF prisoners had quite catholic reading tastes, requesting titles by Yeats, Lady Gregory, George Russell (Æ), George Bernard Shaw, St John Ervine, Mary Shelley, and William Wordsworth.[102]

Those who lived under Spence's routines and have since gone on to play a political role complain that what they relayed of their jail time to Martin Lynch was not included in the final play, with many Loyalists feeling that *Chronicles* indulged in 'typical stereotypes' of uneducated men whose sole cultural interest was in flute bands and drugs. Billy Hutchinson (1955–), who took a degree in Town Planning while in Long Kesh, remembers:

> The reality is that in my compound, at one stage there were nineteen of us doing degree courses and finishing. I think that overall in terms of Loyalism there were thirty-two people who got degrees. The Provos didn't get into degrees until after the Ceasefires, and all of their people who were in prison and did a degree were all people who were told to do that because they were being put into positions of power. But we were doing it well before then. The Open University statistics prove when UVF men were doing degrees Republicans actually wouldn't take education because they thought it was a British plot to convert them. We were the first people to do education, and he [Martin Lynch] ignores all of that.[103]

Even those UVF volunteers who did not avail of the Open University still followed Spence's procedures, and while these may have seemed mundane and 'a bit like Groundhog Day, the highlight of it wouldn't have been fighting with screws over drink on the Twelfth morning'. All seemed to translate that 'Republicans were idealistic young men who were fighting

---

[101] Billy Hutchinson, *Transcendental Art—A Troubles Archive Essay* (Belfast: Arts Council of Northern Ireland, 2011), 1–2. Michael Longley, Letter to James Magee, 5 December 1973. Privately held archive. Longley's letter is written in green felt-tip pen on the Arts Council of Northern Ireland's official paper. My thanks to James Magee, ex-UVF prisoner in Long Kesh (Compound 12), and Dr Gareth Mulvenna for access.

[102] See their call for books in *Combat*, Vol. 4, Issue 25 (1979), n.pag.

[103] Interview with Billy Hutchinson, Belfast, 12 November 2012. See also William 'Plum' Smith, *Inside Man: Loyalists of Long Kesh—The Untold Story* (Newtownards: Colourpoint Books, 2014), 112.

for Ireland', while Loyalists were 'sectarian bigots who when in prison pumped steroids and lifted weights'.[104]

It is not entirely fair to see the play in such stark terms. Leaving aside the central chorus of Freddie, a Protestant Prison Officer, *Chronicles* contains two Loyalists, one a conventional tough who lifts weights, the other a Bob Dylan-loving UVF man who is well read and interested in left-wing thought (reminiscent of the real ex-UVF and PUP activist William Mitchell). This dichotomy provides both the humour and dramatic spark:

> HANK: Thumper, still no chance of you puttin' your name down for the Open University thing?
> THUMPER: You away in the head? University's only for people who don't know things.
> HANK: It's you who's losin' out. There's five in the cage startin' next week.
> THUMPER: Good luck to yiz.
> HANK: The CO says he wants us to find out why we're fightin' for loyalism. He says the loyalist working class have to start relyin' on themselves, instead of always voting for solicitors and businessmen in the Unionist Party.
> THUMPER: The CO's head's full of wee white mice.[105]

More generally, Lynch emphasizes how 'there's something in the Catholic, nationalist side that allows the Long Kesh thing to be regarded as a badge of honour. Whereas in the Loyalist side there's the opposite experience.' This broadly negative dimension not only undercuts the humour for Loyalists but also, rather crucially, goes to the heart of a cultural reading of the prison experience in the wider community: 'One Official [IRA man] I met, who was interned for ten months said to me "Martin—what a fabulous human experience, the most enriching experience of my life," because of the comradeship he shared. That spoke volumes to me about the Republican side generally.'[106] Tellingly, those who joined the paramilitaries and served time in jail were not embraced to anywhere near the same extent in Protestant working-class communities—quite the reverse.[107]

While the significance of prison to Loyalism should not be derided, it was what the men did when they were released, what they did with

---

[104] Interview with Bobby Niblock, Belfast, 30 August 2012. Other ex-UVF volunteers reacted more philosophically, accepting that 'If you have a different story, write it yourself' (interview with Robert Rodgers, Belfast, 15 August 2012). Several Loyalists acted on this, launching their own theatre group in the summer of 2013. See Connal Parr, 'Etcetera Theatre Company: An Exercise in Ulster Loyalist Storytelling', *New Hibernia Review*, Vol. 20, No. 4 (Winter 2016), 91–112.

[105] Lynch, *Chronicles*, 28–9, 48–9, 72, 85.

[106] Interview with Martin Lynch, Belfast, 9 November 2011.

[107] See the data and comments in Colin Crawford, *Defenders or Criminals? Loyalist Prisoners and Criminalisation* (Belfast: Blackstaff Press, 1999), 121–2.

Spence's training, which mattered. His voice was now fixed in the back of their heads: 'Lose this martyr/victim sense. If you don't like it, do something about it when you get out.' One who fell under his supervision was George Morrow, who painted in Crumlin Road Gaol and became an artist on his release. At an exhibition at the scene of his one-time incarceration, Morrow confirmed that Spence 'imposed a structure on everyone', facilitating the ambience and his art. Unable to create around prison violence, 'Spence was the only one who was able to come down and quell everything.'[108] Eventually released from the Maze in December 1984, Spence immediately began working in community schemes in the Shankill area.[109] His lengthy incarceration, even when it was known that he was inwardly and publicly renouncing militarism, was because he had absconded (or was 'kidnapped', as his organization phrased it) on release to attend his daughter's wedding. It was at this time that the UVF was reorganized.[110]

Spence ultimately traversed Loyalism to emerge representative of an older Belfast working-class profile, articulating the kind of bread-and-butter socialism of John Hewitt, Sam Thompson, and the NILP (his brother Eddie had been a member of the Communist Party). His attendance at the British Labour Party conference in Blackpool in 1994 reflected his view that 'We have a culture beyond flute bands and lambeg drums.'[111] Above all Spence became a champion for the Shankill Road, declaring at a conference at Queen's University in 1991, 'If any good has come from the troubles, it certainly has been the rise of community groups within the Protestant areas,' and while constitutional politicians had 'failed' it, his affection for the area and its 'misguided pride' shone through: 'The people are doing the double in the Shankill. They realize now that they are underprivileged, they realize now how much they have been conned.'[112]

However, even this predilection for the Shankill was to diminish as the years passed. Spence could do little to prevent spikes in Loyalist violence, and a devastating 2000 feud—when his home was badly damaged—'near killed him', according to his daughter.[113] His health deteriorated and the

---

[108] Quoted in *Irish Times*, 1 April 2013, 6; interview with George Morrow, Bangor, 18 June 2014.

[109] *The Guardian*, 14 December 1984, 4.

[110] *The Observer*, 5 November 1972, 1. Spence is the clear inspiration for Maurice Leitch's novel *Silver's City* (1981), reportedly saying years later that Leitch 'got me right in that' (interview with Maurice Leitch, London, 31 July 2015).

[111] Quoted in *The Guardian*, 6 October 1994, 2.

[112] Quoted in Bernard Cullen (ed.), *Discriminations Old and New: Aspects of Northern Ireland Today* (Belfast: Institute of Irish Studies, 1992), 32–3.

[113] *Irish Times*, 17 May 1988, 11; *The Guardian*, 18 March 1999, 1; Liz Rea, quoted in Bill Rolston, *Children of the Revolution* (Derry: Guildhall Press, 2011), 84. This prompted

death of his wife (prompted in large part by the feud trauma) only exacerbated his disillusionment. Spence was always aware that he had been a pawn in a wider game and carried this grievance in him until his death in September 2011. In 1965 a Unionist Party politician approached him to take charge of a reactivated UVF on the Shankill. This figure, who went on to become politically prominent, informed Spence that the IRA planned to take over the north and murder ministers in Terence O'Neill's government, and so Spence realized that the real reason for the revival of the UVF, and thus his life in jail, was a Unionist power struggle between hardliners—who opened this chapter destabilizing Terence O'Neill—and the O'Neillite reformers themselves.[114]

With the die cast on Spence's iconic militant status he was understandably never forgiven by relatives of those the UVF killed in their campaign, including the family of Peter Ward, an eighteen-year-old Catholic shot dead in June 1966, and Matilda Gould (an elderly Protestant lady who died following the attempted petrol-bombing of a Catholic bar).[115] Spence always denied the Ward murder but was convicted and, pre-empting the prison protest of the following decade, undertook his first hunger strike in 1966 against the 'Victorian' conditions of Northern Irish prisons. It was the experience of being ignored by 'those political leaders that were in a position to actually get conditions changed' that led to Spence's long-running contempt for 'Super Prods' and Unionist hardliners,[116] surfacing especially through his involvement with the PUP, whose conference he addressed the year after his ultimate progeny of the historic Loyalist Ceasefire: 'What have these wretches ever done for Ulster? What will they ever do for Ulster except shout at the dark from their trenches or dream up another crazy stunt. They talk a good fight but as my Da used to say "talk is cheap but it takes money to buy drink". The tribal ritualistic incantations and shibboleths of the past are dead.'[117] Having orated the UVF's 2007 statement renouncing violence, Spence was not invited to the June 2009 decommissioning announcement, those he mentored confirming that he had by this time fallen 'out of favour'.[118]

---

his permanent residence in Groomsport, County Down, known locally as 'Shankill-on-Sea'. See also *Belfast News Letter*, 27 September 2011, 9.

[114] *Irish Times*, 27 September 1985, 9; David Sharrock, 'Gusty Wind of Change', *The Guardian—G2*, 16 December 1996, 7.

[115] *Irish News*, 29 June 2016, 10.

[116] Interview with William Mitchell, Belfast, 26 July 2012.

[117] Gusty Spence, Text of Speech to Progressive Unionist Party Conference, 11 February 1995. Linen Hall Library Political Collection.

[118] *Belfast Telegraph*, 27 June 2009, 8; interview with William Mitchell, Belfast, 26 July 2012.

In the year before his passing he called for the organization to put itself out of existence and requested that there be no UVF trappings at his funeral.[119]

CLASS

Returning to May 1974, perhaps the strangest detail is that those who have written about Northern Irish Protestantism, of its disparity and individualism, seem to have passed over the UWC strike, buying into the simple view of one monolith cutting across class. This view has 'Bank managers and suburban golf club secretaries' cheering the strikers on,[120] neglecting the divisions between those involved. British Prime Minister Edward Heath alluded to the way that in popular memory the strike came to be falsely associated with Ian Paisley, who was not involved at all.[121] Though this is an exaggeration—Paisley did end up playing a part—it has been conveniently forgotten that he missed the stoppage's critical first week as he was in North America and was thought to be gauging whether or not it would succeed. A famous story has him sitting in Glen Barr's chair at one of the UWC meetings and, when he refused to move on account of a 'sore back', being physically lifted down the table by two UDA heavies. Treated with 'total disrespect, he was only there because he was part of the Unionist family'.[122] This theme even makes its way into Parker's *Pentecost* when Lenny claims the strike will end soon. 'Strike? This is no strike. [*Paisleyite voice*] This is a constitutional stoppage!', Peter japes.[123]

By 1974 there had already been considerable Unionist fissuring with the formation of the DUP and the Alliance Party, as well as the mild continuance of the Faulkner Unionists. Paisley had always lambasted the 'fur-coat brigade' after the style of Independent Unionists such as Tommy Henderson, and the Executive's Minister for Education Basil McIvor conceded that affluent, pro-power-sharing 'Liberal' Unionists such as himself were particular targets for Loyalist resentment.[124] The strike was

---

[119] *Belfast News Letter*, 11 November 2010, 1; *Belfast Telegraph*, 26 September 2011, 4.

[120] Utley, *Lessons*, 120. See also Bell, *Protestants*, 11, 138–9.

[121] Edward Heath, *The Course of My Life* (London: Hodder and Stoughton, 1998), 445.

[122] Interview with Glen Barr, Derry, 28 November 2012. See also Ed Moloney, *Paisley: From Demagogue to Democrat* (Dublin: Poolbeg Press, 2008), 258–66.

[123] Parker, *Pentecost*, in *Three Plays*, 172.

[124] Basil McIvor, *Hope Deferred: Experiences of an Irish Unionist* (Belfast: Blackstaff Press, 1998), 121.

thus directed, as the UDA's former Supreme Commander confirms, against the way:

> The Unionist politicians—Captain Terence O'Neill, Brian Faulkner, and all the rest—just took it for granted. The fascinating thing was this was the first time that people had said 'Hold on, we've had enough of this carry-on.' The Council of Ireland was imposed on us. We weren't told. We weren't considered in the argument at all. It wasn't about them [the SDLP] being in government; it was about the attitude of the Unionist politicians. They never were used to making decisions from Partition here. They allowed the civil service to run the place, and it got that bad that we were the lesser known people within the British government. Our politicians hadn't the sense to realize that they weren't important. They were ambushed.[125]

It is important to remember that effigies of Faulkner, as well as Gerry Fitt, were burned in Newtownabbey's Rathcoole estate on the fall of the Executive.[126]

One of the strangest of appropriations, therefore, has seen Unionist politicians trying to take credit for the stoppage's success, in John Laird's case with a retrospectively preposterous claim that it represented an extension of his incarnation as an 'Ulster Scots rebel'. In this reading the strike was, again, a uniform effort where 'everyone in the Unionist community worked together, from the richest businessman to the most humble lowly paid worker'.[127] *De facto* leader Glen Barr (1932–) confirmed that such men, aside from precipitating through their absence of leadership his entry into politics in the first place, were opportunistically keen to be photographed with the strikers: 'But if you'd have dared mention the fact you were thinking of marrying one of their daughters, they would run a mile.'[128] Barr's hostility to the Unionist establishment clearly moulded him:

> I was brought up on these [Derry] back streets, two-up two-down, the youngest of ten. Two died so there was eight of us, two girls and six boys. We had a Catholic [family] on one side and a Protestant on the other, therefore I could never understand this complaint about the Protestants having all the wealth in Northern Ireland. I wasn't brought up in a Protestant ghetto or a Catholic ghetto: I was brought up in a mixed ghetto. I saw the poverty across the two back walls and there was no difference between us.

---

[125] Interview with Andy Tyrie, Dundonald, 9 August 2012.
[126] Fisk, *Point of No Return*, 224.
[127] John Laird, *A Struggle to Be Heard* (Exeter: Global & Western, 2010), 89–90, 96.
[128] Speaking at the conference '40 Years On: The Strike Which Brought Down Sunningdale', co-organized by the author and held at Queen's University Belfast on 19 May 2014.

We were leaderless in the Protestant community. I detested the Official Unionists and still do to this day, because they exploited the ordinary working-class Protestant people. They made us believe we were better than the Catholics. I was a trade union leader before the Troubles started, so I was already facing the faceless Unionist men in Derry.[129]

The apparent class animosity chimes with the estimation of an Executive Minister that the strikers were motivated 'as much by a crude class hatred of the landed gentry and local business tycoons who for years had dominated Unionist Party politics as by their fears of a united Ireland via Sunningdale'.[130] Even during the secret talks which took place between the UVF and the Provisional IRA earlier in 1974, at a hotel in Mountnugent, County Cavan, the Loyalist group's delegates Billy Mitchell and John Hanna 'stated that they had their belly full of the fur-coat brigade and were resolved to seek some form of Government and leadership that excluded the landed Gentry and the Upper/Middle class'.[131]

The UWC strike accordingly ushered in a new phase in that incredibly ambivalent, often tortuous relationship which has existed between Loyalist paramilitaries, and Unionist politicians. When the Reverend Martin Smyth insisted that Protestants had no time for 'thuggery and socialism', Andy Tyrie rounded that men like Smyth 'did politics for a hobby and now they come crawling to us from under their flat stones; they should be ashamed to show their faces'.[132] One UVF volunteer recalled talking with Tyrie at a time when Unionist politicians had stopped coming to meetings of the UWC. They pondered calling all the politicians, 'the Harry Wests, the Bill Craigs, the Paisleys', to a meeting at Hawthornden Road:

We'll take them in to a room and tell them: 'Look, gentlemen, there'll be no more split parties. We don't care what youse call it, but there's going to be one party. There's going to be one leader. We're leaving the room—youse have got an hour to pick the name of a party and a leader, and we'll be back in an hour.' And Andy says, 'Yeah, and we'll go back in an hour and there'll all be sitting squabbling and fighting. What do we do then?' I says, we take Big Ian's fur hat and we put the names into the hat and we draw a name out. Andy says, 'And he's the leader?' I says: 'No, no. Take him out the back and we'll shoot him. And we'll come in and give them another hour to pick a leader, and we'll shoot every fuckin' one of them until there's one left and he

---

[129] Interview with Glen Barr, Derry, 28 November 2012.
[130] Paddy Devlin, *The Fall of the N.I. Executive* (Belfast: Paddy Devlin, 1975), 83.
[131] Billy Mitchell, 'Discussions with the Provisional IRA' (n.d.), 6. The IRA delegation, who found common ground with the UVF in seeing 'no difference between Green Tories and Orange Tories, between the Fur-coat Brigade and the Castle Catholics', included Dáithí Ó Conaill, Brian Keenan, Seamus Twomey, and Martin McGuinness.
[132] Quoted in *The Observer*, 2 June 1974, 11.

can't be backstabbed then we'll know we have a true leader!' (*Pause*) You know the only thing about that? I'm sorry we didn't fuckin' do it![133]

Despite this 'Lead us or we'll kill you' psychosis, Loyalists were happy to use expedient politicians, Andy Tyrie cheerfully claiming that Minister for the Environment Roy Bradford tipped off the strikers with the Executive's plans: 'He was floating information between the Loyalist groups, not just Ken Gibson, but I was getting the phone calls from Stormont itself, direct. They were telling me the state of affairs up there, "the Executive's going to fall, the fight's been won".'[134]

   In an important nexus, Unionist politicians of Bradford's brand were in the early 1970s supporters of redevelopment plans including the building of the Belfast Urban Motorway, a scheme entailing the destruction of Protestant working-class housing in the Shankill, Sandy Row, and Lower Ormeau to provide a ring road around Belfast city centre. Bradford was a particular advocate of the programme, overruling the objections of residents in favour of 'freedom of choice for car owners'.[135] The UWC played a critical role in thwarting this process through the 'Save the Shankill' (STS) campaign, as at a local level 'it was now recognized that traditional Unionism aided by the British government was prepared to destroy the Shankill and it was up to local people to save it'.[136] The UWC's Jim Smyth was approached to chair the movement, which also brought together the Shankill Traders' Association, members of the United Ulster Unionist Coalition (UUUC), church representatives, and Loyalist paramilitary groups. A community worker prominent in the campaign remembered approaching 'them as community organizers to say, "Listen, you've just had your strike, but this is going on right below you—your own community—and you need to agree also to get involved in this struggle here."'[137] When the Housing Executive announced it would knock down all remaining shops in the lower Shankill, the STS responded by 'blacking' all incoming demolition work, that is, smashing up any machinery (such as bulldozers) which were to be used for demolition. The UWC was the body which actually carried this out, and, with the British government wanting to avoid direct confrontation as

---

[133] Interview with James Magee (ex-UVF volunteer), Belfast, 26 November 2014.

[134] Interview with Andy Tyrie, Dundonald, 9 August 2012. Tyrie noted of Bradford that 'What he thought and what he said was always different. So many of them dealt with the Unionist community that way, "We'll be tough, we'll do this." They sort of looked down at me because I knew all their business.'

[135] Wesley Johnston, *The Belfast Urban Motorway: Engineering, Ambition and Social Conflict* (Newtownards: Colourpoint Books, 2014), 106.

[136] See Ron Weiner, *The Rape and Plunder of the Shankill* (Belfast: Published by the author, 1975), 64, 66, 145.

[137] Interview with Jackie Redpath, Belfast, 19 February 2013.

in May 1974, the initiative successfully halted both the Urban Motorway and the wider Shankill redevelopment scheme by the end of March 1975.[138] Though senior civil servants aver that the strike was 'not an anti-Catholic thing; it was an anti-government thing',[139] the baser elements in its disposition should not be dismissed. Jackie Redpath, who remains active in community work, acknowledges its populist charge, 'foaming up' against the Unionist establishment and the constitutional nationalism of the SDLP: 'Populism does not necessarily equate to working class stuff; they're two distinct things. There was a thing within the Ulster Workers' Council Strike that was basically saying "We won't have a Taig about the place", that was against Catholics and especially nationalists in government.'[140] The phenomena of sectarianism and class-consciousness historically co-existed within the Protestant working class, and this was present in 1974 too. The militancy of 'combative sectarianism' often 'brought the working-class Orangeman into conflict with the state and with those members of the local ruling class who viewed such conflict with distaste and attempted to control it'. Echoing Thomas Carnduff's associations, this occasionally entwined with the Labour movement, generating 'a militant populism which expressed class conflict in terms of upper class "betrayal" of the Protestant cause'.[141] May 1974 lay in the clash between this militant populism and the middle-class liberal consensus highlighted at the start of this chapter.

Instructive is the caste of O'Neillite Unionists who served as Ministers in the Executive, who were all, in different ways, utterly scattered following the collapse of Sunningdale. Basil McIvor, Herbert Kirk, and John Baxter retired almost immediately from politics to careers in law and accountancy, while both Leslie Morrell and Roy Bradford lost their seats in the Constitutional Convention election the following year. Other O'Neillites like Sir Robert Porter had departed even earlier, meaning that the modernizing guard, the logical culmination of O'Neillism, had been categorically decimated. Duncan Pollock, who soldiered on in Faulkner's newly formed Unionist Party of Northern Ireland (UPNI), believed 'They saw the Executive working and they decided to wreck it. I was hammered in the elections to the Convention. I expected it, but they really hammered me.'[142] Brian Faulkner's private secretary was certain that the strike was in essence a *putsch* against the generation of Unionist modernizers and reformers, under enormous personal and physical threat during the period, who began their own long march from around the time

---

[138] Weiner, *Rape and Plunder*, 146.
[139] Interview with Maurice Hayes, Belfast, 26 November 2012.
[140] Interview with Jackie Redpath, Belfast, 19 February 2013.
[141] Henry Patterson, *Class Conflict and Sectarianism: The Protestant Working Class and the Belfast Labour Movement 1868–1920* (Belfast: Blackstaff Press, 1980), 144.
[142] Quoted in *Irish Times*, 12 July 1979, 10.

of O'Neill's ascent.[143] Reflecting on why Protestant workers then handed power back to the same politicians they resented, one trade unionist believed 'They didn't know what to do with it. They didn't know they had that much strength.'[144] The secretary of the NILP, who also met with Loyalists at the time, recalled: 'Once the Executive resigned, it was over—they didn't *want* anything else. Whereas they were in a position to say "We want some sort of devolved administration that's going to be different, not Sunningdale but Sunningdale minus the Council of Ireland," or something like that. They asked for three Labour Exchanges in north Belfast. It was crazy.'[145]

With the strike's motor located in the way the Protestant working class had felt 'Catholics had been "winning" consistently since 1968',[146] the victorious momentum was invariably destructive, as captured—again—by Stewart Parker. Surveying the jubilation which greeted the destruction of Sunningdale, Peter in *Pentecost* despairs: 'You'd think they'd given birth, actually created something for once, instead of battering it to death, yet again, the only kind of victory they ever credit, holding the good old fort, stamping the life out of anything that starts to creep forward.'[147] The euphoria, relief even, expressed in Protestant areas on the fall of the Executive would appear to verify this, Glen Barr now stating that:

> People have lost sight of the fact that we did not beat the British government in 1974. I remember the night that we went home after the Executive collapsed. We left Hawthornden Road, Andy Tyrie and myself, driving through East Belfast and the people were lighting bonfires. As far as they were concerned it was a victory: Faulkner had collapsed. We were looking for new elections, which we didn't get.[148]

CONCLUSION

In the context of the Troubles a break of some importance had taken place, as a new breed of 'Loyalist'—now firmly separated by phraseology—traded

[143] Interview with Robert Ramsay, Cultra, 2 February 2012. The former Prime Minister himself believed that the riots of August 1969 irrevocably damaged relations between the communities. Eight people were killed and over 1,800 (mainly Catholic) families displaced across Northern Ireland, leading O'Neill to mournfully accept that all he and his supporters had worked for 'was then lying in the gutter . . . it is sad that my policies were not more widely supported.' Letter to Robert Porter, 14 March 1971. Sir Robert Porter Papers.
[144] Interview with Joe Law, Belfast, 26 June 2013.
[145] Interview with Douglas McIldoon, Belfast, 27 January 2012.
[146] David W. Miller, *Queen's Rebels: Ulster Loyalism in Historical Perspective* (Dublin: University College Dublin Press, 2007; 1st edition 1978), 163.
[147] Parker, *Pentecost*, in *Three Plays*, 199.
[148] *Irish Times*, 3 June 1974, 6; interview with Glen Barr, Derry, 28 November 2012.

barbs with mainstream Unionists. Up until this point, 'Unionist politicians would have spoken to us in smoky rooms, where you had to come in the back door and out the same way.'[149] It was disingenuous for representatives like Roy Beggs to retrospectively pretend that the strike 'could have worked without them (Loyalist paramilitaries)'.[150] Yet the condemnation was understood in class terms; their 'middle class, fur-coat vote wouldn't allow it'.[151] Beggs was one of many to begin distancing themselves from young Protestant working-class males entering the jails in numbers, some to the mentorship of Gusty Spence. Though it is worth noting that moderate Unionists were 'quite unwilling to share a platform' with paramilitaries who had 'stated that <u>no politician is to be trusted</u>',[152] on the other hand Loyalist ex-prisoners assert that high levels of apathy in the constituency derive in part from the way Unionist leaders, having roused them to action, 'spoke with forked tongues' at this time, condemning them 'as quickly as anyone else'.[153] Those paramilitaries who do vote tend to cast their ballots in favour of Paisley's Democratic Unionist Party (the DUP has returned the favour by running the odd UDA affiliate as an electoral candidate), while those Loyalists who have set up parties discovered that 'Unionist voters simply don't vote for paramilitaries'.[154]

Just over a decade after the UWC strike, Stewart Parker's *Northern Star* was first staged at the Lyric Theatre. A quintessentially Protestant exercise, it seemed emblematic of his 'liberality' with ideas as well as a 'willingness to forgive characters and their crimes'.[155] Parodying seven styles of Irish theatre from the eighteenth century to the present day, Parker explores the 'cruel joke' history has played on the north, turning 'the dream of unity of the men of no property regardless of religion, into a force which was instrumental in creating the lines of division between the two tribes'.[156] 'We never made a nation,' despairs Henry Joy McCracken. 'Our brainchild. Stillborn. Our own fault. We botched the birth.'[157] McCracken was seen to have 'fumbled the birth of the new Ireland by allowing his Jacobin uprising to become "a Catholic riot"'. History itself would yield 'from the

[149] Interview with Billy McQuiston (ex-UDA volunteer), Belfast, 14 June 2013.

[150] Quoted in Susan McKay, *Northern Protestants: An Unsettled People* (Belfast: Blackstaff Press, 2000), 10.

[151] Interview with Billy McQuiston, Belfast, 14 June 2013.

[152] Robert Porter, Letter to Stanley Morgan (Ulster Vanguard Secretary), 17 March 1972. Sir Robert Porter Papers. Original emphasis.

[153] Interview with Bobby Niblock, Belfast, 30 August 2012.

[154] *Irish News*, 2 May 2014, 12; interview with Hugh Smyth, Belfast, 15 February 2012.

[155] Robert Johnstone, 'Playing for Ireland', *Honest Ulsterman*, No. 86 (Spring/Summer 1989), 64.

[156] Fintan O'Toole, 'Northern Star', in *Critical Moments: Fintan O'Toole on Modern Irish Theatre*, ed. Julia Furay and Redmond O'Hanlon (Dublin: Carysfort Press, 2003), 32.

[157] Parker, *Northern Star*, in *Three Plays*, 75.

same womb, terrible monsters'.[158] This raised 'the crucial question for
Stewart. You can explain the resort to violence but you really can't
condone it because it never, ever worked. It perpetuated those horrific
vendettas'.[159] Like Gusty Spence, who also knew he had reintroduced a
certain militancy to northern Protestant politics, Parker's McCracken
realizes the consequences of his movement shortly before his fate at the
end of a rope:

> MCCRACKEN: So all we've done, you see, is to reinforce the locks, cram
> the cells fuller than ever of mangled bodies crawling round in their
> own shite and lunacy, and the cycle just goes on, playing out the
> same demented comedy of terrors from generation to generation,
> trapped in the same malignant legend.[160]

When the play was performed in Belfast's First Presbyterian Hall on the
bicentenary of the 1798 rebellion, a new dispensation appeared within
reach. The production's director Stephen Rea chose the venue as an ideal
'way of using a location to highlight historical ironies'. Not only was the
church aesthetically beautiful and historically potent—containing a secret
room used to hide priests, constructed during the Rebellion era—it was
'meant for theatre. It's meant for debate because the Presbyterian Church
was, as the elders told me, not a sacred building. It was where they
discussed.' But Rea also seemed unwilling to entertain *Northern Star*'s
ambiguity: that the Rebellion itself may have contributed to the two
hundred years of sectarian division and bloodshed which followed. 'I
know he says "We botched the birth" and all that. I'm not standing up
for violence, but you have to look at where it comes from—and everyone's
implicated.'[161] The play, and Rea's own work, is larger than this. With the
exception of Brendan Behan, the writers whose styles are imitated in
Northern Star were almost uniformly Protestant—Beckett, O'Casey,
Shaw, Farquhar, and Synge—and so through sheer virtuosic plurality—
and the individual historical example of figures such as Jemmy Hope, a
proxy Sam Thompson—'the best way to escape from the prison of the past
lies in celebrating art and reason rather than mythologizing violence'.[162]

A more capacious understanding of the varying attitudes within
Ulster Protestantism during historical events presented in the likes of
Pentecost may also try the locks, though this also requires a magnanimity

[158] O'Toole, 'Northern Star', 33.
[159] Interview with Lynne Parker, Dublin, 24 March 2012.
[160] Parker, *Northern Star*, in *Three Plays*, 65.
[161] Interview with Stephen Rea, Dublin, 14 August 2014.
[162] *Irish Times*, 7 November 1998, 49; Michael Billington, 'He Had a Dream', *The Guardian*—G2, 18 November 1998, 12.

within the community itself. NILP stalwarts agree that had Unionism displayed even a 'modicum of generosity' during the 'lost opportunity' of the 1960s, the ferocity of the violence from 1969 onwards might have been averted.[163]

> PETER: Can you not see, this whole tribe, so-called Protestants ... all that endless mindless marching, they've been marching away with the lambegs blattering and the banners flying straight up a dead-end one-way blind alley, self-destroying, the head's eating the tail now, it's a lingering tribal suicide going on out there, there was no need for any of it, they held all the cards, they only needed to be marginally generous.[164]

Though some fellow Ulster Protestant writers disapproved of 'a fashion then to be ashamed of your own tribe',[165] there is a self-examination going on which was impossible to imagine taking place through or between Unionist politicians, whose careers would be ended by expressing such sentiments.

Rea had played Lenny in the original production of *Pentecost*, always drawing on Brian Friel's aphorism that the Irish problem was 'all about language'. Ulster Unionists and Loyalists, in this view, have subsequently fixed to 'create a language for themselves which is not negotiable. It has to mean that one thing.' This is not outlandish and is connected, some Protestants feel, to the literalism of the group; of wanting 'every "I" dotted and every "t" crossed before moving to the next stage', in contrast to the suppler workings of Irish Republicans.[166] Touring *Pentecost* around Ireland, north and south, Rea observed:

> the impact it had—a feeling that some truth was being told. It started with Parker really. There's *Pentecost*, there's [Seamus Heaney's] the *Cure at Troy* [1991], but *Pentecost* precedes the *Cure at Troy*, and it's only in that small microcosm and room where there are these people that find it impossible to live, who end up determining to be reconciled. I believe those plays, even though the writers might not have intended them as interventions, become interventions. This filters into people's consciousness. It's not that suddenly everybody says 'Ah Jesus, come on boys', throw down their weapons and run and embrace, it doesn't happen like that. But it can adjust something in the ether. At the time when *Pentecost* was set you couldn't imagine a future. All you could imagine was people huddling in their houses, hiding from the very frightening violence that was outside.[167]

---

[163] Brett, *Long Shadows*, 153.   [164] Parker, *Pentecost*, in *Three Plays*, 184.
[165] Interview with Maurice Leitch, London, 31 July 2015.
[166] The Reverend David Cooper, quoted in Graham Spencer, *Protestant Identity and Peace in Northern Ireland* (Basingstoke: Palgrave Macmillan, 2012), 90.
[167] Interview with Stephen Rea, Dublin, 14 August 2014.

In the year of the Enniskillen bombing and the ongoing fallout from the 1985 Anglo-Irish Agreement, the essence of *Pentecost* was its imagining of some kind of reconciliation when none appeared in sight. The play was again revived in the autumn of 2014 at Belfast's Lyric Theatre, its themes of intransigence within Protestant politics as pertinent as ever. Aware that drama is one of the hardest of art forms, Parker probably needed 'a better dramaturge' to develop his material.[168] His at-times dazzling intellectualism, offensively seen as 'non-working-class', does not always win the crowd, but he remains one of the most significant of Northern dramatists for his 'broad vision' and saying 'things about Ulster which had not been said before'.[169] In what is commonly viewed as Parker's finest play, misgivings almost always centre on *Pentecost*'s ending. Lamenting its 'evangelical' aura, Fintan O'Toole found the final scene's 'leap beyond realism into some kind of metaphor of transcendence' lacked credibility.[170] The *agape* of this sequence, beginning with Peter telling the story of going with a university friend to dump a stash of LSD into the Silent Valley reservoir—Loyalists reach the installation before them (as they did in 1969) to blow it up, so Belfast is 'dry' rather than high—fuses a sanguine 1960s spirit with biblical verse in a way only a radical East Belfast Protestant could manage. Past history's bloody crossroads, Marian has reached a settlement with Lily and her ghostly rage, allowing for the final cleansing vision of nude, singing nuns on an Irish beach who 'are experiencing their sex'. Pleading to live in the present and move away from the perpetual blaming of the other for all grievance, Marian requests that the dead—both innocent and malevolent—cease being 'our masters', echoing Parker's own realization that the arts were indispensable in subverting an ideological 'deathwish'.[171]

---

[168] Interview with Jimmy Fay, Belfast, 25 November 2014.

[169] John Keyes, 'Theatre Days', *Fortnight*, No. 388 (September 2000), 59. A well-reviewed *Pentecost* production by Tinderbox Theatre Company had an audience of only eleven people at one performance in Whiterock, West Belfast. *Fortnight*, No. 334 (December 1994), 44.

[170] Fintan O'Toole, 'Pentecost', in *Critical Moments*, 60–1; Richtarik, *Parker*, 320–7. O'Toole concurred with the consensus that *Pentecost* was a major work after seeing Lynne Parker's 1995 production (*Irish Times*, 31 October 1995, 10).

[171] Parker, *Pentecost*, in *Three Plays*, 200–1, 203, 208; Stewart Parker, '*Dramatis Personae*: John Malone Memorial Lecture', in *Dramatis Personae*, 27.

5

Ron Hutchinson, Graham Reid,
and the Hard Eighties

Those happier decades we were dominant,
but now that mastery has flaked away,
those trades and crafts which fed us have grown scant;
too many waken to a workless day.

> John Hewitt, 'A Little People' (1986)

We were never a Unionist family. I used to resent the idea that
because you were a Protestant, people assumed you were ok. We
never benefited from that because we were never part of that
bandwagon.

> Graham Reid (Interview with the author, May 2012)

The fortunes of the Lyric Theatre began to change when Leon Rubin took
over as artistic director in 1981. Hitherto the Yeatsian preserve of its
founder Mary O'Malley, the movement afforded Stewart Parker, whose
relations with the company had long been strained, the opportunity of a
fresh start. In November 1982 the Lyric mounted a production of his
Kingdom Come and shortly after Rubin commissioned Parker's *Northern
Star*. The theatre had a new director by the time it was staged two years
later, with Patrick Sandford more than happy to proceed with the
'McCracken play'.[1] This also had implications for Parker's friend Graham
Reid (Fig. 5.1), who had a 'a very unsatisfactory brief encounter' with
Mary O'Malley, swiftly understanding that her concept of a national
theatre ('Hail Mary, full of Yeats') did not include working-class Protest-
ants. Reid still chafes at the memory of the Lyric's literary advisor John
Boyd keeping Parker, Bill Morrison (1940–2011), and himself 'out of the
Lyric', encapsulated by an incident where Boyd read one of his scripts and
informed him that the play would 'not be good enough for the Abbey

---

[1] Marilynn Richtarik, 'Living in Interesting Times: Stewart Parker's *Northern Star*', in
John P. Harrington and Elizabeth J. Mitchell (eds), *Politics and Performance in Contemporary
Northern Ireland* (Amherst: University of Massachusetts Press, 1999), 17.

Fig. 5.1. Photo of Graham Reid.

Note: Author's own

Theatre—it's not good enough for the Lyric'.[2] 'Looking back', Reid told the *Irish Times*, 'the Lyric's constant rejections did me a favour because they sent me into the arms of the Abbey, where I learned my craft.'[3] Reid's *The Death of Humpty Dumpty*, featuring Colm Meaney and a young Liam Neeson, debuted on the Peacock stage of the Abbey in September 1979, transferring to the main stage three months later.[4]

In the decade which followed it was observed that the 'powerful pull of television and the lack of a really top-class local theatre offering plays all the year round inevitably draws Northern writers out of the theatre and away',[5] a condition met by Reid and Ron Hutchinson (Fig. 5.2), who left to work in England—the former settling in London, the latter eventually

---

[2] Interview with Graham Reid, London, 17 May 2012.

[3] Quoted in *Irish Times*, 29 August 1995, 10. Boyd's worst habit was favouring his own work. When choosing scripts for production, 'It helped if it was written by somebody called John Boyd, or possibly Sean O'Casey, with whom he would mention in the same breath as John Boyd' (interview with Patrick Sandford, London, 13 October 2015).

[4] See Lionel Pilkington, 'Violence and Identity in Northern Ireland: Graham Reid's *The Death of Humpty Dumpty*', *Modern Drama*, Vol. 33, No. 1 (Spring 1990), 15–29.

[5] Fergus Linehan, 'Wanted: A New Generation of First-Rate Dramatists', *Irish Times*, 24 September 1988, 22.

Fig. 5.2. Photo of Ron Hutchinson.

Note: Permission of Ron Hutchinson

in the United States. Both therefore began their careers outside Ulster, with Reid at the Abbey and Hutchinson a Royal Court writer. Hutchinson's subsequent Hollywood experience rendered him—as he once put it—'a lucky hooker with posh clients', but even when adapting something as exotic as Mikhail Bulgakov's *Flight* for the National Theatre in 1998, he seemed to allude to some kind of eventual return: 'I can understand why Bulgakov's white Russians eventually chose to go home rather than live in exile. The homeland exerts a powerful pull.'[6]

---

[6] Quoted in *The Guardian—G2*, 8 January 1997, 14. See Mikhail Bulgakov, *Flight* (adapted by Ron Hutchinson) (London: Nick Hern Books, 1998). A recent Hutchinson adaptation was *The Captain of Köpenick*, which ran at the National Theatre at the start of 2013.

Politically, Northern Ireland experienced a light influx of enlightened Tory 'Wets', including James Prior, as Secretaries of State during the 1980s, banished for being on the wrong side of the prevailing Thatcherite ideology. Prior remembered the Official Unionists in thrall to the integrationism of Enoch Powell, almost always blaming the British government and Northern Ireland Office, 'who they hated and regarded as a kind of den of serpents. They were very anti-English at the time.'[7] While not an economic 'Wet', Dublin-born Grey Gowrie was a notable member of Prior's NIO coterie and possessed a politico-cultural understanding the Prime Minister did not share, trying to convey to her the differences between Ireland and England: 'I recognized through the conversation that this was somebody to whom the concept of cultural politics simply did not exist. It wasn't a case of being difficult or obdurate or stupid: it wasn't there. It was a real blank in her.'[8] One of the ironies of the eulogies paid by Unionist politicians to Margaret Thatcher in April 2013, aside from the viciousness of their opposition to the 1985 Anglo-Irish Agreement, was that the policies of Thatcherism actually exacerbated the effects of the 1979–81 recession on Northern Ireland. This had begun with the second oil price shock as unemployment rose, but the hangover of unemployment from the Thatcher years continues to burden Belfast as it does the north of England, Scotland, and Wales.[9]

As in other times of political and economic duress there was a correlation between strife and creativity. Gerald Dawe drew a line between the economic recession and the burgeoning literary scene, with it being 'much easier to get a poem published in Ireland in the '80s than it was to find a job. Indeed, there must be some kind of curious link between an economic recession and the number of people who started to write.'[10] This was also felt in the theatre with both Hutchinson and Reid included in the wave of writers acclaimed by the *Guardian*'s theatre critic as part of 'a substantial Irish revival'. By the start of 1986 Michael Billington felt confident enough to declare that 'out of a sense of history, social turmoil and enlightened subsidy, have come the stirrings of what looks like a theatrical re-birth'.[11] The emergence of a new crest of dramatists contrasted

[7] Telephone interview with Lord James Prior, 6 June 2012.

[8] Interview with Lord Grey Gowrie, London, 19 September 2012.

[9] North Belfast Westminster MP Nigel Dodds described Thatcher as 'truly a great patriot, a great unionist, a great Briton' (quoted in *Belfast Telegraph*, 11 April 2013, 5); Frank Gaffikin and Mike Morrissey, *Northern Ireland: The Thatcher Years* (London: Zed Books, 1990), 43, 74, 205.

[10] Gerald Dawe, *False Faces: Poetry, Politics and Place* (Belfast: Lagan Press, 1994), 83, 85.

[11] Michael Billington, 'The Irish Fringe Takes Centre Stage', *The Guardian*, 8 February 1986, 13. This also coincided with Brian Friel, Tom Murphy, Thomas Kilroy, and Stewart

starkly with the political atmosphere. The culmination of the prison protest inside Long Kesh arrived with the second Hunger Strike of 1981, when seven Provisional IRA and three INLA prisoners starved themselves to death, decimating the moderate, non-sectarian political networks which had been developing. From 1977 to 1981 Belfast City Council had witnessed an unofficial caucus of left-leaning Unionists, the SDLP, the Workers' Party, and Independents casting aside their constitutional differences to combine on working-class issues relating to housing, education, and health. However, in the municipal elections which took place during the month of Bobby Sands's death, this group was sundered and Ian Paisley's Democratic Unionist Party marginally outpolled the Official Unionist Party for the first time province-wide (though this was in terms of the popular vote and only by 0.1 per cent, meaning that the UUP still retained more seats).[12]

It would also be unwise for the 1980s Irish theatrical scene, north and south, to be sentimentalized as a 'golden era'.[13] After the successes of Leon Rubin and Patrick Sandford, Richard Digby-Day's rapid exhaustion of the budget meant that by late 1986 the Lyric Theatre had fallen into serious debt and had to shut for a period of five months to avoid bankruptcy as local actors and practitioners struggled to find work.[14] The Board of Trustees lost John Hewitt in June 1987, but the remaining cadre—Thomas Kinsella, O'Malley, her husband Pearse, and spokesman Ciaran McKeown—were thought to be outstaying their welcome, as well as 'chronically geared to not doing the one necessary deed, of employing a really talented Artistic Director and giving him/her a free hand'.[15] Playwrights were faced with the familiar prospect of exile, a route taken by Hutchinson who found a home (via the Royal Shakespeare Company) in the Royal Court—'Mecca for troublemakers, for those who can't conceive of art that isn't in some way political'[16]—then under the directorship of Max Stafford-Clark. Famously, 'the Court' incubated a siege mentality with a troupe memorably framed as 'entrenched and beleaguered by what we see as an often

---

Parker producing key works, as well as the northerly emergence of Martin Lynch, Anne Devlin, Christina Reid, and Charabanc (see Chapter 7).

[12] Interview with Hugh Smyth, Belfast, 15 February 2012. See Andrew Pollak, 'Graveyard of the "middle ground"', *Irish Times*, 29 December 1981, 5.

[13] Interview with Martin Lynch, Belfast, 20 March 2014.

[14] Interview with Patrick Sandford, London, 13 October 2015; *Irish Times*, 19 March 1987, 10. The Board removed Digby-Day and cancelled the last two productions of the season in December 1986.

[15] James Simmons, 'Belfast Drama: The Year Until June', *The Linen Hall Review*, Vol. 5, No. 2 (Summer 1988), 14–15.

[16] Ron Hutchinson, 'A Walk up the Alley', in *Rat in the Skull* (London: Methuen, 1995; 1st edition 1984), n.pag.

hostile economic and critical world beyond Sloane Square',[17] and its impact on Hutchinson was matched only by the medium of television. Thus Hutchinson's best-known play *Rat in the Skull* (1984) was first performed in London, not Northern Ireland, and when the play received its Belfast premiere at the Stranmillis Theatre in March 1987 it was 'left to a group of unemployed actors surviving on the dole to put it together'.[18] Generally the way an impressive set of writers emerged during the 1980s, or delivered what many regarded as their best work, was the result of artistry engaging with social and political tumult, in spite of the theatrical scene in Ulster, not because of it.

TELEVISION AND INFLUENCE

In the context of Northern Ireland the influence of television ensured that the 1980s was 'the decade when plays became the thing. Before that it was the poets.'[19] Though this was to change drastically, the emphasis on gritty, naturalistic television drama exemplified by the BBC's *Play for Today* series ensured that the proportion of the British population actually watching drama was 'greater than in any previous age'.[20] Through a paternalistic kind of public service broadcasting, other television drama pioneers recalled an era 'filled with men and women who mostly cared about the programmes rather than the dividend'.[21] Most drama from the corporation in Northern Ireland, radio and television, was at this time produced for network consumption—as opposed to regional transmission—and thus tended to be of quite a high standard. For numerous reasons it was more expensive to make than in the rest of the UK, but this was considered a price worth paying for the insight the work itself could lend to audiences within and beyond Northern Ireland.[22] This was doubly ironic as there had hitherto been a remarkable avoidance of the Troubles by British broadcasters, as if 'it was all happening in another world, hundreds of miles away' (when war broke out in the Falkland Islands in 1982, it appeared closer to British

---

[17] Max Stafford-Clark, quoted in *London Times*, 22 August 1985, 13.

[18] Helen Shaw, 'Hard Times at the Lyric', *Irish Times*, 19 March 1987, 10. This was Actors Wilde, comprised of director Roy Heaybeard and actors John Hewitt (not to be confused with the poet), B. J. Hogg, and Eoin O'Callaghan.

[19] Interview with Christina Reid, Belfast, 24 June 2013.

[20] John Carey, *The Intellectuals and the Masses: Pride and Prejudice among the Literary Intelligentsia, 1880–1939* (London: Faber and Faber, 1992), 214.

[21] Dennis Potter, 'The James MacTaggart Memorial Lecture', Edinburgh Film Festival (1993), in *Seeing the Blossom* (London: Faber and Faber, 1994), 55.

[22] Rex Cathcart, *The Most Contrary Region: The BBC in Northern Ireland 1924–1984* (Belfast: Blackstaff Press, 1984), 261–2.

viewers than Northern Ireland on television).[23] BBC Northern Ireland's drama was a natural corrective to this.

UK-wide, Graham Reid was placed in a line of writers including Jim Allen, Alan Bleasdale, and Trevor Griffiths, who illustrated 'the capacity of naturalism to show social conflict, highlight inner contradictions and adopt a resolutely critical stance toward the status quo'.[24] More specifically Reid prospered from a particular set of circumstances at the BBC when a brand of 'risk-taker' producers including Neil Zeiger, Ken Trodd, Chris Parr, David Rose, and Innes Lloyd fought the necessary battles with the Head of Programmes—in Northern Ireland's case Cecil Taylor—with the upshot that 'the directors and the writers were allowed to get on with it'. Taylor had decided that 'he wanted to leave his mark', and that the best way to achieve this was through television drama.[25] Kenneth Branagh, who made his screen debut in Graham Reid's *Billy* plays (1982–4), recognized that they were in tune with BBC Northern Ireland 'taking pride in this new drive to establish a first-class drama output'.[26] Ron Hutchinson also embraced the *Play for Today* platform, the tone of *The Last Window Cleaner* (1979) anticipating the black humour of Martin McDonagh (a resemblance noted by actors who performed the work of both writers).[27] Interspersed with scenes of fantasy, D. C. Denis Deacey (Ken Campbell) is guided by his British Army handler, Captain Wigmore (John Bird)—full of useful observations such as 'If you find you're not being shot at, you're in a safe area; if you are, you're not'—and takes a guest house room in order to keep an eye on Sammy (Joe McPartland), ostensibly a window cleaner but suspected of paramilitary ties.

Deacey's predecessor is West Indian Leroy (Norman Beaton), who explains why Sammy must be spied on: 'The window cleaning's only a front, Deacey. Wise up, man. No money in that in this town—no windows in this town!' The Army are unable to fathom how Sammy lives in a reasonably affluent area of Belfast when the continuous bombing campaign must have deprived him of the windows he cleans for a living. Leroy has his own unique take on the Troubles which he explains to Deacey on a drive around the city:

> You gotta speak two languages in this place . . . three: English, Irish, and Rubbish. Wise up. Protection means getting bombed. I mean this is the

[23] John Bull, *New British Political Dramatists* (London: Macmillan, 1984), 203–4.
[24] Elmer Andrews, 'Graham Reid's Ties of Blood: A Failure of Realism', *Honest Ulsterman*, No. 83 (Summer 1987), 73.
[25] Interview with Graham Reid, London, 17 May 2012.
[26] Kenneth Branagh, *Beginning* (London: Pan Books, 1990), 81.
[27] See the comments of Mick Lally in *Irish Times*, 23 July 1998, 13.

place where the war didn't start 'til they sent in the peace-keeping force. Whatever you read in the papers, man, this is a *pre-post-colonial* situation. And whatever you hear on that magic box: they ain't gonna keep them crazies in the cage any longer than they have to.

The Last Window Cleaner's final line—'It might look like Birmingham: but it ain't,'[28] spoken by Deacey as he looks out onto a suburban Belfast street, was appropriate for the year in which the Conservative leader who declared that Northern Ireland was 'part of the United Kingdom—as much as my constituency is' became Prime Minister.[29] James Prior asserts that this often-misquoted remark illustrated 'how little she [Margaret Thatcher] actually understood the place',[30] but Deacey's quip also reflected the bemusement of many in a British audience towards a decade of conflict. Hutchinson sees the blackness of the humour as quintessentially Northern Irish but also part of 'the bigger Irish tradition. God forbid I'm putting myself up against those guys, but Beckett is a knockout comedian; he's a stand-up. Joyce: you read *Ulysses*, there's a laugh on every page. It's just hilariously funny—and you know that's our tradition as well.'[31]

Both Reid and Hutchinson cite Shaw and O'Casey as influences, an Irish dimension to their identities as northern Protestants. In Reid's case, because of his enthusiasm for O'Casey and Shaw, 'the Abbey Theatre meant a hell of a lot to me',[32] while for Hutchinson this is based even more than the plays on personal fragments and 'the quiddity of biographical information', as his recollection of a chance meeting with a milkman in the coastal English town of Torquay makes clear. The milkman related to Hutchinson the story of how he used to deliver his bottles to an affluent part of the town where, through an ajar window, he would 'hear a voice and then a hand would wave at me. I never saw the guy but I saw the hand, and I'd have a little conversation with this Dublin accent. Then I didn't see it anymore, and I asked somebody who it was and they said it was quite a well-known writer from Dublin who lived there.' This was Sean O'Casey, who had retired to the town with his wife and would pass away there shortly after. Hutchinson viewed this as a direct line to theatrical legend: 'like a link in some way to more than the plays almost; that image of O'Casey's good humour in bothering to acknowledge the milkman

[28] Ron Hutchinson, *The Last Window Cleaner* (Belfast: BBC Northern Ireland, 1979). Author's transcriptions.
[29] Quoted in Paul Bew, Henry Patterson, and Paul Teague, *Between War and Peace: The Political Future of Northern Ireland* (London: Lawrence & Wishart, 1997), 52.
[30] Telephone interview with Lord James Prior, 6 June 2012.
[31] Interview with Ron Hutchinson, Belfast, 2 August 2012.
[32] Interview with Graham Reid, London, 17 May 2012.

after a sleepless night. That's *my* O'Casey story—that he bothered to say good morning to the milkman on his rounds.'[33]

THE *BILLY* PLAYS (1982–4)

Graham Reid held a number of different jobs including as a nurse orderly, machinist at James Mackie & Sons ('Mackie's'), a bin man, and schoolteacher—in between periods on the dole—before finally becoming a full-time writer in 1980. A memorable incident on his Mackie's night shift confirmed that Sam Thompson was not the only Protestant proletarian in Belfast hankering for Harold Wilson's election victory in October 1964. Twinning it to the liberation of toilet breaks, the excitement grew 'as the Labour Party made further and further gains. Spilling out onto the Springfield Road the following morning we, the workers, the victors, were jubilant. Thousands of men, who wouldn't dream of voting anything other than Unionist in Northern Ireland, were celebrating, if only with inward joy, the victory of the Labour Party.'[34] Like almost all the writers considered in this book, Reid vouches for a Labour background: 'My father was always a Labour man and it was only with O'Neill and his "Crossroads" election and supporting Brian Faulkner (twice) when I voted Unionist. Most times I didn't vote at all.'[35]

More generally part of Reid's ability to translate working-class Protestant life onto the stage stems from lived experience on the Shankill Road, where he did 'vigilante duty' with the UDA's Tommy Lyttle,[36] and then later during his time as a teacher. Leaving behind manual work, he returned to education to gain a degree in Education from Stranmillis College, which helped to land him his first teaching job in Bangor, County Down. Affirming that his principal ambition was to be an historian, Reid recalled at the school:

---

[33] Interview with Ron Hutchinson, Belfast, 2 August 2012.
[34] Graham Reid, 'Comings and Goings', *Threshold*, No. 35 (Winter 1984/5), 22.
[35] Interview with Graham Reid, London, 17 May 2012.
[36] Tommy 'Tucker' Lyttle (1939–95) was the UDA's spokesman for fifteen years. Running the kind of routines with which he came into contact with Reid—he was also a machinist at Mackie's—Lyttle became a founder member of the UDA, participated in the 1974 UWC strike, and helped to found the New Ulster Political Research Group with Andy Tyrie and Glen Barr. Sentenced in 1991 for terrorist-related offences, he saw out his sentence as a conventional criminal after amassing a murky reputation during the UDA's evolution into 'a mafia-style criminal gang'. Widely believed to be a Special Branch informant, Lyttle died of a heart attack in a Donaghadee bar (*The Guardian*, 21 October 1995, 32).

this staff meeting where I was critical of the History syllabus. In the Third year the pupils had their subject choices—most of them dropped history because it was a reading subject, and most of them were not into reading—so they never got to the twentieth century or to Irish politics, ever. I complained about this, and the headmaster banged the table: 'No surrender! You'll never convince me there was fifty years of Unionist misrule!'[37]

Reid was struck by the 'visceral sectarianism; this idea we were teaching kids in this war-like situation who were not equipped to know what they were fighting for'. The scene of the headmaster rejecting Irish history was replicated verbatim in his play *The Hidden Curriculum* (1983).[38] Echoing Gusty Spence's questioning within the compounds of Long Kesh, Reid's pupils were unsure of what precisely as Protestants they were commemorating each year, and he felt personally responsible for their 'ignorance— the kids were out at night, some of them were rioting, some of them ended up in prisons, some of them became killers. And that hurt because you felt you were part of the problem. You weren't contributing to the solution as I saw it, which was education.'[39] The Head of the English department character would appear to be speaking on behalf of Reid when he says to his class, 'Some of you are in the Orange Order, I'm not. Does it not strike you as odd . . . that I should care more about your backgrounds than you do? (*Pause*) It is high time you all became a lot more aware of the world around you.'[40] There was naturally a social dimension to this, the play pinpointing how a middle-class system with middle-class professionals remains apart from their working-class pupils, a system continuingly perpetuated through Northern Ireland's grammar schools.

With the *Billy* plays, Reid was to make an important distinction between the largely non-sectarian 'hard man' profile and the paramilitaries who emerged from the mid-1960s. Billy Martin (the young Kenneth Branagh) is the eponymous figure but the central character is really his father Norman (James Ellis), a traditional Belfast 'hard man' whose 'answer to everything is his fists—that was his language'.[41] Reid's work recalls an older, oral remembrance of the city; a neglected period of social history crowded out by a legion of balaclavas. The morality of the plays is pre-Troubles, harking back to an earlier era of Belfast characters including Buck Alec, Stormy Weatherall, and Silver McKee. Though the profile

[37] Interview with Graham Reid, London, 17 May 2012.
[38] Graham Reid, *The Hidden Curriculum*, in *The Plays of Graham Reid* (Dublin: Co-op Books, 1982), 157–8.
[39] Interview with Graham Reid, London, 17 May 2012.
[40] Reid, *Hidden Curriculum*, 103.
[41] Interview with Graham Reid, London, 17 May 2012.

pre-dates 1969, this does not mean that the 'hard men' lacked their own political relevance. The case of Buck Alec is particularly instructive. A legendary figure who kept lions (obtained from Dublin and Belfast zoos, apparently named Roger, Sheila, and Joey) in his back garden,[42] Alec left for the United States in the 1920s to participate in Chicago's mob underworld, including as a bodyguard—it was claimed—to Al Capone. On his return in the latter part of the decade he was caught up in the upheaval of the time, especially in a society like Northern Ireland where those prone to violence will always be useful to those in positions of power. Alec had been involved in the 'A1' Ulster Special Constabulary ('A Specials'), and was later drafted into the reconstituted UVF in 1935 to 'promote a sectarian war'.[43] Alec became disillusioned with the Unionist politicians behind the group and at one stage threatened to take the information he had to the authorities. Desisting when he was reminded that the authorities were the same people behind the outfit, it was nonetheless a foreshadowing of a future generation of Loyalist paramilitaries who also resented being cajoled into action by their 'betters'.

Though the violence of the Troubles also moulded Reid, the earlier, domestic scenes of violence were more timeless, giving way to public discord, the kitchen to the street:

> Men used to be paid on the Thursday or Friday night, and we had four or five characters on the street who would get drink and they'd come home and you'd hear the window smashing either from the outside or the inside, you'd hear the shouts and roars, families screaming, kids crying, wives being battered, fights at the corner of the street. That was the world we grew up in and that's the world I set out to portray.[44]

Reid's sketch of the obstinate set of 'hard men' who populated his street included an ex-Royal Marine who would fight for half an hour straight with two other males, akin to the famous donnybrook between John Wayne and Victor McLaglen in John Ford's *The Quiet Man*. A sense of honour also characterized the duels and contrasted with the later Troubles, whereby 'they'd knock each other down and somebody would say, "That's enough, stop."'[45]

Reid maintains that 'throughout the first bloody years of the Troubles the hard men still existed', but 'the gunman did away with the hard men of Belfast really'. The *Billy* plays dramatize the clash of codes, with the

---

[42] See James Galway, *An Autobiography* (Bath: Chivers Press, 1978), 25.
[43] Gusty Spence, quoted in Roy Garland, *Gusty Spence* (Belfast: Blackstaff, 2001), 44–5.
[44] Speaking on *Arts Extra*, BBC Radio Ulster (broadcast 2 March 2009).
[45] Interview with Graham Reid, London, 17 May 2012.

archetypal Norman defying the paramilitaries ('To hell with the UDA'). In an early scene he approaches the UDA '*drilling half a dozen local teenage boys*', their sergeant John Fletcher (John Hewitt) looking on as 'NORMAN *continues to approach his troop. He walks straight on, scattering them. We see* JOHN FLETCHER's *reaction of impotent rage.*'[46] One English critic grasped the difference, noting that 'Neither Billy nor Norman have belonged to Protestant paramilitaries, though both are known as hard men.'[47] Like his father, Billy rejects paramilitarism, acknowledging that joining such a group relates to status within a community and a sense of power. He is challenged on this by the aforementioned UDA sergeant:

JOHN: You Martins all think you're hard men, don't you?

BILLY: That's right, and we don't have to dress up to prove it.[48]

Receiving rapturous reviews on its original broadcast, *Too Late to Talk to Billy* (1982) was rescreened on its thirtieth anniversary in February 2012, attracting a record audience share for BBC Northern Ireland.[49] Not everyone greeted the screening with enthusiasm, Malachi O'Doherty complaining of 'great flaws in the play' which rendered it 'clunky and inadequate'. His criticism stemmed from its attitude to violence and 'the basic principles that these characters were assumed to live by: chiefly the notion that a son who can't speak to a father who resorts to kicking him round the living room, is the one with the problem'.[50] The point— clunkily conveyed—was partially valid. The *Billy* plays did glamorize a certain kind of Belfast working-class life and macho culture where fighting defines male interactions, Billy telling his friend Ian (Colum Convey), who is being pestered by UDA man Fletcher, 'You don't gain anything trying to reason with the likes of him. You're better just lashing out and taking your chances.'[51]

---

[46] Graham Reid, *Too Late to Talk to Billy*, in *Billy: Three Plays for Television* (London: Faber and Faber, 1984), 18. Reid remembers one story of a giant hard man whose brother was assaulted on the Shankill Road confronting the attackers and it taking 'seven bullets to kill him, like killing Rasputin'.

[47] Hugh Herbert, 'Irish Ties', *The Guardian*, 22 February 1984, 13.

[48] Reid, *Too Late*, 41.

[49] Chris Dunkley called the play 'hugely powerful' and 'almost Learlike in the intensity and bleakness of its gaze' (*Financial Times*, 24 February 1982, 11); *Belfast Telegraph*, 7 February 2012, 8.

[50] Malachi O'Doherty, 'Sadly, it's Too Late to Take an Axe to the Billy Trilogy', *Belfast Telegraph*, 6 February 2012, 25.

[51] Reid, *Too Late*, 42. In the final play, *A Coming to Terms for Billy*, when Norman and Billy bond to fight two local UDA toughs, the former urges his son to 'never negotiate with the likes of them . . . Round here hard men are the ones who get the first dig in' (*Billy: Three Plays*, 163–8; original ellipsis).

However, aside from underestimating the universality of the plays, O'Doherty's assessment ignored the separation—as throughout Reid's work—of working-class Protestant life from Loyalist paramilitarism. Of all the series the first engaged most directly with political motifs, and the failure of the rest of the series to emulate its tough undertones was lamented by the playwright Gary Mitchell at a discussion of the plays held in Omagh in February 2009. The second and third plays Mitchell felt were particularly guilty of 'ignoring certain elements of the Protestant community' which had led to a 'disappointment' towards media portrayals from the same group.[52] In an interview printed days before the Anglo-Irish Agreement was signed, Reid remarked:

> There are people I was brought up with who would consider me possibly an even greater threat to them than a Catholic, because, in their eyes, I don't know what I am. But the *Billy* plays have been so popular, you see, particularly among Protestants who feel whether they agree with me or not, that the plays are honest and genuine and that they are being seen for what they are for once. Because Protestants always felt they had a bad press. These plays showed there were ordinary Protestants who are as much the victims of social deprivation and lack of opportunity as Catholics.[53]

Mitchell's criticism of the *Billy* plays is also countered by Loyalists who remembered viewing them in Long Kesh and finding them 'fantastic, so realistic'.[54]

In the final play of the initial trio, one of the Martin daughters, Maureen (Aine Gorman), insists 'we're not Irish . . . we're Protestants', and it is established right from the opening directions of the first. Zooming in on '*a street of small, two-up, two-down houses in the Donegall Road area of Belfast*',[55] the audience encounters a zone strongly associated with the Protestant working-class community. Initially this was reflected in a different first draft, 'an apocalyptic vision in which all the main characters were killed off', intended as a direct response to the Troubles. Reid appreciated the change to the 'much more domestic play', arguing that the *Billy* plays, and specifically the first, 'justified itself in terms of the drama, which didn't depend on having to take a position on Northern Ireland. For the audience they didn't have to think through the politics. It's a bit like America with Vietnam for a long time. You couldn't get anything on Vietnam done because people felt forced into a stance which

[52] *Arts Extra*, BBC Radio Ulster, 2 March 2009.
[53] Quoted in *The Guardian*, 12 November 1985, 11.
[54] Interview with Billy Hutchinson, Belfast, 12 November 2012.
[55] Reid, *Coming to Terms* and *Too Late*, in *Billy: Three Plays*, 152, 15. Original ellipsis.

they didn't feel comfortable with.'[56] *A Matter of Choice for Billy* (1983) was praised for 'moving his central characters on and developing others into unexpected relationships',[57] while the third, *A Coming to Terms for Billy* (1984), wrapped up the initial trilogy. On the denouement the *Guardian* critic assessed they were 'not overtly political plays, but studies of a family beset by almost overwhelming personal afflictions: loss, sickness, unemployment, drink, uncontrollable tempers and male pride'.[58] A television colleague credits Reid as 'a great writer of human weakness because he understands that people fail', though Reid himself concedes that the plays were essentially 'about my family'. While Norman was not based on his own father, Lorna (played by Brid Brennan) is 'very much my mother', a resemblance which provoked disagreements with his siblings.[59]

By far the most vital aspect of the *Billy* plays is that they universalized Belfast life at a time when the province was regarded as an international trouble spot. We are always aware of the Troubles, but they rest in the background so that the 'humour and warmth and passion in working-class family life was made accessible to everyone, and not just to people living in Ulster'.[60] While they were considered 'the most memorable and powerful account of life in working-class Protestant Belfast that British television has so far offered',[61] their characters and themes were recognizable in working-class cities of the UK and could easily have transferred to London, Liverpool, Glasgow, or Birmingham. In Gary Mitchell's view this universality was liable to omit the actualities of Protestant working-class life. Yet it was also the case that at the end of the original trio, with Billy and Norman reaching a moment of harmony, an Orange band can be heard approaching the street (*'really banging out* Derry's Walls *by this stage'*), the shot lingering 'to frame an image of what amounts to a defiant emergence of a loyalist identity that was submerged in earlier episodes'.[62]

Another dramatist who emerged in the 1980s from the opposing community wrote that the shared experience of television drama ensured 'We saw into each other's living rooms for the first time,' potentially

---

[56] Interview with Graham Reid, London, 17 May 2012.
[57] Peter Fiddick, 'Choice for Billy', *The Guardian*, 11 May 1983, 11.
[58] Hugh Herbert, 'Irish Ties', *The Guardian*, 22 February 1984, 13.
[59] Telephone interview with Robert Cooper, 15 August 2014; interview with Graham Reid, London, 17 May 2012.
[60] Branagh, *Beginning*, 97.
[61] Hugh Herbert, 'The Mask of Violence', *The Guardian*, 12 November 1985, 11.
[62] Reid, *Coming to Terms*, in *Billy: Three Plays*, 171; Lance Pettit, *Screening Ireland: Film and Television Representation* (Manchester: Manchester University Press, 2000), 235–6. The fourth televised play, *Lorna* (1987), produced by Danny Boyle, has her joining the Royal Ulster Constabulary and selling the family house against the wishes of Billy and Norman; its heroine reflects Ulster Loyalist isolation following the 1985 Anglo-Irish Agreement.

sowing the seeds for a common Northern Irish identity beyond division.[63] The *Billy* plays were also significant in elevating actors from Northern Ireland to a wider cultural awareness, becoming for the first time 'a saleable product',[64] and the series even came to be retrospectively praised by the surprising source of Ronan Bennett as one of the few dramas working-class Protestants had produced of quality because 'Reid's tone is driven, enraged and denunciatory, the voice polemical . . . it is an angry reaction to the prevalence of bigotry.'[65] Aside from misconstruing the tone, the Orange parade that closes the end of the original trilogy—which the family watch, but do not join—manages not to feel menacing, emblematic of the popularity of the plays across the sectarian divide in Belfast.

RATS IN THE SKULL

In the 1970s Ron Hutchinson worked at a number of jobs in Coventry including as a social security visiting officer, fraud investigator, and even in a zoo. Nonetheless the Troubles 'would have been pretty immediate, the Irish thing in Coventry; very, very immediate'.[66] The Hunger Strikes did not particularly impact ('noises off I think'), but as his theatrical career got into gear he was approached by Max Stafford-Clark, artistic director of the Royal Court, to write a new play. Hutchinson's response was ' "Max fuck off, I'm sick to death of the whole Irish thing," because I was getting my TV career going. I was writing thrillers for the TV, I was going to Hollywood for the first time. I wrote *Rat in the Skull* under protest in a way, to get it off my chest: to get rid of it.'[67] This accords with contemporaneous interviews Hutchinson gave where he conceded to being wary of re-entering a dialogue he had been 'trying to disengage from'.[68] Aware that London theatre audiences had with the exception of Stewart Parker's *Spokesong* (1975) only really been exposed to a view of Northern Ireland invariably sympathetic to Republicanism, Stafford-Clark saw the play as 'important because it articulated the voice of the Ulster Protestant',

[63] Anne Devlin, 'Writing the Troubles', in Brian Cliff and Éibhear Walshe (eds), *Representing the Troubles: Texts and Images, 1970–2000* (Dublin: Four Courts Press, 2004), 19.
[64] Interview with Patrick Sandford, London, 13 October 2015.
[65] Ronan Bennett, 'An Irish Answer', *The Guardian Weekend*, 16 July 1994, 55.
[66] Interview with Ron Hutchinson, Belfast, 2 August 2012.
[67] Hutchinson wrote television pieces for the BBC before moving to Hollywood in 1986. He worked for Home Box Office (HBO) and won an Emmy Award in 1989 for *Murderers Among Us: The Simon Wiesenthal Story*.
[68] Quoted in *London Times*, 1 September 1984, 20.

reflecting 'a piece of history that was being missed'. He remembered going to the Greater London Council (GLC), then under the tenure of Ken Livingstone, in an attempt to secure funding for the project. Encountering an anarchic environment, Stafford-Clark was kept waiting for over an hour to see the GLC's Arts Minister Tony Banks, whose assistant finally confirmed, '"Listen, don't worry—Royal Court, Irish play, it's absolutely fine, I guarantee you'll get £30,000." And we did, because we ticked the right boxes. If they'd known in fact that it was a play that gave a voice to the Ulster Protestant they would have fined us £30,000.'[69]

The more immediate Troubles backdrop to *Rat in the Skull* were the 'Supergrass' trials of late 1981 and early 1982, when members of para-military groups informed on fellow volunteers to the courts in return for reduced jail time (or immunity). With two hundred people convicted under the scheme, these had initially proved successful, especially in relation to Loyalists, but many of the original convictions were overturned on appeal when the testimony of informers was deemed unreliable.[70] Hutchinson confirmed that the play became 'yrs. truly arguing with himself, trying to square his Northern Irish Protestant heritage with a deeper sense of all-Irishness, setting his head against his heart, trying to find a position'.[71] Like many of the playwrights in this book, Hutchinson is always rowing with himself, symptomatic of a Protestant tendency towards self-examination and dissent (and contrasting, arguably, with the mainstream Republican view of the theatre as a didactic tool to advance politics). In something which gets to the heart of why a number of Protestant working-class dramatists have written for the theatre, Hutch-inson explained how:

> Everybody was pretty convinced we were the bad guys, you know that cliché—the Sash, the bowler hat, the stone-faced men, the Lambeg drum—and that kind of puzzled and pissed me off. So I think *Rat in the Skull* came out of me trying to work that out. Certainly I didn't go into it with any political axe to grind the way if I'd been Coventry Catholic Irish—it would have been 'Brits out' and 'Send the troops home in a box', all that. All easy: an identity already forged rather than one you have to piece together

[69] Stafford-Clark, quoted in Ruth Little and Emily McLaughlin, *The Royal Court Theatre Inside Out* (London: Oberon Books, 2007), 245–6.

[70] Mark Urban, *Big Boys' Rules: The Secret Struggle Against the IRA* (London: Faber and Faber, 1992), 134–7. A worker on the Loyalist prisoners' appeal saw the trials as a form of internment and 'knew for a fact that there were fellas there who weren't involved in the charges that were put against them' (interview with David Overend, Belfast, 28 April 2015). Sixty-seven of the 120 paramilitaries who appealed against the evidence of the ten major supergrasses were released on appeal.

[71] Ron Hutchinson, 'A Walk up the Alley', in *Rat*, n.pag.

for yourself. I had to piece that Protestant background together. I had to begin to understand what my family history was, and discovered this bifurcation between my dad from rural Protestant heartland, my mother from urban Protestant heartland, the city rats versus the farmers' sons. That was something to explore rather than just *arrive* at.[72]

Set in the interview room of a London police station and devoted to the extensive interrogation of an IRA man by an RUC detective, *Rat in the Skull* won plaudits when it opened at the Royal Court in August 1984. Its original cast included Brian Cox and Gary Oldman, the former receiving an Olivier Award for his performance as Nelson. The Irish premiere of the play took a further two years, courtesy of the actor and director Ronan Wilmott, to whom Hutchinson gave the Irish rights in a bar ('a drinker's deal, honour amongst boozers'), infuriating his agent. Wilmott staged *Rat* at the Project Arts Centre and called it 'the best play in 25 years about the dilemmas of Northern Ireland', as well as the first Troubles piece to show 'sympathy for the Protestant situation'. He also pointed out that the play's success had been critical, not commercial: English audiences, in 1984, 'didn't want to know'.[73] Stafford-Clark clarified that *Rat* was not a box-office winner but a 'Royal Court hit, full on Mondays and Saturdays',[74] and the acclaim retrospectively amused Hutchinson in light of the play's original gestation. 'Max used to take great glee in pointing out to me the first reader's report on *Rat* had said, "A very great disappointment: Hutchinson fails to understand the theatrical space!"' Neither were all critics unanimous in praise. The following year *Rat* transferred for a short season to the Public Theater in New York, where it was caught by another English critic who complained of a 'fulsomely wordy play' and 'over-writing'.[75]

A decade later, as the Royal Court's headquarters were being refurbished, the play was revived by artistic director Stephen Daldry as part of a series of Court 'Classics' at the Duke of York's on St Martin's Lane. This production had critics revert to their original effusive commendation,[76] though Mark Lawson qualified that 'the exact cultural situation to which those plays were a provocative response no longer exists'. The previous year's historic Republican and Loyalist ceasefires dictated that Hutchinson was required to rewrite parts of the original script, altered circumstances

---

[72] Interview with Ron Hutchinson, Belfast, 2 August 2012.
[73] Quoted in *Irish Times*, 9 May 1986, 12.
[74] Quoted in Little and McLaughlin, *Royal Court*, 246. Stafford-Clark also directed the Central Television film of the play broadcast three years later, with Cox, Oldman, Colum Convey, and Peter Jackson reprising their original roles.
[75] Martin Cropper, 'Rat in the Skull', *London Times*, 3 July 1985, 10.
[76] Nicholas de Jongh, 'Unlikely Winner in an Explosive Game of Cat and Mouse', *London Evening Standard*, 12 October 1995, 7.

which meant that a play which 'seemed to be about the impossibility of peace in Northern Ireland now appears to be about the ultimate hopelessness of the peace process'.[77] Aside from rewriting being a common theatrical procedure, such analysis rather misses the point. The essence of *Rat in the Skull*, as noted by Michael Billington in his original notice, is that 'whatever the constitutional position of Northern Ireland, Catholic and Protestant are far closer to each other than they are to the people on the UK mainland',[78] a condition which comes through most forcefully in a confrontation between RUC man Nelson and Detective Superintendent Harris towards the end:

> NELSON: (*Easily, taking his measure of Harris*) There's something about our brand of bully boy that irritates at the best of times, isn't there? Our brand of Brit, our brand of Prod that irritates the hell out of *you*. Seeing the worst of yourselves in us. Not comfortable to live with, are we? The clockwork Orangeman, bobbing behind tribal banners, our ranting reverends, ya-hooing down the steer, so damn confusingly loyal we'd blow up every last one of you if we had to—
>
> HARRIS: I don't really want to talk about your ranting reverends and your tribal banners, DI Nelson. I'm a Londoner mate, and I resent what's basically a quarrel between two brands of Irishman has done to my town, my life, both as a copper trying to do his job and as an ordinary fucking human being.[79]

Nelson echoes John Hewitt's poem 'The Colony' ('this is our country also, nowhere else; / and we shall not be outcast on the world') in stating: 'I *belong*. My people *belong* and we have been all the way back.'[80] But the similarities between Nelson and IRA man Roche are temperamental, even spiritual, making their perpetual animosity all the more tragic. Nelson realizes he is more in tune with the man he is meant to be breaking than those in the system he is loyal to: 'Me, in the parade with all the dead men, a little deader every day than I was the day before. The rat in my head shut up. And there's his smirking, knowing face. He knows exactly how I'll jump. He'll go along, in his parade, like me in mine.' With this recognition he assaults the captive Roche, aware his brutality will collapse the prosecution case and secure the IRA man's immediate release from the police station. The British detective is livid, accusing him of 'Turning on

---

[77] Mark Lawson, 'The Time Bandits', *The Guardian—G2*, 11 October 1995, 15.

[78] Michael Billington, 'Rat in the Skull', *The Guardian*, 5 September 1984, 9.

[79] Hutchinson, *Rat*, 42.

[80] John Hewitt, 'The Colony', in *The Collected Poems of John Hewitt*, ed. Frank Ormsby (Belfast: Blackstaff Press, 1991), 79; Hutchinson, *Rat*, 35.

your own', prompting Nelson's quietly defiant: 'He's my own.' Politically the final scene locates that the violence of the Troubles ultimately boils down to a clash between Catholics and Protestants, a simple but important acknowledgement resting outside the classic Republican narrative of the IRA versus 'the Brits'. It is accepted the British 'will leave' one day, and the proceeding dilemma reaches to the heart of both Hutchinson's most celebrated play and Ulster's division.

Colour starts to glow as the entire back wall becomes a montage of the hills and loughs and cliffs and narrow lanes and green glens of Ulster, the object of this passion, cockpit of this hate.

ROCHE: We've another date, him and me. When the Brits pull out. When the gloves come off.

NELSON: We've another date. Him and me.

ROCHE: You've seen nothing yet ... Down from the hills, out of the back streets with a chance to finish it. A chance to put it right for once and for all.

NELSON: (*echoing the words, with a different tone*) A chance to finish it. A chance to put it right once and for all.[81]

In the final, dream-like scene of the rewritten version,[82] Roche appears to return the favour. The retired Nelson is being set up for assassination, the mention of a few IRA volunteers 'ordered to bump off this RUC man', but Roche 'doesn't show' for the operation, sparing his interrogator's life. While Nelson has plenty of sectarian venom which he unleashes over the course of the play, the rat in the skull—though a disturbing image—suggested the potential for a new relationship. The rat will indeed 'gnaw away at fixed attitudes and hardened ideals', so while the conflict was perceived as an infinite cycle—'Never an end to it. A condition. Like the weather,'[83] in Nelson's words—shrewder critics detected an odd hope. As the 'two men become symbiotic aspects of an agreed identity, almost one split Irish identity',[84] an escape route, onto mutual ground, could be envisioned. Loyalist militants anticipated the above in calling for the 'crutches' of the British and Irish governments to be dispensed with, so that:

---

[81] Hutchinson, *Rat*, 47–9, 52–3. Original ellipsis.

[82] The original ending is slightly different, indicating that the IRA man intends to go through with the operation. We are left with Nelson's ambiguous 'Me and Rochey have a date ... maybe an Irish brand of chance,' as Roche walks away. *Rat in the Skull* (London: Methuen, 1984), 32. Original ellipsis.

[83] Billington, 'Rat', 9; Hutchinson, *Rat*, 46.

[84] Michael Coveney, 'Caught Red-Handed', *The Observer*, 15 October 1995, 13.

the two strongest groups could get out of their ditches and get up on to the bank, and then make decisions. That's why the Good Friday Agreement [1998] was very important, because the two groups had eventually arrived there, Sinn Féin and the DUP, and they couldn't go anywhere else. They had to start hating each other all over again after coming through the whole system—or learning to live with each other.[85]

Rat in the Skull also tapped into the continuous theme that disturbance was largely acceptable, and manageable, for the British state when it was happening in Northern Ireland, but not when it was transposed to the mainland. 'Whatever you might have been up to back in Belfast, it's more important that you get done for breaking a few shop windows in Oxford Street or disturbing the traffic in Horse Guards Parade,'[86] Nelson reminds Roche, and the play's audience, early on. It is a reservation Hutchinson himself has always shared, voicing just before the play's original run how 'It is not enough to be woken to the problem every few months by a big bang. We have a responsibility to nudge around the problem.'[87] Injecting this sentiment into *Rat in the Skull*, the apparent reality behind the Provisional IRA's reckoning that 'one bomb in London is worth ten in Belfast',[88] leads Nelson to conclude that meaningful exchange with his sworn foe is inevitable.

ORDINARY LIVES

The unrelenting anger Graham Reid holds on behalf of the victims of Troubles' violence, for those who stayed clear of paramilitary groups, was announced from the outset with his first play *The Death of Humpty Dumpty* (1979). Painting a hellish picture of pain and self-pity, George Sampson is shot by paramilitaries when he accidentally witnesses gun dumping. Paralysed from the neck down, the revelations of the infidelities of his yesteryear gradually dismantle his family unit.[89] Imelda Foley perceptively argues that Reid's work is 'informed by an unusual intimacy with both working and middle-class cultures', a quality he shared with St John Ervine who had also experienced life on both sides of the tracks. Reid was thus able to chart a 'nuclear, middle-class family' deteriorating in

[85] Interview with Andy Tyrie, Dundonald, 9 August 2012.
[86] Hutchinson, *Rat*, 13.
[87] Quoted in *London Times*, 1 September 1984, 20.
[88] Gary McGladdery, *The Provisional IRA in England: The Bombing Campaign 1973–1997* (Dublin: Irish Academic Press, 2006), 2–3.
[89] Graham Reid, *The Death of Humpty Dumpty* (Dublin: Co-op Books, 1980).

The Death of Humpty Dumpty. This 'disintegration of social units' is conveyed through 'recurring states of siege both literal and metaphorical, with paramilitaries as the wielders of power', a power which guarantees 'them literal freedom of movement while victims are trapped behind varieties of closed doors'.[90] In the *Billy* plays the Martin family does survive; it survives the shock of their mother dying and social pressures, thanks mainly to Lorna holding it together. But *The Closed Door* (1980), which Reid wrote in an experimental haze over a fortnight, is a bleaker exploration of the same vein as Stewart Parker's: of citizens trying to lead ordinary lives in a vicious atmosphere. A rarely examined, underrated work in Reid's oeuvre, *The Closed Door* presented 'an extraordinarily disturbing account of cowardice, of a man exposed by the violent circumstances of Ulster life to a severe test he was unable to meet'.[91] In its critical scene Victor hears his childhood friend Slabber—who is flash and full of tall tales, his opposite—outside his house trying to gain entry to escape the Loyalist paramilitaries he owes money to.

Slabber is subsequently murdered by men completely cognizant of their power and anonymity. When one of the Loyalists urges the other to 'get on with it before somebody calls the cops', the killer replies: 'There's probably a dozen pair of eyes on us right now, but they're all shit scared. Nobody's going to call the cops. They know better, we'd blow the whole fucking street up if they dared.' Victor is so wary of being entangled that he cannot even bring himself to call an ambulance. Talking to Slabber, bleeding to death on the other side of the door, he confesses:

> I hate you, Slabber, do you hear that? I've always stayed out of it . . . I dirtied myself the day they shot my foreman, Billy Gillespie. (*Pause*) He died without speaking a word . . . because he was one of the first men to join the UDR. Well, what bloody good did it do him? 'Join up, like a man.' What for? To end up like him? A hero sprawled out on a dirty, cold old concrete floor, his head blown to pieces. When they catch the one who did it he'll get twenty years. It'll be described as a 'brutal and senseless act'. But it wasn't brutal. It was quick and clean, and thorough. It wasn't senseless. He knew why he was doing it, so did Billy. (*Pause*) It's like a game you're all playing. A game for heroes.[92]

Reid has vacillated in his pronouncements on northern Protestant identity. At the time his single television drama *The Precious Blood*

[90] Imelda Foley, 'Theatre and the Conflict in Northern Ireland', *A Troubles Archive Essay* (Belfast: Arts Council of Northern Ireland, 2009), 13.
[91] Angela Wilcox, 'Briefings', *The Irish Review*, No. 1 (1986), 123.
[92] Graham Reid, *The Closed Door* (Dublin: Co-op Books, 1980), 30, 32–3.

(1996) was transmitted, he commented that 'Protestants, if they realise it, are in a fortunate position. Unlike Republicans, we can pick and choose from two cultures, the British and the Irish, and I think that, rather than have this mad search to discover a possibly mythical Protestant/Unionist/ Ulster identity, we should just enjoy cherry-picking.'[93] This has hardened in recent years as he has spent time living in England. While he will 'always acknowledge that my theatrical home is the Abbey Theatre' (echoing Thomas Carnduff and John Hewitt's concept of Dublin as a 'literary capital'),[94] Reid is now adamant that:

> Unlike John Hewitt I would say I'm British first, Ulster second. I was born in 1945, Ulster was solidly British then and has remained so. I knew a couple of people who were ambiguous because they'd been born when Ireland was one country, before partition, and I can totally understand that. Hewitt was of course pre-partition. I'm not sure if I'd go to the cross for it, but I would insist. A bit of bolshiness perhaps creeps in. I suppose I became a bit ballsy. I actually say to Brian Friel and Seamus Heaney: 'You know you're British because all your social experiences are British. Education system, social service system, the legal system—it's all British. You can't say you're Irish, not in your experience growing up as British,' which didn't go down well as you can imagine. I'm very, very proud being British because I believe in British history and the Empire and all the rest of it. Both my grandfathers fought on the Somme. All of that means a hell of a lot to me.[95]

Field Day Theatre Company founders confirm Reid's hostility to their project ('I think he called us Provos,'[96] remembers one director), and like Carnduff and novelist Maurice Leitch, a friend and fellow Ulster expat based in London, Reid becomes defensive of Ulster Protestant staples not because of his own personal activities but when such institutions are under attack. The violence against forces and symbols associated with Ulster Protestantism shook Reid's sense of Irishness, even when he worked there in the 1980s. During rehearsals for one of his plays in Dublin, Reid remembers a bomb attack on the border which resulted in the deaths of several policemen, and the subsequent feeling that 'there was nobody in that city who gave a shit. Nobody I could talk to, share the heart of the experience with.'[97]

---

[93] Quoted in *The Daily Telegraph*, 6 June 1996, 12.
[94] Interview with Graham Reid, London, 17 May 2012; John Hewitt, 'No Rootless Colonist' (1972), in *Ancestral Voices: The Selected Prose of John Hewitt*, ed. Tom Clyde (Belfast: Blackstaff Press, 1987), 150.
[95] Interview with Graham Reid, London, 17 May 2012.
[96] Interview with Tom Paulin, Oxford, 7 July 2015.
[97] Interview with Graham Reid, London, 17 May 2012.

The *Billy* plays had been interpreted as part of what Edna Longley called the 'cultural corridor'—'part of what we have abstracted from all the influences and made our own',[98] ultimately deriving from a pool of cultures. Reid either cut himself off from this or has evacuated a previous Irish connotation to Protestant identity. This is stranger still in light of Reid's recognition that, along with his friend Stewart Parker, Dublin was artistically a city 'where both of us Northern Protestants were welcomed, when "our own" didn't want to know us.'[99] His echoing of Parker's principal theme of 'ordinary people trying to live ordinary lives'[100] has an ongoing resonance in a 'Victims' voice outside the uneasy tent of the current political dispensation in Northern Ireland, problems Reid anticipated in the period immediately following the 1994 ceasefires. Some of Reid's political attitudes—along with an increasing conservatism—were reinforced by his physical distance from Northern Ireland. 'It is a terrible ordeal for those who have lost loved ones to see people running about in suits and briefcases, joining delegations to Stormont, pleading the case for peace,' Reid commented in 1995. He had conversed with people who 'feel betrayed by the ceasefire', under the impression that 'in this new atmosphere of goodwill to all, those who killed their loved ones will not be pursued'. It was surely little accident that he came to echo Margaret Thatcher's famous sentiment that 'In any society, crime remains crime, murder remains murder, whatever spin you put on it and no amount of peace-chasing will change that.'[101]

In a comprehensive essay on his *Ties of Blood* (1985) television plays, Elmer Andrews generally interprets Reid's work as a 'typical product' of an Ulster theatre tradition 'marked by a condescending treatment of sectarianism as antiquated prejudice and bigotry'. While personal life is bruising, 'the important thing is that these characters do not let their differences interfere with social duty or the maintenance of public order. This is the supreme virtue . . . the responsibility to preserve life.'[102] Though an intended critique, this identifies Reid's dedication to personal, character-driven as opposed to didactic political drama. 'You can have a politically correct line on the big issues, like nuclear war, yet in your domestic world, you can be an absolute disaster. We may never see a nuclear war, but we can destroy each other much more completely in our private lives,' Reid has said.[103] This also resembles his original desire with the *Billy* plays to

[98] James Hawthorne, quoted in Damian Smyth, 'Cultural Pluralism, or Plain Sectarianism?', *Fortnight*, No. 278 (November 1989), 29.

[99] Graham Reid, 'A Northern Star', *The Irish Review*, No. 7 (Autumn 1989), 88.

[100] Quoted in *Belfast Telegraph*, 27 April 2013, 27.

[101] Reid, quoted in *Irish Times*, 29 August 1995, 10.

[102] Andrews, 'Ties', 83, 85.

[103] Quoted in *The Daily Telegraph*, 6 June 1996, 12.

stage ordinary life in a Protestant working-class district of *pre*-Troubles Belfast. When Norman tells Billy 'I go out to work every day. Your ma never knew what it was like to have a broken pay,' his son responds, 'No, but she knew what it was like to have a broken jaw, and a broken nose.'[104] Fundamentally, for Reid, 'it always comes down to one woman and one man and how they relate to each other. It's politics in the background, people in the foreground, never the other way around.'[105]

Thus violence in Reid's work is not entwined with the later Troubles but firmly grounded in an emotional and historical context. The former is 'domestic and endemic; unemployment, drunkenness, deprivation, preju-dice, sexual arrogance',[106] while the latter echoes the sectarian strife of the 1920s and 1930s. Reid's own family were forced out of the Ardoyne, North Belfast in 1935, his father playing 'The Sash' as loudly as he could on a wind-up gramophone, 'an act of defiance as they left the area'.[107] His grandfather's experience of communal brutality was similarly formative. As a cart-driver for Bass during the 1920s, he helped to move a Catholic neighbour's furniture off the Donegall Road, drawing hostilities from his own side. Later, driving up York Street 'with a moving partition' and sniper fire, his assistant helper, a sixteen-year-old youth, 'was shot dead as he was sitting beside him. He just rode on, waiting, thinking I'm next.'[108] It is this kind of story, burned into Belfast's constitution, which underpins Reid's vision of working-class life in the city.

PAISLEY AND THEM

The staging of *Paisley & Me* in Belfast's Grand Opera House at the end of October 2012 marked Ron Hutchinson's subjective return to Northern Ireland. As a Unionist leader, architect of his own political party (the Democratic Unionist Party), and founder of his own Church (the Free Presbyterian Church of Ulster)—as well as the man responsible, many people contend, for stirring up the Troubles in the late 1960s—the Reverend Ian Paisley was a formidable subject for Hutchinson to grapple with. The play is a domestic, familial imagining of an encounter between

[104] Reid, *Too Late*, in *Billy: Three Plays*, 44.
[105] Quoted in *The Guardian*, 7 June 1996, 4. In *A Coming to Terms for Billy*, Norman's new, redemptive love Mavis was played by actress Gwen Taylor, whom Reid married in real life.
[106] Hugh Herbert, 'The Mask of Violence', *The Guardian*, 12 November 1985, 11.
[107] Despite this, Reid points out that his father 'was never an Orangeman, voted Labour all his life and cried when Joe Stalin died!' 'Author's Note', *Love, Billy* Theatre Programme (Belfast: Lyric Theatre, April 2013), 10.
[108] Interview with Graham Reid, London, 17 May 2012.

himself, his deceased parents, and the historical figure. Heavily influenced by Samuel Beckett's *Happy Days* (1961) and W. R. Rodgers' radio play *The Return Room* (transmitted in December 1955), *Paisley & Me* was the second part of an 'Ulster Trilogy' commissioned by Green Shoot Productions to explore Northern Ireland eighteen years after the Ceasefires. Whereas Graham Reid is an enthusiast of local Ulster politics, Hutchinson was never bound by this interest and was reluctant to renew a gaze. Having worked in Hollywood for thirty years there was, however, a sense of 'unfinished business'; a searching 'for an identity to confirm some existential things: signposts maybe to who we are or why we react in certain ways'. He remained invigorated by 'how complex it is, that particular identity, which is meat and drink if you're a writer. You can go to the well two or three times.' Nevertheless, Hutchinson found this revisiting emotionally as well as mentally draining: 'I guarantee this is the last bloody time, because *Paisley's* nearly killed me. It's the hardest thing I've ever written.'[109] Its changing titles—even uncomfortable at the start to use the name directly—were instructive. Beginning with *Big Martin*—a reference to Martin Lynch, who produced the play—progressing to *The Big Man*, then *Paisley*, before ending with the insertion of the most important character. *Paisley* became, quite literally, *Paisley & Me*.

Early drafts were a more straightforward, biographical exploration of the man Paisley. They contained him duelling with a figure (Donald) possibly based on the Reverend Billy Hyndman, the real-life minister of Drumreagh Presbyterian Church and 'a liberal cleric with no liking for the evangelicals of Presbyterianism'.[110] By explaining an early power struggle in his life we were witnessing the later Paisley's ambitions and mutability writ large. The appropriateness of this motif, prior to his prominence, was the sense that people—in Paisley's mind—are mere stepping-stones. Donald is a modernizer, keen for the Church to adapt to meet the demands of the modern age. With this progressive mentor a possible course, Paisley rejects him.[111] In these drafts Hutchinson was making a statement about how Paisley's rise to power was littered with the personalities of those whose position he desired and whose friendship he was willing to discard to reach a pinnacle. The third character is Jimmy MacMurtrey, a streetwise Belfast Unionist politician with more than a hint of Desmond Boal. The Paisley protagonist assimilates qualities from both Donald and Jimmy—the former's humour and oratorical ability, the latter's savviness and edge—then dispenses with them. They think they

---

[109] Interview with Ron Hutchinson, Belfast, 2 August 2012.
[110] Ed Moloney, *Paisley: From Demagogue to Democrat?* (Dublin: Poolbeg Press, 2008), 40.
[111] Ron Hutchinson, *The Big Man* (Unpublished: 24 May 2011), 5–29, 32–42.

are using him and all the while the opposite is the case. In the final scene the three Protestant men are joined for an ominous game of cards by a fourth character, Sean MacGlattery—a composite of Gerry Adams and Martin McGuinness—whom Donald and Jimmy urge Paisley to 'forgive' and come to terms with.[112] Hutchinson walked past all of this and decided it was not the play he wanted to write.

As *Paisley & Me*'s producer Martin Lynch exasperatedly notes, Hutchinson's current practice of writing for the screen led to constant rewriting, shifting emphasis, and the accompanying foibles the play suffers from:

> It's not unusual for twenty drafts to be done for a screenplay, that's been Ron's life for thirty years. So it's a mad thing for me to say about somebody as brilliant as Ron Hutchinson, but his inability to structure a stage play was blatant with every draft. So he never, ever found the structure that allowed him to tell that story well enough. He kept fucking about with structure after structure after structure. And the big problem was that every time he did a draft, there was maybe forty, fifty, sometimes sixty per cent of it very good, and forty, thirty or twenty per cent shite. So when you sent him notes, what did he do? He went away, threw out *everything* that he had and came back with a brand new structure, Hollywood-style! Screenwriting-style, ah fuck! Brand new fucking structure—brand new play![113]

Perhaps the principal development in the change of emphasis was the death of Hutchinson's father in January 2012. Early on the character 'My Dad' turns to the audience, 'Died January the second, this year. Rolled over in bed and that was that.'[114] In some ways the play is Hutchinson burying his father, with one reading of the final production as 'postdramatic theatre'.[115] In an introduction to a collection of his plays, Stewart Parker discussed how 'Plays and ghosts have a lot in common. The energy which flows from some intense moment of conflict in a particular time and place seems to activate them both,'[116] and the ghosts of Hutchinson's parents lead to a wider examination of Ulster Protestant identity. 'I realized that my mum and dad argued, really argued, about one thing and that was Ian Paisley. It was still a part of their identity struggle,' said Hutchinson. 'So this play is about me listening to their quarrel and trying to figure out what it means to me because of what it meant to them.' He

---

[112] Hutchinson, *Big Man*, 43–51, 119–49.
[113] Interview with Martin Lynch, Belfast, 20 March 2014.
[114] Ron Hutchinson, *Paisley & Me* (Unpublished: 2 October 2012), 19.
[115] Interview with Jo Egan (theatre director), Belfast, 6 December 2012. Coined by Hans-Thies Lehmann, 'Postdramatic Theatre' often jettisons plot to emphasize a performative process whose impact on the audience is more important than the text.
[116] Stewart Parker, 'Introduction' to *Three Plays for Ireland* (Birmingham: Oberon Books, 1989), 9.

confirmed in subsequent press interviews he was 'returning to confront a few old ghosts that have been following me about the world'.[117]

Ultimately Hutchinson's inspiration originated from re-encountering the language of his idyllic childhood in Islandmagee (an 'extraordinary remote place, no running water'), on the east coast of County Antrim, and its dichotomy with the Midlands city where his parents moved when he was a child. He specifically recalls the back of the Courtaulds chemical plant, still being able to 'taste the smell of that horrible place. It was being snatched from Eden. I could never accept the sentimentality of Coventry or those roots. Coventry was great to a lot of people and gave my dad a living but I just don't feel loyalty to it; it was a wasting.' If the *Billy* plays were Graham Reid walking round the streets with his mother off the Donegall Road, *Paisley & Me* is Hutchinson:

> going back to that Eden—I'm hearing my mother's voice in the cottage at Mullaghbuoy. I'm hearing my father in his father's farm house, and I'm hearing rows and fights and all while words spoken with that very strong, strange, adhesive accent that we have here in the north. My money has been made more than anything writing dialogue for American television and movies. It forced me to go back and listen to my language—to the inflections of my childhood that I heard. Those deep structures of language, inflection, delivery—the violence with which even most of my parents' conversational exchanges took place, in terms of energy but also the vividness of imagery that they used. I think lodged in the memory of writers is the first music of language that they heard. So for me getting back to writing on an Irish subject again is an act of reclaiming that, which makes it very primal for me, very elemental. This whole thing is not only in the head; it's visceral. Because I'm only hearing the voices of my childhood and that Eden that I still at some level am ferociously angry about having been plucked from.[118]

The play becomes a trafficking of ghosts, surveyed towards the end by the author's character glancing across a sea mist 'where the ghost of my dad was headed, from Stranraer, the boat train', to 'the ghost of my mother waiting for him with an oil lamp flickering in the window'—and, finally, 'somewhere the ghost of me heading for another boat, the one that took me unwilling, hot with tears, to England, to that exile that's never ended, that never will'.[119]

Both Hutchinson's parents emerge from the earth, their graves, to talk to their son, the author of this play. All are awaiting an arrival: 'do you

---

[117] Interview with Ron Hutchinson, Belfast, 2 August 2012; quoted in *Belfast Telegraph*, 4 October 2012, 3.

[118] Interview with Ron Hutchinson, Belfast, 2 August 2012.

[119] Hutchinson, *Paisley & Me*, 82.

think he'll come?' *Paisley & Me* is an extended argument in much the same way as *Rat in the Skull*, but this argument goes on between Hutchinson, his parents, and their (in)famous guest. The latter arrives to deliver his opening address as renowned orator, reeling off a list of Secretaries of State, 'errand boys' of successive British Prime Ministers he has seen off, as well as 'their big pals in Dublin, Lynch, Cosgrave and Haughey'. Hutchinson asks Paisley 'if any words you said stoked the flames?'

> PAISLEY: Then I'll have to face my Maker and answer for it on the Day of Judgement—not here—not at the hands of a sun tanned scribbler. Where were you when murder had us by the throat? On your yacht?
> ME: I don't have a yacht and I don't know anybody who does. Can you look inside yourself—look at your actions—your rhetoric—the Paisley thing—and say it had no part to play? If we can't be honest among ourselves, if we can't ask the hard questions about our responsibility for what blew up here—not excepting me because that day when I saw you in person—when I stood on the edge of that Glasgow Orange gang I don't think that there's anything you could have asked of me that I wouldn't have given you. That's how *confirming* it was, to be there. To be exposed to the full blast of you. The drums of my tribe were beating. I was home. I was back in Islandmagee in the Revival tent again. I'd have followed you along with the rest of them where you pointed. I was touched by that Immensity, too.[120]

Hutchinson clarified that his 'mother saw Paisley as a defender, while my father saw him as an alien presence from an Ireland he didn't really recognize, even though it was another Protestant Northern Ireland'.[121]

If the play is a series of challenges, Hutchinson to Paisley and vice versa, his father has most to confront Paisley about. He is irritated by his wife's adoration ('I could hug him to death, so I could,' she says), as well as the men he inspired to acts of 'loyalty'. This included his wife's Uncle Billy, who was physically abusive to his spouse and emigrated to Canada in dubious circumstances, though his resentment of Paisley is altogether more deep-rooted:

> MY DAD: My dad was a Grand Master of the Lodge and as stout an Orangeman as you'd meet in a day's hike. I had that come-all-ye up

---

[120] Hutchinson, *Paisley & Me*, 2, 4, 7–8, 34–6.
[121] Quoted in *Irish News*, 30 October 2012, 28. This parental political division mirrored that of the Progressive Unionist Party's David Ervine, whose mother was a proud Paisleyite and his father a socialist NILP supporter who told Paisley to 'fuck off' when he canvassed at their East Belfast home. See Ed Moloney (ed.), *Voices from the Grave: Two Men's War in Ireland* (London: Faber and Faber, 2010), 312–13.

to my ears, the same kind of claptrap you gave out which was why I could never stand you and I still can't. I know very well, Mr Paisley, what your religion means. The excuses it gives a man to do what's blackest in him and still think he's white as snow. What's behind those fine words? I saw it at first hand. Is it any wonder I took the first chance out that I got? Adolf Hitler might have had his faults but he did me a favour. If it hadn't been for him I'd still have been here. Wouldn't have seen the world. Seen how you can live with your fellow man, whatever foot he digs with.[122]

A common criticism of the play was that its eponymous historical figure was 'a supporting character', Paisley 'reduced to little more than super-natural psychoanalyst for our tortured expat hero'. There is much veracity in this assessment. Paisley does get lost somewhere in the whole toil, the biography of Hutchinson gradually obliterating that of his subject. But the same critic realized that in invoking 'the spirits of his dead parents and Paisley himself', Hutchinson holds 'a sort of inquiry on behalf of the Northern Ireland Protestant community at large'.[123] With the present political dominance of his party (the DUP), it is tempting for many to see Paisley as some kind of tribal avatar, finally risen to the top by 2003 as always promised.[124] But if the play is not strictly about Paisley, it is certainly a play about Paisleyism—the ideology as opposed to the individual—and thus about an Ulster Protestantism which has reacted profoundly against, as well as in favour of, this vein. It has often been pointed out that Paisley's main original target was the Unionist establish-ment, embodied by Prime Minister Terence O'Neill and elite individuals like the Governor of Northern Ireland Lord Erskine, who was bitterly harangued (along with his wife) by Paisleyites in June 1966, years before the outbreak of the Troubles and the emergence of the Provisional IRA.[125]

While his authentic appeal to the Protestant working class—for his charisma and ability to tell 'it the way it really was'—should not be discounted, the fact is that Ulster Protestants have always disagreed internally over their politicians and are far 'too diverse' to be represented by one redoubtable man alone.[126] Colin McCusker confirms that his

---

[122] Hutchinson, *Paisley & Me*, 24, 61.
[123] Joe Nawaz, 'The Big Man is Relegated to a Supporting Role', *Belfast Telegraph*, 31 October 2012, 9.
[124] See for instance Newton Emerson, 'Paisley Rise-to-Power Myth Distorts Facts', *Irish News*, 16 January 2014, 16; Steve Bruce, *Paisley: Religion and Politics in Northern Ireland* (Oxford: Oxford University Press, 2007).
[125] Moloney, *Paisley*, 123–7.
[126] Bobby Niblock, '1955–1972' (Unpublished: n.d.), 9; Patrick Mitchel, *Evangelicalism and National Identity in Ulster, 1921–1998* (Oxford: Oxford University Press, 2003), 173.

father Harold, the former Ulster Unionist MP for Upper Bann, 'had no tolerance of Paisley at all. He didn't perceive him as being particularly intelligent, just somebody who roared and shouted.'[127] The current leader of the UVF-aligned Progressive Unionist Party argues that with Loyalists acting on his inflammatory speeches, Paisley 'was responsible, in an indirect way, for young men going to the graveyards and to prisons'.[128] Aside from the inherent diversity of Protestantism, the most severe estimations tend to be found within, and the way such sentiments are continually voiced by Loyalists—not to mention other Unionist dissenters barracked and usurped in Paisley's ascent—is illustrative of the complicated, frequently turbulent relationship between them and the late Baron Bannside. In a strange sense, Hutchinson's *Paisley & Me* reflects this prevailing divisiveness, which was simplified and mostly downplayed in public tributes when Paisley passed away in September 2014.

In publicizing the play Hutchinson emphasized how 'the simple accretion of fact on top of fact doesn't necessarily result in any kind of truth about a character or the times he or she lived in'.[129] His laboured insistence on this masks a simple lack of interest in Paisley's biography. The journey and justification for doing a deal with Sinn Féin—the political twist at the heart of the Paisley story—is somehow beside the point, and when Hutchinson approaches it we encounter the least convincing scenes of the play. He is always shoehorning a different dynamic into the narrative. After referencing his fine constituency record as an MP, Paisley's vaunted charm and memory for detail is touched on:

ME: Wouldn't they just be more of those useless faces? Is he asking to be judged on those?

MY MOTHER: Why not?

ME: Because it's no concern of ours what happens when he closes the door behind him—only when he's in the street or in the pulpit or on

---

Andy Tyrie recalled the antagonism of his father—who had signed the Ulster Covenant and fought in the First World War—towards Unionist representatives during election time on the Lower Shankill: 'This big flat-back lorry came round and it had all these people with their great crumply coats and nice hats all sitting in the back. But they always had a wee drummer—this was the nearest the Loyalists got to it—and he played for the people to come out so that people could listen to the politicians. My own father was very much a Labour person in the years of Harry Midgley, and he used to say to us, "Come on in and don't be listening to them people, they're only here looking after themselves." He used to say "Have you ever seen them here before?", and that was always the question' (interview with Andy Tyrie, Dundonald, 9 August 2012).

127 Interview with Colin McCusker, Portadown, 29 November 2011.
128 Interview with Billy Hutchinson, Belfast, 12 November 2012.
129 Ron Hutchinson, 'Playwright's Foreword', *Paisley & Me Souvenir Programme* (Belfast: Green Shoot Productions, October 2012), 4.

the TV or on that platform in Trafalgar Square because it's there that he troubles the world. So I'll take it for granted that he's a family man and a funny man and can look you in the eye and remember the name of your second cousin third removed.

PAISLEY: Says the Man of Words who went on his knees but who still closed his ears to the greatest truths ever spoken. Could that be why you're back? From Neverland? Maybe it's time to swap the beach for what? A field? The sun of Califor-ni-ay for—shall we say?—a light rain— Armagh—Down—Antrim—Islandmagee?—and God to speak to you. *God.*[130]

Graham Reid has penned one of the prospective film biopics on Paisley, though this is in an onerous development phase which will see many alterations (and may be delayed or even never see the light of day if the Paisley family object). Reid's suitability for the project may have been at question because on a profound level he objects to the subject: 'I'm convinced that as soon as the opportunity to be First Minister was on the horizon Paisley was prepared to do a deal with anybody, because it's money and power. I think Paisley has done more damage to Northern Ireland than Gerry Adams and the IRA ever did.'[131] Early drafts see Reid working through this hostility and coming out the other side through finding the one area he can truly relate to its protagonist on: the love of his family. Paisley's upbringing in 1930s Ballymena and later devotion to his own children become touchingly reminiscent of the affectionate boisterousness of the Martin family in the *Billy* plays. When his father James tells him the 'Lundy' story, of that 'enemy within', the child Paisley panics: 'I'm going to slam our garden gate and keep it closed.'[132] Contrary to the clichéd reading of a basic monolith, in something Reid shares with Ron Hutchinson, it is the emotional as well as the ideological splintering which defines Ulster Protestantism.

CONCLUSION

As the more lukewarm critical responses noted, *Paisley & Me* presupposed an interest not so much in Paisley and Protestant politics but in Ron Hutchinson himself, as a writer and man.[133] There were production difficulties with abrupt casting, and the actor who played Paisley pointed

---

[130] Hutchinson, *Paisley & Me*, 27–8.
[131] Interview with Graham Reid, London, 17 May 2012.
[132] Graham Reid, *Paisley* (Revised 2nd draft: June 2009), 8, 101–16, 111–12.
[133] Anne Hailes, 'Intense Tale All about Him and Paisley', *Irish News*, 1 November 2012, 34.

to the unsuitability of the Belfast Opera House as the play's venue. In a neutral environment such as the Royal Court, where an audience 'didn't come with an expectation of "Woops, there goes my Paisley"'—in other words, where judgements were not based on their entrenched fondness/animosity for the political figure—*Paisley & Me* might have prospered.[134] The play's real pitfalls, however, derived from a mixture of personal loss as well as Hutchinson's apparently idiosyncratic screenwriting profile, with its concentration on structure and moving from script to script in a 'totally un-unionizable business'. Hutchinson compares this with the rural, labouring profile of his father, shifting from building site to building site, also cementing structure,[135] the constant rewriting ensuring that a different play slipped through his fingers.

Graham Reid's fifth and final play about the Martin family, *Love, Billy* arrived—after a sixteen-year hiatus—at the Lyric Theatre in May 2013. Ironically the universality of the first four has started to recede to the local, and aspects of the new piece such as Billy's career in the British Army were underdeveloped,[136] though it received good audiences. Billy's new line of work signified Reid's own mental allegiance, as had been the way for St John Ervine dwelling on British forces at Dunkirk. Norman now resides in a wheelchair and with his memory lapsing we discover he is dying. Referring constantly to the way the site of his old house is 'part of the City Hospital now', Billy is asked by his sister Lorna why he is so 'obsessed' with the building,[137] and the same question could be directed at Reid himself. Reid's mother, like Billy's in the plays, died in the hospital, and he is similarly fixated by the way it has literally enveloped his old neighbourhood. Another of the Martin sisters says 'Coolderry Street was redeveloped, not blown up',[138] the now-vanished warren of working-class housing recalling Stewart Parker's debut *Spokesong*: 'If the bombers don't get it, the planners will.'[139]

This final *Billy* play is really a lament for a Belfast which is no more. There are even references to Buck Alec taking his toothless lion for walks, as well as the residue of the violent reputation Norman lived by. The malaise had set in years before but the 1980s confirmed the permanent decay of a peculiarly Protestant working-class way of life. The security of employment—'I worked in the shipyard. I built ships,'[140] Norman

---

134 Interview with Dan Gordon, Belfast, 5 April 2016.
135 Interview with Ron Hutchinson, Belfast, 2 August 2012.
136 See Grania McFadden, 'When Talking is Done, It's Hard to Love New Billy Play', *Belfast Telegraph*, 2 May 2013, 7.
137 Graham Reid, *Love, Billy* (Unpublished: 6th draft, February 2013), 22, 69–70, 98, 100.
138 Reid, *Love, Billy*, 86. The finale of the initial trilogy pulled back to reveal the same street.
139 Stewart Parker, *Spokesong*, in *Plays 1* (London: Methuen, 2000), 57.
140 Reid, *Love, Billy*, 4, 33, 59, 61–2, 67–8. By the mid-1990s Belfast's shipyard workforce had plummeted from a peak of 42,000 to 1,700. Mackies Engineering Foundry

defiantly reminds us—as well as the very streets themselves are gone. If some Ulster Unionists chose to forget the disintegration of the industries which provided the bedrock of working-class Protestant employment, some Loyalists could not:

They destroyed communities and you saw it happening in the shipyard here. When I worked at the shipyard in the late 1970s eleven thousand people worked in it. Before that it was twenty odd thousand people. As a kid I can remember all the men walking to Mackie's—that's what you seen. You aspired: 'When I grow up I want to work at Mackie's,' or 'I want to work in the shipyard.' Now that's no longer an option for kids because the shipyard only employs something like two hundred people. In the mining villages it was the same. From you were a kid, you're growing up and see your father going out every day and the same here in the shipyards, Sirocco works, and all those places. When the mines closed down in the UK, it led to long-term unemployment. People didn't realize the effect it would have on the society. A lot of people saw their father and grandfather not going to work, so then they get into that long-term unemployment thing. They go on to working benefits schemes to survive, and then you get a whole generation used to that. When you get people on a train it's very hard to get them off it, but that's what Thatcher did.[141]

The Conservative government of the time became the first since the Second World War to abandon the aim of full employment, with unemployment rocketing to 10 per cent by 1982, hitting adult males and young people especially badly.[142] Bypassing contemporary references to aspiration—a seeming shorthand for making a lot of money—we see above a different, perhaps original use of the term: the aspiration to work.

Mirroring this deterioration was the virtual disappearance of the once significant NILP. The party which challenged the Unionist Party for the Belfast vote ran 11 candidates out of 1,000 in the 1981 municipal elections, returning one councillor.[143] Even David Bleakley, disenchanted

had reduced from 7,500 to 450 employees (closing in 1999), while many of the foreign companies with local Northern Irish plants—Courtaulds, ICI, British Enkalon, and Michelin—had departed. The artificial fibre industry, a mainstay of Ulster employment, almost completely vanished. Shankill Think Tank, *A New Beginning*, 13 (Newtownabbey: Island Publications, 1995), 27.

[141] Interview with William 'Plum' Smith, Belfast, 14 March 2012. Others stress that the problem cannot be laid solely at the door of Conservative administrations, with some Protestant males returning 'to this notion of apprenticeships and trades as what we need', while the rest of the world has 'moved on' through education (interview with Dawn Purvis, Belfast, 20 January 2012).

[142] Selina Todd, *The People: The Rise and Fall of the Working Class, 1910–2010* (London: John Murray, 2014), 320.

[143] Sydney Elliott and W. D. Flackes, *Northern Ireland: A Political Directory* (Belfast: Blackstaff Press, 1999), 551.

by empowered extremes, had left the stage, though he continued writing and welcomed the 'Rolling Devolution' initiative of James Prior (who incidentally strove to 'keep the Yard going' as long as he could as Secretary of State).[144] At the height of the 1981 Hunger Strike, Bleakley wistfully told an old NILP comrade, 'Our policies were never tried. We can look back on 30 years of election addresses without wincing and how many politicians in Northern Ireland can do that?'[145]

In *Love, Billy*'s pivotal scene, Norman rises from his wheelchair and surveys:

> NORMAN: Coolderry Street, gone! I never thought I'd outlive the whole street. (*reckons*) Aye, the front would have been about here. When we lived here I knew everybody in the street. Not all their kids mind, but the parents, the grown-ups. (*points with his stick*) Coolbeg Street was there . . . Coolmore Street . . . a laundry there. An organ pipeworks there . . . all gone . . . Coolderry Street. Aye, we did some living in this wee street all right. A lot of things happened. Belfast's changed . . . big changes.[146]

Norman has always embodied an older Belfast: of hard men, vibrant shipyards, jobs for (overwhelmingly) Protestant males—a state which does not exist anymore, except in memory and legend. When Norman dies, therefore, a certain Belfast dies with him. Like Ron Hutchinson's *Rat in the Skull*, therein lies a curious optimism; that the city's violence and segregation may not be determined or immoveable, just as the structures and certainties which once characterized a particular Protestant working-class way of life are not either.

---

[144] David Bleakley, 'Ulster—the Next Step', *Socialist Commentary* (July/August 1977), 6; telephone interview with Lord James Prior, 6 June 2012.

[145] Quoted in Sam McAughtry, 'Northern Ireland Labour lives on', *Irish Times*, 20 May 1981, 12.

[146] Reid, *Love, Billy*, 90–1. Original ellipses.

6

The Anger and Energy of Gary Mitchell

> They attacked my family because of what they'd heard about my plays, but if they think their actions will create an impotence in my work they are sadly mistaken: my weapons are not baseball bats and petrol bombs, they are words, and I have an abundance of them.
>
> Gary Mitchell (2007)

> His unique contribution is very much his own life. The fact that he was born and bred on the housing estate that is Rathcoole; that he lived the life of that microcosm of Northern Irish Unionism as a boy, as a young man and into his youth, and he had the skills and the ability to be able to transfer those stories and put them on stage in a way that completely engrossed people and that they hadn't seen before.
>
> Stuart Graham (Interview with the author, September 2011)

Graham Reid continued writing for television into the 1990s, visiting the Maze prison on several occasions to research the single television drama *Life After Life* (1995). His initial reflections conform to a traditional reading of the prison experience, embraced by Republicans, whose book-shelves were 'geared to study' and academic works, while Loyalists had 'trashy' novels.[1] As we have seen, Reid came from a Labour family, but his view of Loyalist paramilitaries proceeded along oversimplified and conventional Unionist lines: 'Young Protestants who were involved tended to be in the security forces, in the police or the Army, so the quality of the Irish Republican in that range seemed to be higher than Loyalists. That was the difference in calibre. Protestants had legitimate outlets if they wanted to serve their country whereas Republicans didn't.' Inside Long Kesh, Reid observed an apparent drawback with Loyalist prisoners in there being 'a lot of different, disparate little groups', and on a tour round the complex was half-jokingly warned by a prison officer that Republicans

---

[1] Interview with Graham Reid, London, 17 May 2012. *Life After Life* was based on the real 'Work Out' system where prisoners were introduced to employment schemes following their release.

would 'be very well-mannered, very disciplined, will offer you a cup of tea', while Loyalist prisoners 'may hang you from the lights!'

He met a number of volunteers including Gusty Spence (who had 'tremendous charisma'), John 'Grug' Gregg, and several Provisional IRA figureheads including Raymond McCartney. Despite having little time for the paramilitaries, Reid refused to morally cauterize them with many reminding him of 'lads I grew up with, on both sides, who'd gotten involved in all this socially. I found them very personable and people I could have related to in different circumstances.' His research coalesced with a particularly vibrant political period where Secretaries of State entered Long Kesh to negotiate with Loyalist prisoners and the profile was invested with the kind of prestige which it has seldom possessed within the Protestant community. This would eventually lead to tension,[2] and the time was also marked by intra-communal violence as Loyalism began to fragment. Not dissimilar to F. S. L. Lyons's framing of the post-Irish Civil War atrocities as 'the last convulsive spasm of the fever that had been wasting the land',[3] developments from the Downing Street Declaration of 1993 to the Provisional IRA's decommissioning in 2005 can be seen to encompass the final convulsive spasms of the Troubles. While the intensity of the conflict which preceded it is unlikely to be matched, as with the Irish Civil War it continues to influence life and politics in Northern Ireland.

RATHCOOLE

Rathcoole, Newtownabbey, is situated to the north of Belfast. The geographical and social development of the estate was closely linked to the period of expansion presided over by Terence O'Neill, which 'strengthened the socio-economic fortunes of the working class and made them more willing to disperse from traditional segregatory living conditions and into new housing estates'.[4] The locality was heavily patrolled by the UDA during the 1974 Ulster Workers' Council stoppage, when its potential as a Loyalist no-go area became clear (Andy Tyrie and the late Bill Craig made

---

[2] *The Guardian*, 10 January 1998, 1. The PUP's Billy Hutchinson recalls: 'Mo Mowlam said she wanted to go into the prison to talk to the prisoners and we met with her and said "Mo, prisoners don't make the decision about this—we do. We've already consulted with our constituency and we have told the prisoners that they're hostages."' The voice of the prisoners was therefore subsumed to that of the party (interview with Billy Hutchinson, Belfast, 12 November 2012).

[3] F. S. L. Lyons, *Ireland Since the Famine* (London: Fontana, 1985; 1st edition 1963), 536.

[4] Aaron Edwards, *A History of the Northern Ireland Labour Party: Democratic Socialism and Sectarianism* (Manchester: Manchester University Press, 2009), 103.

Fig. 6.1. Photo of Gary Mitchell.

Note: Author's own

personal visits to rally the troops).[5] Rathcoole was also the birthplace of Bobby Sands, whose family left following intimidation in 1972. The acclaimed playwright Gary Mitchell (Fig. 6.1) was born and brought up in the estate and was 'seen early on as a lone voice grassroots loyalist'.[6] In November 2005, however, Mitchell was forced to leave when his home and family were attacked. Despite appearing publicly he has lived in hiding ever since, initially in a safe house arranged by the Progressive Unionist Party's David Ervine.

The assault on Mitchell's house and car was accompanied by attacks on his niece and disabled uncle, the latter being informed by a carful of men that he had several hours to leave Rathcoole. Mitchell's grandmother had passed away days before and her subsequent funeral service was marred by the family requiring a police escort, at the same time as an orchestrated posse of adolescents made their presence felt by chanting Loyalist songs (one shouting 'One Mitchell dead' as his grandmother's coffin was brought out).[7] While there was a personal component to the attacks—which for obvious ethical reasons will remain private—the reasons for the

---

[5] Ian S. Wood, *Crimes of Loyalty: A History of the UDA* (Edinburgh: Edinburgh University Press, 2006), 43–5.

[6] *The Guardian*, 13 June 2000, 8.

[7] Gary Mitchell, 'Rathcoole Ranger', in Ronnie Esplin and Graham Walker (eds), *It's Rangers for Me? New Perspectives on a Scottish Institution* (Ayr: Fort, 2007), 112.

expulsion were twofold. Firstly, rogue elements within the UDA took exception to Mitchell's exploration of Protestant working-class identity, leading to his plays being performed and revered in Ireland.[8] Paramilitaries 'would stop you in the street, ask you what you were doing in Dublin and accuse you of selling out. They [the gang] sent a message that I was banned from Rathcoole and had defied them, but I never even knew there was a ban.'[9] Accordingly 'the people who threatened his life never went to see his plays, believing that such activity was essentially identified with the other side',[10] a theme Mitchell returns to repeatedly, almost as a preamble: 'Protestants don't see the arts as belonging to them … plays are seen as silly things that can't change people's minds. When I was growing up the over-riding feeling was that everyone involved in the arts is gay or Catholic. There was no room for a heterosexual Protestant.' Speaking several years after the onslaught, Mitchell revealed that David Ervine had remarked to him shortly before his death in 2007 that he was suffering for his drama's success, 'because I was more popular than they were'.[11]

Ironically his play *Remnants of Fear* opened the 2006 West Belfast festival *Féile an Phobail*, with Mitchell even asked to launch the event that year (he joked that he felt safer on the Falls Road than in his home estate).[12] This was seen by its director Pam Brighton as a sign of a naturally enlightened community embracing the 'other', but it has more convincingly been argued that Mitchell's Rathcoole, with its absence of state law and 'Henchmen with grandiose titles' issuing 'instructions for day to day activities'—where the dole pays the rent for a flat used for punishment beatings—is essentially the Loyalist mirror of West Belfast.[13] After seeing a performance of Mitchell's *In a Little World of Our Own*, Sinn Féin's former director of publicity remembered thinking 'I wouldn't like a play written about the IRA in that way, and it could be because of things the IRA did.'[14] The crossover was reinforced in March 2012 when Mitchell's *Love Matters* was performed at the Lyric Theatre before going on tour. There has been a tradition of Irish-speaking in East Belfast,[15]

---

[8] Mitchell's *In a Little World of Our Own* was awarded the *Irish Times* award for Best New Play.
[9] Quoted in *The Observer*, 29 January 2006, 7.
[10] Roy Foster, 'Who Betrayed the Lundys?', *The Guardian Review*, 11 February 2006, 7.
[11] Quoted in *Irish Times*, 2 May 2009, 49. See also *Belfast Telegraph*, 12 May 2014, 24–5.
[12] *Irish Times*, 2 August 2006. 11.
[13] Imelda Foley, 'Theatre and the Conflict in Northern Ireland', *A Troubles Archive Essay* (Belfast: Arts Council of Northern Ireland, 2009), 17.
[14] Interview with Danny Morrison, Belfast, 29 August 2013.
[15] Linda Ervine, 'The Protestant Community and the Irish Language', *Social Justice Review* (Spring 2013), 35–8. Ervine runs Irish classes at the East Belfast Mission on the lower Newtownards Road.

naturally downplayed as the years have passed, but the play was uniquely translated and performed in Irish by the Aisling Ghéar company: a thriller about Loyalism played out in the Irish language.

Mitchell had been adamant that to extricate himself from Rathcoole would damage both his writing and the ability to reflect his community authentically. When warned of the early hackles being raised against his work from within the estate, Mitchell was defiant: 'Why should I leave? It is important for me to stay here and keep in touch with the people I'm in touch with. If you are not aware of things are changing, you'll lose the detail and you'll write a lot of nonsense.'[16] The paradoxical irony of Mitchell's international acclaim in the UK and Ireland is that it has mentally and physically transported him out of Rathcoole. Yet his point remained that 'in order to understand the complexity of Northern Ireland, you must live here'.[17] A local councillor who has also since departed agrees Mitchell's 'source was that area, and it's actually quite hard for a playwright if you're mainly writing about where you live in and round. Probably more than most playwrights it would have drawn him away from his well.'[18] Nevertheless those who have worked with him were actually surprised by how long Mitchell was able to survive in Rathcoole 'because he seemed to be so out there in terms of his criticisms of the leadership of the Loyalist paramilitaries, and the absolute failure to look after and protect their own communities'.[19] His original mentor remembered fearing for his safety even during his early radio work: 'I said "Are you not frightened Gary? If I were you I would be terrified—the stuff you write which is totally critical of Loyalism, of where everyone sits." And then of course, ultimately in the end they did come and get him.'[20]

The second element in the attacks was related to one of his main subjects: the fragmentation of Loyalism. As the UDA inches towards political channels, Freddie in *As the Beast Sleeps* (1998) suggests to his friend 'Maybe now's the time for another wee job,' and when he is rebuffed puts it down to 'all this shite that's going on. We need to do something about that, Kyle. Maybe start doing things on our own.'[21] Rumours of the UVF moving towards completely standing down were mooted in 2010–11, but anonymous Loyalists also warned of trouble

[16] Quoted in Susan McKay, *Northern Protestants: An Unsettled People* (Belfast: Blackstaff Press, 2000), 113.
[17] Quoted in Paddy Logue (ed.), *The Border: Personal Reflections from Ireland, North and South* (Dublin: Oak Tree Press, 1999), 130.
[18] Interview with Mark Langhammer, Belfast, 21 September 2011.
[19] Interview with Patrick O'Kane (actor), Belfast, 2 November 2011.
[20] Interview with Pam Brighton, Belfast, 25 March 2014.
[21] Gary Mitchell, *As the Beast Sleeps* (London: Nick Hern Books, 2001), 14. See also Tom Maguire, *Making Theatre in Northern Ireland: Through and Beyond the Troubles* (Exeter: University of Exeter Press, 2006), 145–9.

ahead because of the way 'Someone was a military commander—now he is nothing. They feel disempowered,'[22] a feeling of contemporary resonance in Loyalist circles. Freddie is the embodiment of such a mentality, reminiscing that in the old days,

> FREDDIE: Everybody knew where they were. Not like now. We used to walk into that club and every fucker in the place would be patting us on the back and yelling our names out—the drink would just flow all night. And then, all of a sudden...
> *Stops.*
> SANDRA: Everything changed.
> FREDDIE: Too fucking right it did. (*Pause*) Well fuck change that's what I say. Why can't everything stay the same?

Later, a character prominent in a Loyalist political party outlines how he needs to raise funds for an American tour.

> ALEC: How are the Yanks supposed to know what's going on, from our point of view, if there's no-one available to tell them? Five-star hotels, top class restaurants all cost money. We can't just turn up to dinner with American businessmen in our jeans and an aul' t-shirt. We can't grab fish and chips and head down the pub for a few pints and a bit of a laugh. This isn't fucking eejits wearing masks, burning cars, blocking roads and singing 'God Save the Queen' round a bonfire with a crate a beer each. This is the future.[23]

Alec, the new breed of Loyalist politician who seemed to be close to a breakthrough during the peace process, was not as it turned out articulating the future. The images of Loyalists ridiculed are still prevalent, while parties like the Ulster Democratic Party (UDP) ended up dissolving and the Progressive Unionist Party has also struggled.[24] Despite their fortunes, such parties interacted profoundly with the theatre which depicted them. After a performance of *As the Beast Sleeps*, the actor playing Loyalist hardliner Freddie remembered catching sight of the UDP's Gary McMichael afterwards,

> seeing him being visibly shaken by what he had witnessed. He had a very apprehensive look, and I didn't hear this but it was reported to me that he had said to Gary [Mitchell], 'A bit close to the bone that'. What he did say to me was 'Very scary man'—which I thought was very ironic, because I was actually terrified of him. But I remember being impressed by the fact he was

---

[22] Quoted in *Belfast Telegraph*, 17 January 2011, 33.
[23] Mitchell, *As the Beast*, 55, 76. Original ellipsis.
[24] *The Guardian*, 7 November 1998, 14.

there because he was precisely the type of person who needed to see that. The challenge facing the Alec character was how to effectively re-engage or engage differently the Freddies of this world into a new political landscape, and it was a challenge which Alec was abdicating responsibility for. That's why it was so provocative on Gary's part. Living within that community, that was a very direct challenge to that political leadership: 'Don't forget.'[25]

The aspiration to civilianize Loyalist groups unsettled those who refused to buy into the new project. 'You just talk to them out there. Talk on TV. Talk in big debates. Preach your new brand of Unionism anywhere you want, but these ears are closed to you,' another UDA man tells Alec. This is the beast that sleeps: those who do not accept the new dispensation outlined by most modern politicians in Northern Ireland, refusing to adapt to changed circumstances. Freddie warns of the way he's always 'waiting. Waiting on Paisley. Waiting on Robinson taking over. Waiting on the call. Well I'm all waited out. It's time.'[26]

Tension was to climax in a devastating 2000 feud in Belfast, wreaking particular havoc on the Shankill area. In extraordinary scenes over two hundred families with any alleged UVF association (and many with none) were forced out of the small area of the Lower Shankill by a column of UDA men loyal to paramilitary figurehead and tabloid newspaper favourite Johnny Adair. 'With hindsight you see an inevitability about this,' community worker Jackie Redpath comments. 'Once people who were engaged in violence like the Loyalist paramilitaries against the IRA, once that went as a struggle, where was all that stuff going to go? What it did was it turned in on itself.'[27] Both Redpath and Chris McGimpsey, a councillor for the area at the time, believe 'the community never got over it', the latter agreeing that the Ceasefires ensured 'Loyalists had lost their *raison d'être*. Loyalism's historic mandate was to effectively defend Northern Ireland against the Provos but they didn't have to do it anymore because the Provos had called a ceasefire.' The relentless feuding derived from 'all this jockeying for a position', with figures attempting to gain control of the area's drugs trade to 'build up an empire. Part of it was fuelled by personal ambition, money—but they didn't have an enemy.'[28] Gusty Spence, whose home was ransacked while he was away, remembered the same thing being meted out to what was known as 'red flaggers' and 'socialist houses' on the Shankill.

---

[25] Interview with Patrick O'Kane, Belfast, 2 November 2011.
[26] Mitchell, *As the Beast*, 78, 82.
[27] Interview with Jackie Redpath, Belfast, 19 February 2013. See *The Guardian*, 22 August 2000, 1.
[28] Interview with Chris McGimpsey, Belfast, 18 January 2012.

A LITTLE WORLD

One of Mitchell's most formidable plays *In a Little World of Our Own* premiered in Dublin in 1997 and was credited with bringing Protestant working-class life and politics to an Irish audience for the first time since Graham Reid's work of the early 1980s. The play is a Greek-style tragedy with all the violence and action taking place off stage. While theatres in Northern Ireland deemed the material too dangerous to handle,[29] the play did arrive in Belfast on tour towards the end of the year to rave reviews and sell-out performances, its brutal cacophony enhanced when Billy Wright was assassinated by the INLA in the Maze prison in December 1997. Stuart Graham, who portrayed protagonist Ray in the original production at the Peacock Theatre, establishes that the play was coterminous with the Abbey's wish to engage with Northern Irish politics at a 'frightening' but also 'immensely interesting' time: 'When the peace process kicked off, the Abbey were very quick to invite all of the political parties in the north to come to the opening night. None of them came from the Unionist side other than David Ervine, who from that moment become quite a regular visitor to the Abbey Theatre.'[30]

It was Graham who first took the play to the Abbey, though he initially feared that it would fail in Dublin, as 'people might have absolutely no interest whatsoever in these people who were as alien to them as a family living on a working-class housing estate in Newcastle upon Tyne or Glasgow'. But because the essence of the play is 'a domestic drama about individual human beings, the Dublin audiences adored it on a level like I have not witnessed before or since. We had people sitting on the stairs, probably illegally, in the performances. The Peacock only holds 120, 130 people—there literally were lines of people sitting on the steps as well to watch it.'[31] With his father once active in the UDA, Mitchell had always been around the paramilitaries and understood them, wanting to universally highlight 'that this was just one group of people fighting themselves in really bad, ugly ways'.[32] Politically, *In a Little World of Our Own* catches Loyalism on the cusp of the Good Friday Agreement,

---

[29] Mitchell remembers the Lyric Theatre's initial response: 'We love the play, love the characters, love everything about it—could you set it in Birmingham?' (interview with Gary Mitchell, Antrim, 6 June 2013).
[30] Interview with Stuart Graham, Belfast, 8 October 2011.
[31] Interview with Stuart Graham, Belfast, 8 October 2011.
[32] Interview with Gary Mitchell, Antrim, 6 June 2013.

dramatizing tensions within a strand of the community as to whether to pursue peaceful methods or remain wedded to militarism.[33] Ray, a classic, fatalist Loyalist volunteer, is dismissive of political manoeuvring symbolized by the unseen character of Monroe (a PUP or UDP representative). Publicly Mitchell praised such parties for 'trying to give a voice to the angry men',[34] but Ray speaks differently at the start of the play:

RAY: Pricks like Monroe are just shit. What people don't understand is this. The world is a violent place. We know that better than anybody. Whether it's dealing with the IRA or dealing with petty theft or glue sniffing. See, I'm not just talking about beating people up. I'm talking about common sense. We've helped everybody. Even those young fellas. Years from now, when those young fellas have grown, they'll look back and realize that they could have been going to prison for years. And they could've returned to the streets worse and tried to do bigger jobs, got caught again and ended up spending most of their time in and out of prison. I saved them from that. A few broken bones and bruising will be forgotten about in a couple of months. And they won't do it again.[35]

Such sentiments are of course highly dubious. A young delinquent tends not to be revitalized by being badly beaten up. Yet this is a prevalent practice in areas such as Rathcoole and one which takes place with a level of support in Protestant working-class communities. A councillor whose power base was formerly the Shankill estate observes how the paramilitaries are 'not incapable of recognizing how to do stuff which is popular with the communities'.[36] Most of all 'the world is a violent place' mentality was—and largely remains—the Loyalist mindset. In a sense this is emotive as well as a product of history. 'A lot of people during the conflict basically lived on adrenaline; you can't just turn that tap off overnight,'[37] remembers an ex-UDA volunteer who intermediated during the worst of the feuding. Despite this, an *Irish Times* writer dubbed Mitchell's play a 'tentative sign that something has changed', detecting an odd optimism linked to an ongoing process: 'The dashing of hopes that it enacts implies at least that there was in the first place some possibility of hopes being fulfilled . . . the relentlessness of Gary Mitchell's gaze and the quality of

---

[33] See Gary McMichael, *An Ulster Voice: In Search of Common Ground in Northern Ireland* (Dublin: Roberts Rinehart, 1999), 55, 165–6.

[34] Quoted in McKay, *Northern Protestants*, 114.

[35] Gary Mitchell, *In a Little World of Our Own*, in *Tearing the Loom and In a Little World of Our Own* (London: Nick Hern Books, 1998), 3–4.

[36] Interview with Chris McGimpsey, Belfast, 18 January 2012. See, for instance, the UVF beating two teenagers accused of anti-social behaviour in the Greater Shankill area in January 2008 (*The Observer*, 13 January 2008, 3).

[37] Interview with Billy McQuiston, Belfast, 14 June 2013.

his vision suggest that his play may in its own way mark the beginning of the end.'[38]

Friction depicted in the play is not antagonism between Loyalist and Unionist politicians, also a dynamic of the time, but within Loyalism itself: the straight choice between violence and politics. The play dramatizes once more the clash between those trying to pacify and those reluctant to renounce the old ways: 'The thing obviously with David [Ervine] and Billy [Hutchinson] is that they've done some bad shit in their lives, and they regret and they've apologized for that and they've moved on,' but the central presence of *In a Little World of Our Own* 'hadn't got to that place. Ray was still just as unapologetic about what he'd done. Ray was still in a position where he'd quite happily go out and murder again if he had to, if he felt it was necessary.'[39] Such voices tend not to appear prominently in the news media or public records, rendering Mitchell's articulation of them particularly valuable. The emergence of Billy Wright as a figurehead who eschewed socialism, and politics generally—in contrast to the UVF's affiliated PUP organization—brought these tensions very prominently into the political arena.[40] The UDA, meanwhile, at a time in the early 1990s 'used the Hume–Adams talks process as an excuse to target the entire nationalist community' and had begun to out-kill Irish Republican paramilitaries in the years preceding the 1998 Belfast Agreement.[41]

The play is built on the filial relationship between Ray and his handicapped brother Richard who idolizes him, and it is precisely because Ray is capable of a loving relationship with his brother that jars and disturbs interpretations. A key insight into Mitchell's own world view, a complex and often murky place, was highlighted at a discussion after a showing of the play during its original Dublin run. Mitchell recalled:

> This wee Catholic woman started saying 'You created this character of Ray, I fell in love with him. Do you really expect me to believe that he raped and murdered a thirteen-year-old girl? I'm afraid not. The Taig did it.' This woman shouts this out and [the play's director] Conall Morrison had to say to her 'You do know what a Taig is?', and people in the audience were shouting 'no, no we don't'. He said, 'Well, I'm a Taig, and you're probably a Taig—a Taig means a Catholic,' and then the horror started to go through the audience, who had just said how much they loved the play! That was the

---

[38] Fintan O'Toole, 'Doomed Dreams of Decency', *Irish Times*, 18 February 1997, 12.
[39] Interview with Stuart Graham, Belfast, 8 October 2011.
[40] See David Ervine's account in Ed Moloney (ed.), *Voices from the Grave: Two Men's War in Ireland* (London: Faber and Faber, 2010), 452–8.
[41] *Belfast Telegraph*, 11 January 2010, 27.

point. That you can love a character and think: 'Guy's fantastic-looking, looks after his brother, wait a second—what did he do?' This is what people are really afraid of. They're afraid that ordinary people kill and hate another group of ordinary people. They're down on their luck, they're squeezed, they've no money, they've no food, they're dying, and they're looking at the same people in the same streets who have everything. Guess what's going to happen? They're going to try and take it. If you don't allow them to earn it, if you don't allow them to even aspire to having it, then they're going to try and take it by force. That's normal.[42]

The director of Mitchell's *Trust*, which premiered at the Royal Court in 1999, remarked, 'We disagree on a load of issues, but it's those differences that form the strength of our friendship,'[43] a dynamic of the creative process for Mitchell generally. Conflict informs the way he works with others. 'I went to the bother of writing these plays, so I am going to be accurate. If there are words in the play it is because I have heard them. I am writing what people say.'[44] Whilst this dedication to verisimilitude has often served Mitchell well, effective drama is very often about what has not happened rather than what has, illuminating what British playwright Howard Barker has called 'the politics of the emotions'. Barker asserted 'that the only things worth describing now are things that do not happen, just as the only history plays worth writing concern themselves with what did not occur'.[45] Mitchell's work is powerful because it makes its audience, in his own words, 'feel something', not because it occurred in real life (it also recalls Thomas Carnduff's insistence that his work was only 'drawn from life').[46] An actor who remembers Mitchell defiantly saying 'that actually did happen' during a read-through at the National Theatre notes that it 'doesn't actually address the problem, which is that if you don't believe it, it doesn't matter whether it happened or not'.[47] This problem has been overcome by an accomplished director, which Mitchell has had at some points but not others in his career.

---

[42] Interview with Gary Mitchell, Antrim, 6 June 2013. See Mitchell, *In a Little World*, in *Tearing*, 7–18, 28–31.

[43] Mick Gordon, quoted in *The Guardian—G2*, 20 January 1999, 14. See Gary Mitchell, *Trust* (London: Nick Hern Books, 1999).

[44] Quoted in Tim Miles, 'Fighting the Peace: Counter-Narrative, Violence, and the Work of Gary Mitchell', in Lisa Fitzpatrick (ed.), *Performing Violence in Contemporary Ireland* (Dublin: Carysfort Press, 2009), 78.

[45] Harold Barker, *Arguments for a Theatre* (London: John Calder, 1989), 19.

[46] Interview with Gary Mitchell, Antrim, 6 June 2013; quoted in *Irish Times*, 12 October 1932, 5.

[47] Interview with Patrick O'Kane, Belfast, 2 November 2011.

DESCENT

In tandem with Gary Mitchell's theatrical breakthrough, Rathcoole was increasingly regarded as the fiefdom of John 'Grug' Gregg, who almost killed Gerry Adams in an assassination attempt in March 1984.[48] On his release from prison in 1993, Gregg assumed command of the South-East Antrim brigade of the UDA and presided over increased recruitment during the ceasefire period before being shot dead during another internal feud in 2003.[49] Mitchell encountered him during a documentary being filmed in Rathcoole early in his career, Gregg delivering the semi-psychotic remark that the programme makers could film on the estate if they did not use cameras.[50] Politically, however, Rathcoole possessed something of an independent streak when between 1973 and 2005 the area returned a minimum of one Labour councillor—and often more—in every municipal election. One such representative was Mark Langhammer (1960–), the son of a socialist printer father from pre-war Czech Sudetenland and a Belfast Protestant mother from the Shankill Road, who was an independent Labour councillor in Newtownabbey from the early 1990s until 2005:

> I started being politically active in the early eighties. The Northern Ireland Labour Party was to all intents and purposes over and this little remnant was left in Newtownabbey which survived long after the rest of the Labour Party fell apart. So there was a little flame there that was still going. The fact that in Newtownabbey there was such a strong strain of traditional or mainstream Labour was connected to manufacturing and industry. There'd be quite a lot of industry in Newtownabbey with Mackie's, Shorts, the Shipyards, Spalding, ICI, Standard Telephones—all unionized. The culture of trade unionism ran through the place. There wouldn't be a street in the estate that didn't have a shop steward or a Health and Safety Rep or a convenor in it.[51]

Former residents of the Shankill who resettled in Rathcoole also carried their Labour outlook with them when they moved to take up residence in the new estate.[52] But if Langhammer represented the residue of this

---

[48] Richard English, *Armed Struggle: A History of the IRA* (London: Macmillan, 2003), 247.
[49] *The Guardian*, 3 February 2003, 6.
[50] Interview with Tony Rowe, Belfast, 6 June 2009.
[51] Interview with Mark Langhammer, Belfast, 21 September 2011. Other Labour figures from the area included Bob Kidd, who had been an NILP councillor since the early 1960s, serving as an independent prior to his retirement in 2001. Kidd refused on socialist principle to own his own house (interview with Mark Williamson, Belfast, 24 November 2014).
[52] Interview with Jackie Hewitt, Belfast, 19 August 2014.

Protestant Labour culture, his tenure on the Council coincided with a time of increasing UDA muscle. Intrinsically related to the collapse of the traditional industries, middle-class Unionists had concurrently 'retreated to the golf courses' leaving the churches behind.[53] While impressed with certain UDA-affiliated spokespersons such as Gary McMichael and David Adams, Langhammer believes that the majority of the group were 'far more interested in using the cover of the peace process to deepen their criminal activity'. Gregg in particular was 'just nakedly sectarian', his political aspirations extending little further than 'shooting Fenians'.[54] This was exacerbated by the fact that policing in Rathcoole was virtually non-existent since attacks on the RUC following the 1985 Anglo-Irish Agreement,[55] with the result that hardly any officers lived locally. Those who joined the force could afford to move out of the estate and did, ensuring that the community lacked any low-level flow of information and communication with the police service, a void stepped into by the UDA. With the paramilitary group 'effectively subcontracted to the police', a 'blind eye to one degree or another was turned to their criminal activities, whether that's selling contraband cigarettes, vodka, or minor drug-dealing. They had a free hand in all of that in order that there was some flow of communication to Special Branch or whoever they were reporting to.'[56] The subsequent lack of order or any semblance of 'fairness', Langhammer believes, accounted for why people who would not normally support Labour kept voting for him. The atmosphere naturally energizes Gary Mitchell's work, which frequently touches on themes of the rule of law, policing, and justice in a dangerous environment.

When Langhammer arranged for an official police presence to return to the area, his home and car were attacked:

> There was a phase where I got letters and threats and the constituency office was stoned and windows broken, and then eventually they placed a bomb under my car. But it was particularly to do with support that I had given and initiated with the police. Basically the new Superintendent in Newtown-abbey was a Catholic and I went to talk to him and said 'Isn't it about time we reintroduced proper policing into Rathcoole?', i.e. policemen walking about the place. He was prepared to give that a try so I found him a

---

[53] Wood, *UDA*, 308–9.

[54] Interview with Mark Langhammer, Belfast, 21 September 2011.

[55] Paul Bew and Gordon Gillespie, *Northern Ireland: A Chronology of the Troubles 1968–1999* (Dublin: Gill & Macmillan, 1999), 198–9.

[56] Interview with Mark Langhammer, Belfast, 21 September 2011. See also *The Observer*, 5 April 1998, 5. A similar relationship is thought to exist at present between the police and the UDA-linked Lower Shankill Community Association (LSCA) in Belfast.

community building out of which to operate. It was a Churches Association building so the police were going to come to this weekly clinic and people could drop in and say their dog was lost or whatever. It was very low-level but the purpose was to re-establish normal policing, normal communication between the community and the police and the end to paramilitary policing. On the day in which it was going to open the building was graffitied, 'Touts in here', and my car was bombed. It was Gregg's mob. Basically he was putting out the message 'I run this fucking estate—you don't.'[57]

Not the only local political figure to be subject to these methods,[58] Langhammer was to follow Gary Mitchell out of Rathcoole. Before he left he looked into the dramatist's case and saw some of the plays, which he found 'very explicit, so I can see how the UDA wouldn't have liked to have seen themselves portrayed that way. The typical Loyalist reaction to Gary's play would have been, I heard it said a number of times, "He's making a cunt out of us, fucker's making a cunt out of us." That's about as much sense as I could get.'[59]

As the attacks on both playwright and councillor, identical in their hallmarks, took place in the years after the Good Friday Agreement, Mitchell deeply resents the suggestion that Northern Ireland is politically 'solved'. The assaults on elected political representatives and himself have ensured his work represents 'a counter-narrative to the hegemonic narrative of a movement towards peace'.[60] The sectarianism and violent antecedents are still present, in Mitchell's vision, despite the determination of a great many who maintain they are not: 'How could I write a positive drama about the peace process when terrorists are blowing up my car?' Just months after art met life and he was driven from his home, Mitchell appeared as a character from one of his own plays:

You're a second-class citizen if you don't come from London or Metro-land. If I was a Muslim writer whose work upset members of my community so much that some were threatening to kill me, then it would be a cause célèbre. There would be questions in parliament, writers would stage protests and Salman Rushdie would write letters of support. But because this is Northern Ireland what's happening to my family isn't part of the peace process narrative.[61]

[57] Interview with Mark Langhammer, Belfast, 21 September 2011. See also Wood, *UDA*, 269.
    [58] The Progressive Unionist Party spokesman Ken Wilkinson's house was pipe-bombed in December 2010 after he condemned sectarian attacks in Newtownabbey: 'If you speak out within your community, this is the price you pay' (quoted in *Belfast Telegraph*, 13 December 2010, 11).
    [59] Interview with Mark Langhammer, Belfast, 21 September 2011.
    [60] Miles, 'Fighting', 80.   [61] Quoted in *The Observer*, 29 January 2006, 7.

This statement directly echoes the view of a former leader of the Progressive Unionist Party: the Protestant working class never truly considered itself a part of the peace process narrative. This did not equate to wishing for a return to violence, only that 'working-class Unionists seem to be scapegoats of this whole process. They've had no dividend from the peace process.'[62] This has been sharpened by what Loyalists perceive to be partial historical and judicial investigations into the past, including a large-scale 'Supergrass' trial and the occasional prosecution.[63] Despite the statistic of 60 per cent of Troubles killings being carried out by Republicans, 30 per cent by Loyalists, and 10 per cent by British security forces, 'it's all going one way. The majority of enquiries that actually take place and prosecutions that follow are in the working-class Unionist areas. And it's breeding terrible resentment too because the British are now being perceived to have been reneging on the deal that they made.'[64] This erupted in October 2010 when upwards of two hundred young people threw stones and petrol bombs following police searches of homes in Rathcoole as part of an Historical Enquiries Team investigation into killings committed by the Mount Vernon UVF.[65] It was further aggravated by the 'On the Runs' scandal several years later, when it emerged that letters of assurance signed by the British government were sent to 187 Republican volunteers effectively guaranteeing *de facto* amnesty and that they would not be questioned by the police in Troubles investigations.[66]

Along with trite predictions of Catholics overtaking Protestants within the Northern Irish workforce on account of the birth rate,[67] a report by the Equality Commission charting employment levels from 1990 to 2006 showed that the share of Catholic full-time jobs rose from 34.9 to 43.1 per cent, while Protestant full-time jobs declined from 65.1 to 56.9 per cent, losing out particularly in manufacturing.[68] Commentators have observed that this has less to do with local political developments and is more attributable to 'globalisation and the move of heavy industry to Asia', though the same writer acknowledges that the more universal factors will not wash: 'Irish unity has been put on the never-never, but in every other way the community they represent sees improvement in its standing, in its

---

[62] Interview with Brian Ervine, Belfast, 28 January 2011.

[63] *Irish News*, 19 March 2012, 7. In the autumn of 2011, a large-scale 'Supergrass' trial of fourteen UVF men centred on a feud-related killing of the UDA's Tommy English in 2000. All but one was acquitted of all charges the following February (*Belfast Telegraph*, 23 February 2012, 4).

[64] Interview with Brian Ervine, Belfast, 11 January 2011.

[65] *Irish News*, 27 October 2010, 6–7.   [66] *Irish News*, 27 February 2014, 10.

[67] *Belfast Telegraph*, 31 March 2016, 8.

[68] *Belfast Telegraph*, 18 December 2007, 9.

prospects, in the quality of life and in its self-regard. Loyalist areas, in contrast, see recent years as a history of loss—of power, of status and political control and, crucially, of employment.'[69] In a scene from the film of Mitchell's *As the Beast Sleeps* (2002), Kyle and his UDA companions find themselves in a congested job centre. He is asked by a clerk if he has any qualifications, prompting sniggering from his friends, before being informed that he needs to have 'a high standard of education' to be able to apply for certain jobs. On their way out Freddie jokes 'No jobs for bank robbers, no?', leading to an existential exchange:

KYLE: We're not exactly looking for jobs are we?
FREDDIE: We've got jobs.
KYLE: Have we?[70]

Patrick O'Kane, who played Freddie in both the film and the first theatrical production, noted that the scene 'clarified a point which was being made in the original stage play, which is that they had been willing followers of a cause at the expense of their own personal education, and in some sense their own personal development'. When they were 'suddenly dropped, they were left with nothing'—except a future of unemployment.[71]

INFLUENCES AND POLICING

When it is suggested that his work echoes a particular dramatist or play such as Tom Murphy's *A Whistle in the Dark* (1960), Mitchell is adamant: 'I've never seen it. You go on the internet and type in "Gary Mitchell" and I guarantee after about ten clicks you'll come to a thing going, "Gary Mitchell—heavily influenced by..." and then a list of Irish writers. I never saw a play! And if I did see a play, you can bet I didn't like it. So that's "influenced by no one".'[72] This lack of a theatrical basis is essential to understanding Mitchell's theatre. His real influences are cinematic, especially the work of directors such as Martin Scorsese and Quentin Tarantino. While Mitchell is credited by some actors with 'writing Tarantino for the stage',[73] Scorsese is tonally more appropriate

[69] Maurice Hayes, 'Is UDA Taking the Peace Pledge?', *Belfast Telegraph*, 13 November 2007, 14.
[70] Gary Mitchell, *As the Beast Sleeps* (Belfast: BBC Northern Ireland, 2002). Author's transcription. This scene does not feature in the play.
[71] Interview with Patrick O'Kane, Belfast, 2 November 2011.
[72] Interview with Gary Mitchell, Antrim, 6 June 2013. The ellipsis represents a pause.
[73] Interview with Laine Megaw (actress), Belfast, 14 May 2012. Martin McDonagh, who emerged at around the same time, was also influenced more by film than by theatre.

because the violence has serious morals behind it which do not glamorize its personnel. Films like *Mean Streets* (1973) and *Goodfellas* (1990) also achieved the disorienting complexity Mitchell strives for 'where suddenly the bad guys were the good guys as well'.[74] The refusal of any theatrical lineage, while occasionally a little contrived, lends Mitchell a useful 'outsider' perspective which allows him to 'make outsiders' observations about his own community, and about the theatrical community within Northern Ireland'.[75]

Like Ron Hutchinson, Mitchell would find a spot at the Royal Court Theatre, which staged both *Trust* and *The Force of Change* (2000), the latter a taut work exploring policing and reactions to the 1999 Patten Report, which had changed the RUC's name to the Police Service of Northern Ireland (PSNI). A senior officer scorns:

> BILL: 'The Patten Report', what a joke that is. Take the guns off the police but let the terrorists keep theirs for 'personal protection'. I've sat in this station and watched my own organisation crumble. We even have Catholics involved these days. And the government wants more and more of them brought in. If they had their way the IRA would take over the Police force. Promotion and recruitment is going to be at least fifty-fifty. Is our population even fifty-fifty? No. That's reverse discrimination. In short who is going to be protecting your community? No-one. Every decision about a march. Every decision about anything is going to go their way.[76]

The play explains Protestant attitudes to the policing reforms to a London audience which was interested (briefly) in knowing how, or if, the peace was holding. Mitchell immediately identified the tensions of a force which now had 'to start policing Protestants'. The detritus of a 'confused and isolated organisation which doesn't know where it belongs'[77] presided over the flashpoint Drumcree dispute of 1995 and continues to exhibit a worryingly deteriorating relationship with Protestant working-class communities. *The Force of Change* played to full houses and would be transferred onto the Court's main stage after its initial run, representing a high point of Mitchell's time in London. Unlike most other writers considered in this book, Mitchell also prospered from

---

[74] Interview with Stuart Graham, Belfast, 8 October 2011.

[75] Interview with Patrick O'Kane, Belfast, 2 November 2011.

[76] Gary Mitchell, *The Force of Change* (London: Nick Hern Books, 2000), 49.

[77] Mitchell, quoted in Ruth Little and Emily McLaughlin, *The Royal Court Theatre Inside Out* (London: Oberon Books, 2007), 395. See also Michael Billington, *State of the Nation: British Theatre Since 1945* (London: Faber and Faber, 2007), 374.

circumstances at the Lyric Theatre under then-artistic director Robin Midgley. While he had his detractors and the theatre's finances remained precarious, Midgley sought to encourage local talent and so Ulster's principal theatrical venue was cautiously receptive to Mitchell when he emerged.[78] The departure of sympathetic television producers like Robert Cooper, on the other hand, means that the BBC now has little disposition to produce drama, in Mitchell's words, 'about the Protestant community of Northern Ireland by a Protestant',[79] invariably reflecting a slanted view of the 'post-conflict' society. Cooper confirms that he left at a time when Northern Irish drama was being phased out, a sea-change courtesy of then Director-General Greg Dyke, who rechannelled funding from BBC2's regional drama to mainstream BBC1 productions.[80] The resulting debris is shallow, glitzy series like *The Fall* (2012–) in which Northern Ireland and its people are an appendage of the story, basking in the strikingly unmemorable visuals of affluent Belfast cityscapes, projecting a place few of its inhabitants know or experience.

PUNK

In *Energy*, which premiered in Derry in 1999, Gary Mitchell deals with punk music in the context of Northern Ireland. If the route suicidally pioneered by Sid Vicious ended in self-immolation or teenagers hurling rocks at one another every Friday night at Belfast interfaces, those who took the other road—represented by punk's natural intellectual John Lydon—ended up writing, and Mitchell has more than a little of *The Sex Pistols* frontman's spiky intellect. Patrick O'Kane, who has acted in some of Mitchell's most important plays, notes that his 'writing has a similar rawness to it, that visceral edge in terms of its energy which punk music had'.[81] The attacking rhythms reverberate through the language, and O'Kane intriguingly confirms that he listened to fast, upbeat punk music as a way to get into the character of Loyalist renegade Freddie in *As the Beast Sleeps*. In the face of much hostility ('Your gigs were shut down by paramilitaries, the community frowned upon you'), Mitchell played in as many as fifteen different punk bands growing up in Rathcoole. Prior to his leadership of the UDA's 'C Company', Johnny Adair also played in a

---

[78] *Irish Times*, 27 January 1994, 8. Midgley chose Graham Reid's *The Hidden Curriculum* as the opening play of his tenure.
[79] Mitchell, 'Rathcoole Ranger', 125.
[80] Telephone interview with Robert Cooper, 15 August 2014.
[81] Interview with Patrick O'Kane, Belfast, 2 November 2011.

punk group and was attracted to the 'white power' revival of the early 1980s, attending skinhead discos in Rathcoole and Monkstown.[82] Aside from the way these details—popularly recycled by journalists—elide the more progressive Protestant punk bands of the era,[83] Mitchell reminds us that 'punks were the weak people in the community: the non-violence people who just liked music. They liked the fact that they could lift guitars and play something. No voice, no intelligence, no way of explaining or communicating. But you can bang the hell out of a drum; you can strum the hell out of a guitar; and you can bounce up and down and reveal all your frustrations with life.'[84]

The 2013 release of the film *Good Vibrations*, based on the life and memoir of Terri Hooley, saw a renewed interest in Northern Ireland's punk scene, encapsulated by Hooley himself. Punk seemed to represent the most considerable movement to vault sectarian barriers since the Labour advance, a continuum seemingly enhanced by the way Hooley's father was a devotee of the NILP and even won a municipal seat for it in East Belfast just after the Second World War.[85] Some held that the movement was 'viewed with suspicion by paramilitaries from both sides of the divide, because organically, unplanned and unstructured, punks and their hangers-on crossed every religious and social divide',[86] a view Mitchell characteristically rejects:

> The music was brilliant but again, I know the myth surrounding the punk movement in Northern Ireland and I can tell you—I am a Protestant and I was a punk—it's all nonsense. Because the reality is that the Protestant communities hated punk, and that's why I wrote *Energy*—to show that if you were a Catholic and you wanted to play punk music, what happens? You're encouraged. You're supported all the way. This is how you end up with all these bands like *The Undertones*. But suddenly it becomes political. Suddenly it becomes anti-British. 'Anarchy in the UK', 'God Save the Queen'—'Let's make fun of the Queen, let's make fun of the Army. Let's *use* music, for *us*'—and that's what it became. I agree that the music could

[82] David Lister and Hugh Jordan, *Mad Dog: The Rise and Fall of Johnny Adair and 'C Company'* (Edinburgh: Mainstream Publishing, 2004), 32–4.

[83] Gareth Mulvenna, 'The Protestant Working Class in Northern Ireland: Political Allegiance and Social and Cultural Challenges Since the 1960s', PhD thesis, Queen's University Belfast, 2009, 54.

[84] Interview with Gary Mitchell, Antrim, 6 June 2013.

[85] Terri Hooley (and Richard Sullivan), *Hooleygan: Music, Mayhem, Good Vibrations* (Belfast: Blackstaff Press, 2010), 14, 16–19. In October 2012 Hooley was jostled by two Loyalists on the footpath where he was walking his dog, recalling that he 'used to get this at every election because my father was in the Labour Party' (quoted in *Irish News*, 30 October 2012, 7).

[86] Henry McDonald, 'Punk Memorial Idea Has Some Hits and Misses', *Belfast Telegraph*, 6 November 2012, 29.

have done it. We could have had this huge movement and the myth could have been true. But the reality is that, sadly, again to me it was a very Catholic thing in terms of Belfast and Northern Ireland. They grab it, they own it, and they rewrite it. The music became another weapon in the same way I believe as the theatre. But if it's used as a weapon then it's no use: it becomes just as blunt as any other weapon.[87]

This is part contrariness, part over-sensitized suspicion of nationalist appropriation, and completely rooted in the Rathcoole vicinity. Much as Mitchell has understandably swum against the tide of the peace narrative, the consensus surrounding Ulster's punk scene—fostered by the Hooley biopic—represents another fashionable bubble to burst.

Nevertheless, the way the legendary Derry punk band *The Undertones* entered the fray with 'It's Going to Happen', released days before Bobby Sands died on hunger strike in 1981, would appear to confirm Mitchell's qualm. The group had prided itself on being apolitical, but after Sands's passing, guitarist Damian O'Neill wore a black armband when the group appeared on *Top of the Pops* to play the song, which hazily beckons the British government to change track: 'Happens all the time / It's going to happen, happen / Till you change your mind.' Over a decade prior to the *Good Vibrations* hype, not always helped by Hooley's glib deportment, *Energy* entertainingly captures the sense that punk was not impervious to political pressures, with the traditional certainties always liable to corrupt.

PETE: Fuck politics, don't even go near it. What you should be writing about... is us.[88]

The UDA demands protection money from the shop where the band practices, and sectarian divisions (the band is mixed) also intrude. Politics keep recurring, as when the band's guitarist comes up with a new song:

HUMPER: What's it called?
DAVE: It's called 'Starving'... because it's about the Hunger Strikers.
PETE: No way.
HUMPER: How's it about the Hunger Strikers?
DAVE: Well the first verse is about being thirsty and the second is about being starving.
HUMPER: No, Dave.
PETE: When you asked me to join this group a big part of the deal was that we wouldn't touch politics—ever.

---

[87] Interview with Gary Mitchell, Antrim, 6 June 2013.
[88] Gary Mitchell, *Energy* (Unpublished: 3rd draft, November 1998), 72. Original ellipsis.

DAVE: What do you mean when I asked you to join this group?

HUMPER: Pete's right, we've always said that we wouldn't touch politics. Everything is only political if you make it political.

DAVE: A song about people starving could for some people be the hunger strike or it could even be the famine.

PETE: What the fuck would you know about the famine?

HUMPER: I think you should stick to the love songs you do.[89]

The UDA man Glen assures the record store owner he is intimidating that 'This is a Catholic thing, scummy rebel music is for the scummy rebels.' Consulting a notebook with his lines, Glen robotically claims, 'This is anti-Christian and therefore Anti-Protestant. Just another example of the dirty Fenian psychology that's rampant in our society. This Punk Rock rubbish can't be allowed to get a foot hold in this community. Nobody likes it and nobody wants it.' Oblivious to the retort that 'the Kids do', Glen loses patience and strikes a cymbal with a gun; music played by weapons and hijacked, like many things in Northern Ireland, by gunmen literally calling the tune. Despite this the band make their first gig, each member individually splurging out their politics on stage. Before the music overwhelms language, Dave outlines a median humanism which equates ultimately to being left alone: 'I just want to say that I agree with Pete about the victims and I agree with Alison about the criminals and redemption . . . but I don't want to fuck with or agree with fucking any paramilitary organisation that still has arms or still carries out punishment beatings.'[90]

Its sequel *Reenergize*—staged at the Derry Playhouse in 2013—is a largely comic piece, though even here Mitchell's recent past looms large. Beyond the enjoyment of seeing the characters again fourteen years on, still largely the same (actors Andy Moore and Chris Corrigan reprised their performances), they remain financially squeezed with a UDA surrogate in the form of debt collector 'Young' Cecil. He extracts what he is due by simply taking the post office cards, bank cards, and PIN numbers off the main characters. Cecil pressures Pete to apply for a higher level of Disability Living Allowance (DLA) so that he can in turn be paid, deepening a benefit trap.

CECIL: Do you think my da retired from the club because he wanted to? He didn't. He was told to retire. And now that I've been given this chance I have to make sure nobody forces me to retire. Do you understand? We're not a big high street bank, I'm not on a million pound bonus whether I fuck things up or not. My job is to lend money

---

[89] Mitchell, *Energy*, 67–9. Original ellipsis.
[90] Mitchell, *Energy*, 108–10, 158. Original ellipsis.

to people so that when they pay it back I can charge them a lot of interest, make a lot of money and keep everybody above me happy.[91]

Though the main characters get the better of Cecil, at the end they still owe him money, albeit with their cards returned and repayment at a better rate. Mitchell always appears to be writing about the financially pushed because it is the experience he continues to know. His initial purist desire for control over his work led to his demanding final cut—ultimately shared with producer Robert Cooper—of the film of *As the Beast Sleeps* at the expense of a more substantial fee ('Nowadays because I'm skint, I would never be able to do that'). A former mentor pointed out that he writes prolifically to support a young family and 'lived virtually on fresh air for the last few years',[92] a condition he has navigated through the unswerving support of his wife Alison.

MODERN BRITAIN

The poet and former UK Cabinet Minister Grey Gowrie has noted that multiculturalism ensures that the citizens of the United Kingdom now understand cultural politics in a way they did not when he served as a Minister in Northern Ireland. The continuing exposure to Islam, Hinduism, and Sikhism, and highlighting of institutions such as arranged marriage, mean that the modern British populace now has a surer handle on cultural issues.[93] Back in the era of the government Gowrie served, another poet provocatively asserted that official Unionism 'clings to a concept of nationality which no longer satisfies many of the British people whom the Ulster Unionists wish to identify with',[94] pre-empting an insight Gary Mitchell had while on attachment at the National Theatre in London:

> In London I found the exact same thing [as Northern Ireland] except it was very much race rather than sectarianism. I remember having this argument when I was Writer-in-residence in the National, making my observations of how I felt and people weren't happy with it at all. Because they kept promoting this 'Oh we're multicultural, we all work together'. Black and white people, Asian people, all of them work together because they're being paid. What happens at night time? As soon as they walk out of work they go to their own ghettos. The black people go to a black area, the Irish people go to an Irish pub. Everybody goes to their own place afterwards. It's not multicultural. If you pay people enough money they'll say anything and they'll get on with

---

[91] Gary Mitchell, *Reenergize* (Unpublished: 29 April 2013), 2, 15–18, 53.
[92] Interview with Pam Brighton, Belfast, 25 March 2014.
[93] Interview with Lord Grey Gowrie, London, 19 September 2012.
[94] Tom Paulin, 'A New Look at the Language Question', in *Ireland's Field Day* (London: Hutchinson, 1985), 13.

anybody. It is a myth and you've only to look at what happens in the street. Suddenly you have this incident; a solider gets killed in the middle of the street and suddenly people go 'Oh it's an isolated incident, because racism doesn't exist'. Multicultural? Fucking nonsense. People don't want to face up to it.[95]

The difficulty with this is that London is demonstrably not the same as Belfast or Rathcoole, and Mitchell's struggle with the capital of the United Kingdom is symptomatic of the problems many from the Protestant working class (and Loyalism) now share: a vision of the identity they are adamant they uphold which does not correspond to the modern reality of a diverse and cosmopolitan British city. 'Whatever they think they are, or want to remain, is changing—but they can't,' as a trade unionist from the same background phrased it.[96] Mitchell fundamentally did not, perhaps could not, grasp what a place like London represents; the pluralism of races existing side by side in a turbulent, contested, but finally coherent experiment. The strength of uniquely exploring an inward-looking community does not transfer to the metropolis of a global capital. Sometimes Mitchell has confronted the dichotomy and he was struck by the racially mixed nature of London's theatre audiences, trying 'to listen to as many people and talk as much as I could with members of the audience'.[97] After a performance of Mitchell's *Trust* at the Royal Court, a theatre critic noticed how 'many people emerged commenting that such a situation could equally arise in minority communities in Britain. But they then quickly observed that in Northern Ireland, these people come from the majority population—at which point, the focus hardens and sharpens.'[98] Mitchell told the same journalist that this heightens the community's intransigence. British people do not recognize them as British: 'They just think of them as crazy people.'

The modern UK's multicultural identity and chequered history was encapsulated in Danny Boyle's opening ceremony to the 2012 Olympic Games in London, an event which former Irish Republican hunger strikers (albeit of a dissenting variety) managed to laud as 'brilliant' and a 'real history of these Isles'.[99] At the same time, the wider UK's relationship with multiculturalism remains ambivalent. London elected a Muslim Mayor (Sadiq Khan) in May 2016 but has not been impervious to tension, as a surge of race hate attacks following the 2016 'Brexit' vote illustrates,[100]

---

[95] Interview with Gary Mitchell, Antrim, 6 June 2013. The killing was that of Drummer Lee Rigby in Woolwich, London, in May 2013.
[96] Interview with Joe Law, Belfast, 26 June 2013.
[97] Interview with Gary Mitchell, Antrim, 6 June 2013.
[98] Jane Coyle, 'Another Ireland', *Irish Times*, 23 March 1999, 12.
[99] *The Observer*, 6 February 2011, 8–9; Tommy McKearney, 'State of the Union', *Social Justice Review* (Winter 2012), 37.
[100] *London Evening Standard*, 29 June 2016, 8.

and it also possesses a certain exceptionalism compared to the rest of England, as evidenced by its majority vote to remain in the European Union. In this sense the Ulster Protestant working class can be located alongside the wider white working class of the UK who are also 'searching for an identity' and find themselves 'abandoned by their political leaders'.[101] It would therefore be helpful to view the Protestant predicament within a broader UK framework, as 'a class which has been subject not simply to economic immiseration but to a systematic devaluation of its moral worth by a commentariat in the media and academia which focuses on its sectarianism/racism, threatened masculinity and general "identity crisis"'.[102] On the mainland this has manifested in voluble anger towards the 'centrist convergence' of both major political parties, generating 'left behind' white working-class communities who consider themselves voiceless in mainstream politics. In England and Wales these voters have partly turned to radical Right alternatives such as the United Kingdom Independence Party (UKIP) which provides a solution—and scapegoat—through anti-immigrant rhetoric, and like older blue-collar UK voters 'with obsolete skills and few formal qualifications', the Ulster Protestant working class has negotiated the post-industrial barriers of austerity Britain.[103]

When in December 2012 a volatile series of protests began in the wake of the democratic decision of Belfast City Council to fly the Union Jack on no more than eighteen designated days instead of all year, trade and local business in Belfast city centre were badly disrupted.[104] The damage to the economy was marked but the essence of the protest was missed. The agitation chaotically impacted on economic activity, obstructing routine and affecting the night life of the more affluent citizens enjoying a drink and going to expensive restaurants. There was thus a distinct class-charge to the protest, which may be connected to the way members of the dominant Unionist Party such as Sammy Wilson—once known as 'Red Sammy' for his apparent sympathies—are considered to have left their working-class constituents behind.[105] The former Finance Minister counters that while difficulties are universal, he admits to finding Protestant

---

[101] Sarfraz Manzoor, 'The Forgotten People', *The Guardian—MediaGuardian*, 3 March 2008, 9.
[102] Henry Patterson, 'Interests and Identities in Northern Ireland', *Dynamics of Asymmetric Conflict: Pathways toward Terrorism and Genocide*, Vol. 4, No. 1 (2011), 75–6.
[103] Robert Ford and Matthew Goodwin, *Revolt on the Right: Explaining Support for the Radical Right in Britain* (Abingdon: Routledge, 2014), 145, 135–8, 176.
[104] *Belfast Telegraph*, 17 December 2012, 4–5. Business of pubs and restaurants was down 28 per cent and retail sales down 14 per cent.
[105] *Irish News*, 18 January 2012, 1.

working-class 'disengagement' worrying: 'There are a lot of people who would be in the lower-end of the economic spectrum who disengage from everything. They disengage from Churches, from education, from community activity, from political activity. And you need people who are embedded in those communities, even if you can't get them out to vote, to at least keep the foot in those communities so they're articulating what the needs are.'[106] Another DUP representative for East Belfast, formerly of the Northern Ireland Labour Party, concedes that 'over the years we had lost touch and become too middle class. The reality to some degree is that we're up at Stormont and my major concern is that I become detached. Four miles down the road those people are not seeing the dividend.'[107] Sammy Wilson claims, however, that the problems 'started a long, long time before the current economic situation' and relate to the way 'as families got successful they moved out', so 'the natural leaders were disappearing. Increasingly you saw that more and more of the people who were left in those areas were people who didn't have a great deal of motivation.'[108] Wilson does not therefore accept that his own party has left behind its original urban working-class base and rather feebly passes the buck to a previous generation of Unionist politicians, that is, the Official Unionist Party, for not maintaining a presence in these areas. There is even some suggestion that the DUP's close relationship with the UDA—occasionally running ex-paramilitaries as candidates and backing organizations which are headed by UDA personnel[109]—is a way of wresting back working-class support.

Gary Mitchell on the other hand has for years written about the marginalized and disillusioned underclass ('my group') thrown up by the 'Flag Protests', relating it to an old dynamic:

They're suckered in with this nonsense about the 'master race'. It happened in America. The myth is that you're better than somebody just by being white. In Northern Ireland you're born and told: 'You're better than these other people just because you're Protestant. Don't forget—those people there, no matter what happens to them, they'll always be Irish. They'll always be Catholic, they'll always be scum.' So you should just be happy—*quietly*, happy. Sitting in your shitty wee house with no money and no food. 'Remember—you mightn't have anything, but you're still a Protestant.' You have to buy into that. The distraction is: don't worry about politics.

---

[106] Interview with Sammy Wilson, Carrickfergus, 10 February 2012.
[107] Interview with Sammy Douglas, Belfast, 3 February 2012. Douglas stepped down from politics in 2017.
[108] Interview with Sammy Wilson, Carrickfergus, 10 February 2012.
[109] *Irish News*, 30 September 2016, 4. One such group is Charter NI.

Don't worry about anything that's real. 'You have to vote for us because we're going to stop *the monster.*' What's the monster? 'A United Ireland'.[110]

Mitchell is interrogating a long-standing myth perpetuated by Unionist politicians, displaying the same anger as Protestant trade unionists who agree that whereas the Catholic community could demonstrate against the state, 'We had to suffer our poverty in silence.'[111] As has been noted, nothing provokes resentment within the Protestant working class in Northern Ireland more than the notion that life within this bracket was, or remains, in any way privileged.[112]

At the tail end of New Labour rule the British playwright Richard Bean bemoaned an increasing number of plays featuring 'a load of people in a flat doing stuff, and you never find out where they get their money from'.[113] In a Northern Irish context playwright Daragh Carville actually called for even more stories about Belfast's 'swanky apartment blocks, of coffee shops and the new culture',[114] exemplifying Bean's observation that the hardships of daily living for those on the bottom rung of society seldom seemed to preoccupy theatre practitioners in those years. This is not a complacency Gary Mitchell's work has ever suffered from. If it is a low-paid or unskilled job, paramilitary activity, or the dole which provides income, we are made aware of it very early on. We know exactly the importance of money and economic status because it affects daily working-class life; a culture where 'you tend not to plan ahead because you live for today'.[115] This generally hinders those negotiating an increasingly penurious welfare system, with difficulties budgeting, and, in general, simply 'making ends meet'.[116] This book has dealt with class in traditional terms but the time-frame of this chapter takes in new stratifications, including the advent of one at the very bottom, below the old working class: the 'precariat'. With 'Poor economic capital' (as well as low cultural and social capital),[117] this is a group resounding through Gary Mitchell's work before they were even designated as such.

---

[110] Interview with Gary Mitchell, Antrim, 6 June 2013.

[111] Interview with Glen Barr, Derry, 28 November 2012.

[112] Graham Walker, 'Old History: Protestant Ulster in Lee's "Ireland"', *The Irish Review*, No. 12 (Spring/Summer, 1992), 69.

[113] Quoted in *The Guardian—G2*, 28 January 2009, 24.

[114] Quoted in *The Observer*, 26 April 2009, 12.

[115] Interview with John Kyle, Belfast, 11 November 2010.

[116] Lisa McKenzie, *Getting By: Estates, Class and Culture in Austerity Britain* (Bristol: Policy Press, 2015), 47.

[117] Mike Savage, Fiona Devine, Niall Cunningham, Mark Taylor, Yaojun Li, Johs Hjellbrekke, Brigitte Le Roux, Sam Friedman, and Andrew Miles, 'A New Model of Social Class? Findings from the BBC's Great British Class Survey Experiment', *Sociology*, Vol. 47, No. 2 (April 2013), 230.

Part of the broader tension is that paramilitaries who did well materially during the 'war' years are peering into an uneasy future where their operations and funds will be questioned. It became for Loyalism about 'putting our own house in order', a process which led to some catastrophic feuding,[118] and with present promises from the British and Irish governments to combat paramilitarism on the horizon, there is likely to be further discord ahead. In a row towards the end of *As the Beast Sleeps*, the domestic is fused with the broader climate when its conflicted protagonist insists:

> KYLE: Money's part of it. We need money. Money to get this place done up properly—to pay your Ma off—to give Joe a better life—to get the car sorted out. This is about all that. We all need money, Sandra. We might not like it but that's the way it is.[119]

This slip into the personal also reflects the life Mitchell faces as a writer, anticipating the expense of living with a young family after the Rathcoole attacks when he and his wife 'continued to pay a mortgage for a bungalow we were not allowed to return to'.[120] This may seem trivial to some but for the vast majority of working-class Protestants it is day-to-day life. In Mitchell's case, with lost deposits through hasty house moves and new school uniforms for new schools, 'it's not even about safety any more. It's about money. You can't write a play or film when you're in the middle of this. I've lost maybe two or three years' worth of work. That's how clever that organisation is.'[121]

FLAGS

In November 2012, the current leader of the Progressive Unionist Party Billy Hutchinson called a meeting with approximately three hundred standing UVF Volunteers where he explained that 'They either work with us and get politicized, or they'll be criminalized. It has to be politics pure and simple.' A matter of weeks before the 'Flag Protests' commenced in December 2012, he explained exactly where he was planning to take his constituency if the opportunity arose:

> The problem at the minute for the PUP is that both classes are so far apart it's unbelievable and what we need to do is some of this stuff and play to our

---

[118] Mitchell, *As the Beast*, 80; *The Guardian*, 18 March 1999, 1.
[119] Mitchell, *As the Beast*, 63, 96. By the end the political has morphed into the domestic, as Sandra sides with Freddie against her own husband: 'Fuck talk.'
[120] Mitchell, 'Rathcoole Ranger', 111.
[121] Quoted in *Irish Times*, 2 May 2009, 49.

own audience, until we get them ready—and then we bring them down the road. We're going to have to do some of that; we're going to have to do stuff which I don't particularly like doing. But at the same time, it's about lining them all up and saying 'Here's where we're going . . .'.[122]

Developments on Belfast City Council provided Hutchinson with the opening he was looking for. To harness the momentum of the ensuing protests was a gamble and one which initially paid off. The PUP doubled its council seats in the May 2014 municipal elections—Hutchinson topping the poll in Court, North and West Belfast—and even more importantly the conversion strategy ('bringing them down the road') appeared to be working when at the October 2013 annual conference the party passed a motion in favour of 'Equal', that is, same-sex marriage,[123] with those directly recruited from the protests appearing to have changed their minds on this issue following speeches in favour of the motion.

However, the minimal aspiration for the PUP was to take back the Northern Ireland Assembly seat for East Belfast, and this was where the strategy came unstuck. Most of the figureheads who came to prominence in 2012–13 were based outside East Belfast, and despite the goodwill for the PUP from academia and the media (which other Unionists say is 'disproportionate' to the political strength the party has),[124] the Flag Protests were complex and took in disparate, almost frenziedly different strands of Protestant politics. Left-wing elements were present, and were nurtured by the PUP, but the protests also encompassed the far-right Britain First and other extreme Loyalist groups.[125] The leaders proved themselves adept self-publicists but whenever they have dipped the slightest toe into electoral waters they have been found wanting.[126] Despite an able candidate in Dr John Kyle, the PUP fell short of taking East Belfast in the May 2016 Assembly election, and, more problematically, its involvement in the Flag Protests led many to glean that the party of David Ervine appeared to have shed its socialist credentials in favour of precisely the kind of flag-waving its leaders once denounced.[127] This extended to a change in Hutchinson's previous contrition for past Loyalist actions,

---

[122] Interview with Billy Hutchinson, Belfast, 12 November 2012. The ellipsis represents a pause.

[123] *Belfast News Letter*, 14 October 2013, 10.

[124] Interview with Sammy Wilson, Carrickfergus, 10 February 2012.

[125] *Belfast Telegraph*, 20 June 2014, 6. One far-right campaigner involved was Jim Dowson, also a member of the 'Protestant Coalition'.

[126] In the local government elections of May 2011, Jamie Bryson (born in 1990), chairman of the Ulster People's Forum (UPF) and one of the Flag Protest leaders, gained 167 votes in Bangor West, finishing second bottom of the poll.

[127] See Hutchinson's comments in Feargal Cochrane, *Unionist Politics and the Politics of Unionism Since the Anglo-Irish Agreement* (Cork: Cork University Press, 1997), 45, 57.

seemingly playing to a new hard-line gallery. His 1995 statement that 'We achieved absolutely nothing through violence' was replaced by insistences that he had 'no regrets in terms of my past because I believe I contributed to preventing a united Ireland'.[128]

Nonetheless with obituaries for the PUP already penned, its involvement in the Flag Protests was a way of keeping the organization relevant. Hutchinson downplayed the reactionary connotations and condemned the accompanying Loyalist violence which overtook East Belfast, often directed at the centrist Alliance Party, who had offered the compromise motion on the Council ensuring the flag came down. He pointed out how public regenerative campaigns such as 'Backin' Belfast', which arose to specifically counter the commotion, 'should have been done long before there was any flag protest' to make an increasingly gentrified city centre more accessible to everyone. Hutchinson recalled a specific incident in late December 2012 when the protests were well underway, as a gathering became heated. After being pushed by a police officer, 'I asked where the boss was and he said "he's behind me"—and when I looked over his shoulder, between him and another officer what I could see was hundreds of people running about with shopping bags in the town. That image stuck with me; because people were so resilient.'[129] The 'boss' is indeed the economic situation, the flag dispute symbolizing above all 'what people felt they were losing'.[130] Others perceptively deduced that the storm may 'actually be about the fact that demographically this is becoming a different city and is going to become a majority Catholic nationalist/Republican city, and nobody's looking at how that change is managed'.[131]

Neither should the role the main Unionist parties played in stirring the situation be ignored. The *Belfast Telegraph* carried a letter from the minister of the Adullam Christian Fellowship in Sandy Row three days after the protests ignited, drawing attention to 'weeks of yellow leaflets' (the colour of the Alliance Party) which had been printed by both the Democratic Unionist Party and Ulster Unionist Party. Conveying the statement 'No Union Jacks being flown again over City Hall', these had been distributed across East Belfast, leading the same pastor to doubt 'the politicians [who] condemn the violence that happened, but none said they were sorry for lighting the fuse that brought the violence about, by the words they had uttered in the run-up to the crucial vote'.[132] Fifteen police

---

[128] Quoted in *The Observer*, 27 August 1995, 12; quoted in *Irish News*, 20 March 2014, 4.
[129] Interview with Billy Hutchinson, Belfast, 21 March 2013.
[130] Interview with Jackie Hewitt, Belfast, 19 August 2014.
[131] Interview with Jackie Redpath, Belfast, 19 February 2013.
[132] Pastor Paul Burns, 'City Hall Flags Dispute Leaves Me in Despair', *Belfast Telegraph*, 6 December 2012, 34.

officers were injured in initial street clashes (rising to 146 by February 2013), with Unionist politicians apparently satisfied to 'incite and then condemn'.[133] Seeing his group on television again, Gary Mitchell at first reacted humorously ('You shouldn't put microphones in front of teenagers'), before cutting to the heart of the problem:

> It's the easiest thing in the world to go 'Look at these eejits. They want their flag put up, haha, look at them, they're scum!' That's not helping anybody. Something needs to be done to actually go in and look at it, try to examine it, and find out how did you reach this point. To be totally honest, the first thing that comes into my head, and maybe it's because we have kids, when I see people on TV rioting about a flag is 'What's wrong with the education system?' Because nobody can explain what they're *really* talking about. Nobody can identify the real issues.[134]

While the protests exposed sneering middle-class attitudes on social media, ridiculing the underprivileged for how they dressed and spoke ('fleggers', a play on how 'flag' is pronounced, became a derogatory term for the protesters), they were also accompanied by a new rash of self-appointed 'community leaders', raising parallels with the wider UK. In 1981 Bradford City Council set up the Bradford Council of Mosques, encompassing various sects to act as the intermediary between that community and public bodies in the northern city, but ultimately designed 'to present itself as the true voice of the "Muslim community"'.[135] The problem was that this allowed hardliners within what was a diverse community to present themselves as the authentic voice of *all* Muslims in the city. The resulting 'community leaders', whose main loyalty was to Islam, were essentially 'installed as the custodian of the Muslim community, a community that did not exist in this form until council policy has parcelled it up and given it as a gift to the Council of Mosques'.[136] It is not hard to identify the resonances in Northern Ireland, with assorted victims' campaigners and Loyalist activists vying to present themselves as the mouthpieces of the entire, so-called 'Protestant/Unionist/Loyalist' (PUL) community.

By the time the same energetic, youthful 'community leaders' were imprisoned and requested to be moved to the Loyalist paramilitary wings of Maghaberry prison,[137] it became clear that what was playing out was the impulsive fury of young men who wished to emulate the violent

---

[133] Interview with Billy Hutchinson, Belfast, 21 March 2013.
[134] Interview with Gary Mitchell, Antrim, 18 September 2013.
[135] Kenan Malik, *From Fatwa to Jihad: The Rushdie Affair and its Legacy* (London: Atlantic, 2009), 73.
[136] Malik, *From Fatwa to Jihad*, 76–7.
[137] This was the aforementioned Jamie Bryson (*Irish News*, 15 March 2013, 14).

heyday of the Troubles. Far from a new dispensation moving beyond past antagonisms, some juveniles in Protestant working-class areas feel they have 'missed out' and are echoing the rhetoric of Gary Mitchell's Loyalist dissidents. 'Fuck politics, fuck talking, fuck all that shit... Taigs hate us and we hate them. That's the way it is and that's the way it's going to stay,'[138] Freddie blazes in *As the Beast Sleeps*. The actor who originally portrayed the character grasped that though there was a euphoric feeling in 1998, 'the notion that there's a lot of work to do was useful. Just because we've signed this piece of paper and stopped fighting doesn't mean we want to be friends with each other. We're still in that situation now, frankly.'[139] Young Protestant males remain prey to Loyalist paramilitary leaders who have the cool audacity to sit in the office of an elected MLA and inform him they will 'have hoods on the streets of East Belfast if they didn't get things they wanted done'.[140] Though deprivation and social problems in working-class Catholic areas are as severe if not more so, a PUP councillor bluntly concedes that Loyalist politicians failed to match Sinn Féin's ability 'to engage with the next generation of younger people coming up. Younger people got involved in paramilitary organizations because it gave them a sense of camaraderie and identity. But there was not a healthy connection between the Loyalist paramilitaries and the PUP in terms of mentoring and influencing young people.'[141]

CONCLUSION

Trade unionists have pointed out that in Rathcoole and other Protestant working-class areas the loss of the manufacturing industry was particularly devastating 'because it stripped out a layer of people who used to be shop stewards, convenors, and health and safety reps'. Combined with the decline of Churches, which provided some of the glue in Protestant communities, the collapse of these 'very large, almost unseen influences' has had dire consequences for the social fabric of such areas.[142] At a time when it has become less important to the Protestant working class, Christian faith has become increasingly relevant to Gary Mitchell. He

---

[138] Mitchell, *As the Beast*, 81.
[139] Interview with Patrick O'Kane, Belfast, 2 November 2011.
[140] Interview with Sammy Douglas, Belfast, 3 February 2012. Following rioting on the lower Newtownards Road in the summer of 2011 (see *Belfast Telegraph*, 22 June 2011, 4), this was the promise of a UVF leader in East Belfast.
[141] Interview with John Kyle, Belfast, 11 November 2010. Kyle is his party's representative for Pottinger.
[142] Interview with Mark Langhammer, Belfast, 21 September 2011.

was approached by a group of sympathetic Loyalists after he left Rathcoole who said they could take revenge on those who attacked his family and home. Initially vengeful, this feeling had subsided. 'I didn't want anything like that at all. I said, "I write plays mate, hopefully that will be my revenge." The more I can convince people to stay away from these organisations... That's how I win.'[143] He has always been alert to the situation, confirming not long after he was driven out of his home that young working-class Protestants 'don't feel they have any stake in society. The paramilitary organisations have to go away—but they also have to be replaced. Teenagers need to be given other opportunities.'[144]

Representatives of the party linked to the UVF remain guarded on how a civilianization process might pan out. Any inclination the organization has to 'leave the stage', in David Ervine's words, is thought to be offset by 'individuals and groups who don't want to go away—who get kudos, significance and benefit from the continued existence of the UVF'.[145] In May 2010 a conspicuous murder on the Shankill Road prompted the departure of Dawn Purvis as leader of the same party. Once involved in transformation initiatives, she is under no illusions as to the future:

> Unfortunately there were other forces at work which meant that there was never going to be an endgame. Now it took me a while to see that and certainly the murder of Bobby Moffet just hit it on the head for me. That was my tipping point, because Bobby Moffet posed no threat to the peace process, no threat to the Union, no threat to the PUP. He posed a threat to the authority of someone within the UVF—and I just thought to myself there are individuals there who are not going away. They've no notion of going away. No matter what the PUP do, no matter what initiatives we put in place, no matter what endgame and what conflict transformation processes there are, there are people there who continue to thrive on power and they've too much vested in it to ever leave it behind.[146]

If recent evidence is anything to go by, Loyalist violence, especially from a particular locus within the East Belfast UVF—reaching the heart of Belfast city centre in August 2013[147]—represents a continuing fixture in Northern Ireland for some time to come.

Reflecting on a moment when international audiences looked to his work for an insight into the Protestant working class, Mitchell thinks he

[143] Mitchell, 'Rathcoole Ranger', 110–11; quoted in *Irish Times*, 2 May 2009, 49. Original ellipsis.

[144] Quoted in *Irish Times*, 2 August 2006, 11.

[145] Interview with John Kyle, Belfast, 11 November 2010.

[146] Interview with Dawn Purvis, Belfast, 20 January 2012. See *Belfast Telegraph*, 29 May 2010, 1.

[147] *The Observer*, 11 August 2013, 6; *Irish News*, 26 August 2013, 1.

was embraced 'because you were getting something real, challenging. What I wrote wasn't backing up one side, or letting down one side. It was basically saying "this is reality".'[148] There is an implicit challenge in his ability to stand back and present his people to themselves. In the radio drama *Drumcree* (1995), about the long-running Orange marching dispute, the contentious parade splits Dave and Jimmy, the former an RUC man who tackles his Orangeman brother for the violence it has generated:

DAVE: The world was watching Jimmy, and we let ourselves down so much! People might have had time for us in the past, but not anymore. The whole world now thinks *we're* scum. It's not only the rioting. Have you ever sat down and thought about the whole thing? Drunks and whores dancing round bonfires. The next day the same drunks and whores line the streets while all those old men, some carrying swords for God's sakes—swords! . . . I suppose we can thank our lucky stars there were no white horses riding over the horizon. I mean, where do we live? Are we in the dark ages, some kind of medieval lost kingdom? What kind of image is that to show to the world?[149]

Mitchell defended that if his work was critical then it represented a general criticism of humanity and 'not the Protestant community of Northern Ireland alone', but perhaps more than anything he had reached the stage where he was in tune with Pier Paolo Pasolini's statement that 'It is better to be an enemy of the people than an enemy of reality.'[150]

Mitchell's continuous rejection of the mythology of the peace process confirms that he still has his finger on his community's pulse, projecting too some of the traditional deficiencies in Unionist conceptions of modern Britishness. As a favoured collaborator argues, his personal situation in many ways reflects his community's contemporary limbo:

His foundations were rocked a little bit whenever his own domestic events happened, because that left him in a place where he wasn't quite sure what he was anymore—because his own community was telling him that they didn't want him. It's probably quite confusing for him in a time when the Loyalist community doesn't quite know what it is anymore either. They are literally in this place where they are seeking to find an identity for themselves that is more than just simply saying 'no'.[151]

[148] Interview with Gary Mitchell, Antrim, 6 June 2013.
[149] Gary Mitchell, *Drumcree*, directed by Roland Jaquarello, broadcast on 16 July 1996 (BBC Radio 4). Author's transcription. The ellipsis represents a pause.
[150] Gary Mitchell, 'Balancing Act', *The Guardian Review*, 5 April 2003, 19; Pier Paolo Pasolini, *Lutheran Letters*, trans. Stuart Hood (Manchester: Carcanet Press, 1983), 13.
[151] Interview with Stuart Graham, Belfast, 8 October 2011.

The loss of former PUP leader David Ervine following a fatal heart attack in January 2007 deprived Loyalism of a particularly important voice who had developed 'a way of saying things without changing the essence of the thing, but saying it in a way that could bring people in', a man aware of the Paisleyite/Labour dichotomy within the Protestant working class (embodied by his parents), and articulate in a political culture which does not value articulacy. 'Leadership is to lead and hope that more of your people follow on, and that probably would have happened with David. He was a strong character, outspoken, condemned things when they needed to be condemned,'[152] prepared where so many are absent to actually lead. Mitchell agreed that 'Since David Ervine's death, everything has been up in the air because we don't know what's really going on.'[153] He was talking of his personal situation but the personal, as ever, seemed to mirror the political.

Mitchell is on the cusp of cinema projects, one of which sees a former Loyalist paramilitary returning to Northern Ireland from the United States to confront the past. In *Return*, Peter is a Pentecostalist preacher who has found God since killing a man during the Troubles, and on encountering a mob back in Belfast ('teenagers on either side perched like Gargoyles') is physically attacked. Though in this story it is Peter who has committed the past atrocity, his response reflects Mitchell's heightened faith and forgiveness of those who assailed him in Rathcoole. Conversing with his American wife via the internet, he says, 'I think I'm changed. Completely, I mean. I didn't hit any of them, Angela. I didn't fight back. I don't feel anything for them. I don't feel like going back there and getting revenge.'[154] In another film script, set during the 1974 football World Cup, a teenager (suitably nicknamed after the German striker Gerd Müller) walks away from a 'bonfire burning ever so brightly with the flames stretching up to the clouds dominating the rest of his peripheral vision'. When his father asks where he is going, Gerd tells him he's returning home to watch a film on television. He turns his back on the bonfire of his community and 'dashes up as fast as he can towards home and the possibility of replacing reality with the fantastic world of films'.[155]

[152] Interview with Chris Hudson, Belfast, 20 January 2011; interview with Jackie Hewitt, Belfast, 19 August 2014.
[153] Quoted in *Irish Times*, 2 May 2009, 49.
[154] Gary Mitchell, *Return* (Unpublished: n.d., probably 2009), 63–6. Mitchell has not been able to forgive everybody. His film biopic of Ian Paisley collapsed soon after the Paisley family withdrew their support on discovering the script was a critical 'warts and all' venture (*The Observer*, 22 June 2008, 12).
[155] Gary Mitchell, *Get the Pope* (Unpublished: 2 August 2010), 89. This script won a pitching award at the Galway Film Fleadh in 2009. See also *Belfast Telegraph*, 26 September 2015, 3.

7

Loyal Women? Marie Jones
and Christina Reid

JANET: There are no women in Ireland. Only mothers and sisters
and wives.

Christina Reid, *The Belle of Belfast City* (1989)

The willingness of Loyalist paramilitaries to silence women, 'keep them at
home, protect them—don't allow them to do anything', has always
appeared to Gary Mitchell 'a lack of respect. Shame even.'[1] Criticism of
his plays being 'dominated' by men accordingly led him to write *Loyal
Women*,[2] which premiered at the Royal Court in November 2003. The
female brutality depicted was not uncommon during the Troubles, repli-
cating as it did 'the fierceness, violence and flinty intransigence of their
monolithic male counterparts' in certain Protestant working-class communities.[3] Those who fraternized with British soldiers were famously
tarred and feathered in nationalist areas, but violence occurred between
women in Protestant districts too. A particularly disturbing case was that
of Ann Ogilby, a single mother in her early thirties who was beaten to
death in July 1974 by a unit of UDA women for having an affair with a
married volunteer.[4] The nature of the killing in one of the organization's
notorious 'romper rooms' conjures up disturbing parallels with the violence in Mitchell's *Loyal Women*.

This chapter transcends the silence and brutality by concentrating on
two women, Christina Reid (Fig. 7.1) and Marie Jones (Fig. 7.2), whose

---

[1] Quoted in Susan McKay, *Northern Protestants: An Unsettled People* (Belfast: Blackstaff
Press, 2000), 117–18.
[2] Interview with Gary Mitchell, Antrim, 18 September 2013. See Grania McFadden,
'Mitchell's "marching season" Lacks Edge and Menace', *Belfast Telegraph*, 14 June, 2000, 25.
[3] Nicholas de Jongh, 'Union of Troubled Natures', *London Evening Standard*, 12
November 2003, 49. See Gary Mitchell, *Loyal Women* (London: Nick Hern Books,
2003), 53, 63, 100–3.
[4] Sarah Nelson, *Ulster's Uncertain Defenders: Protestant Political, Paramilitary and Community Groups and the Northern Ireland Conflict* (Belfast: Appletree Press, 1984), 126. The
women's UDA section was apparently stood down following the incident.

Fig. 7.1. Photo of Christina Reid.
Note: Permission of Alan Brodie Representation

Fig. 7.2. Photo of Marie Jones.
Note: Permission of Curtis Brown Group Ltd

theatre has aired an array of female voices, more generally locating the intersections between their lives, work, and gender politics. From the outset it is worth stressing that class is for both writers as instrumental as gender, with their best work usually fusing the issues. Reid's widower claims that his late wife would stop short of using the term working class: in her world view 'There were ordinary people who did ordinary jobs.'[5] As references to social class saturate Reid's work, this therefore appears more a comment on her own mobility. In *Did You Hear the One About the Irishman...?* (1985), Allison observes of her sister-in-law that she had 'married into the middle classes; got herself out of those mean back streets', with the arrest of her brother forcing 'her to look back to what she came from'.[6] Reid, too, had been born in the initially mixed, working-class Ardoyne area of North Belfast, escaping from the back streets but never afraid to look back on their inhabitants. Though she regularly declared her Irishness, Reid's work is undoubtedly 'rooted in affection for the community she came out of'.[7] The only playwright considered in this book to have had an overwhelmingly positive experience with the Lyric Theatre, she remembered John Boyd—who had kept Graham Reid and others at bay for years—being 'very, very good to me when I was there'.[8] Playfully dubbing the infamous Lyric Board the 'Old Men at the Zoo' (after the Angus Wilson novel), Reid was particularly impressed by John Hewitt, who asked her to sign his programme of her debut play *Tea in a China Cup* (1983) on its opening run, his encouragement symbolic of his championing of Protestant working-class voices in the arts.

Marie Jones hails—like St John Ervine, Sam Thompson, and Stewart Parker—from East Belfast, though she too voiced the familiar mythology that 'you didn't often hear of people making it as playwrights—people from my background didn't seem to do that sort of thing'. More accurately her work 'concerns the survival of the ordinary individual against the odds', a concept behind one of her more underrated plays, *Rock Doves* (2007)—the eponymous birds reflecting the way so many people in Belfast's concrete clusters, especially women, 'live on their wits, adapting to what life throws at them'.[9] If Reid's dramatic influences were Irish (Sean O'Casey, again), Jones leans more towards Arthur Miller as her

[5] Interview with Richard Howard, London, 22 February 2016.
[6] Christina Reid, *Did You Hear the One About the Irishman...?*, in *Plays: 1* (London: Methuen, 1997), 73.
[7] Interview with Patrick Sandford, London, 13 October 2015.
[8] Interview with Christina Reid, Belfast, 24 June 2013.
[9] Marie Jones, 'Conversations with the Writer', *Rock Doves* Theatre Programme (Belfast: Rathmore Productions, 2010), 13.

model.[10] Memories of her humble upbringing resemble those of West Belfast trade unionist and community worker May Blood, whose family were unaware they were poor until social workers told them, 'but it was happy because we were taught that people were people', chiming with Jones's recollection of 'a very happy childhood. We were poor, but so was everyone else.'[11] The humour in Jones's work is renowned but behind the comedy lies a supreme darkness:

> I don't set out to write a comedy per se, but I've lived a life and sometimes it's a very Irish thing that you use humour as a tool to deal with whatever's around because you can't deal with certain things. We always say that without tragedy in Ireland there'd be no humour—funerals are the funniest kind of places you could go. I'd always say I actually write tragedies: people laugh at them.[12]

CHARABANC

As with Graham Reid, a pre-Troubles vernacular infuses Marie Jones's plays via an older vein of storytelling, comedy, and sectarianism. Stories of the Harland and Wolff shipyard (where her father worked), the Labour movement, and the Second World War all played a key role in Jones's development as an actress and playwright.[13] Educated at Orangefield Girls' School in Belfast, her work in some respects harks back to the musical and cultural scene in the city prior to the onset of serious violence at the end of the 1960s. Above all it was the audio of her mother and aunts gossiping when she was a child that turned her into a playwright. Lubricated by a bottle of Sandeman port, 'there'd be the same stories every week, but with different variations, depending on who was in the room and what had been happening. Just ordinary women, talking about their hopes and fears, joys and dreams. Nobody cared what they thought. They didn't know that they were handing me down my livelihood.'[14] At the age of nineteen Jones married a lorry driver and had a child two years later, though her path away from the semi-detached suburbia set out for young mothers of her class was sealed when she joined the Young Lyric Drama Studio in response to a newspaper advertisement. Already struggling to

---

[10] *London Times*, 8 March 1990, 20; *Irish Times*, 24 June 1999, 15.
[11] Quoted in *Belfast News Letter*, 15 February 2010, 20; quoted in *Irish Times*, 24 June 1999, 15.
[12] Interview with Marie Jones, Belfast, 26 November 2014.
[13] Philip Johnston, *The Lost Tribe in the Mirror: Four Playwrights of Northern Ireland* (Belfast: Lagan Press, 2009), 187.
[14] Quoted in *Irish Times*, 5 March 2014, 14.

blend in with other young couples, she felt unhappy and took the bold decision to walk out on her marriage—and seven-year-old son—before she turned thirty.[15]

The interregnum between this time and her commercial success in the theatre is the key to Jones's core. In 1983 she co-established Charabanc Theatre Company, which was credited with bringing new audiences into the theatre and paving the way for a thriving community theatre scene.[16] But this is to miss the essence of struggle and fear of not being heard which is so central to Jones's story. She attributes the foundational discontent of working—or more precisely, not working—as an actress in Belfast to her drive. At the beginning of the 1980s, the Lyric and Arts Theatres were still prone to producing the classics and bringing 'English actors over to perform them. They probably thought we couldn't do an English accent and or that if we were local and available, we were no good.'[17] Those actresses who were active then point to 'a lot of jealousy and competition in those days' between actors,[18] but the Charabanc women responded by creating their own work in the face of what Maurice Leitch views as the local inferiority complex of 'the colonial cringe'. 'We just wanted an actors' centre', confirms Jones. 'We just wanted to act. We have to thank them [the Lyric and Arts Theatres]—we have to thank them for that sort of fucking colonialism, because if we'd have got parts in here we probably would never have started Charabanc.'[19] Another founder confirms that employment was foremost in their minds, but that 'It wasn't just the quantity or the lack of roles, but I think the quality of the roles that we were frustrated about.'[20]

Charabanc received vital support from Belfast playwright Martin Lynch. Even more formative than the advice he gave the group to write their own material was the experience of seeing his *Dockers* premiere in the Lyric Theatre in 1981. Jones recalled administrator Winifred Bell being front of house, as Lyric founder Mary O'Malley's 'confidante':

---

[15] *Irish Times*, 24 June 1999, 15.

[16] David Grant, *Playing the Wild Card: A Survey of Community Drama and Smaller-scale Theatre from a Community Relations Perspective* (Belfast: Community Relations Council, 1993), 35; Ophelia Byrne, *The Stage in Ulster from the Eighteenth Century* (Belfast: Linen Hall Library, 1997), 73.

[17] Quoted in 'Marie Jones in Conversation with Pat Moylan', in Lillian Chambers, Ger FitzGibbon, and Eamonn Jordan (eds), *Theatre Talk: Voices of Irish Theatre Practitioners* (Dublin: Carysfort Press, 2001), 213.

[18] Interview with Stella McCusker, Belfast, 5 April 2016.

[19] Interview with Maurice Leitch, London, 31 July 2015; interview with Marie Jones, Belfast, 26 November 2014. This interview took place in the Lyric Theatre.

[20] Interview with Carol Moore, Belfast, 13 August 2014.

She was still there—sort of like the residue that was left—horrified. Buses piled up here at the Lyric. Fucking big dockers coming in, trying to get their beer into the theatre. It was the most brilliant night of my life. I couldn't believe it. It was like old Shakespeare in the fucking Globe with people throwing tomatoes going 'Hey that's me!', shouting up at the stage! People hearing about their own lives in theatre. For me it was just that's the kind of plays I want to be in, never mind write. This is it. This was just immediate, and it [*Dockers*] was Shakespearean. It was a fucking big story with everybody involved from that street, the unions, everybody.[21]

Lynch confirms that Jones was alone among the Charabanc founders in being enthralled by the 'class badge' of *Dockers*, but that 'her prime motivation in getting together with Brenda Winter and the others was to get work as actresses. It was about work: nothing else.'[22]

Though an overwhelmingly male enterprise, Lynch's play emboldened the Charabanc women—comprising Jones and Eleanor Methven, Carol Scanlon, Brenda Winter, and Maureen McAuley—to illuminate another working-class record in danger of being forgotten: the story of Belfast women in the linen industry. The company 'all had aunts, mothers, or sisters who at some time worked in the mills', a virtual all-female employment preserve.[23] Lynch counters that at this stage 'there was nobody into politics with them' and that none of the women knew the history of Belfast: 'Marie's great strength is that she's a great observer of human beings and how they behave with each other, and of course her great sense of humour. But politics, history? Fuck all. Nothing,' an assessment Jones concurs with:

It didn't become like 'We want to do plays about our people.' Fuck, our people, I didn't even know who we were. I mean people talked about Outdoor Relief as being our history, and I thought it was like an outside toilet! It didn't occur to me that it was a movement. It was the theatre, Charabanc, that politicized us. Once we started to research who we were, we went: 'This is not right. Nobody's ever written about these women—these're our grandmothers.' So it was theatre that politicized me as opposed to I came in and wanted to do political theatre.[24]

Lynch also claims that it was his idea to explore the 1911 Belfast mill strike, though only Jones was supportive and 'at least two of them didn't want to go near this stuff because strikes were *me*. They saw me as a

---

[21] Interview with Marie Jones, Belfast, 26 November 2014.
[22] Interview with Martin Lynch, Belfast, 20 March 2014.
[23] Jones, quoted in 'Conversation with Pat Moylan', 213.
[24] Interview with Martin Lynch, Belfast, 20 March 2014; interview with Marie Jones, Belfast, 26 November 2014.

left-wing IRA man.' He also introduced the group to a person who would have a major influence on the development of both Charabanc and Marie Jones. Lynch had first met Pam Brighton at the Edinburgh Festival, where she had impressed him with her political outlook: 'She'd worked for 7:84 and all the radical groups. Then when we wanted a director, I rang Pam and got her in, and of course she pushed them in a political direction as well.'[25] At this stage Brighton's politics aligned with a British Communist Party position, though—as we have seen—this was eventually to morph into support for modern day Sinn Féin. Because of the acrimonious nature of the breach—in 2001 Brighton took an ultimately unsuccessful High Court legal action against Marie Jones, claiming a share of the profits of Jones's highly successful play *Stones in his Pockets*[26]—it is understandable that Brighton's part in Charabanc's history has ebbed. Her existence towards the end of her life, put bluntly by Lynch as 'a propagandist for the Provos on the Falls Road', has further clouded her importance. Following her passing in February 2015 it is now time for Brighton's formative part in the story to be rewoven into the narrative.

One of the five original Charabanc women insists that she 'hadn't a political bone in my body until I met Pam Brighton'. Being working class and from a family which had not gone to university, Brenda Winter-Palmer admitted to 'a bit of a second-class citizen feeling about where I came from and what I was. I think the gift that both Pam and Martin gave me was that allowing me to take a pride in my own heritage.' Brighton's political compulsions—which earned her the nickname 'mein pamf' in the corridors of the BBC—were judged both 'her greatest strength and her greatest weakness', though they saved Charabanc's first play *Lay Up Your Ends*,

> from a certain degree of sentimentality. I remember at one point the character of Ethna loses a child, and the temptation when you're writing something like that is to write a scene in which she gives full vent to her emotion. She wouldn't let us do this. She said, 'This is not a play about a child dying. This is a play about an ideological commitment to trade unionism and all that that stands for.' So she had the nuance, because we were quite inexperienced at that time, to pull us back from that, but by the same token in her later work I think she crossed over that fine line between politics and propaganda. Sometimes she lacked compassion for the individual. I watched Pam (during Charabanc's tour to the Soviet Union) at the Leningrad memorial stand and cry for the masses who had died. The ideology is what moved her. What didn't really move her was compassion

[25] Interview with Martin Lynch, Belfast, 20 March 2014.
[26] *Irish Times*, 19 May 2004, 7.

for people. It was that whole thing of the individual must be subservient to the grand narrative and scheme of things.[27]

Brighton remains enigmatic to the Charabanc women, appearing by turns cruel and fascinating to them. But aside from her impressionable politicking, she also made practical suggestions which contributed to their productions, introducing the group to the ideas of John McGrath and the radical Scottish theatre group 7:84.[28] Her background with the like-minded Hull Truck Theatre Company moulded *Lay Up Your Ends* as 'very much rough theatre, because that was all we could afford—and that was Pam. Pam said "You don't have any money, you don't need a set."'[29]

The group researched the history of working-class women in Belfast by studying old newspapers and seeking out relevant interviewees who were still alive, leading them in the direction of the legendary peace activist Saidie Patterson (1906–85). Born in Woodvale Street, Patterson had worked as an outworker in the linen trade, moving on to Ewarts Mill on the Crumlin Road at the age of fourteen. In 1940 she led a momentous strike at the Mill and was appointed the first full-time official of the textile branch of the Transport and General Workers' Union in Belfast, with a portfolio for women. Patterson's reputation extended beyond Northern Ireland to trade unionist circles across the United Kingdom and Ireland, her Moral Re-Armament outlook emblematic of a Christian socialist as opposed to a Marxist perspective ('The Lord is on our side and we cannot fail,' she said, justifying the 1940 strike).[30] Determined to locate this stalwart of the Labour movement, Charabanc tracked Patterson down to her small terraced house in West Belfast for an interview. By now in her eighties, she talked of the pervasive sectarian situation (both Protestants and Catholics were employed in the mills) and the 'difficulty of uniting women who were afraid of losing what, in many cases, was the only income coming into the house'.[31] Patterson was 'prescient in some way; she knew it was important politically that she told us her story. She actually said to us "There's a story here to be told and youse are the girls that are going to tell it." It was the most inspirational thing that anybody has ever said to me in my life.'[32] This capturing of a story which might have been lost was a crucial engine behind Charabanc and, later, Marie

---

[27] Roland Jaquarello, *Memories of Development* (Dublin: Liffey Press, 2016), 193; interview with Brenda Winter-Palmer, Belfast, 20 October 2015.

[28] John McGrath, *A Good Night Out: Popular Theatre: Audience, Class and Form* (London: Methuen, 1981).

[29] Interview with Carol Moore, Belfast, 13 August 2014.

[30] David Bleakley, *Saidie Patterson* (Belfast: Blackstaff Press, 1980), 32–44, 46–51.

[31] Jones, quoted in 'Conversation with Pat Moylan', 213.

[32] Interview with Brenda Winter-Palmer, Belfast, 20 October 2015.

Jones's solo work. The group 'reflected the lives of "insignificant" people, women who are supposed to have no place in history other than as extras for the crowd scenes',[33] and the rediscovery of figures like Patterson was essential, therefore, in telling a story that might otherwise have been buried.

Charabanc followed a 'learn-as-you-go' approach, lending their productions the inchoate energy which comes from grappling with new concepts:

> There was no mission statement. We wrote *Lay Up Your Ends* and wanted to tour within the community, so that became part of reflecting back the oral history they were giving to us. I don't think you could call *Lay Up Your Ends* a polished play in any sense, and because it uses agit-prop—sometimes we are talking directly to the audience—and elements of music hall and working-class culture, and because of the way we worked in pulling research from everywhere, in many ways it was a mish-mash. But it had a passion that was unquestionable and a rawness that somehow mirrored the women we were reflecting.[34]

The group's activism went beyond theatrical productions to take its place as part of the Labour culture discussed throughout this book. The late historian and activist Bob Purdie recalled Jones and Eleanor Methven organizing election material with him, filling envelopes and canvassing on behalf of the Labour Party of Northern Ireland (LPNI), a tiny post-NILP grouping which unsuccessfully ran candidates in Coleraine, North Belfast, and South Belfast in the local elections of May 1985.[35] A frail John Hewitt was also known to sit in on the LPNI's Belfast meetings.

Jones had always classed David Bleakley as one of the few political figures in Northern Ireland 'who could spake for you'—that is, those able to articulate working-class demands and represent the same bracket in the public arena.[36] Carol Moore continues to view her acting career from a unionized perspective, noting that in each of her acting jobs she identifies the Equity (actor's union) representative and is alarmed to discover actors who are not involved, particularly in a business of freelance contracts where the prospect of exploitation is rife. Moore also points out that Charabanc's original board included trade unionists Terry Carlin and the late Inez McCormack, while veteran socialist and Irish Transport

---

[33] Fintan O'Toole, 'Unsung Heroines Take a Bow', *Irish Times*, 2 June 1990, 27.

[34] Interview with Carol Moore, Belfast, 13 August 2014. See Martin Lynch and Charabanc Theatre Company, *Lay Up Your Ends: A Twenty Fifth Anniversary Edition* (Belfast: Lagan Press, 2008).

[35] Interview with Bob Purdie, Belfast, 25 April 2012. Veteran Belfast trade unionist and Labour councillor Jack Macgougan attended a performance of Charabanc's play *Oul' Delf and False Teeth* at London's Drill Hall Theatre in 1984. They turned to applaud him at the curtain call.

[36] Quoted in Marie Jones, '"People who could spake for you"', in Lynch and Charabanc, *Lay Up*, 129.

and General Workers Union organizer Paddy Devlin was instrumental in backing the group's funding applications on Belfast City Council.[37] Actor and director Ian McElhinney had approached Equity to get the group onto the ACE (Action for Community Employment) Scheme, which provided the critical financial springboard, and so 'right from the beginning the union was really important to the company and always was all the way through'.[38] The stance informed the theatre and vice versa:

BELLE: There's two thousand weemin [women] on the streets. You heard what [James] Connolly said—it's the workers in any great city that makes it great. Great industrial Belfast would be nothin' without the workers. D'ye know somethin' Florrie? This has to stop somewhere or the bloody machines we're workin' will be gettin' more respect than us.

FLORRIE: Well, just look at us, Belle. It's us what makes the finest linen in the world but we can't afford to bring it home w'us.

BELLE: Linen? I've two sheets of brown paper on my windys [windows] and the *Telegraph* coverin' the table.[39]

Their pro-trade union sentiment brought Charabanc into further contrast with the historical ethos of the Lyric, as Mary O'Malley publicly criticized the influence of Equity and unions in her theatre.[40]

AUDIENCE

Lay Up Your Ends opened at the Arts Theatre on Botanic Avenue—in a building which is now a bingo hall—on 15 May 1983 and would go on to be seen by over 13,000 people in fifty-nine different venues, including community centres and professional theatres. Though Jones attributes the success of the play to 'something that people had never seen before. Belfast women being funny, being bawdy and being strong,'[41] other practitioners argue that Charabanc harked back to other provincial companies such as the Group Theatre in 'the reassertion of the Ulster voice. As the Troubles wore on and the Lyric became the last man standing, obviously you had this imported Celtic Twilight stuff that Mary O'Malley was so obsessed with, and people actually stopped hearing the Belfast or local Ulster voice

37 Interview with Ian McElhinney, Belfast, 31 August 2010.
38 Interview with Carol Moore, Belfast, 13 August 2014. To qualify for ACE support actors had to have been out of work for six months, meaning that all five members were eligible.
39 Lynch and Charabanc, *Lay Up*, 73.
40 Mary O'Malley, 'Life and Role of the Lyric Theatre', *Irish Times*, 25 March 1975, 8.
41 Jones, quoted in 'Conversation with Pat Moylan', 214.

on stage.' This had been a core element of the Group's work—St John Ervine' *Boyd's Shop* (1936) was a staple of this—where 'people were hearing their own voices on stage. So Charabanc tapped into that and Marie then continued it.'[42] Farmers and ex-mill workers, constituting by the 1980s an untypical theatrical audience, were among the most frequent Charabanc attendees over the following years, and while the gender aspect was pronounced, its 'appeal to a broader base, one which includes the working-classes',[43] was even more essential.

The central paradox of Marie Jones's theatre is that she personally cautions against the use of labels at the same time as prospering from stereotypes. The initial caution was especially useful when it came to getting Charabanc off the ground, as when it began she recalled 'a lot of English theatre companies, trendy, middle-class... calling themselves feminists. It could be alienating and we were trying to encourage people to go to the theatre, people who had never been before.'[44] Such labels had particularly negative connotations in Protestant working-class areas. At a March 1986 symposium held in Belfast, Craigavon Women's Group founder Patricia Morgan was suitably 'critical of many feminists for being insensitive to women with less experience as political activists, through being too theoretical and remote from everyday problems'.[45] Jones always fears the academic overwhelming an audience 'because there's politicians and lecturers out there that can beat people over the head with facts and figures', and so as a cohort Charabanc cannot be separated from being defined against the emergence of Field Day Theatre Company a few years before, in all its masculine 'intellectual origins'.[46] At the same time Jones was aware that they needed 'the political weight round there, to say: "It's not just a wee story."'[47]

Another of the founding members agrees that in the early 1980s Charabanc were 'going into working-class areas—UDA clubs, Republican clubs, community centres—so to call ourselves a feminist theatre company, I don't mean to be patronizing but they might have said "what does

---

[42] Interview with David Grant, Belfast, 20 October 2015. Paddy Devlin, who allowed the women to hold meetings in his house, agreed that they were 'the natural heir of the Group Theatre'. Paddy Devlin, 'Let's Get Back to the Groupie Days!', *Sunday World*, 18 June 1989, 37.

[43] Maria DiCenzo, 'Charabanc Theatre Company: Placing Women Center-Stage in Northern Ireland', *Theatre Journal*, Vol. 45, No. 2 (May 1993), 180.

[44] Quoted in Imelda Foley, *The Girls in the Big Picture: Gender in Contemporary Ulster Theatre* (Belfast: Blackstaff Press, 2003), 30.

[45] Margaret Ward, 'Feminism in the North of Ireland—A Reflection', *Honest Ulsterman*, No. 83 (Summer 1987), 62–3.

[46] DiCenzo, 'Charabanc', 176. See also Brenda Winter, 'Charabanc, Cultural Capital and the Men of Recognized Credit', *Ilha do Desterro*, No. 58 (January/June 2010), 439–58.

[47] Interview with Marie Jones, Belfast, 26 November 2014.

that have to do with us?"' Carol Moore agrees that many women in
working-class areas are feminists 'in practice' because 'in Protestant and
nationalist/Republican communities they were the glue that kept their
families and communities together, when their men were on the barricades or involved in campaigns or in jail or on the run', something
abundantly clear to the founders when they researched their play *Somewhere Over the Balcony* (1988) by going to live amongst the women of
Divis Flats in West Belfast. 'At that time—I can't speak for anyone else—
but at twenty-four I wasn't calling myself a feminist,' remembers Moore.
'On the public airways we didn't want to get into that whole debate about
feminism: it was implicit in our plays.'[48] Another Charabanc architect
puts it even more succinctly: 'We fudged it. We were scared then of losing
our credibility in the community.'[49]

Though it was reported that Charabanc had 'reached a point of creative
exhaustion' by 1988,[50] this is an overstatement. The following year the
company staged an ambitious production of Darrah Cloud's *The Stick
Wife*, set in early 1960s Birmingham, Alabama, about the lives of women
married to Ku Klux Klan members. The group's eventual demise was
more down to the founding members pursuing their own projects. It had
achieved its primary aim of providing work. Now in demand for their
abilities, the collective armour was no longer essential. By the time they
gathered together again for *The Stick Wife*, Eleanor Methven had been
working with Druid Theatre Company in Galway. Carol Moore had
teamed up with the San Francisco Mime Troupe and appeared as the
eponymous heroine in Joe Comerford's acclaimed film *Reefer and the
Model* (1988), while Jones had continued writing and acting in theatre,
television, and film. Yet all guarded against the idea that things had
improved for women in the theatre: 'The situation is still no better for
actresses in the North of Ireland. The work just isn't there. If Charabanc
did not exist now, we would have to form it.'[51] The outcry which greeted
the announcement of the Abbey Theatre's 2016 season of plays on the
Easter Rising centenary—featuring one play, for children, written by a
woman—would appear to confirm that the situation remains as depressed
for women in Irish theatre as it was in 1983. Similarly, Charabanc's
extensive touring practices have never been emulated.[52]

---

[48] Interview with Carol Moore, Belfast, 13 August 2014.
[49] Interview with Brenda Winter-Palmer, Belfast, 20 October 2015.
[50] DiCenzo, 'Charabanc', 182.
[51] Speaking as one in Jane Coyle, 'Charabanc Motors On', *Theatre Ireland*, No. 18 (April–
June 1989), 42.
[52] *Irish Times*, 10 November 2015, 2; interview with Carol Moore, Belfast, 13 August 2014.

MEMORY

Christina Reid left school at fifteen, starting a family and working in a range of jobs (including in the clothing trade and as a civil servant), before returning to education in her thirties. She often referred to the fortuity of the era when she emerged as a time when Irish drama was in vogue, but as with Jones her background almost always shapes her plays. In *Tea in a China Cup* (1983), the character of Beth insists: 'I couldn't possibly remember it, I was only an infant, but I've heard that story and all the other family stories so often that I can remember and see clearly things that happened even before I was born.'[53] This is something Reid perpetually returned to as a definitive condition for many across the divide in Northern Ireland, challenging communal memory: 'It's not your experience—it's what you've been told.'[54] *Tea in a China Cup* is oftentimes described as a 'memory play',[55] and Reid had her own memories of pivotal events such as the UWC strike of 1974, which she recalled

> split a lot of Protestant families asunder because it was 'Shut your shop or support the strike,' and there were a lot of Protestants who were anti-any sort of Agreement with Dublin, any sort of Agreement with anything Catholic— but they didn't support the strike! There was, I always call it, a sort of working-class Protestant grandeur. 'We don't behave like that; Catholics behave like that.' I heard those sorts of conversations within my family.[56]

Reid's work often features such voices, overwhelmingly female, going back and forth to disseminate both the entrenched and shifting political currents to be found in her original community.[57]

The 'verbal storytelling' of her grandmother and sisters, which made them '*seanchaí* [storytellers] without knowing it', was remarkably similar to Jones's recollections of her aunts and relations gossiping. She grew up between two homes, her parents' house in the formerly mixed but now strongly Catholic working-class Ardoyne (North Belfast) and her maternal grandparents' house on the Donegall Road (South Belfast), where the same women lived a largely gendered existence revolving around child-rearing

---

[53] Christina Reid, *Tea in a China Cup*, in *Plays: 1*, 10.

[54] Interview with Christina Reid, Belfast, 24 June 2013.

[55] Wei H. Kao, 'Remapping Protestant Women and Interracial Minorities in Christina Reid's War Dramas', in Gillian McIntosh and Diane Urquhart (eds), *Irish Women at War: The Twentieth Century* (Dublin: Irish Academic Press, 2010), 208.

[56] Interview with Christina Reid, Belfast, 24 June 2013.

[57] Reid, *Tea*, in *Plays: 1*, 23–6. See Elizabeth Doyle, 'Men Don't Cook in West Belfast', *Fortnight*, No. 337 (March 1995), 30–2.

and the home. When the men left the household for work, the pub, or Orange parading, Reid noticed that the women behaved differently, becoming 'More relaxed, bawdier, full of life and banter'. She pointed out that her grandmother's house was on the same street as her namesake Graham Reid (no relation), but that 'we have completely different memories, probably because of gender', more generally suggesting that men are 'more entrenched, politically and socially, whereas women, in general terms, seem to find it easier to cross boundaries and move on'.[58] While men can appear caricatured, it must be remembered that Reid's plays are a deliberate corrective to the predominance of men in Irish drama, also representing a challenge to the subservience of women in Northern Ireland who assume that they are in some way responsible for the bad behaviour of their husbands and sons.

> SARAH: I sometimes think if I'd been a stronger sort of person, you know, took him in hand a bit more, that he'd of turned out all right. I was always too soft.
> BETH: You, and all the other women like you. No matter what a man does wrong it's always some woman's fault, isn't it?[59]

Though the standard of male roles in Reid's work has been criticized,[60] it is a charge resisted by those men who have acted in the plays. *Tea in a China Cup* appears to have touched males from her background precisely because it reminds them of a matriarchal society with a length of tradition when citizens frequented fortune tellers, superstitiously covered mirrors around the dead, and knew people in their street who washed bodies and delivered babies: 'It was the women who held it and kind of ran it from a distance, socially. Kept it functioning, kept the pawn-shop going, the money being sorted, the economy running, the borrowing, the trading.'[61] Reid recalled another production of the play which she directed at the Riverside Studios, Hammersmith, when a West Indian company was following in rehearsals. Its cast and crew came to see *Tea* and in the bar afterwards one of the men said of the character Aunt Maisie, ' "I got an aunt in Jamaica like that. She calls alla you lot whiteys! There they were, my aunts, sitting there with their arms folded, watching the world go by, talking about everybody." I thought, you have no idea what a big compliment that is; that you recognized this family of women.'[62]

[58] Quoted in Foley, *Girls*, 58, 60–1.   [59] Reid, *Tea*, in *Plays: 1*, 38.
[60] Lynda Henderson, 'Two New Plays from Belfast', *Theatre Ireland*, No. 5 (December 1983–March 1984), 97–8.
[61] Interview with Dan Gordon, Belfast, 5 April 2016.
[62] Interview with Christina Reid, Belfast, 24 June 2013.

Reid's women's lives are 'characterized by [men's] absence and (it is implied) by neglect'.[63] This can be twinned to criticism of 'masculine' associations of the Orange Order, but *Tea in a China Cup* is far subtler than this. The play opens with the terminally ill figure of Sarah joyously listening to the sounds of an Orange marching band, yearning to see the Twelfth festivities 'one more time before I go'.[64] Former artistic director of the Lyric Patrick Sandford, who helmed the Lyric's 1984 revival of the play, viewed it in opposition to Graham Reid's *Hidden Curriculum*, which premiered two years earlier and was

> fundamentally an intellectual piece of work, written to make an intellectual statement—it attracted a lot of attention. But it was a piece of moderately high-brow theatre. A Christina Reid play so obviously was not. There was something about *Tea in a China Cup* that the audience went 'Oh, we're not being talked to—we're just watching ourselves.' And it was entirely Protestant, but it didn't wave a flag. Of course it talked about going to the field, it talked about what it was to be a Protestant, but it was just a story of Belfast people written by a woman, and I think there were certain people who patronized it for that reason. Some of the London press wouldn't come because it was not a strident play in any way. I think probably therein lay its greatness as well as its misfortune.[65]

While reviews were actually resoundingly positive (with the praise occasionally gendered),[66] Sandford's judgement is astute. Beth gently voices the commonly made criticisms of the more sectarian Orange traditions, but 'what Sarah's carnivalesque enjoyment conveys is the personal and communal view rather than the overtly political or demonized perspective on the Twelfth of July. The history of her experience of previous memorable Twelfths is passed on from mother to daughter as an oral legacy, a transmission of storytelling through the generations.'[67] Reid liked to puncture Protestant shibboleths in interviews, but the plays themselves revere the traditions passed down; Sarah longingly urging Beth to 'mind all the old family stories, tell them to your children after I'm gone'.[68] This was borne out by the excited reaction of a Protestant

[63] Anthony Roche, *Contemporary Irish Drama: From Beckett to McGuinness* (Dublin: Gill & Macmillan, 1994), 235.

[64] Reid, *Tea*, in *Plays: 1*, 8.

[65] Interview with Patrick Sandford, London, 13 October 2015.

[66] Lisa Fitzpatrick, 'Disrupting Metanarratives: Anne Devlin, Christina Reid, Marina Carr, and the Irish Dramatic Repertory', *Irish University Review*, Vol. 35, No. 2 (Autumn–Winter 2005), 330. See Anthony Masters, 'A Play that Never Raises its Voice', *London Times*, 15 October 1984, 12; Ray Rosenfield, 'Tea in a China Cup at the Lyric, Belfast', *Irish Times*, 12 April 1984, 12.

[67] Roche, *Contemporary*, 234.   [68] Reid, *Tea*, in *Plays: 1*, 10.

actor who saw *Tea* and declared that he had 'never seen this view on the stage before! This is how it really was!'[69] It is not therefore the case that the women of *Tea in a China Cup* are 'disempowered within a community of Orangemen'; the whole point is that they embrace their communal myths and are, as the same author acknowledges, 'mostly proud of their Protestant unionist identity'.[70] An actress from the original production believes that Reid's return to education—taking A Levels and then a degree in English, Russian studies, and Sociology, abandoning it to become Writer-in-residence at the Lyric—in some sense reinforced these roots.[71]

Tea in a China Cup was compared with Stewart Parker's *Pentecost* in stretching back through two World Wars to represent the experience of a Protestant family, and its ambitious time-framing and structure was duly praised.[72] But if Reid's structure was radical, her ultimate cultural message was far more traditional. Unlike Reid herself, the play carefully evades judging the communal myths and practices, leaving the audience to make up their own minds. Reid appeared to be asserting that 'you cannot deny that this human richness and culture and existence is there and has been there. She wasn't saying "Fuck the Pope". She was saying: "This exists. This is particularly true for these women. This is a jewel, and the implications of it are for you to consider, I'm just going to tell you it's here."' *Tea in a China Cup* is consequently 'full of tenderness and love for a caste of Irish people without judging it'.[73]

Those who identify the play as a critique of Protestant 'respectability', illuminating a sectarian group vying to avoid sinking 'to the level of Catholics',[74] entirely miss the import of this detail. Positive Orange undertones are present in *Tea in a China Cup*, rendering its politics more complex than previously thought, perhaps accounting for why Pam Brighton politically (and unfairly) termed Reid a 'trivial' writer.[75] They are embodied by the sympathetic, sentimentalized figure of senior matriarch Sarah, who hints at Reid's own belief 'that marriage and motherhood do

[69] John Keegan, quoted in Claudia Harris, 'Community Conscience or Reflection? Theatre in Northern Ireland', in Alan J. Ward (ed.), *Northern Ireland: Living with the Crisis* (New York: Praeger, 1987), 199.

[70] Kao, 'Remapping', 208–9.

[71] Interview with Stella McCusker, Belfast, 5 April 2016.

[72] Diderik Roll-Hansen, 'Dramatic Strategy in Christina Reid's Tea in a China Cup', *Modern Drama*, Vol. 30, No. 3 (Fall 1987), 393; Roche, *Contemporary*, 229–30.

[73] Interview with Patrick Sandford, London, 13 October 2015.

[74] Roll-Hansen, 'Dramatic Strategy', 392; Roche, *Contemporary*, 233. A sharper reading identifies 'how women put other women down' and subjugate themselves within the Unionist community (interview with Dawn Purvis, Belfast, 20 January 2012).

[75] Interview with Pam Brighton, Belfast, 25 March 2014.

not necessarily stifle women's independent lives'.[76] As with Marie Jones, humour was critical to the overall task because it allowed the largely middle-class Protestant audience of the Lyric to absorb the message without instinctively rejecting it, as if recognizing the faint beat of a drum they once knew. Reid was deeply in touch with these elements, her widower pointing out how excited and charmed she was to meet Prince William and Kate Middleton at an event organized by Youth Action (of which she was a patron) in Belfast in March 2011.[77] While there was an element of the Belfast girl made good, affectionately dropping the names of the famous and powerful, Reid understood Ulster Protestant royalist traditions and respected the inheritance.

THE POLITICAL SPHERE

The hundreds of thousands of women who campaigned forcefully on behalf of the Union in the early part of the twentieth century are now seen to represent 'a significant phase in the evolution of political activism among Irish women'.[78] Though significantly less prevalent than men, women were not completely non-existent at Stormont (six women Unionist MPs were elected between 1921 and 1972, among them Dehra Parker),[79] and Protestant activists who featured in the public eye such as Saidie Patterson, Betty Sinclair, and Sadie Menzies (the latter two Communist Party members) tended to be avowedly left wing. The modern manifestation of this spirit is May Blood (1938–), now a peer in the House of Lords and patron of the Labour Party in Northern Ireland. Upholding a commitment to all working-class women across the state, Blood led a prominent campaign against the continuous reductions in the levels of Sure Start, which had set aside £16 million pounds for projects which would have benefited deprived areas in the province.[80] Protestant women have not therefore been totally absent from public politics, and it is no coincidence that—like Mark Langhammer—Blood is strongly involved in

---

[76] Jozefina Komporály, 'The Troubles and the Family: Women's Theatre as Political Intervention', in Brian Cliff and Éibhear Walshe (eds), *Representing the Troubles: Texts and Images, 1970–2000* (Dublin: Four Courts Press, 2004), 70.

[77] Interview with Richard Howard, London, 22 February 2016.

[78] Senia Paseta, *Irish Nationalist Women, 1900–1918* (Cambridge: Cambridge University Press, 2013), 34.

[79] See Rachel Ward, *Women, Unionism and Loyalism in Northern Ireland* (Dublin: Irish Academic Press, 2006), 117.

[80] Anne Moore, 'Blood Speaks Out', *Fortnight*, No. 385 (May 2000), 9.

the campaign to advance integrated schooling in Northern Ireland, coming into conflict with vested interests in the Catholic Church.[81]

Blood had not been afraid to show her independent streak during the 1974 UWC strike by working every day at the Blackstaff Mill (even traipsing along with Len Murray's ill-fated 'back-to-work' march),[82] and she was later involved in the non-sectarian Women's Coalition. Though the group dissolved fairly innocuously in 2006, and its impact has often been dismissed by those who viewed it as a gimmick of the Northern Ireland Office,[83] the NIWC nonetheless impressed powerful individuals (including Hillary Clinton and Tony Blair) during the 1998 Good Friday Agreement negotiations. Back when Blood began her community work in West Belfast at the start of the Troubles she found gender cooperation difficult to establish beyond the sectarian gridlock. Aware of the mobilizing influence of Internment on women in Catholic working-class areas from August 1971, she noticed a similar dynamic in Loyalist areas when men were lifted and many women gradually emerged from kitchen routines 'to all of a sudden being in complete charge of her family's needs and responding purposefully to those needs with whatever energy and creativity the situation required'.[84] In many ways the impact of the Women's Coalition in politics was precipitated in community work by organizations such as the Women's Centre on the Shankill Road, which Blood founded in 1987.

Though the Women's Coalition spluttered out—and was on the receiving end of scorn from senior Unionist politicians, one of whom insisted that women being in politics 'will change family life as we know it'[85]—May Blood suggests that Northern Protestants have not lacked articulate and voluble female working-class voices. Like many considered in this book she defies categorization as a Loyalist and is instead emblematic of being Protestant working class. Yet, even within Ulster Loyalism itself there are signs of change. The Progressive Unionist Party was partially rejuvenated by their involvement in the 2012–13 Flag Protests and has since promoted young women as spokespersons and electoral candidates. Surveys on the protests outlined the importance of women in

---

[81] *Belfast Telegraph*, 4 June 2011, 17.

[82] Baroness May Blood, *Watch My Lips, I'm Speaking!* (Dublin: Gill & Macmillan, 2007), 77–80.

[83] Suzanne Breen, 'A Political Trailblazer who has Shattered Glass Ceiling in Record-breaking Fashion', *Belfast Telegraph*, 18 December 2015, 26. See Kate Fearon, *Women's Work: The Story of the Northern Ireland Women's Coalition* (Belfast: Blackstaff Press, 1999).

[84] Baroness May Blood, 'Recollections', *Grassroots Leadership* (1) (Newtownabbey: Island, 2005), 7.

[85] Blood, *Watch*, 153.

the agitation, reporting how 'several of the female participants were openly critical of the men within their communities for not doing more'. One man conceded that 'It's been the women from the start. They have stood in the street in the rain and snow and kept this issue alive. The men have been absent.'[86] Julie-Anne Corr Johnston was a direct discovery of the protests and would go on to win a seat for Oldpark, North Belfast, in the local government elections of May 2014. One of the city's few openly gay representatives, she has not been afraid to highlight socialist, pro-choice, and pro-refugee positions on Belfast City Council, connecting her involvement in the Flag Protests to her status as a young gay woman:

> I always felt segregated, marginalized, and had hid my true identity and who I was in the closet. But the one time that I had felt that I was part of something, that I was accepted regardless of anything, was when I was with my family. It sounds ridiculous but that euphoric atmosphere when you're standing on the Lisburn Road or in the city centre on the Twelfth of July with your wee flag and everybody's cheering when the bands are going past. That's the one time I just felt like I belong. And I guess that symbolism meant when the flag came down I thought: 'No.' Because my family were angry I became angry, and it was almost like we had a shared hurt. Now my relatives were angry because we'd family that fought in the armed forces and so that hurt them because that was what they fought for. I always think of those British values I believe in—of multiculturalism, pluralism, inclusivity, and mutual respect. The flag epitomizes that for me because regardless of any of the conflict that has happened in Northern Ireland, everyone has a part in that flag regardless of who they are.[87]

Though there has been talk of Loyalist females as 'backbone' before,[88] there is unquestionably a different dialogue going on within Loyalism which is being spearheaded by women. Dawn Purvis (1966–) led the PUP for over three years following the death of her mentor David Ervine in January 2007, increasing the party's share of the vote in the March 2007 Assembly election in East Belfast, even if it is often forgotten that she did so—as with Billy Hutchinson's decision to recruit via the Flag Protests— by flagging up the British credentials of the party.[89] Though her relationship with the PUP soured, the original 'motivational leadership' of Ervine and

---

[86] INTERCOMM and Dr Jonny Byrne, *Flags and Protests: Exploring the Views, Perceptions and Experiences of People Directly and Indirectly Affected by the Flag Protests* (Belfast: Intercomm, 2013), 12.

[87] Interview with Julie-Anne Corr Johnston, Belfast, 7 April 2016.

[88] Dawn Purvis, 'Female Future', *Fortnight*, No. 377 (March 1999), 8.

[89] Aaron Edwards, 'The Progressive Unionist Party of Northern Ireland: A Left-wing Voice in an Ethnically Divided Society', *British Journal of Politics and International Relations*, Vol. 12, No. 4 (2010), 597.

Gusty Spence represented a 'blanket of encouragement and positivity'
running parallel with the Democratic Unionist Party's shabby treatment
of the Women's Coalition during the Northern Ireland Forum and 1998
power-sharing Assembly. At the same time Purvis was always on the back
foot in the 'male world that is the UVF',[90] often discussing gender with
Ervine, especially as she began to receive increasing publicity from 2006
onwards:

> We were always doing this self-analysis. We were always sitting down,
> talking, and analysing what went on. Gusty did that with him, then he
> passed this on to me and it was always 'Get on the balcony DP'. So we'd get
> on the balcony, review what happened, and he once said to me, 'People will
> be wondering how you got to where you are within the PUP,' and I went
> 'Yes I've often thought about that,' and he said, 'And what have you
> thought?' I said, 'Well, I wouldn't like to say,' to which he said, 'Well I'll
> say it for you. They'll say either you held rank in the UVF or you slept your
> way to the top. You have to be conscious that that's the way people will
> think. And, given that the UVF had no women members, there'll be
> thinking the other one.' So I'm always conscious of how people view me
> as a woman and getting to the level that I got as PUP leader, and there are
> those who will not understand how I got to be PUP leader and will fill in the
> gaps themselves. I know how I got there and other colleagues know how
> I got there, and I'm fine with that.[91]

Historically Protestant working-class women were disproportionately
taken to court for abortion-related offences in comparison to Catholic
females,[92] and when Purvis took over the reins following Ervine's prema-
ture death she noticed that the party's pro-choice policy began to receive a
higher profile 'than when David ever talked about it'. Though Ervine had
always articulated the PUP's call for the extension of the 1967 Abortion
Act, the new spotlight led to complaints from fellow party members,
'saying "Is it all about this?", and I was actually saying "Yes it is all
about this, because that's what the PUP's about." It's about equality. It's
about human rights. And it is about policy after all.'[93] Purvis's gender
accentuated a pro-choice stance in the minds of the electorate and even her
own party.

   In the summer of 2014, Purvis's first theatrical effort was performed as
part of Green Shoot Productions' *Flesh and Blood Women*, a trio of new

---

[90] Interview with Chris Hudson, Belfast, 20 January 2011.
[91] Interview with Dawn Purvis, Belfast, 20 January 2012. While there was no formal
female wing, the UVF did in fact have some women members.
[92] Leanne McCormick, ' "No Sense of Wrongdoing": Abortion in Belfast, 1917–1967',
Journal of Social History, Vol. 49, No. 1 (2015), 125–48.
[93] Interview with Dawn Purvis, Belfast, 20 January 2012.

short plays.[94] *Picking Up Worms* is a minor piece and limited by the very regression of its central character to childhood. Seven-year-old Lisa also seems too articulate for her age, but the enterprise and Purvis's offering received good notices.[95] What is most interesting is her choice of time: May 1974, again confirming how burned into the psyche of the community the UWC strike remains. Purvis remembered how 'exciting' May 1974 was, 'like an abnormality'. There was 'always something happening in the street', but also 'the palpable fear for a child of scary things in the shadows, though we didn't know what they were'.[96] The play also allows Purvis to signal her own dissent through its young protagonist, who asks her mother what a 'strike-breaker' is, before deciding 'I want to be a strike-breaker! I want to go to school!' 'Don't say that and don't ever let me hear you saying that again,' her mother snaps back.[97]

Despite the Democratic Unionist Party's nomination of Arlene Foster as its first female leader (and subsequent first woman premier of Northern Ireland), this does not of course entail that conservative, gendered inclinations within the largest political party of Northern Ireland are dissipating.[98] The 2016 Assembly election saw an increased share of women in the chamber, but the DUP remains opposed to the extension of that famous piece of British legislation, the 1967 Abortion Act, to Northern Ireland, and when Foster was welcomed into her new job by Assembly representatives, her party colleague Edwin Poots rose to declare: 'In congratulating Arlene on her elevation to the post of First Minister, I should say that it is the second most important job that she will ever take on. Her most important job has been, and will remain, that of a wife, mother and daughter.'[99] As Rose contends in Christina Reid's *The Belle of Belfast City*, in an assessment which seems to have entered the lexicon, the 'right-wing Protestant church is in total agreement with the right-wing Catholic Church on issues like divorce and abortion, on a woman's right to be anything other than a mother or a daughter or a sister or a wife'.[100]

[94] *Irish News*, 14 April 2014, 36–7. The other two plays were by Jo Egan and Brenda Murphy.

[95] See Jane Coyle, 'Real Women, Talented Youths, and a Comedy that Doesn't Come Off', *Irish Times*, 13 May 2014, 12.

[96] Quoted in *Sunday Life*, 27 April 2014, 30–1.

[97] Dawn Purvis, *Digging Up Worms* (Unpublished, 2014), 23.

[98] Máire Braniff and Sophie A. Whiting, ' "There's Just No Point Having a Token Woman": Gender and Representation in the Democratic Unionist Party in Post-Agreement Northern Ireland', *Parliamentary Affairs*, Vol. 69, No. 1 (2016), 93–114.

[99] Quoted in *Belfast Telegraph Online*, 12 January 2016.

[100] Reid, *Belle of Belfast City*, in *Plays: 1*, 221.

STEREOTYPES AND IDENTITY

An essential detail, echoing others in this book, is that Christina Reid, while acknowledging her Irish identity, has not fallen into the trap of conveying that the ways of the opposing political tradition in Ireland are more enlightened than Ulster Unionism. In *Did You Hear the One About the Irishman . . . ?*, nationalist and loyalist male are shown to mirror one another, reinforced by the way the Loyalist and IRA paramilitaries Hughie Boyd and Joe Rafferty are intentionally played by the same actor.[101] Some commentators have misguidedly concluded, in a view naturally encouraged by nationalist leaders, that the imagery of mainstream Irish Republicanism furnishes it with progressive feminist credentials, a view resting on the visibility as opposed to volubility of women.[102] Others have noted that while Sinn Féin pays lip service to women's rights, real power in the party has always resided with a small cadre of men. Martin McGuinness confirmed that he was 'personally opposed' to both 'abortion on demand' and the extension of the 1967 Abortion Act,[103] while it is also worth remembering that for all the 'political correctness' displayed towards the Women's Coalition during the Good Friday Agreement negotiations, Sinn Féin 'froze them out when it came to discussion on crunch issues'.[104]

Marie Jones's exploration—a more appropriate word than 'interrogation'[105]—of stereotypes works because they are universal currency, and the aim is always to expand the audience. Such stereotypes are also what both the local and international audience knows (or thinks). Post-Charabanc Jones branched out as a solo playwright and began working with DubbelJoint Theatre Company, which she founded with Pam Brighton and actor Mark Lambert. One of the early fruits was the one-man show *A Night in November*, first performed in August 1994 in Whiterock, West Belfast, as part of the *Féile an Phobail* festival. It embarked on a commercially successful tour for over a year throughout Ireland and the United Kingdom, being seen by an estimated 30,000 people and picking up several awards. Like Christina Reid, Jones is

[101] Maria Delgado, Introduction to *Plays: 1*, xiii. See Reid, *Did You Hear the One*, in *Plays: 1*, 88–9, 90–1.

[102] Margaret Ward, 'Finding a Place: Women and the Irish Peace Process', *Race & Class*, Vol. 37, No. 1, Ireland: New Beginnings? (July–September 1995), 48–9. Gerry Adams has written of how the Republican community is a 'matriarchal' one. See Adams, *Before the Dawn: An Autobiography* (Kerry: Brandon, 1996), 235.

[103] Quoted in *Belfast Telegraph*, 7 December 2012, 4–5.

[104] Fionnuala O'Connor, *Breaking the Bonds: Making Peace in Northern Ireland* (Edinburgh: Mainstream, 2002), 132. See also Blood, *Watch*, 153.

[105] Foley, *Girls*, 145.

unthreatened by notions of Irishness. Though insisting that she understands Unionist 'fear', Jones has said, 'I'd like to see a united Ireland if it happened peacefully.'[106] The charge most often levelled at her, in colloquial idiom of the kind she would appreciate, is of 'guilty Prod'—the Ulster Protestant who has risen from their class, takes to heart the oppressive mantle of Stormont (*circa* 1921–72), and frequently ends up siding with his/her opposite.

A Night in November features an uptight, middle-class Protestant, Kenneth McAllister, a dole clerk who turns away from tribal elements within his own community to discover a new identity as a 'Protestant... Irish Man',[107] symbolized by his abandoning support for Northern Ireland and following the Republic of Ireland during the 1994 football World Cup in the United States. The symbolism of this conversion has been much criticized over the years but is reflective of Jones's own journey. Gary Mitchell, perhaps unsurprisingly, 'can't stand' *A Night in November*:

> It's tapping into a thing that I hate; the idea that being British is evil/being Irish is fantastic. Guess what we're going to do? We're going to have a play that starts off with the stage red, white, and blue and then at half time we're going to change the stage into green, white, and gold, and the audience are all going to stand and give us a standing ovation. They're not. The play isn't getting a standing ovation: the politics is. What they're saying is: 'A Protestant has written a play where a Protestant person suddenly realizes that Protestants are evil and shit and realizes actually we should all be Irish Catholics. Awesome! That's fantastic!' It's not challenging; it's confirming. But the point is it's still a shit play and nonsense, because no one does that, and anybody who does do that—they get called traitors.[108]

While typically caustic, this analysis was not far removed from Fintan O'Toole's withering assessment. Admiring its 'very skilful script', O'Toole nevertheless agreed with Mitchell that 'It tells a Catholic audience exactly what it wants to hear,'[109] fostered by 'representative Protestant' Kenneth, with a family mechanically forged in his image:

> KENNETH: We are the perfect Prods, we come in kits, we are standard regulation, we come from the one design, like those standard

---

[106] Quoted in *Irish Times*, 24 June 1999, 15.

[107] Marie Jones, *A Night in November*, in *Stones in His Pockets/A Night in November* (London: Nick Hern, 2000), 108.

[108] Interview with Gary Mitchell, Antrim, 6 June 2013. The set designer was artist Robert Ballagh, who—like Pam Brighton—has made no secret of his political sympathies. When a debate about the Irish government potentially removing Articles 2 and 3 from the Constitution resumed in 1992, Ballagh complained that their removal would alienate northern nationalists (*Irish Times*, 3 December 1992, 12).

[109] Fintan O'Toole, 'Insulting Both Sides', *Irish Times*, 5 December 1995, 12.

kitchens with the exact spaces for standard cookers and fridges, our dimensions never vary and that's the way we want it.[110]

Former Charabanc admirers deemed that the stereotypes of conformist Protestants rendered 'a work of high bigotry',[111] and aside from the lack of challenge to a southern audience, there was also a disturbing gender component in the form of the caricature of Kenneth's wife 'Debrah'. Not only does *A Night in November* recommend escaping from the confines of Ulster, it required its protagonist to rid himself of his 'stupid empty-headed bitch' wife to join the 'lads' of Irish football fans.[112] It is possible (though not likely) that this could appear as a displacement of Jones's own early marriage, but the more considerable problem is that Kenneth's 'great act of rebellion involves taking all of the money he can lay his hands on, slipping out of the house in secret, and leaving his wife and children behind. The play's sexual politics, in other words, are about as profound as its ethnic politics are.'[113]

Even Jones's supporters found *A Night in November*'s politics hard to stomach. Martin Lynch saw the first production of the play and witnessed 'quite a number of Protestant people who walked out, despised it'. He disliked its affirming effect: 'All the Catholics up here think it's great because it tells them that their community's beautiful and flawless and the Protestants are all pigs.' On the other hand, he judged it 'Marie's best-written play in craftsmanship—in terms of a character developing and going from being this and becoming that; the journey.'[114] Dan Gordon must also be considered a major factor in *A Night in November*'s success. It was by all accounts 'a performance of extraordinary virtuosity',[115] and it was his real-life bad experience with a 'little hard woman' in the Carrick-fergus unemployment office who made him fill out a holiday form when he was going to work on a play in Donegal which determined the character's profession, importantly in light of the self-sufficient assumptions attached to the particular job. Jones was outraged ('Fuckin' right!'), and so the most famous dole clerk in Irish theatre was born.[116]

A Night in November's original director remembered that 'it was a very personal play for Dan in that he had been a Unionist. I'll never forget the moment where he was looking at the Catholic guy and suddenly breaks down and says "I'm sorry". It was in the Opera House, which was packed,

---

[110] Marie Jones, *Night*, in *Stones*, 81.
[111] John Keyes, 'Theatre Days', *Fortnight*, No. 388 (September 2000), 30.
[112] Jones, *Night*, in *Stones*, 75.   [113] O'Toole, 'Insulting', 12.
[114] Interview with Martin Lynch, Belfast, 20 March 2014.
[115] O'Toole, 'Insulting', 12.
[116] Interview with Dan Gordon, Belfast, 5 April 2016.

and was just one of those moments in the theatre you pay for.'[117] Pam Brighton referred to being a Unionist here the same way one might speak of being an alcoholic, but this did have significance for Gordon, who performed the play over five hundred times from 1994 to 2003, because it came out of him 'coming to terms with my own identity; realizing that I don't have to march on the Twelfth. There are elements of my upbringing that I love dearly and would never change, but there are other elements where you go "My community behaved badly and did the wrong thing."'[118]

A Night in November marked the beginning of the end of Jones's association with Brighton. The latter's legal action claiming that she should be recognized as a joint author of *Stones in His Pockets* was finally settled in Jones's favour in 2004. The split was personal but also political. Not only did Brighton feel that she was due a share of the *Stones* spoils, she also objected to Jones's populist move away from the theatre Charabanc and DubbelJoint had initially pursued: 'She felt I was becoming too Republican and too committed to West Belfast, and I thought she was becoming too ambitious and kind of thoughtless in a way. She'd probably be more ambitious than I was, Marie, in wanting to be seen as a great playwright and earning some money. I've always been absurdly careless about money.'[119] Yet for Jones this was simply coterminous with her fear of labels estranging, and thus diminishing, the audience: 'It comes down to the same problem which we avoided with Charabanc. Once you label, you alienate. Plays speak for themselves.'[120] Jones apparently finds it difficult to mention Brighton's name these days, but 'If everything was to calm down for Marie, she would acknowledge that Pam is probably the decisive influence on her life as a writer.'[121] Yet in forcing the politics, Brighton had performed the cardinal sin of losing the audience. Jones contemporaneously noted that DubbelJoint came to be 'run by Pam, and she has the right to label it, define it, as she sees appropriate. But my plays for the company could never be defined as nationalist or any other form of "ism".'[122] She must briefly have forgotten about *A Night in November*.

---

[117] Interview with Pam Brighton, Belfast, 25 March 2014. Marty Maguire, Conor Grimes, and Patrick Kielty have also performed the monologue.
[118] Interview with Dan Gordon, Belfast, 5 April 2016; Jones, *Night*, in *Stones*, 107.
[119] Interview with Pam Brighton, Belfast, 25 March 2014. See also Brighton's piece in *Theatre Ireland*, No. 23 (Autumn 1990), 41–2.
[120] Quoted in Foley, *Girls*, 34.
[121] Interview with Martin Lynch, Belfast, 20 March 2014.
[122] Quoted in Foley, *Girls*, 33–5.

GENERATION

Confirming how she came 'from this Protestant background of being proud to be Irish, but more English than the English all at the same time', Christina Reid insisted that she 'would always call myself an Irish writer'. Her work often turns out to be a very close reflection of the dynamics of her own family, with humour deriving from her brothers and the friction stemming from her grandfather, a proud Orangeman and Battle of the Somme enthusiast: 'I remember asking him questions about the Somme and he said "Your problem is you don't know what you are."' Reid's response to her grandfather's barb was that the 'problem in Northern Ireland is everybody *is* so sure'. Her cordial defiance was inspired by the other women in her family, led by her grandmother, who sang Irish rebel songs not out of any political inclination but 'just to annoy my grandfather'.[123] Though she naturally talked down the parallels, a grandfather figure well set in dedication to Queen and country crops up in several of Reid's plays, including *Tea in a China Cup* and *My Name, Shall I Tell You My Name?* (1989). Reid questioned him good-naturedly about the Somme, but he could not complete the process because it would be to question 'Everything he'd lived and survived by'.[124] As a young person she remembered seeing large amounts of Union Jack bunting around her father's house in the lead-up to the Twelfth of July, 'and then I began to ask questions about it. Parts of it really puzzled me. I don't know what that was to do with, probably to do with my granny singing old rebel songs. I was just questioning it.'[125]

In interviews Reid liked to play her grandmother, stating how her younger characters realized 'that the Somme wasn't a great victory but more like slaughter on a huge scale',[126] with the result that her theatre has been read as 'a conflict of generations that contrasts differing perspectives on most major aspects of life, including sexual politics', reflected by the young who refute patriarchal influence in contrast to Reid's senior women, like Sarah in *Tea in a China Cup* and Vi in *The Belle of Belfast City*.[127] This is, again, an oversimplification. Dissent is offered generationally by the youthful Beth and Theresa in *Tea in a China Cup*, and Dolly (and, of course, Belle herself) in *The Belle of Belfast City*, but the

---

[123] Interview with Christina Reid, Belfast, 24 June 2013.
[124] Quoted in Foley, *Girls*, 60.
[125] Interview with Christina Reid, Belfast, 24 June 2013.
[126] Quoted in *Irish Times*, 18 September 1989, 9.
[127] Komporály, 'Troubles and the Family', 70.

plays display an unquestionable empathy with the dwindling customs. *The Last of a Dyin' Race* was first broadcast on radio in 1986 and was read by friends at a special remembrance event for Reid in June 2015 at the Orange Tree Theatre in Richmond, London. Featuring a tight-knit community essentially taking over an undertaker's funeral parlour ('Right girls, she's in here') to ensure their recently deceased friend 'gets a proper send off', they casually eat and drink next to the cadaver, pondering the dead generations.

> AGNES: My father was an ould bugger... drove two good women to an early grave. Lizzie had no childhood worth talkin' about, what with takin' care of me and tryin' to keep my da sober.
>
> *A cup and saucer ratting.*
>
> I wouldn't mind my tea toppin' up if you've a minute Sarah, them buns are nice, but they're awful dry in the middle.[128]

The women refer in a disparaging way to the absent men, a throwaway remark that birth gets 'easier every time' leading another to quip: 'It'll be some man said that.' They jovially reminisce over old wakes, including one where mourners took the dead man and 'propped him up in the coffin with a bottle of stout in his hand so that he could join the celebrations'. Here again is a decidedly sympathetic view of the elders' traditions, passing by the younger generations with 'no time for the old customs',[129] all conjuring up a vanishing but proud community.

A common abrasion in Reid's work concerns different kinds of audience. Charabanc broke down this wall by their very *raison d'être*, but Reid's more individual exploration of the same subject is revealing. She got the idea for *Joyriders* (1986) from an evening at the Lyric when a group of young people from Divis Flats made their first ever trip to the theatre to see Sean O'Casey's *Shadow of a Gunman*. The lads smoked, ate food, cheered when Donal kissed Minnie, and tried to get served at the bar afterwards even though they were under-age. When Reid asked one what he made of the play, 'A load of shit' was his reply. The young skinhead was, however, clipped by one of the girls present ('How would you know? You got put out for smoking'). Reid went up to the group's Youth Training Project (YTP) on the Falls Road in West Belfast, which she noted was ironically a disused linen mill: 'Most of the kids are only on the

---

[128] Christina Reid, *The Last of a Dyin' Race*, in *Best Radio Plays of 1986* (London: Methuen/BBC Productions, 1987), 48, 52, 60. The play won a Giles Cooper Award for 1986. Original ellipsis.

[129] Reid, *Last*, 46–7, 53, 57.

scheme for a year, training for jobs they won't get because of their background. Then they're back out on the street.'[130] In the play Big Sandra likens the YTP to a 'government joyride. A good laugh for a year, an' then ye grow up.'[131] *Joyriders* has structural deficiencies but also possesses an 'unselfconscious energy' which 'carries the play and the audience forward without strain or pompousness',[132] and its theme of a receding state ultimately having no answers for disenfranchised and unemployed youth remains powerfully relevant to the UK at large.

Reid was aware that young working-class males in Northern Ireland are always susceptible to the paramilitaries and never backed away from addressing the coercive tendencies within her own community, engaging with them 'because they're there'.[133] This was complicated by some of her relatives being involved with the UDA, and she recalled a group of Loyalists from the same outfit, clad in brown leather jackets, attending *en masse* a performance of *The Belle of Belfast City* at the Lyric Theatre, sitting in the back row and cheering a 'sexist, racist speech'. One of the group, realizing what the play was conveying about a certain type of Loyalist, questioned her about it in the bar afterwards, all of which taught her that the paramilitaries narcissistically 'love seeing themselves on stage and on screen, because then they exist: they are real. "Great to see our wans [ones] on stage."'[134] Charabanc also encountered the paramilitaries on tours of Northern Irish community centres, Marie Jones remembering dilapidated venues where 'the sinks were hanging off the wall', and 'halfway through the UDA went out and had a meeting and then came back in again when the meeting was over. All you'd hear was the boots coming in, "Sorry love, wee meeting there. Carry on!"'[135]

INVISIBILITY

Behind Jones's comic sway lies a darkness which invades even her most apparently entertaining theatre. *Stones in His Pockets*, which ran to enormous commercial and critical success when it was revived in 1999—largely based, as Jones has admitted, on a remarkable performance from Conleth Hill—exemplifies this in its anticipation of the problem currently blighting her original community of a high level of suicides among young

---

[130] Quoted in *Irish Times*, 8 April 1991, 10.   [131] Reid, *Joyriders*, in *Plays: 1*, 163.
[132] Paul Hadfield, 'Keeping the Kids Amused', *Fortnight*, No. 238 (5–18 May 1986), 25.
[133] Interview with Richard Howard, London, 22 February 2016.
[134] Interview with Christina Reid, Belfast, 24 June 2013. This is Jack's speech (*Belle*, in *Plays: 1*, 209).
[135] Interview with Marie Jones, Belfast, 26 November 2014.

males (in a disturbing statistic, Northern Ireland's suicide rate has doubled since the 1998 Good Friday Agreement).[136] The titular young male walks into an Irish river to drown himself because he 'wanted to be someone'.[137] Though there have been problems in the north of the city, the area with the highest levels of suicide amongst young people is East Belfast, which saw a spate of young men taking their own lives towards the end of 2012. A DUP Assembly representative for the area pointed out that his brother and uncle committed suicide within a short time of each other, constituting a 'major problem' in relation to mental health: 'Those are the real issues; it's not about the flag or needing more parades.'[138] The aforementioned PUP councillor Julie-Anne Corr Johnston confirmed that she too had attempted suicide and self-harmed in her teenage years, partly through anxiety over coming out as a lesbian.[139] There is therefore a serious engagement, even tangentially, with her background which Jones is not always given credit for.

Though she guards against the label, it would be wrong to suggest that feminism does not manifest in Jones's plays, especially in *Women on the Verge of HRT* (1995).[140] In keeping with the subliminal darkness, the play may seem a surprising juncture for such a thesis. First performed with Pam Brighton again directing a DubbelJoint production, Vera (played by Jones herself in many productions) is preoccupied by the memory of former partner Dessie, who left her for a woman twenty-five years his junior. Though the early scenes are filled with comedy via a light-hearted lampooning of the singer Daniel O'Donnell, the play conceals a painful dilemma for its central characters and women their age:

> *HRT* to me was a very sad, dark play because it was about women disappearing when they become a certain age. I remember all this research—women who were menopausal thought they were losing their minds. They started not feeling like a woman anymore. I also remembered when we talked to my mother at the time. She said: 'Er, menopause. No such thing in our day.' What she meant was: you didn't talk about it. They didn't even call it the menopause. They said '*the change*', very quiet words. I remember at the time asking 'What has happened, what are these women suddenly changing into?' As you grow old you realize, 'I know what I should change into: nothing.' You disappear if you allow that to happen. So you no longer feel that you're a sexual entity anymore. At a certain age

---

[136] *Irish News*, 25 July 2012, 15.   [137] Jones, *Stones*, in *Stones*, 37.
[138] *Belfast Telegraph*, 10 December 2012, 14; interview with Sammy Douglas, Belfast, 3 February 2012.
[139] *Belfast Telegraph*, 3 June 2015, 13.
[140] Marie Jones, *Women on the Verge of HRT* (London: Samuel French, 1999).

you start to feel anonymous. There's a line in the play, 'I walk into a room and nobody turns round.'[141]

To the middle-aged band who follow him, O'Donnell represents 'somewhere to put that adoration and love into, and it's alright because you become almost like you're no threat, which is insulting'. Jones noticed that the jokes about Daniel O'Donnell 'are made more about his audience than they are about him'—were O'Donnell's fans young women he would attract less derision. Yet in noticing the middle-aged women of Daniel O'Donnell's fan base, Jones correctly frowns on the mentality: 'It's like "Well they're not relevant anymore, so you can have a laugh at them."' Her own comedy is more often than not about the audience enjoying it, even when they are unaware that they are laughing at themselves. The play opened the 1995 *Féile an Phobail* festival, and Jones was struck by how alleviated its audience felt: 'It's almost like it was subversive. "Somebody's gonna speak about it, now."'[142] Brighton maintained that the humour was 'always central to it. People don't do dreary jobs and then want to go and see dreary plays. People want to go and see something that they can laugh about.'[143] Jones's comedy disarms and defuses, representing a compromise for Northern Irish audiences schooled in sectarian norms. *Women on the Verge*, dressed up as entertainment to enjoy on a night out, therefore represents Jones's most powerful statement about gender politics. That it continues to reach the very group the play is about, who are not a conventional theatre-going audience, was another of her unexpected triumphs.

Like the protagonists of *Women on the Verge of HRT*, young Protestant working-class men also feel invisible. The play which accordingly most reconnects Jones with her roots is *Rock Doves*, which ran at Belfast's Waterfront Hall in April 2010. Wrongly ignored and dismissed by recent scholarly criticism,[144] the play has flaws but also contains some of Jones's most impressive writing of the last decade. She confirmed that Orange festivities had always been 'part of my world' as a young person, though this was as much for the 'opportunity to meet boys' as anything else.[145] Researching *Rock Doves*, Jones went to a bonfire with her sister during the annual Twelfth of July celebrations when her young son Matthew (who would play the nameless nineteen-year-old Boy in the Belfast production of the play) was four years old. She had witnessed a kid climb to the top of a bonfire to cheering, only to jump off before he got burnt, landing badly. Present at the scene was an actor from the area called David McBlain, who also witnessed the incident:

> Davy came round the next day and I said, 'Jesus, Davy, the wee lad up the top of the bonfire', and he says: 'Why? He was like a fucking King. Can you imagine what that's like? He was King for a whole day—that was it,' and it suddenly came to me. I initially called the play 'King for a Day' because it was like: 'Here I am. I'm validated.' Because nobody ever validates them in their lives, so when you get an opportunity it's like 'I'm up here and gonna make the most of it.' The risk of burning himself just to be important. He didn't want to leave because he knew that was it. He's a nobody once he leaves that.[146]

The setting of *Rock Doves* is a deserted apartment frequented by an alcoholic tramp, Knacker, an unnamed Boy (who is on the run from a Loyalist paramilitary leader he has double-crossed), another female vagrant called Bella, and a cross-dressing Loyalist singer, Lillian. The latter two characters are woven into the plot but *Rock Doves* really concerns the unlikely relationship Knacker (who 'can't get no lower') and the Boy strike up after their initial sparring. There are references to internecine Loyalist feuding, while the unseen figure of Top Dog, the Loyalist leader the Boy has become disillusioned with, appears reminiscent of 'Mad Dog' Johnny Adair. Lillian points out that Top Dog's removal from the streets has also eliminated the chief who 'was holdin' this area together. Know what's wrong with them all Bella... they're missin' an enemy.' Confronting similar themes to Gary Mitchell's work, Lillian mentions that 'all them years a being at the front they can't go back to bein the nobodies they started out as'.[147]

The Boy is the product (and victim) of the condition in deprived working-class communities of 'a status attached to being a member of a paramilitary organization, particularly when they're wielding power and control over our community'.[148] Sincerely claiming to 'protect this country', he builds 'the biggest bonfire ever seen in Belfast':

> BOY: You shud a seen it Knacker... six weeks before the celebrations I worked day and night to stack that bonfire... spent m' dole money payin' kids in the street to work for me gatherin' wood... I carried

---

[146] Interview with Marie Jones, Belfast, 26 November 2014.
[147] Marie Jones, *Rock Doves* (Unpublished, 2010), 13, 26. Original ellipses here and in extracts below.
[148] Interview with Dawn Purvis, Belfast, 20 January 2012.

most of it myself on my back. I didn't care, I didn't feel it, it was for us, for the cause, it was for Ulster. Sixty feet high it was and I never left it. I built myself a watchman's hut, my sentry post. I lived there day and night to guard it. The women in the street would bring me dinner. It was great. When I had it built, when it was finished, people from all over Belfast came to take pictures of it, cos like, it was a work of Art.

KNACKER: I am sure it was son, I can see it now.

Jones reminds us that the bonfire 'suddenly becomes a work of art. So even with a bonfire people are still trying to make sense of anything that'll help them feel better about who they are.'[149] The Boy is equally proud of the ceremonial Pope effigy he has constructed, on the night of the bonfire perching at the top next to the imitation of then-Pope Benedict XVI:

BOY: It was dead weird. I know he was a dummy and everything, but sittin there 60 ft up, he was company, and yer not gonna believe this, I started to feel sorry for him getting burned. I thought like, so you're a pope, you haven't done me no harm, I mean like, he's German. When am I ever gonna be in Germany? I nearly wanted to save him, but that's treason. I would have bin kneecapped for that, cos they were all down there lukin' up. The people started to gather from all over Belfast hundreds of them, just standing there cheerin'... and I sat there right at the top of the world.[150]

The boy then catches sight of Top Dog, surrounded by men, women, and youngsters drunkenly cheering. As with the young man at the bonfire Jones witnessed, the Boy then jumps off, landing badly on his ankle. Hearing of a party being organized by Top Dog, the Boy hopes the men will embrace him but instead they refuse him entry: 'laughed at me... took the glory of my bonfire and then they slammed the door in my face'. Vengeful at his treatment, he grasses Top Dog and his men to the police after he sees them get out of a car in his neighbourhood with concealed boxes of drugs. As a 'tout', the Boy is initially made to feel important ('they treated me like I was somebody'), but the raid so soon after the Boy had been seen in the street arouses suspicion. Lillian, the cross-dressing character who performs as a resident act in a Loyalist club, eventually tells the organization of the boy's whereabouts, leading to his fatal shooting. Only Knacker validates the Boy's memory: 'He was a born rock dove Bella, he would have survived, I seen it in his eyes... Only a squab, never had a chance to grow. Who knows what he might have done. Bastards.'[151]

---

[149] Interview with Marie Jones, Belfast, 26 November 2014.
[150] Jones, *Rock*, 35–6.   [151] Jones, *Rock*, 36–7, 43, 46–7.

CONCLUSION

When the Abbey Theatre unveiled its season for the centenary anniversary of 1916, with only one of its chosen plays written by a woman, Christina Reid and Marie Jones were named as female writers (along with others) whose plays could easily have been performed during the programme.[152] In amongst O'Casey, Tom Murphy, and Frank McGuinness, the omission showed that even groups which were not traditionally well represented in an Irish discourse—the working class, homosexuals, Ulster Unionists—were still better represented on the stage and, by extension, in public life, than women. In response to the 'Waking the Feminists' campaign the Abbey's director Fiach Mac Conghail organized a public meeting on 12 November 2015, made a speech, and changed absolutely nothing.[153] Charabanc's Eleanor Methven took to the stage that day to declare that if indeed feminists needed waking up, she had been a 'chronic insomniac' and 'awake since about 1976'. Yet the problem for women in the theatre is not, according to Marie Jones, solely confined to either the Protestant working class or Ireland. 'I think women are very private and a play is very public. A novel is a one-to-one experience but if you have an audience looking at your work you are really exposing yourself.'[154] The collaborative 'group' ethos of Charabanc represented a useful shield in this sense, enabling Jones to build up her confidence, which is also why it has been hard to place Christina Reid alongside the prolific, internationally regarded Jones in this chapter. Nevertheless, Riana O'Dwyer has noted that Reid's work illustrates the 'limitations of gender roles' in inhibiting the 'individual freedom' of women. Those 'who place a high value on personal freedom, will move to England to live. The hardliners, who cling to traditional political and family values, will remain.'[155] This might seem a finite assessment, but there was something instructive about the way Reid achieved her own mobility and chose to live between both London and Belfast, raising her children in a similar dichotomy. It was a mobility of class as well as place.

Jones achieved this mobility too. *A Night in November* and *Stones in His Pockets* remain phenomenally profitable, with regular revivals and tours,

[152] Sara Keating, 'Beyond the Abbey: The Trouble for Women in Theatre', *Irish Times*, 7 November 2015, 45.

[153] *Irish Times*, 13 November 2015, 5.

[154] Quoted in 'Conversation with Pat Moylan', 217.

[155] Riana O'Dwyer, 'The Imagination of Women's Reality: Christina Reid and Marina Carr', in Eamonn Jordan (ed.), *Theatre Stuff: Critical Essays on Contemporary Irish Theatre* (Dublin: Carysfort Press, 2000), 241.

while in early 2016 it was announced that the Lyric's revival of Jones's *Christmas Eve Can Kill You* was the most commercially successful show since the theatre's reopening in 2011.[156] Charabanc had a specific aim which it would be wrong to project an overly ideological view onto. 'It was purely economic,' admits a founder. 'We just wanted to work. For God's sake we were paid on a Work Creation scheme! But, then, workers have the right to work.'[157] The salient detail remains that all the actresses involved are hugely talented performers whose appearances over the last thirty years in Northern Ireland—and beyond—are testament to abilities which the local scene was unable to cater for. There is something which rings true in Martin Lynch's assessment of Charabanc as a 'great growing process' for its women,[158] though a continuum is identified by one of its members: 'Marie's gone a different direction, but underlying a lot of her work is that basic "It's not fair." That was the message of *Lay Up Your Ends*. It's a line of Florrie's and I think that that has driven a lot of what she's done. It certainly has driven a lot of what I've done. "It's not fair that it should be like that." It's a very simple philosophy, but it's at the heart of what we did.'[159]

After a very short illness, Reid died in May 2015. 'Christina, I think, right until her death, was so vulnerable,' remembers a close friend and colleague. Suggesting that she never returned to the heights of her debut, Patrick Sandford believes that Reid 'was somehow reluctant to believe she was good. I wonder if at some level her esteem was still in her own lower, working-class [roots].'[160] As news of her death broke, the Lyric were doing a rehearsed reading of *Joyriders*, the practice for most Northern Irish performances of Reid's work in the last decade of her life,[161] but it seemed scant recognition for a writer whose plays had packed the theatre in the 1980s and revealed a plethora of women's voices—especially within Protestant communities—who would otherwise not have been heard. This quality fundamentally links Reid and Jones, along with the recognition that the theatre is not reducible to a cultured middle class. 'My plays get accused of being low art all the time,' Jones has said. 'Even by the arts establishment in my own city. But what's wrong with being popular?

---

[156] See the discussion of *Stones in His Pockets* in Patrick Lonergan, *Theatre and Globalization: Irish Drama in the Celtic Tiger Era* (Basingstoke: Palgrave Macmillan, 2010), 8–30.

[157] Interview with Brenda Winter-Palmer, Belfast, 20 October 2015.

[158] Interview with Martin Lynch, Belfast, 20 March 2014.

[159] Interview with Brenda Winter-Palmer, Belfast, 20 October 2015; Lynch and Charabanc, *Lay Up*, 59.

[160] Interview with Patrick Sandford, London, 13 October 2015.

[161] Interview with Christina Reid, Belfast, 24 June 2013. Reid pointed out that her plays are now mainly performed in Europe and America because 'they are understood there', especially by young people.

I sometimes feel that people want to keep the theatre as some kind of special preserve for people like them, educated, cultured people; they don't like it when a play packs out the theatre with ordinary people having a good time.'[162] Theatrical practitioners have patronized the 'kind of community drama exercise' Charabanc pioneered, even if its creators knew well John McGrath's dictum that 'there *are* indeed different kinds of audiences, with different theatrical values and expectations', and that these mattered more than the views of 'a well-fed, white, middle class, sensitive but sophisticated literary critic'.[163]

May Blood has continually stressed the necessity of Protestant working-class communities being prepared to 'tell our story' and so gain confidence in the future. Women have been especially vulnerable to submersion, and so the effect of Charabanc (and Marie Jones herself) has been incalculably important in lifting people. Those who previously thought 'Why would anyone be interested in my story?' realized they had a story worth telling. It was no coincidence that Charabanc's principal theatrical venue was the community centre, because it was in such spaces (where 'they are still at home, relatively safe')—as Blood has always argued—that women on both sides of the sectarian divide engaged and mixed during the 1980s and 1990s, keeping 'their communities together, and develop[ing] themselves while they were doing it'.[164]

---

[162] Quoted in *The Guardian*, 11 August 2004, 12.
[163] The phrase of theatre director Rachel O'Riordan, 'Machismo of the Troubles', *Fortnight*, No. 451 (March 2007), 17; McGrath, *Good Night*, 2–3.
[164] Harris, 'Community Conscience', 213; Blood, *Watch*, 203, 205.

Conclusion

> We have 53 entries in the Census of Religious Denominations in Northern Ireland—Pentecostal, Elim Tabernacle, House of God, Free Presbyterian. You may split and maybe you are the better for splitting, but fission is part of the identity which is strange, because an identity should be an enclosing thing.
>
> John Hewitt (*Irish Times*, March 1986)

In one of his most significant works, F. S. L. Lyons referred to how the conflict in Northern Ireland could only be understood through 'the recognition of difference'.[1] This has rarely been followed by political and cultural investigations of Ulster Protestantism, which is why this book has looked to dramatic writing and class separation. The playwrights concerned deal with difference by the very nature of their craft: the consideration of the disparate voices and stances which pervade their own community. From the 'voice and conscience of a fragmented culture', John Hewitt,[2] to Gary Mitchell—who once stated 'We need a new beginning, a re-invention'—it may be argued that Ulster Protestants are, in contrast to stereotypes and received polemic, relentlessly dissenting and inherently creative. At the height of his exposure to an English audience, Mitchell articulated 'a fundamental crisis in Protestant culture. We have been going through an extremely depressing loss of identity, loss of culture, and worst of all, loss of a future. We're hugely divided. Umpteen churches, umpteen political parties.'[3] This assessment is contradicted by the subjects of this book, the splintering he regrets tapping into why a number of playwrights (including, of course, himself) have emerged from the background. Simultaneously, the basic recognition of the prevalence of working-class Protestants in the Labour movement—some of whom also wrote plays and books—further punctures the caricature of a straightforward, reactionary homogeneity.

---

[1] F. S. L. Lyons, *Culture and Anarchy in Ireland, 1890–1939* (Oxford: Oxford University Press, 1979), 145.
[2] Eavan Boland, 'John Hewitt—An Appreciation', *Irish Times*, 30 June 1987, 8.
[3] Quoted in *The Guardian—G2*, 10 April 2000, 11.

Discrimination against Catholics is well documented, but 'there was also discrimination of a different kind against the Protestant working class. There were jobs you'd never have got in the BBC unless you were a middle-class Protestant. There were jobs you'd never have got in the RUC, speaking generally, unless you were upper-middle class.'[4] The NILP channelled some of this class dynamic, even if its Protestant component has now largely evaporated. As a former member puts it:

> Within the Protestant working class they would all say if they lived in England they would support the Labour Party. So there's a block interfering with that here—maybe it's the Republican campaign, maybe it's the campaign against Britishness, maybe it's the parading—and that block means they don't focus on the issues they want to focus on. I try and say to them, 'Look, the Union is safe. Nobody's going to vote for a united Ireland a week tomorrow because it won't be there, so don't worry about the Union. Let's not get drawn into the sectarian conflict,' which is where Sinn Féin would like us to be.[5]

For other NILP veterans a substantial Labour vote persists but is now elderly, the tradition permanently blitzed by the violence of the Troubles, which 'polarized the whole community. Polarized everything.' Another directly compares the collapse of the NILP to social democratic parties in Europe in 1914: 'Once it was faced with a nationalist conflict of some intensity, it essentially disintegrated.'[6]

The central myth this book has challenged, and hopefully refuted, is that Ulster Protestants have no literary imagination or connection to the theatre. But myths are inevitable and do provide, in less-acknowledged definitions, a necessary 'account of origins' which explain 'an active form of social organization'.[7] The new myths circulated by these writers do not evade the past but rather interpret it in original ways, uncovering history which has been missed or deliberately obscured. Lynne Parker draws a line between her uncle and another playwright in this book, as 'in some ways Northern Ireland has moved on from the Troubles, yet it's all still there: Gary Mitchell's not wrong'. She believes Parker's plays suggest that 'unless we are vigilant we will return to it, so it is our responsibility to be very

---

[4] Interview with John Kennedy, Holywood, 17 June 2014. Kennedy served on the parliamentary staff of the original Stormont parliament and was clerk to the Northern Ireland Assembly (1982–6).

[5] Interview with Jackie Hewitt, Belfast, 19 August 2014. Hewitt currently co-ordinates *Farset International* on the West Belfast interface. He is both a trade unionist and an Orangeman.

[6] Interview with David Overend, Belfast, 28 April 2015; interview with Tony Kennedy, Belfast, 14 June 2012.

[7] Raymond Williams, *Keywords* (London: Fontana Press, 1988; 1st edition 1976), 211.

rigorous in our scrutiny of the past',[8] directly echoing his own call to write
historically authentic work: 'I know that Shakespeare travestied history to
creative ends, but he was developing an entire historical ethic within the
framework of the Tudor world-view. I feel rather strongly that historical
plays (or novels) written today ought to be factually accurate—the interpretation of the facts is, of course, another matter.'[9] Far from forgetting,
Parker advocated tackling the 'official versions of reality' which he
regarded as 'malevolent and deceitful' and promoted by those in power:
'I want my work to offer alternative versions.'[10]

While Ronan Bennett predictably claimed that Protestant working-class
culture 'has always tended to the exclusive and inward looking', academic
voices have either focused on the activities of Loyalist paramilitaries and
fundamentalists, or in the case of renowned historians gone so far as to
enunciate a 'herd mentality' fortified by the dearth of the Ulster Protestant
'imagination'.[11] Ripostes to the latter were swift,[12] but the demeaning of
the Protestant working class's written culture, and the willingness to either
ignore or compress this into one homogeneous movement, completely
miss the intrinsic difference within the profile. It is an identity, as one of
these playwrights has outlined, that one has to 'piece together'. Collect-
ively, therefore, it often appears in perpetual crisis—why perhaps many
Protestants feel they have lost—but is toiling in the kind of salubrious
disarray outlined as 'controversy, political, religious, social: all sorts of
controversy. Without it you can have no progress, no life.'[13] All of the
writers in this book are convinced that their group is haemorrhaging and in
crisis, something possibly linked to a dramatic faculty:

> The existential is the political. A state was willed into being that explained
> what being Northern Irish Protestant was. That has now gone. The dream of
> a nation for ourselves that is going to affect Protestant values; that's gone like
> snow off a ditch. Now that's gone you've got something to write about
> because what's going to take its place? They will get their thirty-two counties
> one of these days. We had *our* six counties but we lost them. That seems to

[8] Interview with Lynne Parker, Dublin, 24 March 2012.
[9] Stewart Parker, Letter to John Boyd, 29 January 1968, JBC.
[10] Stewart Parker, '*Dramatis Personae*: John Malone Memorial Lecture', in *Dramatis
Personae and Other Writings*, ed. Gerald Dawe, Maria Johnston, and Clare Wallace (Prague:
Litteraria Pragensia, 2008), 24.
[11] J. J. Lee, *Ireland 1912–1985: Politics and Society* (Cambridge: Cambridge University
Press, 1989), 1–19.
[12] Paul Bew, 'An Iconoclastic History, Yet Partly It's Dated', *Fortnight*, No. 283 (April
1990), 23–4; Graham Walker, 'Old History: Protestant Ulster in Lee's "Ireland"', *The Irish
Review*, No. 12 (Spring/Summer 1992), 65–71.
[13] George Bernard Shaw, 'The Protestants of Ireland' (1912), in *The Matter with Ireland*,
ed. Dan H. Laurence and David H. Greene (London: Rupert Hart-Davis, 1962), 72.

me, to have lost, to be a more interesting place for a writer to be writing from than 'One of these days we'll have our thirty-two counties and it'll all be heaven on earth.' We have something to write about that is both political and existential, and that might be why there's something going on with Protestant writers that can't go on with those from a nationalist, Catholic, or Republican background.[14]

Politically speaking this may seem hard to resist, but have Ulster Protestants really lost? Proceeding with the ice-cold objectivity of John Whyte,[15] the Protestant working class has suffered a major decline in its labour opportunities. Connected to education, it has struggled to acclimatize to a global climate where, as in the entire Western world, manufacturing has 'gone East, and with that have gone jobs. You get the sense that Protestant working-class kids are a bit stranded in this Cerberus-oriented economy where the skills of persuasion and communication and marketing are more important than manual skills.'[16] The move from a mainly industrial society to an informational market system was exacerbated by the newer cultural experience of unemployment, and thus adjustment has been particularly arduous.[17] In one of his later letters, St John Ervine proclaimed:

We Ballymacarrett people had a dim view of anybody and anything on the wrong side of the Lagan. After all, we had the 'Island', and what more did anybody want than that? When I saw Lord Pirrie riding in his carriage along the Newtownards Road, I felt almost as reverent as I should feel if I saw God there. He was a genial looking man. I never saw Harland or Wolff, though how I failed to see them I cannot imagine. I still remember how the Island men spent Sunday morning sitting on the foreshore at Sydenham gazing at the Island as if they feared that somebody might steal it if they did not keep their eyes on it.[18]

Ervine spoke of his people possessing Queen's Island as if it was the only thing they had. As it was, the commercial and industrial virtues he thought seminally in tune with the Ulster identity were a mirage, still indulged in by the investment barons of modern Northern Ireland. The Island was

---

[14] Interview with Ron Hutchinson, Belfast, 2 August 2012. Writers from the Republican movement agree 'There's never going to be an intensification of the Union. But there could be over a period of time, social and economic and political harmonization on the island' (interview with Danny Morrison, Belfast, 29 August 2013).

[15] John Whyte, 'How Much Discrimination Was There under the Stormont Regime?', in Tom Gallagher and James O'Connell (eds), *Contemporary Irish Studies* (Manchester: Manchester University Press, 1983), 1–35.

[16] Interview with Mark Langhammer, Belfast, 21 September 2011.

[17] Eileen Evason, *On the Edge: A Study of Poverty and Long-term Unemployment in Northern Ireland* (London: Child Poverty Action Group, 1985), 66.

[18] Letter to John Boyd, 15 October 1960. JBC.

taken; not by Catholics but by the winds of economics and deindustrial-ization. The dramatists considered in the latter chapters of this book came to terms with that loss.

This is, nonetheless, where specific Protestant deterioration ends. Northern Ireland's highest levels of unemployment and deprivation are to be found in the Catholic areas of Whiterock, the Falls, and the New Lodge in Belfast. Forty-three per cent of children in West Belfast live in poverty against 21 per cent in East Belfast, while the highest levels of recorded crime are to be found—by far—in the same vicinities.[19] Constitutionally, the Good Friday Agreement of 1998 arguably copper-fastened a Union which had been further strengthened by Ireland's economic duress following the financial crisis of 2007–8. The Provisional IRA's primary aspiration, reiter-ated time and again, was 'based purely on the need to secure a withdrawal of the British presence from this island', leading shrewder minds banished to the outskirts of the Republican movement to conclude that Sinn Féin's peace process concessions essentially amounted to the defeat of its armed wing.[20] Yet a feeling of being on 'the losing side' persists, something a former Unionist leader suggests may be a hangover of Paisleyism, where 'in order to build up his support, [Ian] Paisley fed this idea that we were always being betrayed and that Republicans were doing better'. Looking squarely at 'the big picture items, in terms of the constitutional settle-ment, I think Unionism has done pretty well out of it'.[21] An ex-UVF combatant who now works in community development attributes the prevalent pessimism to the natural disorganization within the commu-nity: 'When people say "There's no evidence of Protestant people benefiting from the peace process," there's no evidence of a collective response to the benefits of it, because we're still fractured the same way we have always been in our Churches, in the way we vote, even in our militarism. I just think we aren't as joined up in responding to what we have got from it.'[22]

Until very recently this overall settlement was memorably framed as 'The Unionists have won, They just don't know it,'[23] though this was

[19] Northern Ireland Statistical Research Agency, *Northern Ireland Multiple Deprivation Measure 2010* (Belfast: NISRA, May 2010), 27. The top five and the majority of the top thirty most deprived areas of Northern Ireland are Catholic. West Belfast's high child-poverty rating, the fourth worst in the entire UK, is closely followed by the predominantly Catholic Foyle area on 36 per cent. See also *Irish News*, 20 February 2013, 14.

[20] Quoted in *The Guardian*, 17 November 1981, 32; Anthony McIntyre, *Good Friday: The Death of Irish Republicanism* (New York: Ausubo Press, 2008).

[21] Interview with Lord Reg Empey, Belfast, 11 November 2011.

[22] Interview with William Mitchell, Belfast, 26 July 2012.

[23] Paul Bew, *The Making and Remaking of the Good Friday Agreement* (Dublin: The Liffey Press, 2007), 28.

shaken on 23 June 2016 when a small majority of UK citizens voted to leave the European Union. Ironically the Democratic Unionist Party, along with the other more traditional Unionist representatives, backed the vote which may ultimately jeopardize the future of that which they hold most dear. Typically enough, John Hewitt preferred to embrace the myth of Europe in his hierarchy of values, the review of one of his posthumous collections by another Ulster Protestant poet speaking as much to the present as it did when it was published in 1992: 'As Europe painfully rearranges herself, as Communism retreats discredited, as narrow nationalism and crude religion combine to release their toxins, so Hewitt's big-hearted, open-faced versions of regionalism, socialism and atheism appear ever more relevant.'[24]

It is surely no coincidence that what unites all the playwrights considered in this book, apart from Parker and Graham Reid, is the lack of higher education. For some the prospect was of no interest and avoiding it made them the writers they were.[25] Others were proud autodidacts, reflecting a long-standing Protestant tradition of self-education. A few simply lacked the opportunities, or began degrees they never finished.[26] But in the context of modern Northern Ireland where 'the educational non-progressor . . . is most likely to be a Protestant working class male',[27] it remains a shattering problem and one with deep roots. Reflecting on the 1944 Butler Education Act, Christina Reid's archetypal Aunt Maisie in *Tea in a China Cup* would appear to be speaking on behalf of many from her community:

> MAISIE: No good'll come of this subsidized education, you mark my words. The Catholics will beg, borrow and steal the money to get their kids a fancy education. This country'll suffer for it in years to come when well-qualified Catholics start to pour out of our Queen's University expecting the top jobs, wantin' a say in the runnin' of the country.[28]

---

[24] Michael Longley, 'Pivotal Poetry', *Fortnight*, No. 303 (February 1992), 22.

[25] Interview with Ron Hutchinson, Belfast, 2 August 2012. Hutchinson's parents 'didn't give a shit about my education, thank God'. Leaving school at sixteen, he worked in different jobs which he thinks 'may be a deeper well no matter how good an MFA gets you in Screenwriting'. While living in California, Hutchinson taught the Master of Fine Arts in Screenwriting at the American Film Institute.

[26] Christina Reid started but did not complete a degree at Queen's University, confirming that she 'would not have been the same person, writing the way I do, if I had stayed on at school'. Quoted in *Northern Women* (15 November 1983), 16.

[27] Dawn Purvis and the Working Group on Educational Disadvantage and the Protestant Working Class, *Educational Disadvantage and the Protestant Working Class—A Call to Action* (March 2011), 4.

[28] Christina Reid, *Tea in a China Cup*, in *Plays: 1* (London: Methuen, 1997), 31.

Gary Mitchell actually passed the eleven-plus exam but knew he would only ever be 'going to Rathcoole secondary school around the corner'.[29] Initially excelling, he found himself an outsider and 'uncool' among his peers, so he decided to implode. Deliberately pushing himself to the bottom of the class, he realized:

> that learning things was a bad idea, and being dumb was a good idea. Being stupid was the smart thing to do. I read how working-class Protestants entitled to free school meals have some of the lowest scores in the UK. They are bluffing. They're smarter than that. Protestant working-class boys are doing exactly what I did. They are hiding their intelligence. It's very sad, but it's a macho culture.[30]

Easily striking a chord with the wider United Kingdom, where white working-class boys are also struggling with education,[31] it may help scholars—and indeed Ulster Protestants themselves—to start grounding these travails within a broader UK framework.

The difficulty for working-class Unionists is that the 'culture war' is being pursued legitimately, with British symbols democratically removed and Irish Republican narratives propagated in cultural ways. This is not helped by the process coinciding with the widespread Unionist concern that history is being tendentiously rewritten to downplay or expunge unfavourable details from Irish Republicanism's recent past, simultaneously emphasizing past atrocities committed by the British state.[32] Lacking the electoral success and resources of mainstream Republicanism, and apparently unaware of (or unwilling to promote) their own literary efforts,[33] serious disillusionment has arisen without outlet. Violence and street disturbances remain the easier road. Much harder has been adapting to the moving ground ceded by their ideological opponents. At the same time both major Loyalist paramilitary groups have decommissioned and held mostly steady in the face of ongoing dissident Republican violence, while Unionist representatives believe those groups who live by coercion become so resented that

---

[29] Quoted in Susan McKay, *Northern Protestants: An Unsettled People* (Belfast: Blackstaff Press, 2000), 115. In 1994 eleven children passed the eleven-plus exam from all ten primary schools in the Shankill, though most opted—like Mitchell—not to go to the grammar school with more affluent youngsters two bus journeys away. No school on the Shankill delivered A-Levels at the time.

[30] Quoted in *Belfast Telegraph*, 12 May 2014, 24–5.

[31] See Gillian Evans, *Educational Failure and Working Class White Children in Britain* (Basingstoke: Palgrave Macmillan, 2006).

[32] Arlene Foster, 'Republicans Must Not Be Allowed to Shift Blame', *Belfast News Letter*, 13 February 2016, 6.

[33] See the 'Loyalist Literature' section of Chapter 1.

'eventually the community gets rid of them'.[34] This would appear a long-term, generational aspiration, though the emergence of new artistic initiatives enabling Loyalists to convey their own historical narratives can only aid the process.[35]

It has been observed that 'in destroying [Terence] O'Neill, Ulster Unionism opened an era, uninterrupted since, of de facto administration of Northern Ireland by the very liberal establishment they had so resented'.[36] While a Northern Irish legislature has since returned, the UK's liberal establishment remains intact and especially so in London. The Protestant working class has carried the can for a myopic, ungenerous, and parochial reputation, but it is the leadership of mainstream Unionism which has abrogated its responsibility in making the case for progressive constitutional association with Britain. Those within Unionism who traditionally performed this role were intellectuals and the middle classes, exemplified by such names as Charlie Brett, Bob McCartney, and (the later) St John Ervine.[37] A one-time leader of the Ulster Unionist Party claimed that professional, middle-class Unionists 'deserted' politics during the 1970s for roughly a quarter of a century,[38] and this may be linked to the way the existing abortion laws, marriage equality, welfare state provisions, and mainly cohesive race relations represent quite the antithesis of the Britain envisioned by many Unionists in Northern Ireland.

At the close of his autobiography *A North Light*, John Hewitt recounts his voyage to Coventry. With a few hours to spare before what will be a successful interview to run the Herbert Art Gallery and Museum, he wandered into a café to find himself contentedly surrounded by Irish accents. Handed a menu by an Italian waiter, 'an odd friendly feeling' overtook him, as if, 'in some way, part of me had come home'.[39] This was a broad, inclusive Britishness the mainland represented, exemplified by Coventry itself, bombed out and rebuilt by the post-war Labour government, all realized with that 'novelty to a Belfast man, clear evidence of a

---

[34] *Irish News*, 6 April 2009, 15; *Belfast Telegraph*, 19 June 2009, 1; interview with Chris McGimpsey, Belfast, 18 January 2012.

[35] See for instance the founding of Etcetera Theatre Company (*Belfast News Letter*, 5 August 2013, 9).

[36] Marc Mulholland, *Northern Ireland at the Crossroads: Ulster Unionism in the O'Neill Years, 1960–9* (Basingstoke: Macmillan, 2000), 203.

[37] Ian McBride, 'Ulster and the British Problem', in Richard English and Graham Walker (eds), *Unionism in Modern Ireland: New Perspectives on Politics and Culture* (Dublin: Gill & Macmillan, 1996), 13. Others to have played this part include Professors Paul Bew and Arthur Aughey.

[38] Interview with Lord Reg Empey, Belfast, 11 November 2011.

[39] John Hewitt, *A North Light: Twenty-Five Years in a Municipal Art Gallery*, ed. Frank Ferguson and Kathryn White (Dublin: Four Courts, 2013), 249–50.

civic plan'. Hewitt saw, and understood, the Britain many Unionists still cannot fathom or imagine, which is another reason why he takes his place in this book. His voice and individual myth provide the intellectual, middle-class example and leadership so lacking (with a few exceptions) from many Unionist representatives of the recent past and present.

Though some will continue to doubt what theatre and the arts can really achieve, plays offer us information we would receive from no other source, providing a secure way of experiencing 'what it must be like to be a member of another group'.[40] As significantly for this subject, the absence of serious public, intellectual scrutiny and self-questioning means that it has been left to dramatists (and other writers) to fulfil this role and hold up a mirror to reflect, and probe, what is the 'nature of Protestantism: independent thought'.[41] Sam Thompson actually wandered both of the Ulster Protestant working class's apparently forgotten realms of Labour politics and the theatre. As Stewart Parker reminded us, to be a writer in Northern Ireland 'is to be a public figure, up there in the trenches with the captains and the clergymen. Sam Thompson fully accepted this and he roamed about fearlessly in no-man's land waving a red flag.'[42] The abject failure of Thompson's run for the spectacularly unsuitable seat of South Down was not simply quixotic but illustrative that cultural strides do not always parallel the political. The peak of Protestant working-class political power arrived ten years later with the UWC strike, though this was rapidly and willingly relinquished. Modern political despondency has morphed into a form of cultural depression, but to confuse electoral failure with cultural failure is a critical mistake. In Eric Hobsbawm's estimation 'the wrong side won' the Spanish Civil War, but it was due to 'the artists and writers who mobilized so overwhelmingly in favour of the republic, that in this instance history has not been written by the victors'.[43] These playwrights were the same pens of the defeated, negotiating a polarized political world and responding with new histories and a repository of alternative myths.

One of the reasons it has been vital to distinguish between the Protestant working class and Loyalists in this book is the former's individual, dissenting streak—what Gary Mitchell simply terms 'My politics'.[44] It is entirely symptomatic that Ron Hutchinson set out to explore the life of

---

[40] Claudia Harris, 'Community Conscience or Reflection? Theatre in Northern Ireland', in Alan J. Ward (ed.), *Northern Ireland: Living with the Crisis* (New York: Praeger, 1987), 213. It is always unpropitious to be reminded that the most popular plays for Northern Irish audiences in the decade preceding the Troubles were the suggestive, politically-neutered comedies of Sam Cree. See Richard York, 'Sam Cree: Sex, Sects, and Comedy', *Irish University Review*, Vol. 37, No. 2 (Autumn–Winter, 2007), 352–65.

[41] Interview with Dawn Purvis, Belfast, 20 January 2012.

[42] Stewart Parker, 'Introduction to Sam Thompson's *Over the Bridge*', in *Dramatis Personae*, 59.

[43] Eric Hobsbawm, 'War of Ideas', *The Guardian Review*, 17 February 2007, 4.

[44] Interview with Gary Mitchell, Antrim, 6 June 2013.

Ian Paisley and ended up writing a play about himself and his parents. His father hailed from the rural areas of Ballynahinch and Dromore, contrasting with the Belfast urban working-class profile of his mother, who was born off the Woodstock Road to the east of the city.

A huge red and orange sun begins to glow, flooding the stage with a baleful light—

ME: The setting sun was big and red and orange—appropriately orange—like that class of star which gets bigger and bigger just before it collapses—a bit like you, maybe, swelling up and swelling up and sucking all that energy in from so many places—the church, the fields of green that my dad came from and the fields of brick that my mother came from, all our tangled, bloody, family and national history—you, the right man in the right place at the right time to be the vessel into which all that Fear and Anger and paranoid Protestantness could be poured and, yes, Love, too, I'd have to give you that—[45]

In the end Paisley and the author are left alone, his parents clambering back into their burial ground ('What'd you bury me in, again? The suit?' his father enquires), as Hutchinson shovels earth on their graves in closure. Their emotional attachment overwhelms politics at the heart of a very Protestant dispute, and we discover why they have gathered, at the instigation of Hutchinson's imagination, in the field of a giant grave. If the play is Hutchinson burying his parents he is also burying a way of life. Gesturing to the grave of his parents ('Their Northern Ireland—gone'), he assures Paisley his North 'has gone, too'.[46]

At the same time as recognizing that deindustrialization has had a depressing cultural effect on the Protestant working class, another Belfast playwright is adamant 'that the people who lead them shouldn't mollycoddle that view. They should be actually leading them, saying "You need to create something new now," as opposed to worrying about that flag, and tradition. Because that's what's going to get you out of this.'[47] The educational, political, and economic prospects of this group have given rise to much apprehension and despondency, and individuals within will continue to exhibit their sense of fear, marginalization, and disempowerment. This book reverses that spirit in illuminating a progressive political DNA and a fiercely inventive theatrical heritage, dynamics which often coalesced to a remarkable degree. Even if the map of this alternative Protestant culture has been resolutely abandoned, the important thing is that it exists.

[45] Ron Hutchinson, *Paisley & Me* (Unpublished: 2 October 2012), 80–2.
[46] Hutchinson, *Paisley & Me*, 83.
[47] Interview with Owen McCafferty, Belfast, 28 March 2013.

Bibliography

PRIMARY SOURCES

Private papers

Barr, Glen, 'The Ulidian' (1986).

Barr, Glen, 'The Lamentations of Mother Ulster' (n.d.).

Craig, Patricia, 'Visiting John Hewitt', Lecture delivered at the Crescent Arts Centre, 27 October 2011.

Hutchinson, Ron, *The Big Man* (Unpublished: 24 May 2011).

Hutchinson, Ron, *Paisley & Me* (Unpublished: 2 October 2012).

Jones, Marie, *Rock Doves* (Unpublished, 2010).

Longley, Michael, Letter to James Magee, 5 December 1973.

Lynch, Martin, *Over the Bridge* adaptation (Unpublished, 27 February 2010, Clean Act 2—Scenes 1–5).

McKeown, Laurence, *Those You Pass On the Street* (Unpublished, Performed Script 2014).

Mitchell, Billy, 'Discussions with the Provisional IRA' (n.d.).

Mitchell, Gary, *Energy* (Unpublished: 3rd draft, November 1998).

Mitchell, Gary, *Remnants of Fear* (Unpublished: 4th draft July 2004).

Mitchell, Gary, *Return* (Unpublished, n.d., 2009).

Mitchell, Gary, *Get the Pope* (Unpublished: 2 August 2010).

Mitchell, Gary, *Reenergize* (Unpublished: 29 April 2013).

Murphy, Brenda, and Poland, Christine, *Forced Upon Us* (Unpublished, n.d.).

Niblock, Bobby, '1955–1972' (Unpublished, n.d.).

O'Neill, Terence, Letter to Robert Porter, 14 March 1971. Sir Robert Porter Papers.

O'Rawe, Richard, *Greed* (Unpublished, n.d.).

Porter, Robert, Letter to Stanley Morgan (Ulster Vanguard Secretary), 17 March 1972. Sir Robert Porter Papers.

Purvis, Dawn, *Digging Up Worms* (Unpublished: 2014).

Reid, Graham, *Paisley* (Revised 2nd draft: June 2009).

Reid, Graham, *Love, Billy* (Unpublished: 6th draft, February 2013).

Central Library, Belfast: Sam Thompson Collection

Thompson, Sam, 'Autobiographical Script' (1960).

Thompson, Sam, The Border Line: A Play (n.d.).

Thompson, Sam, The Long Back Street (n.d.).

Thompson, Sam, The Masquerade (n.d.).

Thompson, Sam, The Tea Breakers: A Play for Television (n.d.).

Harry Ransom Center, Austin, Texas: St John Ervine Collection

Ervine, St John, Letter to R. H. Rattray, 20 July 1955.

Ervine, St John, Letter to R. H. Rattray, 26 July 1955.

Ervine, St John, Letter to R. H Rattray, 1 August 1955.

O'Casey, Seán, Letter to St John Ervine, 25 November 1933.

Plunkett, Horace, Letter to St John Ervine, 22 May 1918.

Plunkett, Horace, Letter to St John Ervine, 10 March 1922.

Shaw, George Bernard, Letter to Leonora Ervine, 16 November 1917.

Shaw, George Bernard, Letter to Leonora Ervine, 14 May 1918.

Shaw, George Bernard, Letter to St John Ervine, 22 May 1918.

Shaw, George Bernard, Letter to St John Ervine, 17 August 1948.

Shaw, George Bernard, Letter to St John Ervine, 26 July 1949.

Library of the University of Ulster, Coleraine: The Hewitt Archive

Hewitt, John, Letter to John Montague, spring 1964.

Linen Hall Library, Belfast

Carnduff, Thomas, *Castlereagh* (Unpublished, 1935).

Carnduff, Thomas, *The Last Banshee: A Tragedy of County Antrim Life in Three Acts* (Unpublished, n.d.).

Carnduff, Thomas, *The Stars Foretell: A Play in Three Acts* (Unpublished, n.d.).

Devlin, Paddy, 'Introduction' to *Over the Bridge* Programme (Belfast: Civic Arts Theatre, September 1985). Paddy Devlin Papers. Theatre—Box 4.

Devlin, Paddy, 'John Hewitt—The Ulster Poet' (n.d.). Paddy Devlin Papers. Theatre—Box 4.

Ervine, St John, Letters to John Boyd, 1948–60. John Boyd Collection—Correspondence.

Ervine, St John, Letter to Mr Sandford, 10 March 1941. John Boyd Collection—Correspondence.

Hewitt, John, 'A Question of Identity', in *A Critical Look at Independence: Papers from a Weekend Workshop at Corrymeela* (Belfast: The Workshop, 1976). Linen Hall Library Political Collection.

Hewitt, John, Letter to John Boyd, 8 May 1965. John Boyd Collection—Correspondence.

Hewitt, John, Letter to John Boyd, 21 April 1966. John Boyd Collection—Correspondence.

Hewitt, John, Letter to John Boyd, 14 September 1970. John Boyd Collection—Correspondence.

Hewitt, John, Letter to John Boyd, 11 December 1971. John Boyd Collection—Correspondence.

Morrison, Danny, 'From Novel to Stage', *The Wrong Man*: Theatre Programme (Belfast: New Strung Theatre Company, 2005). Linen Hall Library Political Collection.

Parker, Stewart, Letter to John Boyd, 21 November 1965. John Boyd Collection—Correspondence.

Parker, Stewart, Letter to John Boyd, 29 January 1968. John Boyd Collection—Correspondence.

Parker, Stewart, *The Iceberg* (Unpublished, 1974), 56. Stewart Parker Theatrical Archive.

Spence, Gusty, Text of Speech to Progressive Unionist Party Conference, 11 February 1995. Linen Hall Library Political Collection.

McClay Library, Queen's University Belfast
Carnduff, Thomas, Letters to Mary Carnduff, 1940–3. Thomas Carnduff Archive (MS21).
Costello, Amy, Letter to Mary Carnduff, 15 October 1956. Thomas Carnduff Archive (MS21).
Ervine, St John, Letter to Forrest Reid, 11 June 1940. Forrest Reid Collection (MS44).
Webb, G. (Commodore, Royal Naval Barracks), Letter to Thomas Carnduff, 28 July 1941 (MS21).

National Library of Ireland
Ervine, St John, Letter to Sean O'Casey, 6 June 1928. Eileen O'Casey Papers.
Ervine, St John, Letter to Sean O'Casey, 29 October 1929. Eileen O'Casey Papers.
Ervine, St John, Letter to Sean O'Casey, 13 July 1932. Eileen O'Casey Papers.

New York Public Library: Berg Collection
Ervine, St John, Letter to Lady Gregory, 5 May 1916.
Ervine, St John, Letter to Lady Gregory, 22 May 1916.
Ervine, St John, Letter to Lady Gregory, 29 May 1916.
Ervine, St John, Letter to W. B. Yeats, 1 November 1915.
Ervine, St John, Letter to W. B. Yeats, 4 November 1915.

Public Records Office of Northern Ireland
'BBC Scene Around Six—13 May 1974', OE/1/16.
Broadcast by Brian Faulkner, Chief Minister, Saturday 25 May 1974, OE/1/16.
'Press Notice' (17 May 1974), Statement by the Secretary of State for Northern Ireland, OE/1/16.

Newspapers, Periodicals, and Circulars
An Phoblacht
Andersonstown News
Belfast News Letter
Belfast Telegraph
The Blanket
Books Ireland
Combat
The Daily Telegraph
Financial Times
Fortnight
The Guardian (Manchester Guardian)
The Guardian—G2
The Guardian—MediaGuardian
The Guardian Review
The Guardian Weekend
Honest Ulsterman
Irish News

Irish Political Review
Irish Times
Jacobin
Liberty
Linen Hall Review
London Evening Standard
London Review of Books
London Times
Look Left
The Northern Review
Northern Women
The Observer
Poetry Ireland Review
Socialist Commentary
The Spectator
Sunday Life
Sunday World
Theatre Ireland
The Times Literary Supplement
Unity

Memoirs, Scripts, and Contemporary Publications

Adams, Gerry, *Before the Dawn: An Autobiography* (Kerry: Brandon, 1996).

Barker, Harold, *Arguments for a Theatre* (London: John Calder, 1989).

Bell, Fergus Hanna (ed.), *A Salute from the Banderol: The Selected Writings of Sam Hanna Bell* (Belfast: Blackstaff Press, 2009).

Blood, Baroness May, 'Recollections', *Grassroots Leadership* (1) (Newtownabbey: Island, 2005), 4–17.

Blood, Baroness May, *Watch My Lips, I'm Speaking!* (Dublin: Gill & Macmillan, 2007).

Boyd, John, 'St John Ervine: A Biographical Note', *Threshold*, No. 25 (Summer 1974), 101–13.

Boyd, John, *The Middle of My Journey* (Belfast: Blackstaff Press, 1990).

Branagh, Kenneth, *Beginning* (London: Pan Books, 1990).

Brett, C. E. B., *Long Shadows Cast Before: Nine Lives In Ulster, 1625–1977* (Edinburgh: Bartholomew, 1978).

Bulgakov, Mikhail, *Flight* (adapted by Ron Hutchinson) (London: Nick Hern Books, 1998).

Buñuel, Luis, *My Last Sigh* (Minneapolis: University of Minnesota Press, 2003; 1st edition 1983).

Carnduff, Thomas, *Songs of an Out-of-Work* (Belfast: Quota Press, 1932).

Carnduff, Thomas, *Poverty Street and Other Belfast Poems* (Belfast: Lapwing Productions, 1993).

Carnduff, Thomas, *Life and Writings*, ed. John Gray (Belfast: Lagan Press, 1994).

Chesterton, G. K., *Irish Impressions* (Glasgow: W. Collins Sons & Co., 1920).

Collins, Eamon, *Killing Rage* (London: Granta, 1997).

Cullen, Bernard (ed.), *Discriminations Old and New: Aspects of Northern Ireland Today* (Belfast: Institute of Irish Studies, 1992).

Devlin, Paddy, *The Fall of the N.I. Executive* (Belfast: Paddy Devlin, 1975).

Devlin, Paddy, *Yes We Have No Bananas: Outdoor Relief in Belfast 1920–39* (Belfast: Blackstaff Press, 1981).

Devlin, Paddy, 'No Rootless Colonist', *Threshold*, No. 38, Hewitt edition (Winter 1986/7), 22–3.

Devlin, Paddy, *Straight Left: An Autobiography* (Belfast: Blackstaff Press, 1993).

Dowling, Vincent, *Astride the Moon: A Theatrical Life* (Dublin: Wolfhound Press, 2000).

Ellis, James, *Domestic Flight* (Belfast: Lagan Press, 1998).

Ellis, James, *Troubles Over the Bridge* (Belfast: Lagan Press, 2015).

Ervine, St John, *Sir Edward Carson and the Ulster Movement* (Dublin: Maunsel, 1915).

Ervine, St John, *Some Impressions of My Elders* (London: George Allen & Unwin, 1923).

Ervine, St John, *The Organised Theatre: A Plea in Civics* (London: George Allen & Unwin, 1924).

Ervine, St John, *The Theatre in My Time* (London: Rich & Cowan, 1933).

Ervine, St John, *Sophia* (London: Macmillan, 1941).

Ervine, St John, *Private Enterprise* (London: George Allen & Unwin, 1948).

Ervine, St John, *Craigavon: Ulsterman* (London: Allen & Unwin, 1949).

Ervine, St John, *George Bernard Shaw: His Life, Work, and Friends* (London: Constable, 1956).

Ervine, St John, *Selected Plays of St John Ervine*, ed. John Cronin (Gerrards Cross: Colin Smythe, 1988).

Ervine, St John, 'An Onlooker's Tale', in Keith Jeffery, *The GPO and the Easter Rising* (Dublin: Irish Academic Press, 2006), 163–87.

Farrell, Michael, *The Battle for Algeria* (Belfast: People's Democracy, 1973).

Faulkner, Brian, *Memoirs of a Statesman* (London: Weidenfeld and Nicolson, 1978).

Fisk, Robert, *The Point of No Return: The Strike Which Broke the British in Ulster* (London: André Deutsch, 1975).

Fitzpatrick, Barre (ed.), 'Beyond the Planter and the Gael: An Interview with John Hewitt and John Montague', *The Crane Bag: The Northern Issue*, Vol. 4, No. 2 (1980–1), 85–92.

Foley, Imelda, *The Girls in the Big Picture: Gender in Contemporary Ulster Theatre* (Belfast: Blackstaff Press, 2003).

Galway, James, *An Autobiography* (Bath: Chivers Press, 1978).

Grant, David, *Playing the Wild Card: A Survey of Community Drama and Smaller-scale Theatre from a Community Relations Perspective* (Belfast: Community Relations Council, 1993).

Greacen, Robert, *Even Without Irene* (Belfast: Lagan Press, 1995).

Greacen, Robert, 'John Hewitt: The Search for Identity', in *Rooted in Ulster: Nine Northern Writers* (Belfast: Lagan Press, 2000), 115–25.

Green Shoot Productions (The Board), 'The Ulster Trilogy', *Paisley & Me—Education & Outreach Programme* (Belfast: Green Shoot Productions, October 2012).

Haines, Joe, *The Politics of Power* (London: Jonathan Cape, 1977).

Heath, Edward, *The Course of My Life* (London: Hodder and Stoughton, 1998).

Hewitt, John, *Ancestral Voices: The Selected Prose of John Hewitt*, ed. Tom Clyde (Belfast: Blackstaff Press, 1987).

Hewitt, John, *The Collected Poems of John Hewitt*, ed. Frank Ormsby (Belfast: Blackstaff Press, 1991).

Hewitt, John, *Two Plays: The McCrackens and The Angry Dove* (Belfast: Lagan Press, 1999).

Hewitt, John, *A North Light: Twenty-Five Years in a Municipal Art Gallery*, ed. Frank Ferguson and Kathryn White (Dublin: Four Courts, 2013).

Hicks, Patrick, 'A Conversation with Glenn Patterson', *New Hibernia Review*, Vol. 12, No. 2 (Summer 2008), 106–19.

Hooley, Terri (and Richard Sullivan), *Hooleygan: Music, Mayhem, Good Vibrations* (Belfast: Blackstaff Press, 2010).

Hutchinson, Billy, *Transcendental Art—A Troubles Archive Essay* (Belfast: Arts Council of Northern Ireland, 2011).

Hutchinson, Ron, *Rat in the Skull* (London: Methuen, 1995; 1st edition 1984).

Hutchinson, Ron, 'Playwright's Foreword', in *Paisley & Me Souvenir Programme* (Belfast: Green Shoot Productions, October 2012), 4.

Hyndman, Marilyn (ed.), *Further Afield: Journeys from a Protestant Past* (Belfast: Beyond the Pale, 1996).

INTERCOMM and Byrne, Dr Jonny, *Flags and Protests: Exploring the Views, Perceptions and Experiences of People Directly and Indirectly Affected by the Flag Protests* (Belfast: Intercomm, 2013).

Jaquarello, Roland, *Memories of Development* (Dublin: Liffey Press, 2016).

Jones, Marie, *Women on the Verge of HRT* (London: Samuel French, 1999).

Jones, Marie, *Stones in His Pockets/A Night in November* (London: Nick Hern Books, 2000).

Jones, Marie, 'Marie Jones in Conversation with Pat Moylan', in Lillian Chambers, Ger FitzGibbon, and Eamonn Jordan (eds), *Theatre Talk: Voices of Irish Theatre Practitioners* (Dublin: Carysfort Press, 2001), 210–17.

Jones, Marie, 'Conversations with the Writer', *Rock Doves* Theatre Programme (Belfast: Rathmore Productions, 2010), 12–13.

Keyes, John, *Going Dark: Two Ulster Theatres* (Belfast: Lagan Press, 2001).

Kilfeather, John, 'Remembering John Hewitt', *Threshold*, No. 38, Hewitt edition (Winter 1986/7), 31–6.

Laird, John, *A Struggle to Be Heard: By a True Ulster Liberal* (Exeter: Global & Western, 2010).

Logue, Paddy (ed.), *The Border: Personal Reflections from Ireland, North and South* (Dublin: Oak Tree Press, 1999).

Lynch, Martin, *Chronicles of Long Kesh* (London: Oberon Books, 2010).

Lynch, Martin, and Charabanc Theatre Company, *Lay Up Your Ends: A Twenty Fifth Anniversary Edition* (Belfast: Lagan Press, 2008).

McCafferty, Nell, *Nell* (Dublin: Penguin, 2005).

McElborough, Robert, *Loyalism and Labour in Belfast: The Autobiography of Robert McElborough, 1884–1952* (Cork: Cork University Press, 2002).

McGrath, John, *A Good Night Out: Popular Theatre: Audience, Class and Form* (London: Methuen, 1981).

McIntyre, Anthony, *Good Friday: The Death of Irish Republicanism* (New York: Ausubo Press, 2008).

McIvor, Basil, *Hope Deferred: Experiences of an Irish Unionist* (Belfast: Blackstaff Press, 1998).

McKay, Susan, *Northern Protestants: An Unsettled People* (Belfast: Blackstaff Press, 2000).

McKearney, Tommy, 'State of the Union', *Social Justice Review* (Winter 2012), 32–8.

McKeown, Ciaran, *The Passion of Peace* (Belfast: Blackstaff Press, 1984).

McKittrick, David, Kelters, Seamus, Feeney, Brian, Thornton, Chris, and McVea, David (eds), *Lost Lives: The Stories of the Men, Women and Children who Died as a Result of the Northern Ireland Troubles* (Edinburgh: Mainstream Publishing, 2008; 1st edition 1999).

McMichael, Gary, *An Ulster Voice: In Search of Common Ground in Northern Ireland* (Dublin: Roberts Rinehart, 1999).

Maxton, Hugh (W. J. McCormack), *Waking: An Irish Protestant Upbringing* (Belfast: Lagan Press, 1997).

Mills, Richard, 'Closed Places of the Spirit: Maurice Leitch interviewed by Richard Mills', *Irish Studies Review*, Vol. 6, No. 1 (1998), 63–8.

Mitchell, Billy, *The Principles of Loyalism* (Belfast: Progressive Unionist Party, 2002).

Mitchell, Gary, *Tearing the Loom and In a Little World of Our Own* (London: Nick Hern Books, 1998).

Mitchell, Gary, *Trust* (London: Nick Hern Books, 1999).

Mitchell, Gary, *The Force of Change* (London: Nick Hern Books, 2000).

Mitchell, Gary, *As the Beast Sleeps* (London: Nick Hern Books, 2001).

Mitchell, Gary, *Loyal Women* (London: Nick Hern Books, 2003).

Mitchell, Gary, 'Rathcoole Ranger', in Graham Walker and Ronnie Esplin (eds), *It's Rangers for Me? New Perspectives on a Scottish Institution* (Ayr: Fort, 2007), 109–25.

Moloney, Ed (ed.), *Voices from the Grave: Two Men's War in Ireland* (London: Faber and Faber, 2010).

Montague, John, *The Pear Is Ripe: A Memoir* (Dublin: Liberties Press, 2007).

Morrison, Danny, *West Belfast* (Cork: Mercier Press, 1990).

Morrison, Danny, *On the Back of the Swallow* (Cork: Mercier Press, 1994).

Morrison, Danny, *The Wrong Man* (Cork: Mercier Press, 1997).

Morrison, Danny, *Then the Walls Came Down* (Cork: Mercier Press, 1999).

Morrison, Danny, *All the Dead Voices* (Cork: Mercier Press, 2002).

Morrison, Danny, 'Northern Futures', *The Irish Review*, No. 31 (2004), 79–82.

Murphy, Dervla, *A Place Apart* (Harmondsworth: Penguin, 1979).

Northern Ireland Statistical Research Agency, *Northern Ireland Multiple Deprivation Measure 2010* (Belfast: NISRA, May 2010).

O'Casey, Sean, *Inishfallen, Fare Thee Well: Autobiography: Book 4, 1917–1926* (London: Pan Books, 1949).

O'Connor, Fionnuala, *In Search of a State: Catholics in Northern Ireland* (Belfast: Blackstaff Press, 1993).

O'Driscoll, Dennis, *Stepping Stones: Interviews with Seamus Heaney* (London: Faber and Faber, 2008).

O'Malley, Mary, *Never Shake Hands With the Devil* (Dublin: Elo, 1990).

O'Neill, Terence, *The Autobiography of Terence O'Neill* (London: Rupert Hart-Davis, 1972).

O'Rawe, Richard, *Blanketmen: An Untold Story of the H-Block Hunger Strike* (Dublin: New Island, 2005).

O'Rawe, Richard, *Afterlives: The Hunger Strike and the Secret Offer that Changed Irish History* (Dublin: Lilliput Press, 2010).

Osborne, John, *A Better Class of Person* (London: Faber and Faber, 1981).

Parker, Stewart, 'State of Play', *The Canadian Journal of Irish Studies*, Vol. 7, No. 1 (June 1981), 5–11.

Parker, Stewart, *Three Plays for Ireland: Northern Star—Heavenly Bodies—Pentecost* (Birmingham: Oberon Books, 1989).

Parker, Stewart, *Plays: 1* (London: Methuen, 2000).

Parker, Stewart, *Plays: 2* (London: Methuen, 2000).

Parker, Stewart, *Dramatis Personae and Other Writings*, ed. Gerald Dawe, Maria Johnston, and Clare Wallace (Prague: Litteraria Pragensia, 2008).

Pasolini, Pier Paolo, *Lutheran Letters*, trans. Stuart Hood (Manchester: Carcanet Press, 1983).

Potter, Dennis, 'The James MacTaggart Memorial Lecture', Edinburgh Film Festival (1993), in *Seeing the Blossom* (London: Faber and Faber, 1994), 31–56.

Purvis, Dawn, and the Working Group on Educational Disadvantage and the Protestant Working Class, *Educational Disadvantage and the Protestant Working Class—A Call to Action* (March 2011).

Redpath, Jackie, 'Recollections', in *Grassroots Leadership*, No. 4 (Newtownabbey: Island Publications, 2005), 4–15.

Reid, Christina, *The Last of a Dyin' Race*, in *Best Radio Plays of 1986* (London: Methuen/BBC Productions, 1987), 39–71.

Reid, Christina, *Plays: 1* (London: Methuen, 1997).

Reid, Graham, *The Closed Door* (Dublin: Co-op Books, 1980).

Reid, Graham, *The Death of Humpty Dumpty* (Dublin: Co-op Books, 1980).

Reid, Graham, *The Hidden Curriculum*, in *The Plays of Graham Reid* (Dublin: Co-op Books, 1982), 101–64.

Reid, Graham, *Billy: Three Plays for Television* (London: Faber and Faber, 1984).

Reid, Graham, 'Comings and Goings', *Threshold*, No. 35 (Winter 1984/5), 21–5.

Reid, Graham, 'A Northern Star', *The Irish Review*, No. 7 (Autumn 1989), 86–8.

Reid, Graham, 'Author's Note', *Love, Billy*, Theatre Programme (Belfast: Lyric Theatre, April 2013), 10.

Richardson, Robert, 'Sam & Me: Recollections of Belfast and Playwright Sam Thompson in the 1930s', *Krino*, No. 4 (Autumn, 1987), 20–30.

Robinson, Lennox, *Curtain Up* (London: Michael Joseph, 1942).

Robinson, Lennox, *Ireland's Abbey Theatre: A History, 1899–1951* (London: Sidgwick & Jackson, 1951).

Rodgers, W. R., *The Return Room* (Belfast: Blackstaff Press, 2010).

Shankill Think Tank, *A New Beginning*, 13 (Newtownabbey: Island Publications, 1995).

Shaw, George Bernard, 'The Protestants of Ireland' (1912), in *The Matter with Ireland*, ed. Dan H. Laurence and David H. Greene (London: Rupert Hart-Davis, 1962), 68–74.

Shea, Patrick, *Voices and the Sound of Drums: An Irish Autobiography* (Belfast: Blackstaff Press, 1981).

Smith, William 'Plum', *Inside Man: Loyalists of Long Kesh—The Untold Story* (Newtownards: Colourpoint Books, 2014).

Taylor, Peter, *Loyalists* (London: Bloomsbury, 2000).

Thompson, Sam, *Over the Bridge and Other Plays* (Belfast: Lagan Press, 1997).

Wilson, Harold, Transcript of Televised Address, 25 May 1974, http://cain.ulst.ac.uk/events/uwc/docs/hw25574.htm.

Wilson, Harold, *Final Term: The Labour Government 1974–1976* (London: Weidenfeld and Nicolson, 1979).

Winter, Brenda, 'Charabanc, Cultural Capital and the Men of Recognized Credit', *Ilha do Desterro*, No. 58 (January/June 2010), 439–58.

Workers' Association (The B&ICO), *Strike Bulletin No. 1* (Belfast: 19 May 1974).

Workers' Association (The B&ICO), *Strike Bulletin, No. 5—Fascism* (Belfast: 24 May 1974).

Workers' Association (The B&ICO), *Strike Bulletin No. 7—Wilson Backs Down* (Belfast: 26 May 1974).

Miscellaneous Media Material

Arts Extra, BBC Radio Ulster (broadcast 2 March 2009). Recorded at the Strule Arts Centre, Omagh, 28 February 2009.

BBC Newsline (5 February 2013).

Hutchinson, Ron, *The Last Window Cleaner* (Belfast: BBC Northern Ireland, 1979). DVD.

The Late Show: Telling the Troubles, BBC2 (broadcast 21 September 1993). DVD.

Mitchell, Gary, *Drumcree*, broadcast 16 July 1996 (BBC Radio 4). CD.

Mitchell, Gary, *As the Beast Sleeps* (Belfast: BBC Northern Ireland, 2002). DVD.

Sam Thompson: Voice of Many Men, directed by Donald Taylor Black, aired 29 November 1985 (Channel 4). DVD.

SECONDARY SOURCES

Allen, Nicholas, 'Cultural Representations of 1916', in Richard S. Grayson and Fearghal McGarry (eds), *Remembering 1916: The Easter Rising, the Somme and the Politics of Memory in Ireland* (Cambridge: Cambridge University Press, 2016), 168–80.

Andrews, Elmer, 'Stewart Parker', in *Pentecost* Theatre Programme (Derry: Field Day, 1987), n.pag.

Arrington, Lauren, 'St John Ervine and the Fabian Society: Capital, Empire and Irish Home Rule', *History Workshop Journal*, Vol. 72, No. 1 (2011), 52–73.

Arthur, Paul, 'John Hewitt's Hierarchy of Values', in Gerald Dawe and John Wilson Foster (eds), *The Poet's Place: Ulster Literature and Society. Essays in Honour of John Hewitt, 1907–1987* (Belfast: Institute of Irish Studies, 1991), 273–84.

Aughey, Arthur, *Irish Kulturkampf* (Belfast: Young Unionist Council, 1995).

Beider, Harris, *White Working-Class Voices: Multiculturalism, Community-Building and Change* (Bristol: Policy Press, 2015).

Bell, Geoffrey, *The Protestants of Ulster* (London: Pluto Press, 1976).

Bell, Sam Hanna, *The Theatre in Ulster* (Dublin: Gill & Macmillan, 1972).

Bell, Sam Hanna, Robb, Nesca A., and Hewitt, John (eds), *The Arts in Ulster: A Symposium* (London: George H. Harrap, 1951).

Bew, Paul, *The Making and Remaking of the Good Friday Agreement* (Dublin: The Liffey Press, 2007).

Bew, Paul, Patterson, Henry, and Teague, Paul, *Between War and Peace: The Political Future of Northern Ireland* (London: Lawrence & Wishart, 1997).

Bew, Paul, and Gillespie, Gordon, *Northern Ireland: A Chronology of the Troubles 1968–1999* (Dublin: Gill & Macmillan, 1999).

Billington, Michael, *The Life and Work of Harold Pinter* (London: Faber and Faber, 1996).

Billington, Michael, *State of the Nation: British Theatre Since 1945* (London: Faber and Faber, 2007).

Bleakley, David, *Saidie Patterson: Irish Peacemaker* (Belfast: Blackstaff Press, 1980).

Boyle, Louis, 'The Ulster Workers' Council Strike: May 1974', in John Darby and Arthur Williamson (eds), *Violence and the Social Services in Northern Ireland* (London: Heinemann, 1978), 155–65.

Braniff, Máire, and Whiting, Sophie A., ' "There's Just No Point Having A Token Woman": Gender and Representation in the Democratic Unionist Party in Post-Agreement Northern Ireland', *Parliamentary Affairs*, Vol. 69, No. 1 (2016), 93–114.

Brown, Terence, 'The Majority's Minorities: Protestant Denominations in the North', *The Crane Bag: Minorities in Ireland*, Vol. 5, No. 1 (1981), 22–25.

Bruce, Steve, *The Red Hand: Protestant Paramilitaries in Northern Ireland* (Oxford: Oxford University Press, 1992).

Bruce, Steve, *The Edge of the Union: The Ulster Loyalist Political Vision* (Oxford: Oxford University Press, 1994).

Bruce, Steve, *Paisley: Religion and Politics in Northern Ireland* (Oxford: Oxford University Press, 2007).

Bull, John, *New British Political Dramatists* (London: Macmillan, 1984).

Byrne, Ophelia, *The Stage in Ulster from the Eighteenth Century* (Belfast: Linen Hall Library, 1997).

Carey, John, *The Intellectuals and the Masses: Pride and Prejudice among the Literary Intelligentsia, 1880–1939* (London: Faber and Faber, 1992).

Cathcart, Rex, *The Most Contrary Region: The BBC in Northern Ireland 1924–1984* (Belfast: Blackstaff Press, 1984).

Caulfield, Max, *The Easter Rebellion* (London: Frederick Muller, 1964).

Clyde, Tom, 'A Stirring in the Dry Bones: John Hewitt's Regionalism', in Gerald Dawe and John Wilson Foster (eds), *The Poet's Place: Ulster Literature and Society: Essays in Honour of John Hewitt, 1907–1987* (Belfast: Institute of Irish Studies, 1991), 249–58.

Cochrane, Feargal, *Unionist Politics and the Politics of Unionism Since the Anglo-Irish Agreement* (Cork: Cork University Press, 1997).

Courtney, Roger, *Second Congregation Belfast 1708–2008* (Belfast: All Souls' Non-Subscribing Presbyterian Congregation, 2008).

Crawford, Colin, *Defenders or Criminals? Loyalist Prisoners and Criminalisation* (Belfast: Blackstaff Press, 1999).

Dallat, C. L., 'A Single Flame', in Eve Patten (ed.), *Returning to Ourselves* (Belfast: Lagan Press, 1995), 120–9.

Dawe, Gerald, *How's the Poetry Going? Literary Politics and Ireland Today* (Belfast: Lagan Press, 1993).

Dawe, Gerald, *False Faces: Poetry, Politics and Place* (Belfast: Lagan Press, 1994).

Dawe, Gerald, *Against Piety: Essays in Irish Poetry* (Belfast: Lagan Press, 1995).

Deane, Seamus, *Celtic Revivals: Essays in Modern Irish Literature 1880–1980* (London: Faber and Faber, 1985).

Deane, Seamus (gen. ed.), *Field Day Anthology of Irish Writing, Volume 2: From Poetry and Song (1890–90) Through Prose and Fiction (1880–1945)* (Derry: Field Day, 1991).

Deane, Seamus, 'Irish Theatre: A Secular Space?', *Irish University*, Vol. 28, No. 1 (Spring/Summer 1998), 163–74.

Devine, Francis, *Organizing History: A Centenary of SIPTU, 1909–2009* (Dublin: Gill & Macmillan, 2009).

DiCenzo, Maria, 'Charabanc Theatre Company: Placing Women Center-Stage in Northern Ireland', *Theatre Journal*, Vol. 45, No. 2 (May 1993), 175–84.

Dingley, James, *The IRA: The Irish Republican Army* (Santa Barbara, CA: Praeger, 2012).

Edwards, Aaron, *A History of the Northern Ireland Labour Party: Democratic Socialism and Sectarianism* (Manchester: Manchester University Press, 2009).

Edwards, Aaron, 'The Progressive Unionist Party of Northern Ireland: A Left-wing Voice in an Ethnically Divided Society', *British Journal of Politics and International Relations*, Vol. 12, No. 4 (2010), 590–614.

Edwards, Aaron, and McGrattan, Cillian, 'Terroristic Narratives: On the (Re) Invention of Peace in Northern Ireland', *Terrorism and Political Violence*, Vol. 23, No. 3 (2011), 357–76.

Elliott, Sydney, and Flackes, W. D., *Northern Ireland: A Political Directory* (Belfast: Blackstaff Press, 1999).

English, Richard, *Armed Struggle: A History of the IRA* (London: Macmillan, 2003).

English, Richard, *Irish Freedom: The History of Nationalism in Ireland* (London: Macmillan, 2006).

English, Richard, and Walker, Graham (eds), *Unionism in Modern Ireland: New Perspectives on Politics and Culture* (Dublin: Gill & Macmillan, 1996).

Ervine, Linda, 'The Protestant Community and the Irish Language', *Social Justice Review* (Spring 2013), 35–8.

Evans, Gillian, *Educational Failure and Working Class White Children in Britain* (Basingstoke: Palgrave Macmillan, 2006).

Evason, Eileen, *On the Edge: A Study of Poverty and Long-term Unemployment in Northern Ireland* (London: Child Poverty Action Group, 1985).

Fay, Jimmy, 'St John Ervine: Director's Note', in *Mixed Marriage Theatre Programme* (Belfast: Lyric Theatre, January–February 2013), 13.

Fearon, Kate, *Women's Work: The Story of the Northern Ireland Women's Coalition* (Belfast: Blackstaff Press, 1999).

Ferris, Sarah, *Poet John Hewitt, 1907–1987 and Criticism of Northern Irish Protestant Writing* (New York: Edwin Mellon Press, 2002).

Fiacc, Padraic (ed.), *The Wearing of the Black* (Belfast: Blackstaff Press, 1974).

Finlay, Andrew, 'Defeatism and Northern Protestant "Identity"', *Global Review of Ethnopolitics*, Vol. 1, No. 2 (2001), 3–20.

Fitzpatrick, David, *'Solitary and Wild': Frederick MacNeice and the Salvation of Ireland* (Dublin: Lilliput Press, 2012).

Fitzpatrick, Liza, 'Disrupting Metanarratives: Anne Devlin, Christina Reid, Marina Carr, and the Irish Dramatic Repertory', *Irish University Review*, Vol. 35, No. 2 (Autumn–Winter 2005), 320–33.

Foley, Imelda, 'Theatre and the Conflict in Northern Ireland', *A Troubles Archive Essay* (Belfast: Arts Council of Northern Ireland, 2009).

Ford, Robert, and Goodwin, Matthew, *Revolt on the Right: Explaining Support for the Radical Right in Britain* (Abingdon: Routledge, 2014).

Foster, John Wilson, *Fictions of the Irish Literary Revival: A Changeling Art* (Dublin: Gill & Macmillan, 1987).

Foster, John Wilson, *Between Shadows: Modern Irish Writing and Culture* (Dublin: Irish Academic Press, 2009).

Foster, R. F., 'Protestant Magic: W. B. Yeats and the Spell of Irish History', in *Paddy and Mr Punch: Connections in Irish and English History* (London: Allen Lane, 1993), 212–32.

Foster, R. F., *W. B. Yeats: A Life II: The Arch-Poet, 1915–1939* (Oxford: Oxford University Press, 2003).

Foster, R. F., *Vivid Faces: The Revolutionary Generation in Ireland 1890–1923* (London: Allen Lane, 2014).

Gaffikin, Frank, and Morrissey, Mike, *Northern Ireland: The Thatcher Years* (London: Zed Books, 1990).

Garland, Roy, *Gusty Spence* (Belfast: Blackstaff Press, 2001).

Glenny, Misha, *McMafia: Crime Without Frontiers* (London: The Bodley Head, 2008).

Gordon, Mick, *Theatre and the Mind* (London: Oberon Books, 2010).

Graham, Colin, ' "port-lights / Of a ghost-ship": Thomas Carnduff and the Belfast Shipyards', *UCDScholarcast*, Series 7 (Spring 2013), 1–10.

Hanley, Brian, and Millar, Scott, *The Lost Revolution: The Story of the Official IRA and the Workers' Party* (Dublin: Penguin, 2009).

Harris, Claudia, 'Community Conscience or Reflection? Theatre in Northern Ireland', in Alan J. Ward (ed.), *Northern Ireland: Living with the Crisis* (New York: Praeger, 1987), 195–215.

Heaney, Seamus, 'The Poetry of John Hewitt', in *Preoccupations: Selected Prose 1968–1978* (London: Faber and Faber, 1980), 207–10.

Heaney, Seamus, 'Frontiers of Writing', in *The Redress of Poetry: Oxford Lectures* (London: Faber and Faber, 1995), 186–203.

Hobsbawm, Eric, *Bandits* (London: Abacus, 2000; 1st edition 1969).

Hopkins, Stephen, *The Politics of Memoir and the Northern Ireland Conflict* (Liverpool: Liverpool University Press, 2013).

Hunt, Hugh, *The Abbey: Ireland's National Theatre, 1904–1979* (London: Gill & Macmillan, 1979).

Jackson, Alvin, 'Irish Unionism', in D. George Boyce and Alan O'Day (eds), *The Making of Modern Irish History: Revisionism and the Revisionist Controversy* (Abingdon: Routledge, 1996), 120–41.

Johnston, Philip, *The Lost Tribe in the Mirror: Four Playwrights of Northern Ireland* (Belfast: Lagan Press, 2009).

Johnston, Wesley, *The Belfast Urban Motorway: Engineering, Ambition and Social Conflict* (Newtownards: Colourpoint Books, 2014).

Kao, Wei H., 'Remapping Protestant Women and Interracial Minorities in Christina Reid's War Dramas', in Gillian McIntosh and Diane Urquhart (eds), *Irish Women at War: The Twentieth Century* (Dublin: Irish Academic Press, 2010), 205–22.

Kaufman, Eric P., *The Orange Order: A Contemporary Northern Irish History* (Oxford: Oxford University Press, 2007).

Kavanagh, Peter, *The Story of the Abbey Theatre* (New York: Devin-Adair, 1950).

Kinsella, Thomas, *The Dual Tradition: An Essay on Poetry and Politics in Ireland* (Manchester: Carcanet Press, 1995).

Komporály, Jozefina, 'The Troubles and the Family: Women's Theatre as Political Intervention', in Brian Cliff and Éibhear Walshe (eds), *Representing the Troubles: Texts and Images, 1970–2000* (Dublin: Four Courts Press, 2004), 67–78.

Lee, J. J., *Ireland 1912–1985: Politics and Society* (Cambridge: Cambridge University Press, 1989).

Levitas, Ben, *The Theatre of a Nation: Irish Drama and Cultural Nationalism, 1890–1916* (Oxford: Clarendon Press, 2002).

Lister, David, and Jordan, Hugh, *Mad Dog: The Rise and Fall of Johnny Adair and 'C Company'* (Edinburgh: Mainstream Publishing, 2004).

Little, Ruth, and McLaughlin, Emily, *The Royal Court Theatre Inside Out* (London: Oberon Books, 2007).

Loftus, Belinda, *Marching Workers: An Exhibition of Irish Trade Banners and Regalia* (Belfast: Arts Councils of Ireland, 1978).

Lonergan, Patrick, *Theatre and Globalization: Irish Drama in the Celtic Tiger Era* (Basingstoke: Palgrave Macmillan, 2010).

Longley, Edna, 'Progressive Bookmen: Politics and Northern Protestant Writers in the 1930s', *The Irish Review*, No. 1 (1986), 50–7.

Longley, Edna, 'What do Protestants Want?', *The Irish Review*, No. 20 (Winter–Spring 1997), 104–20.

Longley, Michael, *A Hundred Doors* (London: Jonathan Cape, 2011).

Lyons, F. S. L., *Culture and Anarchy in Ireland, 1890–1939* (Oxford: Oxford University Press, 1979).

Lyons, F. S. L., *Ireland Since the Famine* (London: Fontana, 1985; 1st edition 1963).

McAuley, James W., *The Politics of Identity: A Loyalist Community in Belfast* (Aldershot: Avebury, 1994).

McBride, Ian, 'Ulster and the British Problem', in Richard English and Graham Walker (eds), *Unionism in Modern Ireland: New Perspectives on Politics and Culture* (Dublin: Gill & Macmillan, 1996), 1–18.

McCann, Sean, *The Story of the Abbey Theatre* (London: Four Square Books, 1967).

McCormack, W. J., *Northman: John Hewitt (1907–1987): An Irish Writer, His World, and His Times* (Oxford: Oxford University Press, 2015).

McCormick, Leanne, '"No Sense of Wrongdoing": Abortion in Belfast, 1917–1967', *Journal of Social History*, Vol. 49, No. 1 (2015), 125–48.

McDonnell, Bill, *Theatres of the Troubles: Theatre, Resistance and Liberation in Ireland* (Exeter: University of Exeter Press, 2008).

McDowell, Jim, *The Mummy's Boys: Threats and Menaces from Ulster's ParaMafia* (Dublin: Gill & Macmillan, 2008).

McGarry, Fearghal, *The Abbey Rebels of 1916: A Lost Revolution* (Dublin: Gill & Macmillan, 2015).

McGladdery, Gary, *The Provisional IRA in England: The Bombing Campaign 1973–1997* (Dublin: Irish Academic Press, 2006).

McIntosh, Gillian, *The Force of Culture: Unionist Identities in Twentieth Century Ireland* (Cork: Cork University Press, 1999).

McKenzie, Lisa, *Getting By: Estates, Class and Culture in Austerity Britain* (Bristol: Policy Press, 2015).

McNulty, Eugene, *The Ulster Literary Theatre and the Northern Revival* (Cork: Cork University Press, 2008).

McNulty, Eugene, and Maguire, Tom (eds), *The Theatre of Marie Jones: Telling Stories from the Ground Up* (Dublin: Carysfort Press, 2015).

Maguire, Tom, *Making Theatre in Northern Ireland: Through and Beyond the Troubles* (Exeter: University of Exeter Press, 2006).

Malik, Kenan, *From Fatwa to Jihad: The Rushdie Affair and its Legacy* (London: Atlantic, 2009).

Malone, Andrew E., 'The Rise of the Realistic Movement', in Lennox Robinson (ed.), *The Irish Theatre* (New York: Haskell House, 1939), 89–116.

Maume, Patrick, 'Ulstermen of Letter: The Unionism of Frank Frankfort Moore, Shan Bullock, and St John Ervine', in Richard English and Graham Walker (eds), *Unionism in Modern Ireland* (Dublin: Gill & Macmillan, 1996), 63–80.

Megahey, Maura, '*The Reality of His Fictions*': *The Dramatic Achievement of Sam Thompson* (Belfast: Lagan Press, 2009).

Mengal, Hagal, *Sam Thompson and Modern Drama in Ulster* (New York: Peter Lang, 1986).

Miles, Tim, 'Fighting the Peace: Counter-Narrative, Violence, and the Work of Gary Mitchell', in Lisa Fitzpatrick (ed.), *Performing Violence in Contemporary Ireland* (Dublin: Carysfort Press, 2009), 65–84.

Miller, David W., *Queen's Rebels: Ulster Loyalism in Historical Perspective* (Dublin: University College Dublin Press, 2007; 1st edition 1978).

Mitchel, Patrick, *Evangelicalism and National Identity in Ulster, 1921–1998* (Oxford: Oxford University Press, 2003).

Moloney, Ed, *Paisley: From Demagogue to Democrat?* (Dublin: Poolbeg, 2008).

Morgan, Austen, *Labour and Partition: The Belfast Working Class 1905–23* (London: Pluto Press, 1991).

Mulholland, Marc, *Northern Ireland at the Crossroads: Ulster Unionism in the O'Neill Years, 1960–9* (Basingstoke: Macmillan, 2000).

Mulholland, Marc, *Terence O'Neill* (Dublin: University College Dublin Press, 2013).

Munck, Ronaldo, 'A Divided Working Class: Protestant and Catholic Workers in Northern Ireland', *Labour, Capital and Society*, Vol. 13, No. 1 (April 1980), 104–40.

Murray, Christopher, *Twentieth Century Irish Drama: Mirror Up to Nation* (Manchester: Manchester University Press, 1997).

Murray, Peter, 'Radical Way Forward or Sectarian Cul-de-sac? Lindsay Crawford and Independent Orangeism Reassessed', *Saothar*, No. 27 (2002), 31–42.

Nairn, Tom, *The Break–Up of Britain* (London: Verso, 1981).

Nelson, Sarah, *Ulster's Uncertain Defenders: Protestant Political, Paramilitary and Community Groups and the Northern Ireland Conflict* (Belfast: Appletree Press, 1984).

Nolan, Paul, *Northern Ireland Peace Monitoring Report: Number Three* (Belfast: Community Relations Council, 2014).

Novosel, Tony, *Northern Ireland's Lost Opportunity: The Frustrated Promise of Political Loyalism* (London: Pluto Press, 2013).

O'Connor, Fionnuala, *Breaking the Bonds: Making Peace in Northern Ireland* (Edinburgh: Mainstream, 2002).

O'Dwyer, Riana, 'The Imagination of Women's Reality: Christina Reid and Marina Carr', in Eamonn Jordan (ed.), *Theatre Stuff: Critical Essays on Contemporary Irish Theatre* (Dublin: Carysfort Press, 2000), 236–48.

O'Flaherty, Liam, *The Informer* (London: Penguin, 1936).

Ó Madagáin, Brendan, 'Cultural Continuity and Regeneration', in M. A. G. Ó Tuathaigh (ed.), *Community, Culture, and Conflict: Aspects of the Irish Experience* (Galway: Galway University Press, 1986), 17–30.

Ó Seaghdha, Barra, 'Ulster Regionalism: The Unpleasant Facts', *The Irish Review*, No. 8 (Spring 1990), 54–61.

O'Toole, Fintan, 'Today: Contemporary Irish Theatre—The Illusion of Tradition', in Tim Pat Coogan (ed.), *Ireland and the Arts—A Special Issue of Literary Review* (London: Namara Press, 1983), 132–7.

O'Toole, Fintan, *Critical Moments: Fintan O'Toole on Modern Irish Theatre*, ed. Julia Furay and Redmond O'Hanlon (Dublin: Carysfort Press, 2003).

Ó Tuathaigh, Gearóid, *Ireland Before the Famine 1798–1848* (Dublin: Gill & Macmillan, 1972).

Parr, Connal, 'Etcetera Theatre Company: An Exercise in Ulster Loyalist Story-telling', *New Hibernia Review*, Vol. 20, No. 4 (Winter 2016), 91–112.

Paseta, Senia, *Irish Nationalist Women, 1900–1918* (Cambridge: Cambridge University Press, 2013).

Patterson, Henry, *Class Conflict and Sectarianism: The Protestant Working Class and the Belfast Labour Movement 1868–1920* (Belfast: Blackstaff Press, 1980).

Patterson, Henry, *Ireland Since 1939: The Persistence of Conflict* (Dublin: Penguin Ireland, 2006).

Patterson, Henry, 'Interests and Identities in Northern Ireland', *Dynamics of Asymmetric Conflict: Pathways Toward Terrorism and Genocide*, Vol. 4, No. 1 (2011), 73–6.

Paulin, Tom, 'A New Look at the Language Question', in *Ireland's Field Day* (London: Hutchinson, 1985), 1–18.

Pettitt, Lance, *Screening Ireland: Film and Television Representation* (Manchester: Manchester University Press, 2000).

Pierse, Michael, 'Labour and Literature One Hundred Years after the Lockout: Towards an Archive of Irish Working-class Experience', *The Irish Review*, No. 47 (Winter 2013), 44–62.

Pilkington, Lionel, 'Violence and Identity in Northern Ireland: Graham Reid's *The Death of Humpty Dumpty*', *Modern Drama*, Vol. 33, No. 1 (Spring 1990), 15–29.

Purdie, Bob, *Politics in the Streets: The Origins of the Civil Rights Movement in Northern Ireland* (Belfast: Blackstaff Press, 1990).

Quinn, James, 'Thomas Carnduff', in James McGuire and James Quinn (eds), *Dictionary of Irish Biography: Under the Auspices of the Royal Irish Academy: Volume 2* (Cambridge: Cambridge University Press, 2009), 354–6.

Rees, Russell, *Labour and the Northern Ireland Problem 1945–1951* (Dublin: Irish Academic Press, 2009).

Richtarik, Marilynn, 'Living in Interesting Times: Stewart Parker's *Northern Star*', in John P. Harrington and Elizabeth J. Mitchell (eds), *Politics and Performance in Contemporary Northern Ireland* (Amherst: University of Massachusetts Press, 1999), 7–28.

Richtarik, Marilynn, 'Stewart Parker at Queen's University, Belfast', *The Irish Review*, No. 29 (Autumn 2002), 58–69.

Richtarik, Marilynn, 'Beyond the National Question', in *The Parker Project: Spokesong and Pentecost* (Belfast: Lyric Theatre, 2008).

Richtarik, Marilynn, *Stewart Parker: A Life* (Oxford: Oxford University Press, 2012).

Roche, Anthony, *Contemporary Irish Drama: From Beckett to McGuinness* (Dublin: Gill & Macmillan, 1994).

Roll-Hansen, Diderik, 'Dramatic Strategy in Christina Reid's Tea in a China Cup', *Modern Drama*, Vol. 30, No. 3 (Fall 1987), 389–95.

Rolston, Bill, *Children of the Revolution* (Derry: Guildhall Press, 2011).

Savage, Mike, Devine, Fiona, Cunningham, Niall, Taylor, Mark, Li, Yaojun, Hjellbrekke, Johs, Le Roux, Brigitte, Friedman, Sam, and Miles, Andrew, 'A New Model of Social Class? Findings from the BBC's Great British Class Survey Experiment', *Sociology*, Vol. 47, No. 2 (April 2013), 219–50.

Shirlow, Peter, *The End of Ulster Loyalism?* (Manchester: Manchester University Press, 2012).

Sontag, Susan, 'Literature as Freedom', *Irish Pages*, Vol. 2, No. 1 Empire (Spring/ Summer 2003), 175–91.

Spencer, Graham, *The State of Loyalism in Northern Ireland* (Basingstoke: Palgrave Macmillan, 2008).

Spencer, Graham, *Protestant Identity and Peace in Northern Ireland* (Basingstoke: Palgrave Macmillan, 2012).

Stevens, David, 'The Social Thinking of the Protestant Churches', *Studies*, Vol. 80, No. 319 (Autumn 1991), 259–67.

Stewart, A. T. Q., *The Narrow Ground: The Roots of Conflict in Ulster* (London: Faber and Faber, 1989; 1st edition 1977).

Todd, Selina, *The People: The Rise and Fall of the Working Class, 1910–2010* (London: John Murray, 2014).

Urban, Mark, *Big Boys' Rules: The Secret Struggle Against the IRA* (London: Faber and Faber, 1992).

Utley, T. E., *Lessons of Ulster* (London: J. M. Dent, 1975).

Vance, Norman, *Irish Literature: A Social History: Tradition, Identity and Difference* (Oxford: Basil Blackwell, 1990).

Walker, Graham, 'The Commonwealth Labour Party in Northern Ireland, 1942–4', *Irish Historical Studies*, Vol. 24, No. 93 (May 1984), 69–91.

Walker, Graham, 'Old History: Protestant Ulster in Lee's "Ireland"', *The Irish Review*, No. 12 (Spring/Summer, 1992), 65–71.

Walker, Graham, *A History of the Ulster Unionist Party: Protest, Pragmatism and Pessimism* (Manchester: Manchester University Press, 2004).

Walsh, Patrick, '"Too Much Alone": John Hewitt, Regionalism, Socialism, and Partition', *Irish University Review*, Vol. 29, No. 2 (Autumn–Winter 1999), 341–57.

Ward, Margaret, 'Finding a Place: Women and the Irish Peace Process', *Race & Class*, Vol. 37, No. 1, Ireland: New Beginnings? (July–September 1995), 41–50.

Ward, Rachel, *Women, Unionism and Loyalism in Northern Ireland* (Dublin: Irish Academic Press, 2006).

Weiner, Ron, *The Rape and Plunder of the Shankill* (Belfast: Published by the author, 1975).

Welch, Robert, *The Abbey Theatre, 1899–1999: Form and Pressure* (Oxford: Oxford University Press, 1999).

Whyte, John, 'How Much Discrimination Was There under the Stormont Regime?', in Tom Gallagher and James O'Connell (eds), *Contemporary Irish Studies* (Manchester: Manchester University Press, 1983), 1–35.

Whyte, John, *Interpreting Northern Ireland* (Oxford: Oxford University Press, 1990).

Wilcox, Angela, 'Briefings', *The Irish Review*, No. 1 (1986), 123–4.

Williams, Raymond, *Keywords* (London: Fontana Press, 1988; 1st edition 1976).

Wood, Ian S., *Crimes of Loyalty: A History of the UDA* (Edinburgh: Edinburgh University Press, 2006).

Bibliography

Wright, Frank, 'Protestant Ideology and Politics in Ulster', *European Journal of Sociology*, Vol. 14, No. 2 (December 1973), 212–80.

York, Richard, 'Sam Cree: Sex, Sects, and Comedy', *Irish University Review*, Vol. 37, No. 2 (Autumn–Winter, 2007), 352–65.

Thesis

Mulvenna, Gareth, 'The Protestant Working Class in Northern Ireland: Political Allegiance and Social and Cultural Challenges Since the 1960s', PhD thesis, Queen's University Belfast, 2009.

Index

294 *Index*

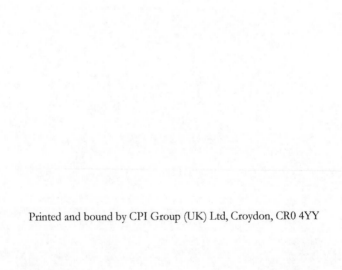

Printed and bound by CPI Group (UK) Ltd, Croydon, CR0 4YY